The Baker's Dozen COOKBOOK

The Baker's Dozen

Flo Braker

John Phillip Carroll

Julia B. Cookenboo

Marion Cunningham

Carol Field

Fran Gage

David Lebovitz

Alice Medrich

Robert Morocco

Peter Reinhart

Lindsey Remolif Shere

Kathleen Stewart

Carolyn Beth Weil

The
Baker's Dozen
COOKBOOK

Become a better baker with 135 foolproof recipes
and tried-and-true techniques

Introduction by Marion Cunningham

Edited by Rick Rodgers

WM
WILLIAM MORROW
75 YEARS OF PUBLISHING
An Imprint of HarperCollins*Publishers*

HarperCollins books may be purchased for educational, business, or sales promotional use. For information please write: Special Markets Department, HarperCollins Publishers Inc., 10 East 53rd Street, New York, NY 10022.

FIRST EDITION

Printed on acid-free paper

Designed by Judith Stagnitto Abbate

Photographs by Beatriz da Costa
Food styling by Liza Jernow

Library of Congress Cataloging-in-Publication Data

The Baker's Dozen cookbook : become a better baker with 135 foolproof recipes and tried-and-true techniques / The Baker's Dozen, Flo Braker . . . [et al.], edited by Rick Rodgers.— 1st ed.
    p. cm.
  Includes index.
  ISBN 0-06-018628-3
  1. Baking. 2. Desserts. I. Braker, Flo. II. Rodgers, Rick, 1953–   III. Baker's Dozen (Group)
  TX763 .B314 2001
  641.8'15—dc21   2001030773

01 02 03 04 05 QH 10 9 8 7 6 5 4 3 2 1

Contents

Acknowledgments   vii

Introduction   1

A Baker's Glossary of Ingredients   3

A Baker's Glossary of Tools   25

The Basics of Cake   44

Cakes for Family and Friends   75

Sweet and Savory Pies   112

Tarts to Tempt   154

A Harvest of Fruit Desserts   180

The Cookie Collection   196

Muffins, Popovers, Easy Quick Breads, and Doughnuts   223

Yeast Breads and Flatbreads   251

Custards and Other Egg-Based Desserts   301

The Finishing Touch: Frostings, Glazes, and Sauces   323

Sources   343

Index   347

Acknowledgments

Our name is The Baker's Dozen, but it definitely took more than thirteen people to get this book to where it is today. We'd like to express our heartfelt appreciation to Michael Bauer, Harriet Bell, David Braker, Doe Coover, Charity Ferriera, Karen Ferries, Carla Fitzgerald, Janet Fletcher, Nancy Kux, Paula Hamilton, Paula Hogan, Jan Makin, Ann Martin, Miriam Morgan, Patti Murray, Pat Motheral, Rick Rodgers, Kim Severson, Kate Stark, Jean Vosti, and Carrie Weinberg.

Thanks to our field trip hosts Alan Scott, Acme Bakery, Cowgirl Creamery and Anna's Bakery, C&H Sugar, Fleischmann's Yeast, Gayle's Bakery, Greenleaf Produce, Guittard Chocolate Company, LaBrea Bakery, McEvoy Olive Ranch, Old Bale Mill, and Strauss Dairy.

For providing warm hospitality to our membership, our sincerest appreciation to Chez Panisse, Picante Cocina Mexicana, the Miyako Hotel, the Mandarin Oriental Hotel, the Pan Pacific Hotel, Raphael House, and The Stratford.

The
Baker's Dozen
COOKBOOK

Introduction *by Marion Cunningham*

If there is one thing I have loved during the last thirty years that I have been a professional cook, it has been belonging to The Baker's Dozen.

The seed for the group was planted in the fall of 1988, when I met Amy Pressman, who then owned a bakery in Venice, California. Whenever I was teaching cooking and baking classes nearby, Amy and I would meet and talk about how wonderful it was to be a baker, but also how mysterious and puzzling baking could be. Through these talks, we often solved some of our baking problems by exchanging ideas and offering suggestions.

Wouldn't it be amazing, we thought, if we organized groups of like-minded bakers in San Francisco and Los Angeles? Baking experiments and comparison tastings to show how the same recipe could be interpreted in many different ways would be our focus.

Forty people showed up with lemon meringue pies at our first meeting of The Baker's Dozen in 1989 at San Francisco's Mandarin Oriental Hotel. The specific topic was weeping meringue, and how we could prevent the weeping and shrinking that occurs on meringue-topped pies. We learned that heating the egg whites and sugar while beating them helps avoid weeping, and using four egg whites instead of the usual recommended three solves the shrinking problem. (A few years later, we discovered another technique that added a cornstarch paste to the meringue.)

But many questions unrelated to meringue kept cropping up throughout the meeting. One person wanted to know how to cut neat slices of cheesecake. Use dental floss, someone counseled. Another baker had problems with grainy caramel sauce. The solution: Add a little lemon juice to the sugar before melting.

Our first meeting was so jam-packed with information that we couldn't wait for the next one. Word quickly spread throughout the baking community about our get-togethers. As we have grown in size to more than three hundred members, The Baker's Dozen continues to run on a simple formula: to share what we know about baking and to learn from one another. There are no officers. We have no dues, but each person is asked to donate $5 to cover the costs of printing and mailing meeting and field trip announcements. There is no newsletter. Members who wish to attend events are asked to return a slip from the mailings so there will be enough room, supplies, and food at each meeting.

Both the Mandarin Oriental and Pan Pacific hotels in San Francisco have generously provided space for our meetings, which are usually held on Monday mornings (often a baker's day off). We are deeply grateful for their hospitality.

We learn by baking and by tasting the results at our meetings. We tested the differences between using cake flour and all-purpose flour in cakes. The surprising result was that most bakers preferred the cakes made with all-purpose flour to the "wimpy" ones made with cake flour. We have tested and tasted different brands of ingredients, including butter and baking chocolate.

Our bake-offs have produced amazing results. When we had an angel food cake bake-off with more than sixty entries prepared from the same recipe, there weren't two cakes that looked alike. They all had different colors, heights, crumb structures, and textures. A second tasting, where the recipe was refined to provide more specific directions, gave results that were only slightly more consistent, proving perhaps that the most important ingredient in a recipe is the personal hand and touch of the baker.

Our field trips are always popular. We visited Fleischmann's Yeast and learned how yeast is cultivated on beds of syrup. At C&H Sugar, we saw the complicated process of transforming raw product into refined brown and white sugars. A trip through the Acme Bread Company in Berkeley revealed every step that goes into making artisan loaves. At the Straus Dairy, we learned about butter. Perhaps the most delicious excursion was our visit to Guittard Chocolate.

With so much information being shared, a cookbook that collected our experiences and favorite recipes seemed to be the next logical step. We divided into committees to write chapters on individual subjects. As the groups gathered and tested recipes to find the best ones, they wrote what turned out to be a primer on each topic. The bakers jotted down tips to clarify the fine points of the recipes, just as if they were attending one of our meetings.

The recipes in this book are more than just recipes. They have been selected and tested by some of the most respected people in the baking business, from cookbook authors, baking teachers, and professional bakers to home cooks who are devoted and passionate about baking. In addition, you'll find information on ingredients, equipment, and techniques that will make you a better baker. We know you'll enjoy trying these recipes.

Most of all, it is our hope that *The Baker's Dozen Cookbook* will inspire our fellow bakers everywhere to form their own baking groups. Surely bakers in certain climates share common problems that could be solved by meetings like ours. How do bakers in humid areas like Florida deal with sticky meringues? What calculations should Denver's bakers make for high-altitude baking? If your experience is like ours, you may start out small and end up big, or your group may never have more than six people meeting in one another's homes. No matter the size of your group, you will learn more about baking than you ever thought possible. Because with a baker's dozen, you always get a little something extra.

A Baker's Glossary of Ingredients

Flour, butter, sugar, eggs, salt . . . a baker uses the same ingredients over and over and over again. But these ingredients never become boring, because the possibilities for combinations and variations are endless.

The more you know about your ingredients, the better baker you will be.

This glossary is meant to be an overview of essential ingredients for general baking. The application of each ingredient, however, may vary from recipe to recipe. Flour is a good example. The flour a baker chooses for bread will usually be much different from the one used for pies. In the introduction to each chapter, you will find details on ingredients specific to the topic and how to use them. The major contributors to this chapter were Fran Gage (Flour), David Lebovitz (Vanilla), Janet Rikala Dalton (Eggs), Gisele Perez (Fats), Cynthia Ware (Leavenings), Alice Medrich (Chocolate), and Carolyn B. Weil (Sugar).

Chocolate

WHAT WOULD THE baker's art be like without chocolate? Over the centuries, it has evolved from a sacramental food for Aztec royalty to a ubiquitous and beloved sweet for the commoner. In spite of its familiar flavor, chocolate remains a mysterious, somewhat temperamental cooking ingredient. It is worth going into a lengthy discussion of chocolate to reveal its secrets, for the more you know about chocolate and cocoa, the easier it is to understand how they behave in a recipe.

Types of Chocolate and Cocoa

Unsweetened chocolate | What home cooks call unsweetened or baking chocolate, professional bakers and chocolatiers refer to as chocolate liquor. Both consist of cocoa beans that have been roasted, ground, molded, and cooled to harden. Unsweetened chocolate is approximately half cocoa butter and half cocoa solids. It contains no sugar or other added ingredients; it should not be confused with or substituted for bittersweet chocolate. Chocolate liquor is the essential ingredient in all other forms of chocolate (except white chocolate): Each category of chocolate is defined by how much chocolate liquor it contains. The more liquor, the more intense the chocolate flavor. More liquor also means less sugar.

Sweet chocolate | This category is too broad to be meaningful to bakers or candy makers. As defined by the USDA, sweet chocolate includes all of the sweetened chocolates for baking and eating that contain at least 15 percent liquor; this is all sweetened chocolates that are stronger than milk chocolate. The category includes chocolates actually labeled "Sweet Dark Chocolate," with up to 35 percent chocolate liquor (such as Baker's German and Ghirardelli Sweet Dark Baking Chocolate), but it also contains semisweet and bittersweet chocolate, with chocolate liquor ranging from 35 to more than 70 percent. Sugar content ranges from less than 30 percent to almost twice that, and milk solids from zero to 12 percent.

Of the sweet chocolates, *semisweet* and *bittersweet* are the most important to bakers. There is no official distinction between bittersweet and semisweet chocolate; manufacturers label these chocolates according to their own standards of sweetness and chocolate flavor. Thus one brand of semisweet might not be sweeter than another brand of bittersweet. Subject to a few cautionary words about high-percentage chocolates (see "High-Percentage Chocolates," below), you can use semisweet and bittersweet chocolate interchangeably in recipes. Semisweet and bittersweet chocolate must contain at least 35 percent chocolate liquor, but most bakers consider 50 to 55 percent to be the minimum-quality benchmark.

Examples of reliable semisweet and bittersweet chocolate with 50 to 60 percent chocolate liquor include Ghirardelli Semisweet, Ghirardelli Bittersweet, Baker's Semisweet, Baker's Bittersweet, Hershey's Semisweet, Lindt Surfin, Lindt Excellence (not to be confused with Lindt Excellence 70%), Valrhona Equatorial, Callebaut Semisweet, and Scharffen Berger Semisweet (which has a chocolate liquor content of 62 percent).

High-percentage chocolates | There is a growing trend to state the percentage of chocolate liquor (also referred to as cocoa mass, cacao, or cocoa beans, depending on the manufacturer) on chocolate labels. The higher the percentage of chocolate liquor, the less sugar there is to sweeten the chocolate, resulting in a deeper, more intense flavor.

"Bittersweet chocolate with high chocolate-liquor percentage" is not an official category as yet. Nonetheless, it is a useful one because these more intense chocolates, with 60 to more than 70 percent chocolate liquor, are increasingly available to American home bakers. They offer exciting choices to the passionate cook, as the complexities and subtle flavor of the cocoa bean are more pronounced in these less sweetened chocolates. Valrhona, Scharffen Berger, El Rey, and Lindt all offer high-percentage chocolates. Look for the percentage on the front of the package. Chocolate with up to 62 percent chocolate liquor usually works nicely in recipes that call for traditional semisweet or bittersweet chocolate. Unless some adjustments are made, chocolate with 66 to 70 percent chocolate liquor cannot always be substituted ounce for ounce in a recipe intended for chocolate with the more common 50 to 55 percent liquor.

There are two main approaches to substituting high-percentage chocolate for the traditional semisweet or bittersweet chocolate in recipes, but both approaches should be considered somewhat experimental.

First, you may attempt to replicate the chocolate intensity and sweetness of the original recipe by using less of the high-percentage chocolate and adding more sugar. Reduce the amount of chocolate by about one-quarter, then add 2 teaspoons of sugar for every ounce of the reduced amount of chocolate. For example, a recipe that calls for 8 ounces of traditional bittersweet chocolate would use 6 ounces of high-percentage chocolate and 12 teaspoons (¼ cup) additional sugar. Ganache recipes require that you reduce the chocolate by one-quarter (although you need not add sugar) because the cream-to-chocolate liquor ratio is critical to achieving a ganache that does not break.

The second approach works for many cake, torte, cookie, brownie, and soufflé recipes: Experiment by substituting high-percentage chocolate for traditional bittersweet chocolate ounce for ounce (with or without adding sugar). This will make a much more intense bittersweet dessert, which must be the intent of the baker who chooses to use a high-percentage chocolate anyway. If you do this without adding sugar, batters are likely to be thicker and less moist and baking time will be shorter, because more chocolate liquor means more moisture-absorbing cocoa solids and less moisture-retaining sugar. Check for doneness early to avoid dry, overbaked cakes and cookies!

Milk chocolate and white chocolate | These two chocolates are similar but different. Milk chocolate has less chocolate liquor than sweet chocolate (but at least 10 percent) and more sugar. The addition of milk and butterfat accounts for its lighter color, milder flavor, and softer texture.

There are two types of white chocolate. The better of the two is essentially milk chocolate (with at least 20 percent cocoa butter) without the cocoa solids. The other type is made with tropical vegetable fats other than cocoa butter, so it contains neither cocoa fat nor cocoa solids. Because neither one contains cocoa solids, the USDA does not consider it chocolate, and it must be labeled "white confectioners' coating."

Milk and white chocolate both scorch easily, so they are rarely found as an ingredient in baked goods, but they can be used in mousses, frostings, and icings. Never try to substitute them in recipes that call for melted dark sweet or unsweetened chocolate. Our favorite milk and white chocolates include Callebaut, El Rey, Valrhona, and Lindt.

Couverture | The finest chocolate, called couverture, melts like silk on the palate. Couverture is subjected to an extended period of conching (a special grinding procedure), during which the ingredients are ground so finely and mixed so intimately together that the palate cannot detect individual particles. Extra cocoa butter is added to ensure a luxuriously smooth texture as the chocolate melts in your mouth.

When chocolate or couverture is used as a candy or cookie coating, it must usually be melted and tempered. Tempering is a process of heating, cooling, and stirring the chocolate in such a way that the cocoa butter crystals form a strong, stable network as the chocolate cools and hardens. Properly tempered chocolate dries quickly, with a shiny surface and a pleasantly brittle texture; dried untempered chocolate looks dull and streaky and has a soft, cakey texture.

Chocolate bars available to the home baker are rarely if ever labeled couverture, but the following bars (ranging in size from 3 ounces to about 1 pound) are couverture-quality chocolate: Ghirardelli Semisweet and Bittersweet; Lindt Surfin and Excellence (including the 70% bar); all Valrhona bars; all Scharffen Berger bars; Callebaut Semisweet, Bittersweet, Milk, and White Chocolate bars; and all El Rey bars.

Chocolate chips | Sometimes called morsels, chocolate chips are especially designed for use in cookies. They can withstand the heat of a hot cookie sheet without burning or losing shape. Chocolate chips are fine when used in cookies or coffee cakes, but because they are usually made of sweeter, coarser chocolate of lower quality, they should not be substituted for melted chocolate in recipes.

Cocoa | There are two types of cocoa available: *natural* and *Dutch processed* (or Dutched). Cocoa in its natural form is quite acidic. Dutch-processed cocoa is treated with an alkali solution to reduce this acidity. (The process was invented in the 1820s in the Netherlands.) The alkalizing process changes the flavor as well as the sharpness of the cocoa. Dutch-processed cocoa can be described as mellower, toastier, and nuttier, some describe it as dull and dusty flavored. By contrast, untreated, nonalkalized natural cocoa is described as both fruity and tart as well as harsh and bitter. Fans of natural cocoa insist that alkalizing mutes the chocolate flavor, while the opposition feels that it actually makes the flavor more chocolaty (probably because baked goods with Dutch-processed cocoa can look darker, and therefore seem richer by visual association). Do not confuse cocoa with hot chocolate mixes, which are sweetened and may contain milk powder.

In older American cookbooks, cocoa always meant the natural variety because only natural cocoa was widely available to the home cook. Today, when you see the phrase "preferably Dutch processed" in a recipe, it often reflects the author's personal taste. But the choice of cocoa can also affect the chemical balance of the ingredients and spell success or disaster. When it is a matter of taste, the two cocoas can usually be used interchangeably, as long as the recipe doesn't include baking powder or baking soda.

The presence of leavening in a recipe sometimes proves it the exception: Cakes or pastries with baking powder and/or soda rely on a balance of acidic and alkaline ingredients for proper rising, flavor, and texture. Especially in recipes with high amounts of baking soda (such as devil's food cake), the substitution of Dutch-processed for natural cocoa can result in a dense, gummy, coal-black cake with a soapy taste.

If a cocoa is Dutch processed or alkalized, it should state it clearly on the package. If not, check the ingredients list and look for "cocoa processed with alkali." Hershey's uses the phrase "European Style" for its Dutch-processed cocoa. Natural cocoa is simply labeled "cocoa" on the package, and the ingredients list will just say "cocoa" or "100% cocoa."

Melting Chocolate

You need no special tools to melt chocolate—just pay attention to what you're doing! Whether you are using a double boiler, a microwave oven, or a bowl in a skillet of barely simmering water, your goal is to melt the chocolate just until it is warm and fluid—not hot.

There are two things to avoid when melting chocolate: excessive heat and moisture. Melted dark chocolate will burn at somewhere near 140°F, but there is no reason to heat it to this high a temperature. Chocolate is completely melted and fluid by the time it reaches body temperature (98.6°F). Burned chocolate gets thick and gritty, which is why chocolate is melted over barely simmering water (or under moderate power in a microwave), never over a direct flame. Take care not to splash water into the bowl, and be sure your utensils are absolutely dry. If just a drop of water gets in the chocolate, it will thicken into a pasty mass. In some recipes chocolate is melted with liquid, but only if the ratio is more than 1 tablespoon of liquid to every 2 ounces of chocolate. Milk and white chocolate contain milk proteins that scorch more easily than dark chocolate, so take special caution to melt them over gentle heat, and do not exceed 115°F.

Always chop chocolate before melting. The smaller the pieces, the more surface area is in contact with the heat, and the less heat and time are necessary to make the chocolate warm and fluid. Chop chocolate on a cutting board with a chef's knife or a sturdy pronged chocolate chipper. Using a food processor may be more trouble than it's worth: You must coarsely chop the chocolate before processing, be sure that the bowl and blade are perfectly dry, and pulse the machine to avoid excessive friction, which would melt the chocolate.

Place the chopped chocolate in a stainless steel bowl (be sure the bowl is dry), then set the bowl in a skillet with about an inch of very hot or barely simmering water. This method applies steady gentle heat over a large surface and encourages a fast melt. (Or use a double boiler.) Do not cover the bowl. Stir frequently with a rubber spatula just until the chocolate is melted and fluid. Safer yet, remove the bowl of chocolate from the water just before the last pieces are completely melted, then stir to finish the melting.

To melt chocolate in a microwave oven, place the chopped chocolate in a microwave-safe bowl. Microwave the uncovered chocolate at moderate (50 percent) power, using 20- to 30-second intervals and stirring after each interval to see how much of the chocolate is melted. The time for each interval depends on the amount of chocolate and the size of the pieces, so as the chocolate melts, change to 5- to 10-second periods. Never try to melt the bowl of chocolate in one zap; it will be likely to burn.

Buying and Storing Chocolate

The best way to choose a chocolate for cooking is to taste it. If you prefer the flavor of one chocolate over another, chances are you will also like the results in your recipe. If your recipe calls for unsweetened chocolate, you may find it difficult to taste, so try different brands of unsweetened chocolate in your favorite brownie recipe and note which one you prefer.

Buy chocolate from a store with a rapid turnover and proper cool storage space that is out of direct sunlight. Bulk chocolate should be wrapped airtight. Be especially wary of random-weight chunks of white and milk chocolate, which can turn rancid quickly. Try to taste a bit before you leave the store. Avoid any that is crumbly or gritty.

Chocolate should be kept well wrapped in a cool, dry place away from pronounced odors (cheese, fish, garlic, herbs and spices, etc.) Stored properly, dark chocolate keeps well for at least 1 year, milk and white chocolates for 3 months.

Chocolate in good condition has a glossy, smooth surface and a brittle snap when broken. If the surface has gray streaks, mottling, or a dull color, the chocolate has been damaged by heat, temperature changes, or moisture (which cause the sugar to crystallize on the surface). This discoloring is called bloom. Bloomed chocolate is not spoiled, unhealthy, or inedible, but a badly bloomed piece may feel crumbly, gritty, or greasy on the palate, and this unpleasant texture can interfere with your nibbling enjoyment. If the chocolate is to be melted and used as an ingredient in a recipe, bloom will not affect the outcome.

Eggs

EGGS SERVE MANY PURPOSES in baking, acting as leavening, binder, and emulsifier. Disregarding the shell, eggs are composed of two disparate components, the yolk (mainly fat) and the white (mainly protein). Eggs are often separated, because the fat in the yolk would inhibit the egg whites from reaching their full volume when beaten.

Eggs have been known to carry salmonella bacteria, which are especially harmful to people with compromised immune systems, the elderly, and infants. Cooking eggs at above 140°F for more than 3 minutes or at 160° kills the bacteria, so all of our recipes that once called for raw or undercooked eggs now use these methods.

All of the recipes in this book were tested with large eggs. The USDA determines sizes on the basis of minimum weight per dozen. A dozen large eggs weigh 24 ounces; the same number of extra-large eggs weigh 27 ounces. Don't substitute one size for another.

The eggs available to consumers are graded AA or A, which are virtually interchangeable. The grade AA egg will have a firm, more round yolk and a small amount of white; the grade A egg will have a larger proportion of thick white to thin white, and the yolk will not stand up as tall. Shell color has no bearing on egg quality. Brown eggs are more expensive because the hens are larger and require more food, so the cost to the consumer is higher.

We often ask for eggs at room temperature. When cold eggs are added to a batter, they can harden the fat, which will change the texture of the batter and the final product, so eggs are rarely used straight from the refrigerator. To quickly bring whole eggs to room temperature, place them in a bowl of warm tap water and let stand for a few minutes.

However, chilled eggs are easier to separate than room-temperature eggs (cold increases the viscosity of the egg). To separate eggs, be sure the metal, glass, or ceramic mixing bowl and any beating utensils are completely grease-free; never use a rubber or plastic bowl, which will retain minuscule traces of fat that can inhibit whipping. To remove residual grease from a bowl, pour a splash of cider or wine vinegar into the bowl and wipe it out with paper towels. Do not rinse out the vinegar, as acidic ingredients (such as cream of tartar and lemon juice) will react with the proteins in the whites to improve whipping.

When opening eggs, crack each one over a small bowl, not directly into batter or dough. Check for any bits of shell in the egg before using, and remove them if necessary (press your fingertip against the shell fragment and bring it up the side of the bowl until you can pick it out). To separate eggs, working over a bowl, transfer the egg back and forth between the two eggshells, letting the egg white flow into the bowl until the yolk is nestled in an eggshell half. Be careful not to catch the yolk on the sharp edges of the shells, or you will get bits of yolk in the white (which can be removed by using the edge of the eggshell as a scoop). When separating many eggs, you may want to try the method used by many professional bakers: Wash your hands, then pour each cracked egg into your cupped fingers, letting the white flow through your fingers until the yolk is sitting in your hand. Wash your hands well with soap and hot water before handling any other food.

Egg whites will beat to their optimum height at about 60°F, which is warmer than chilled but cooler than room temperature. You can separate the eggs, then let the whites stand at room temperature for about 15 minutes. (Use an instant-read thermometer to check.) Or place the bowl of whites in a larger bowl of warm water, and stir with the stem of an instant-read thermometer until they read 60°F. If you are beating large batches of whites, it is helpful to know that the standard 5-quart bowl of a heavy-duty mixer will hold up to 1½ cups of egg whites when they are beaten with up to 1½ cups of sugar.

Every baker needs to master the different stages of beaten egg whites. *Foamy* egg whites form large, very loose bubbles in a cloudy, yellowish liquid. When they reach *soft peaks*, the bubbles are tightening into a white foam with a ribbon that folds back into itself; you can pull the whites into a "peak," but it won't hold one. *Firm peaks* are glossy, firm, and smooth; the whites can be lifted into a peak that will hold and curl at the tip. Stiff peaks are glossy and dry enough to cut with a knife. If whipped until they crackle (indicating breaking bubbles), egg whites are useless. It may be possible to restore over-beaten egg whites by adding one new raw white per one cup of overbeaten whites, and beating it in.

Know how fresh your eggs are. As an egg ages, the white becomes thinner and the yolk flatter. Although this has no bearing on the egg's nutritional value or function, its appearance will change. Most bakers prefer fresher egg whites because they are more viscous and can be beaten into fluffier peaks.

If the carton has a sell-by date, it will never be longer than 30 days past the packing date. The number after the sell-by date is the day of packing, according to the Julian calendar. For example, DEC 20 325 means that the eggs were packed on the 325th day of the year (November 22), and that the sell-by date is four weeks later, on December 20.

Store eggs in the refrigerator, never in the egg-holder shelf of the door, which is one of the warmest spots in the refrigerator. Keep the eggs in the carton, as eggshells are quite delicate and will absorb other refrigerator odors that can transfer to the eggs themselves.

Fats

WHETHER FROM ANIMALS or vegetables, fats act as tenderizers in baked goods. They also add richness and moisture, and often provide flavor. Animal fats, including butter and lard, are solid at room temperature. Vegetable oil is liquid. Vegetable short-ening and margarine are vegetable oils that have been processed to make them firm. All fats (animal or vegetable, solid or liquid) serve the same function and have equal calorie counts, yet their various flavors and properties give them different applications in the baker's kitchen.

Butter | Butter imparts an unmistakable flavor to baked goods that you cannot get from any other fat. It also has a creamy texture that vegetable-based fats wish they had. When creamed, it holds air that contributes to the leavening process. When aeration is not important, melted butter is added to baked goods for its taste.

Butter is sold salted and unsalted. Most bakers have a strong preference for unsalted butter so they can control the amount of salt in a recipe. Salt is added to butter as a preservative, so unsalted butter will always be the fresher choice. Be sure the butter is wrapped in foil or some other impervious material, as it picks up odors easily in the refrigerator.

Margarine | This is artificial butter, created from vegetable oil that has been hydrogenated, a process that chemically alters the liquid to make it firm. Some margarine may also contain animal fats, as well as milk solids. Margarine acts like butter in many ways, but it has a very inferior flavor. We only mention it as a matter of discussion; we never advocate the use of margarine over butter in baking, even if it is less expensive.

Vegetable shortening | A hydrogenated oil product that is nearly 100 percent fat, it has good creaming properties and it melts at higher temperatures than butter, so some bakers do use it in their batters and frostings, and it makes very flaky pie pastry. But again, shortening just doesn't have the creamy, rich flavor of butter.

Lard | It is nothing more than rendered pork fat. It is softer than butter with a sweeter, meatier flavor, and can be used in pie pastries for a very flaky crust. There are supermarket brands, but homemade is far superior (see page 126). Lard is not used as widely as it was in the past because of health concerns associated with a diet high in animal fat.

Oils | These come from many different sources, including fruits (such as olives and avocados), vegetables (corn), nuts (walnuts, almonds, and hazelnuts), and seeds (sunflower, sesame, and rapeseed, which goes by the name canola oil). They vary in flavor quite a bit. An extra virgin olive or walnut oil can add a great deal to the flavor of a yeast bread, while canola oil is virtually flavorless. Oils cannot be creamed, but they are added to yeast and quick breads.

Flour

OF ALL THE GRAINS, wheat is the most important to the baker, because it produces a flour that is capable of determining the texture of a baked product. The invention of roller mills in the second half of the eighteenth century radically changed the way wheat was transformed into flour. Today, huge mechanized rollers shear the wheat berries, separating the endosperm from the bran and germ. The remaining starchy center is sifted from the other ingredients and pulverized. The end result is a uniformly white flour. Prior to this mechanical advancement, grains were ground in hammer or stone mills into a coarse or fine flour that retained all its components. Some millers still use these ancient methods. The results are breads with a chewy texture and earthy taste.

Some grains are now farmed organically, without chemical fertilizers, pesticides, or fumigants in the soil, on the crops, or in the storage tanks. The wheat must be grown in fields that have been chemical-free for three years. Although this commendable approach promotes sustainable agriculture, the baker may not notice any difference in the way flour from organically grown wheat behaves in the kitchen. On the other hand, because organic grain hasn't been treated, it contains naturally occurring yeasts and bacteria that may add depth of flavor, especially in baked products where the taste of the wheat is prominent, such as bread. In addition, these natural substances are responsible for the leavening power and taste of sourdough bread. As much as we often like the results we get from baked goods with organic flour, however, we tested these recipes with supermarket brands of flour because they are readily available.

Although milled wheat contains about 70 percent starch and only 6 to 18 percent protein, it is the protein that affects the personality of a bread, cake, or pie. Without protein, the carbon dioxide produced by the leavening would bubble to the surface and disappear. But when two proteins in the flour, gliadin and glutenin, are mixed with water, then subjected to kneading or mixing, their long, gangly molecules coil and wrap around each other, creating gluten, an invisible superstructure in the dough. This matrix is strong enough to trap the carbon dioxide as the leavening does its work. Gluten gives the dough flexibility, allowing a long baguette to stretch without tearing. (Conversely, it will also make the dough snap back into shape if it is not given time to relax.) In the heat of the oven, the matrix sets and gives texture to the loaf.

Wheat is farmed, making it subject to the vagaries of heat, water, pests, and the skill of the farmer. Some harvests are more plentiful than others; some years produce wheat of poorer quality. All of these factors affect the quality of the proteins in the flour. Milling techniques can also affect the flour. Because wheat kernels are ground by a series of rollers and the proteins are just under the husk, the first pass will yield a flour with more proteins; the flour milled closer to the center will have more starch. Millers mix flours to get the final characteristics they desire.

There are different types of wheat, each variety exhibiting its own characteristics. "Soft" or "hard" describes the protein in the wheat and its baking potential. Hard-wheat flour has sufficient good-quality gliadin and glutenin necessary to develop the strong gluten that forms in bread dough with assertive kneading. Yet this same flour, prized by bread makers, produces tough cakes and cookies. Tender pastries need flour with a lower protein content. In order not to trouble the proteins in the batter, the cake baker mixes it delicately instead of kneading, so the gliadin and glutenin don't join forces to create a strong gluten framework, which would make the cake chewy instead of soft on the tongue.

Cake flour | This is the lowest-protein (8 percent) flour available to consumers. Finely ground and bleached with chlorine to make it whiter, it does make fine-textured cakes, but it is not every baker's first choice. *Pastry flour* is another low-protein flour that some bakers find works well in cakes and pastries. However, as it is difficult to find, we do not use it in this book.

Unbleached all-purpose flour | At the opposite end of the flour spectrum are the higher-protein flours, which are usually reserved for bread making. These higher-protein flours are usually unbleached (the bleaching process reduces the amount of protein). When we use unbleached all-purpose flour in these recipes, we mean a supermarket variety with an average of 10.5 percent protein. (The term "all-purpose" is really a misnomer, as this flour is *not* good for all kinds of baking.) The protein content is listed in the nutritional information on the bag. King Arthur brand flour, which is unbleached, has an 11.7-percent protein content. It will work for most recipes, but you may have to slightly adjust the amount of flour, because flours with different amounts of protein absorb liquid at varying rates. *Bread flour* has more protein than unbleached all-purpose flour (about 13 percent) and is what makes bread chewy.

All-purpose flour | is a blend of soft and hard wheat flours. As its name implies, all-purpose flour can be used for cakes, pastries, and breads. However, professional bakers know its mid-range protein content, which varies from 9 to 10.5 percent, is actually a little too high for silky cakes and a little low for hearty bread. In the South, where tender biscuits are king, the all-purpose flour is often made from soft wheat alone. When a recipe calls for all-purpose flour, we are referring to *unbleached* all-purpose flour with an average of 10.5 percent protein. *Self-rising flour* is a low-protein flour with chemical leavenings already included, so the baker can whip up quick breads in a flash. We don't use it, as we much prefer to add the correct amount of leavening dictated by the particular recipe.

Not all wheat flour is white. The brown flecks in *whole wheat flour* are bits of the bran and germ from the kernel. Because these components contain fats that can turn rancid, whole wheat flour should be stored in a cool place, even refrigerated. Whole wheat flour also contains proteins other than the ones that make gluten, so the protein content printed on the bag may be misleading. For bread baking, whole wheat flour is usually mixed with bread flour to produce a lighter loaf.

Durum flour | Made from a variety of hard wheat, durum wheat makes an interesting addition to breads, but it is primarily used to make pasta dough. Brown durum flour is a whole wheat flour using the entire wheat berry, and white durum flour uses just the endosperm. *Semolina* is the endosperm of durum wheat that has been ground to a granular, sandy texture instead of a fine powder.

Rye flour | This is milled for use in bread and crackers. This grain's gluten lacks the extensibility of wheat, so it won't produce lofty loaves on its own. It is also slightly sticky, even after kneading. For bread, it is usually mixed with about 50 percent white flour, although there are Scandinavian recipes that make very dense rye bread from whole kernels.

Other grains can be used in baking, but because they have low protein and gluten contents, they are usually augmented with white flour. Spelt, kamut, corn, buckwheat (actually more closely related to rhubarb than wheat), and chestnuts (not a grain) are ground and added to baked goods. All these supplements add texture and flavor nuances.

Leavenings

THE THREE MOST COMMON leavenings—ingredients that introduce carbon dioxide into baked goods and make them rise—are baking powder, baking soda, and yeast.

Baking powder and baking soda, considered chemical leavenings, are usually reserved for cakes, quick breads, and other baked goods with a uniform, tender crumb. These leavenings were technology's reliable answer to antique ingredients for getting baked goods to rise, such as hartshorn (made from the hooves and horns of the hart, a male deer) and potash (a by-product of wood ashes). The choice of chemical leavening is determined by the ingredients in the recipe. Usually baking soda is used to neutralize the acidity of ingredients like buttermilk, sour milk, and molasses, creating carbon dioxide in the process. Baking powder works as a leavening without the inclusion of acidic ingredients. The two can also work in tandem, the reaction of the baking soda and the acid creating some of the carbon dioxide, with the baking powder providing the remainder.

There is no set formula for using chemical leavenings, and using more will not make a cake lighter. During the creaming process (see page 48), air bubbles are beaten into the mixture. Baking powder and baking soda will only make those air bubbles larger— they do not create the bubbles. Excess leavening will overactivate and deflate the bubbles before the starch structure is set in the oven, giving the baker a flat, unrisen cake with a chemical flavor.

Baking powder | This is a combination of baking soda and two powdered acids, along with a small amount of starch to absorb moisture in the air that would make the mixture clump. One of these acids, sodium aluminum sulfate, can add a bitter flavor to baked goods. Some bakers prefer aluminum-free baking powder, such as Rumford's, available at natural food stores and many supermarkets. There is no difference in rising power between the non-aluminum and regular brands.

Most commercial baking powder is "double-acting," meaning that it releases its carbon dioxide gas in two stages. The first CO_2-producing reaction occurs when one of the acids reacts with the baking soda as the compound comes in contact with liquid during mixing. The second reaction takes place when the second acid in the mixture is heated during baking, or on a griddle, as with pancakes. (Single-acting baking powder, which is not commonly found in markets, contains baking soda and just one acid, and produces CO_2 only when mixed with liquid.) The advantage of double-acting baking powder is that baking can be delayed; baked goods made with single-acting baking powder must be baked immediately, or all the carbon dioxide bubbles will dissipate before the item has a chance to rise in the oven.

During baking, the second gas-producing reaction is activated. Then, as the mixture is heated, proteins (in the flour and eggs, for example) set up, or gelatinize, forming a network of evenly distributed bubbles.

Be sure to sift the dry ingredients in a recipe to distribute the baking powder evenly.

Nothing, including baking powder, lasts forever, so be sure to check the expiration date stamped on the container. Or dissolve 1 teaspoon baking powder in ⅓ cup warm water; it should fizz dramatically. If not, it's time to replace it. Make your own single-acting baking powder by mixing together two parts cream of tartar and one part sodium bicarbonate (baking soda). If you use homemade baking powder, the batter or dough must be baked as soon as it is mixed.

Using the correct amount of baking powder is critical. It should be between 1 and 4 percent of the weight of the flour, or about 1 teaspoon for every cup of flour. If using heavy ingredients such as whole wheat flour, raisins, chopped fruit, or chocolate chips, increase the amount of baking powder to 1½ teaspoons per cup of flour. These amounts are only suggestions; trial and error will be your best guides.

Baking soda | Also known as sodium bicarbonate or bicarbonate of soda, it is used in baking mixtures that include a high component of acidic ingredients, such as molasses, honey, brown sugar, buttermilk, sour cream, yogurt, fruit juices, natural cocoa (but not Dutch-processed cocoa; see page 6), and even bananas. When baking soda is combined with an acidic ingredient and moisture, it immediately produces carbon dioxide. Therefore, baked goods that use baking soda alone must be baked immediately in order to set the protein structure and trap the bubbles. Baking soda will also darken a batter (think of the rich, dark color of gingerbread or carrot cake).

Even when used without baking powder or in batters and doughs with low acidity, baking soda still has leavening power. When heated, baking soda breaks down into sodium carbonate, water, and carbon dioxide. The drawback is that baking soda can impart an unpleasant soapy taste. But in the presence of an acid, that taste is neutralized.

The amount of baking soda should be 0.5 to 1.5 percent of the weight of the flour in a recipe, or about ¼ teaspoon for each cup of flour. As with baking powder, when the batter includes heavy additions, the baking soda can be increased to ½ teaspoon per cup of flour. To neutralize the acidity in 1 cup of buttermilk, you will need ½ teaspoon of baking soda, which furnishes the equivalent leavening power of 2 teaspoons of baking powder.

Yeast | A living, single-cell organism, yeast is the ingredient that makes breads rise. There are three distinct types of yeast on the market: active dry yeast, instant yeast, and compressed fresh yeast. For information on yeast, see page 253.

Nuts

ADDING FRAGRANCE, texture, and flavor to baked goods, and even replacing flour in some recipes, nuts are one of the baker's best friends.

Nuts (especially pecans and hazelnuts) are very susceptible to rancidity, so inspect them carefully before buying. Purchase them from a source with a rapid turnover, such as a natural food store, where they are usually available in bulk and less expensive. Refrigerate or freeze nuts in airtight containers or plastic bags for only a few months. Always taste nuts before using them.

Coarsely chopped nuts should be chopped into irregular pieces, about ¼ inch square. A simple way to get them to this size actually crushes the nuts without chopping. Spread the nuts on a work surface, then place the flat side of a large knife or cleaver over the nuts. Pressing on the top of the knife, crush the nuts into irregular pieces. If they need to be more finely chopped (finely chopped nuts are less than ⅛ inch square), use the knife to chop them.

In some recipes we use a food processor to chop the nuts with some flour or sugar into a powder of almost flourlike consistency (the dry ingredient keeps the nuts from releasing too much oil from the blade's friction). Other recipes require a rotary nut grinder to grind them into a fluffy texture.

Toasting brings out the flavor of all nuts and is required to remove the skins from hazelnuts. (Skinned, but untoasted, hazelnuts are now available at many markets, and while they are a boon, some bakers miss the toasted flavor.) To toast nuts, spread them on a baking sheet. Bake in a preheated 350°F oven for about 10 minutes, stirring often, until the nuts are fragrant and lightly toasted to a pale golden brown.

Hazelnuts should be toasted until the dark skins are cracked and peeling and the nuts look toasted underneath the skin. Wrap the nuts in a kitchen towel and let stand for a few minutes, then rub in the towel to remove the skins. Do not worry about removing every last bit of skin—they add color and flavor to the batter. If the skins are very stubborn, place the hazelnuts in a coarse-mesh wire sieve and rub them against the mesh to scrape off the recalcitrant skin.

Salt

IN BAKING, a little salt added to a recipe enhances the flavor of the other ingredients. It also strengthens gluten structure, improving the texture of breads. In yeast doughs, it is important to use the amount of salt called for, since salt inhibits yeast growth and controls fermentation. Too much salt added to bread dough will inhibit the activity of the yeast to the point that a heavy, dense loaf will result. When using salted butter in a recipe that calls for unsalted butter, be aware that a pound of butter can contain 1 teaspoon or more of salt, so reduce the amount of salt in the recipe to compensate for the salt in the butter.

When salt is called for in a recipe, it is assumed that table salt is to be used unless otherwise stated. In days past there were not many options when purchasing salt. Today there are many more types of salt available on market shelves. The crystals of the salt types have different shapes, and their weights and volumes vary. A teaspoon of table salt or sea salt may weigh 6 grams, but a teaspoon of kosher salt is 2.8 grams. Individual bakers have formed their own preferences, which we collectively respect, so you will see fine sea salt specified in some recipes. To many cooks, the flavor of sea salt is more delicate than and preferable to table salt.

Table salt | It is finely ground and is mixed with additives so it will flow freely. Iodized salt is table salt with iodine added. This addition is made to prevent the medical condition hypothyroidism, which occurs in geographic areas with no natural iodine. These salts can be used interchangeably in recipes, although some say iodized salt has a distinctive flavor that can be detected in mildly flavored foods.

Sea salt | Processed from the evaporation of seawater and with a higher concentration of minerals, it comes in fine crystals, medium flakes, or coarse grains and ranges in color from dull gray to pure white. It is more expensive than mined salt. Depending on the method of processing, sea salt can weigh more or less by volume than table salt, causing a baked product that is more or less salty than desired. This is especially true with bulk sea salt, which tends to retain more moisture and be heavier than boxed brands. For our bakers who prefer fine sea salt in their recipes, we used a commonly available boxed brand from a natural food store.

Kosher salt | Coarse-grained and additive-free, it is used by both Jewish and non-Jewish cooks. Kosher salt has a large, hollow crystal and blends into savory foods faster than granular table salt. However, because it is coarse, not many bakers use it. If using kosher salt, keep in mind that it weighs less than table salt. It takes from one and one quarter times to twice as much kosher salt (depending on the brand) as table salt to achieve the same amount of saltiness.

Sugar

Granulated sugar | In conventional baking, sugar is the primary sweetener. There are two primary sources for baking sugars in today's market, sugarcane and sugar beets. Sugar from either source will add moisture and flavor to baked goods as well as contributing to crispness and exterior browning. Although the two sugars are considered interchangeable, many bakers prefer cane sugar over beet sugar for baking. Cane sugar does have better flavor and manageability (some cooks find that beet sugar doesn't melt smoothly for caramel).

Molasses | The dark syrup that remains after removing the dry white sugar crystals is a by-product of cane sugar refining. Light molasses comes from the first boiling of the sugar and has a mild flavor. Strong-flavored dark molasses is the result of the second boiling. Bitter blackstrap molasses comes from the final extraction, and is not recommended for general baking. Blackstrap molasses can be found at health food stores, but it has minimal amounts of nutritive minerals. If sulfur dioxide is used in extracting the molasses from the cane, it is considered sulfured molasses. Because some bakers think it has a milder flavor, unsulfured molasses may be recommended in a recipe.

Brown sugar | Refined sugar with cane sugar molasses added back in, brown sugar from beets is white sugar crystals that have been sprayed with brown cane molasses. Cane brown sugar has up to twice as much molasses as beet brown sugar and has a richer flavor. The amount of molasses determines the color of the brown sugar; light brown sugar has less molasses and a milder flavor than dark brown sugar. You can use either, depending on your affection for the taste of molasses. When brown sugar is to be mixed with eggs or liquids, it will dissolve more easily if rubbed through a coarse wire sieve to remove any lumps.

Confectioners' sugar | Commonly known as powdered sugar, it is a very finely ground sugar with a small amount of cornstarch added to prevent clumping. This sugar is well suited for icings and frostings. It is often sifted to remove lumps.

Superfine sugar | Sometimes labeled bakers' sugar or bar sugar, it is a fine white crystal that dissolves easily in meringues, cake batters, and syrups.

Sanding sugar | The large crystal sugar used by bakers for decorating and adding sparkle and crunch to cookies and cakes. It is available in clear or colored crystals. *Pearl sugar* has larger, rounder crystals and is available from specialty grocers (see Sources, page 343). It is considered "non-melting" and is used only for decorating.

Two amber-colored sugars are made from partially refined crystals that still include molasses. *Turbinado sugar* is a large, light brown crystal with a mild molasses flavor. *Demerara sugar* typically refers to the very coarse sugar originally from the Demerara region of Guyana; it is the sugar that fine restaurants often serve with coffee. Both of these sugars are great for caramelizing on top of crème brûlée. For most recipes, these sugars can be ground in a food processor and substituted for granulated sugar, where they impart a mild molasses flavor.

We don't use honey in this book because no one submitted a recipe that used it.

Actually, it poses many problems for bakers. As a liquid sugar, it requires much adjusting of the other wet ingredients, and its acidity can wreak havoc with the leavening in a recipe. Blindly substituting honey for sugar is asking for trouble.

Vanilla

HOW DOES THE FRUIT of an exotic tropical orchid end up in so many desserts, from the humblest pound cake to the richest custard? Vanilla production is very complicated and labor-intensive. Each orchid blossom opens only one day a year and must be hand-pollinated, which certainly makes one appreciate the cost of a bottle of extract or of the vanilla beans themselves. Vanilla extract is often labeled in "folds," which refers to how many vanilla beans are infused in the alcohol base to make the extract. The more folds, the more vanilla beans are used. Two-fold vanilla extract means that twice as many beans were infused per gallon of alcohol as in single-fold extract.

We use only pure single-fold vanilla extract or vanilla beans in our recipes. Many of our bakers prefer aromatic and very flavorful Bourbon vanilla extract, which is available at most supermarkets and kitchenware shops. Imitation vanilla (vanillin) is made from by-products of paper production and has only one of the many flavor and aroma components of true vanilla. Using it means your desserts won't have the same depth and aroma. A small amount of real vanilla extract yields much more flavor and is without doubt worth the difference in price.

The Baker's Dozen was once treated to a presentation by a representative of the McCormick company, who showed the process of vanilla production on the island of Madagascar, from the growing and pollination of the orchids to their three- to six-month curing process and the making of the extracts. Another excellent brand used by many bakers is Nielsen-Massey, which also distributes organic vanilla beans and extracts.

Most extracts have a volatile alcohol base. In order to be sure that the flavor doesn't evaporate, vanilla extract should be added to slightly cooled mixtures. If added at the beginning of heating a custard, the vanilla flavor would literally go up in steam, if not smoke. In baked goods, a healthy amount of extract ensures that enough vanilla flavor remains.

Avoid the inexpensive Mexican vanilla labeled as "extract" available in tourist shops, for most contain coumarin, a toxic ingredient banned in the United States by the FDA. Be aware that other countries don't have the same labeling laws as we do in the United States. True Mexican vanilla extract is very flavorful, and many consider it the best. It is just as costly as other vanillas and should be purchased from a reputable source. See Sources, page 343, for a selection of companies that sell high-quality vanilla. Store vanilla extract in a cool, dark place. It should keep for at least 5 years.

In some recipes, when we want a truer vanilla flavor, we use the vanilla bean itself. The most widely available varieties of beans are Bourbon (from Madagascar and other islands off the coast of Africa), Tahitian, and Mexican. The slender Bourbon beans are the most common and have the most intense flavor. Tahitian beans have a delicate, aromatic fragrance, which some bakers prefer. Tahitian beans contain more moisture, so they are plumper, but they are not necessarily more flavorful than other beans. For most bakers, it's simply a matter of preference. In addition, there are far fewer Tahitian beans cultivated, making Tahitian vanilla extracts and the beans themselves more costly. If you can find them, thick Mexican beans are excellent. Vanilla beans should feel soft and pliable; avoid dry, brittle beans, which have lost their aromatic oils. Wrap vanilla beans well and store in a cool, dark place—but not the refrigerator. They should keep several years.

To use a vanilla bean, split it lengthwise with a small knife. Using the tip of the knife, scrape out the tiny, moist seeds from the bean and add to your batter, dough, or liquid. If the liquid is to be heated for an infusion, add the scraped bean to the saucepan as well so it can release all of its flavor. Remove the bean before using the batter or liquid. Used vanilla beans can be rinsed and stored in a closed jar of rum, bourbon, Cognac, or other liquor for future use. With enough beans, the liquor itself picks up the vanilla flavor, and while not strong enough to substitute for extract, it can be used in recipes that use both alcohol and vanilla. The beans can also be rinsed and dried thoroughly, buried in a jar of granulated sugar and aged for a couple of weeks to make vanilla sugar, which is an excellent substitute for regular sugar.

The Baker's Dozen on the Road

Our field trips are one of the most popular aspects of The Baker's Dozen. These visits to bakeries, farmers, and purveyors are incredibly informative. Invariably, if we have respect for a company when we arrive, we leave awestruck at their devotion to quality. Thanks to Letty Flatt, Fran Gage, David Lebovitz, Alice Medrich, Patti Murray, and Elizabeth Cawdry Thomas for sharing their reminiscences of these excursions.

Greenleaf Produce   Our visit to Greenleaf Produce was planned at the time of year when summer fruits were slowly disappearing and the new fall fruits were just beginning to appear. Greenleaf Produce began almost twenty years ago as an earnest attempt to bridge the distance between farmer and chef. After a few tumultuous years, Greenleaf was purchased by Bill Wilkinson, a seasoned restaurateur who had had little experience with produce.

As we arrived, we were led to a large table virtually overflowing with the most gorgeous produce available: tiny wild strawberries with their stems attached, spicy Muscat grapes, crimson-fleshed Elephant Heart plums, organic and exotic lychees, chewable sticks of sugarcane, and flavorful Pluots, the curious cross between plums and apricots.

Our tasting also brought us together with several small farmers and a few larger ones, who were anxious to show us their finest seasonal produce. Rick Knoll sliced plump brown Turkey figs, notable for their immense size and sweet, syrupy flavor. Sally Schmitt and her daughter Karen Bates had trucked cases of various heirloom apples down from their charming orchard, The Apple Farm, in Anderson Valley. Sally told the group how she became an apple grower after more than ten years in the restaurant business. (Sally and her husband, Don, created the French Laundry restaurant in Napa Valley.) She explained how she never intended to go into apple farming, but how the trees on some dilapidated property she owned slowly became her life. We tasted many varieties of apples, among them crisp King of Tompkins County, russet-colored Wicksons, rosy Pink Pearls, and just about everyone's favorite, Ashmead's Kernel apples. But what impressed us the most was how flavorful a Red or Golden Delicious apple can be when eaten fresh-picked from the tree, in season. We all agreed that it was a completely different apple from what is usually found in the supermarket.

Another farmer, Sally Small of Pettigrew Farms, shared some of the autumnal produce from her farm. Although she insisted that we first try her juicy Gewürztraminer grapes, most of us clamored for slices of her French Butter pears. Sally spoke of how she was encouraged to market these pears, which were just growing on her property (they were considered too fragile to be commercially successful), not realizing that they would be of interest to local restaurants, most notably Chez Panisse. Sally's pears were sweet, yet, at the same time, firmly textured and suitable for baking as well as eating out of hand.

After the tasting, we were handed bags of samples to take home: freshly pressed walnut and almond oils, black Mission figs, and samples of organic apples and plums.

Guittard Chocolate   Over a century old, this family-owned business is well known to bakers on the West Coast and is one of the handful of high-quality American chocolate makers. For many years, most of their excellent chocolates were primarily available to restaurants and candy companies. But in recent years, Guittard has been introducing their bars and chips to home cooks.

Our tour began with a look at fermented and roasted cocoa beans being ground into a paste. Although many of us bakers use pounds of chocolate each day, many had never seen it being made, and we're lucky to have such a facility in our community. But perhaps what most impressed us was the strict quality control; we saw workers unwrapping hundreds of candy bars whose chocolate had not been properly tempered, and they were working diligently to correct the problem. We were also impressed that it took almost a year to calibrate the machine that squirts out the chocolate chips to get the tops of the chips to drip ever so perfectly.

After our tour, we happily sampled the many kinds of chocolates that Guittard produces, from sweet milk chocolate to dark bittersweet and semisweet varieties. We were all definitely up to the task, and we found it interesting and informative to sample the different varieties side by side.

Cowgirl Creamery and Anna's Daughter's Rye Bread   Like kids out of school for the day on a new adventure, we wound our way through Marin County, the gorgeous terrain north of San Francisco. Passing field after field of grazing cows, their faces peering out of the early morning coastal mist, we wondered if these could be the cows that supply the milk to the cheese makers we had come to visit. It was a good guess soon confirmed.

We arrived at our destination, the village of Point Reyes Station, where a group of artisan food producers has established itself. Cowgirl Creamery was started in 1997 by partners Sue Conley and Peggy Smith. Sue and Peggy chose the name because the creamery is, after all, in the Wild West.

The creamery specializes in fresh cheeses (their clabbered cottage cheese is their best seller), processing about 400 gallons of milk a week. We met the assistant cheese maker, Fons Smits, who learned the art of producing artisan cheeses in the Netherlands. One of the new cheeses we tasted was called Mount Tam (named after Mount Tamalpais, which looms over all of Marin), with the flavor of Brie but without the runny texture—kind of like a cross between Brie and heaven.

Around the corner from Cowgirl Creamery, in an outbuilding next to a home, is Anna's Daughter's Rye Bread. Of course, this dense European-style rye bread is a perfect complement to the cheeses, but we all fell in love with the bread just by itself. Only a few members at a time could squeeze into the small baking area to peek into the wood-fired brick oven. The fire is lighted early in the morning and allowed to burn down to coals while the heavy dough is prepared. This dough is made with organic ingredients, with a wild yeast starter for leavening.

We gathered to enjoy a delicious lunch of roast chicken, well-dressed chilled fresh vegetables, and a baker's treat of cookies and ice cream, all washed down with a real thirst quencher, iced black tea combined with Concord grape juice.

Fleischmann's Yeast   Wanting to know more about the production of commercial yeast, The Baker's Dozen went on a field trip to the Fleischmann's Yeast plant in Oakland, California. We assembled on a September day in the parking lot in an industrial part of the city, just off the busy freeway.

The Bay Area's weather, with mild temperatures and low humidity, is perfect for the production of dried yeast. We donned hair nets and, with earplugs at the ready, broke into small groups to tour the plant. Pure yeast cultures, grown on nutrients in test tubes, are what start the process. There are different strains for different baking applications. Sterile wort, made from molasses, is inoculated with the culture. After the culture grows to a specific number of yeast cells, it's transferred to a fermenter. These are huge tanks; we peered into the top of one after climbing up a metal catwalk. Here the yeast is fed a special mix of wort and nutrients so it continues to grow. Sterilized air pumped into the tank provides the necessary oxygen. When the fermentation is complete, large centrifuges separate the yeast cells from everything else; then they are washed to remove waste products. Rotary filters with knife blades remove water from the creamy liquid; we saw it flaking in sheets from the huge rollers. This is either packaged as compressed yeast or further dried to make dry yeast granules. The process is fascinating—within a few days, the contents of a test tube are transformed into thousands of tons of commercial yeast.

Just Desserts   One of the largest commercial bakeries in the San Francisco Bay Area, Just Desserts started in the Noe Valley home of Gail Horvath and Elliot Hoffman in 1974. They quickly became famous for their "just like Grandma used to make" renditions of favorites like chocolate cake (still their best seller), carrot cake, and more. They expanded to include ten retail stores and the acquisition of Tassajara Bakery, but they now concentrate on wholesale baking of desserts in a huge bakery in Hunters Point, near the former home of the San Francisco Giants, Candlestick Park.

It was revealing to hear frank talk about how the business had changed over the years, since many of us are professional bakers who have to balance the books at the same time we're worrying about how our cakes taste. Just Desserts uses only fresh eggs and real butter in their products, and a few cents' cost increase can really affect their bottom line. Observing the production line, we were absolutely stunned at the speed and precision of the cake decorators, who needed only a few seconds to embellish a cake before moving on to the next one.

We always try to fit a meal into our field trip schedule, and this time we all dug into Korean barbecue. But this repast was especially memorable, as Flo Braker broke a front tooth on a bone.

A Baker's Glossary of Tools

A professional baker has a tool kit full of surprises. Not all bakers' equipment comes from kitchenware stores. Along with the expected tools, you might also find a blowtorch for quick browning and carameliz- ing sugar, a wicker basket for shaping bread dough, and almost any other gadget that will make the task at hand easier and quicker to accomplish. When a baker has hundreds of pastries, breads, or confections to make, a creative approach to tool selection is a necessity.

The home baker has an easier job of stocking a kitchen. Many stores carry kitchen tools and appliances, and specialized catalogs offer common wares as well as hard-to-find specialty tools and ingredients. Most professional kitchen supply stores welcome the home baker and provide a large selection of well-made tools and pans at competitive prices. We have listed some of our favorites in Sources, page 343.

Buying good-quality tools and appliances is important. Quality might sometimes cost a little more, but a well-built tool will often last a lifetime. Nothing is more discouraging than to have a tool break or a pan rust after a few uses. A few basics are all you really need, but specialized equipment makes baking easier and a lot more fun.

Following is a compendium of the tools we use in this book. In the opening to each chapter, you will find more details for particular utensils that are used most often to make that particular type of item. Jean Vosti was the author of this section.

Ovens

WHETHER GAS OR ELECTRIC, old or new, an oven that works well produces quality baked goods. It is crucial to use an oven thermometer to verify that the temperature is accurate. Thermometers made just for ovens are readily available in cookware stores (see Sources, page 343). It is easy to compensate for an oven that is off by 5° or 10°F, but it is very hard to adjust for a large degree difference. Serious home bakers should have their ovens calibrated once a year to ensure accuracy. Even a well-calibrated oven will likely have hot spots or cook unevenly. Once you start baking in your oven, it doesn't take long to get to know its idiosyncrasies and adjust for them.

We always recommend a position for the oven rack, which should be set in place before preheating. Remember that heat rises, so items baked in the top third of the oven will brown more quickly. Some suggest using the center of the oven; when in doubt, that is a good bet. But some of our bakers, including Flo Braker and Alice Medrich, prefer the rack in the lower third (just below the center, if you have a choice), because if a baked item is placed in the true center of the oven, the top of the item is actually closer to the top than the center, and it could overbrown. And for pastries like pies and tarts, the lower third is preferable to quickly get heat to the bottom of the pan, to encourage browning.

Allow at least 15 minutes for oven preheating; some bread recipes that require high heat and baking stones suggest a full 45 minutes. For best results, never overload an oven. If more than one pan is cooking at a time, switch pan positions halfway through baking. For cakes baked on the same rack, carefully move them from right to left or front to back midway through the suggested baking time. With cookies, it is best to move sheets from top to bottom and turn them from front to back.

Convection ovens | These have a fan built in to circulate hot air while baking. This air circulation allows faster cooking at lower temperatures and produces more evenly cooked food even when the oven is fully loaded. The thermostat in a convection oven should be set 25°F cooler than the recipe suggests, and the cooking time reduced by one-quarter to one-third. Be aware that ovens with more powerful fans can disturb delicate cookies and cakes during baking and cause less than perfect results.

Microwave ovens | They are not recommended for baking because the items do not cook evenly or brown. But a microwave is a good tool for quickly heating liquids, melting butter and chocolate, and defrosting frozen ingredients. Do not soften butter for creaming in a microwave oven—it is courting disaster.

Small Electric Appliances

Mixers | *A heavy-duty stand mixer* may seem pricey, but it is surely the most useful appliance a baker can own. It can mix batters, knead dough, and whip cream and eggs with a minimum of effort and is especially useful when having to mix for a long period of time.

When buying a mixer, be sure to buy the best quality and most powerful one that you can. The mixer should come with a paddle blade (also called a flat beater), a wire whisk, a dough hook, and a large-capacity stainless steel bowl. The large bowl is not ideal for preparing small amounts, and we sometimes recommend a hand-held mixer for this purpose. Owning a duplicate bowl and beaters is really helpful, since recipes often call for the mixing of egg whites and batter separately. Not having to wash and dry a bowl and beaters midway through a recipe saves time and effort.

A portable *hand-held mixer* is nice to have for certain jobs and an absolute necessity if you don't have a stand mixer. There are times when it is easier and more convenient to use a portable mixer to whip or beat a mixture in a small bowl or in a pan on or off the stove. Be sure to buy a powerful mixer with variable speeds and large beaters.

Food processor | The processor can simplify many tedious tasks, making fast work of chopping, pureeing, slicing, and shredding large quantities. It is especially good for making bread crumbs, finely chopping nuts, and pureeing fruits for sauces. As with a mixer, it is important to buy a food processor with enough power to do the job. An underpowered processor motor can stall or break down when working with large quantities of food (usually not a consideration for most bakers, except for bread dough). The blades of a food processor can become dull after time and should be replaced when worn. When processing a small quantity of food, it is often easier to use a knife or a mini-sized processor.

We believe that bakers should be very selective in choosing what recipes to make in their food processor. While some bakers swear by it for making pastry dough, overprocessing gives less than perfect results. For the baker, a food processor is best used as a prepping tool.

Blenders | Not often used in baking, but they can be helpful for liquefying fruits, chopping nuts, and making crumbs. The more powerful blenders give the best results. An *immersion blender* looks like a fat wand with a whirring blade on the end and is used to liquefy sauces directly in the pot or bowl (it also works for blending custards). It is especially handy to use on larger quantities that won't fit into a conventional blender jar. Professional models are very powerful and do a fine job, but those at the home-cook level are not as powerful and we find that the results can sometimes be disappointing.

Electric juicers | Make juicing large quantities of citrus fruit easy. They can be purchased as freestanding machines or as attachments to some brands of stand mixers and food processors.

Baking Pans

HIGH-QUALITY, HEAVY-GAUGE ALUMINUM baking pans produce evenly cooked, nicely browned results and are worth seeking out. Because they are used by professionals, they are often less expensive than pans of lower quality. Their sturdiness prevents warping in hot ovens, distributes heat evenly, and discourages denting during storage. We never recommend flimsy disposable aluminum foil pans unless you are baking individual baked goods for gift giving.

Pans with black nonstick coatings may seem like an advantage, but the dark color means they retain more heat and can easily overcook or even burn foods cooked in them. The coating can be damaged if sharp tools are used to cut the food in the pan or if other pans are placed on them. Unfortunately, these pans are ubiquitous. If you must use them, reduce the oven temperature by 25°F to compensate for the heat absorption. We will remind you of this a number of times in the book, even at the risk of redundancy. And never use baking pans or sheets that have become discolored with age, as they will also absorb excessive amounts of heat and burn the food.

Some types of pans (such as tart pans, novelty cake pans, and molds) often come only in lighter-weight metal, or glass, or with nonstick coating. They are worth having because of their uniqueness or because their use is specified in a recipe. Be sure they are well made, with well sealed seams. If you are using Pyrex baking pans, this material also tends to absorb oven heat, so reduce the oven temperature by 25°F.

Sheet pans | Also called jelly-roll pans, they are indispensable in a professional baker's kitchen. In fact, the so-called *half-sheet* is surely every baker's favorite all-purpose pan. These flat, rectangular shallow-rimmed pans are used to bake sheet cakes, biscuits, rolls and breads, cookies, and any other item that needs a large, flat surface. They are also useful placed in the oven under pies or other desserts that drip while baking. Professional bakeries use full (also called whole) sheet pans, which measure 17×24 inches, but this size will not fit in most home ovens. Our favorite half-sheet pan measures about 17×12 inches. The dimensions of some brands of pans for home use differ slightly. When we recommend large baking sheets, we mean half-sheet pans.

Cookie sheets | Flat metal pans with one or two ends raised for the baker to grasp. The open sides allow for increased air circulation over the tops of the cookies, which encourages even browning. The design also allows the baker to slide sturdy cookies off the sheet onto a cooling rack. Half-sheet pans turned upside down can substitute for rimless cookie sheets. (If your oven has good circulation, or if you have a convection oven, you do not really have to turn the pan upside down, unless you find that your cookies do not brown properly in the recipe's estimated baking time.) The most common sizes of cookie sheets are 14×10, 15×14, and $17\frac{1}{2} \times 14$ inches.

Insulated sheet pans | These pans have air-filled double metal bottoms and are useful for baking items, such as puff pastry, that require longer baking times or high temperatures. The insulation helps reduce overbrowning during baking, but it can also make for cookies that are actually underbrowned, so these pans aren't recommended for crisp cookies. Stacking a half-sheet pan inside another one of the same size will provide comparable results.

Cake pans | Available in many shapes and sizes; it is important that they have straight sides so that the layers will line up evenly for frosting. Heavy-duty aluminum pans produce good, evenly baked cakes.

Round cake pans | They can be found in sizes ranging from 6 to 18 inches in diameter, but we strongly recommend that you use the size pan recommended in the recipe, as cakes with different diameters often require different amounts of leavening. The most common pan called for in our recipes is a 9-inch round pan with 2-inch-high sides, because we prefer to bake one tall cake that can be cut into the required number of layers instead of baking two or three shallow layers. (This reduces the amount of crust and makes a more tender cake.) Most professional bakers use this type of pan, and while your supermarket probably will not have one (the average household cake pan is $9 \times 1\frac{1}{2}$ inches), it is easy to find at kitchenware and bakery supply stores.

Square cake pans | Square pans hold 25 percent more batter than a round pan of the same diameter. Square pans are often called for in brownie, bar cookie, or crisp recipes.

Cake pans can also be found in heart, daisy, oval, and other imaginative shapes in kitchenware and craft stores that carry cake-decorating supplies.

Springform pans | Used primarily for cheesecakes and other moist cakes that cannot easily be removed from a standard pan. Buy a sturdy one—the spring-operated clips on the sides of inexpensive pans tend to wear out quickly. A 9×3-inch springform is our standard.

A tube pan with removable bottom | This has deep fixed sides, and the cake must be pushed up from the bottom for removal. Do not buy a tube pan with a nonstick interior, as most batters that require a tube pan (such as angel food and sponge cake) also require a tactile surface that gives the batter enough traction to climb up the pan as it rises. Most of these recipes, use a 10-inch-diameter tube pan, but the Dried Cherry and Almond Cake on page 88 uses a smaller 8-inch pan.

Fluted tube pans | Sometimes called by their copyrighted name, Bundt pans are used to bake cakes with a distinctive scalloped design. If the pan is coated with a non-stick material, be sure to reduce the oven temperature by 25°F.

A 13 × 9-inch baking pan | Available in metal or Pyrex glass and handy for baking large cakes, crisps, and bar cookies. It can also be used as a water bath when baking custards or cheesecakes.

Pie pans | Made in metal, Pyrex glass, and ceramic. Most recipes call for a standard 9-inch round pan that is 1½ inches deep. Deep-dish pans, with sides that can be 2 inches or higher, hold more filling than a standard pie pan and are best suited for double-crusted fruit pies. Most bakers argue over the advantages of metal versus Pyrex, and no clear winner has been declared.

Pyrex glass pie pans | Easily available and inexpensive, these pans can go from freezer to oven with a little caution. The glass conducts heat evenly and produces a nicely browned bottom crust even when the pie needs a long baking time. The clear glass allows the baker to judge the degree of browning of the bottom crust, which is a big plus.

Metal pie pans | Come in many sizes, thicknesses, and finishes, and their prices vary. Since they are unbreakable, they are handy to use when transporting pies. Thinner shiny metal pie pans brown crusts quickly and are good to use for single-crust pies or when blind baking an unfilled pie shell, but may not do as good a job on pies that need a lot of baking time. Steel pans conduct heat more evenly and produce an excellent pie.

Ceramic or pottery pie pans | Available in many decorative designs, they are nice to use when bringing a pie to the table to serve. Most have a fluted rim, which helps you easily create a decorative edge on the piecrust. Ceramic does not always brown the bottom crust as well but is nice to use for crisps and cobblers as well as pies that need a lot of time in the oven. (A word of caution: Be sure to measure the height of the sides. If they are more than 1½ inches deep, as many imported pans are, you must adjust the amount of filling and the baking time. Also, the crust may overbrown or burn by the time a custard-based filling cooks through. If this starts to happen, cover the exposed crust with a strip of aluminum foil to protect it.)

Tart pans | Two-piece pans made of shiny or dark metal with shallow, straight, fluted sides and removable bottoms that allow the unmolding of the tart. Most tart pans are made in Europe. They range in size from a 4-inch individual tart to a 12½-inch pan. They are usually no more than 1 inch deep, although deeper pans can occasionally be found. In our tart recipes, we use a 9 × 1-inch pan.

Miniature tart or tartlet pans | These come in 1- to 3½-inch diameters and do not have removable bottoms because the crusts are easily unmolded at these smaller widths. The tartlet crusts are unmolded after baking and before filling.

Quiche pans | Usually made of ceramic or Pyrex, they do not have removable bottoms and are usually used for quiches or other savory pies that can be served at the table. When we make savory pies, we prefer to make them in free-form shapes or in a pie pan.

Muffin pans | Sold in a variety of sizes, from mini bite-sized muffins to jumbo muffins that are more like small cakes in size. We use the standard $2\frac{3}{4} \times 1\frac{1}{2}$-inch pans. They are usually made of aluminum or steel and can be coated with a nonstick material, but there are also ceramic and cast-iron pans. A product line of cast-iron pans is available that comes in many decorative and whimsical shapes, such as hearts and teddy bears.

Madeleine pans | Scallop-shell–shaped cupcake tins, these are usually used to bake madeleines, French pastries that are a cross between a cookie and a small sponge cake, but we also like them for some cookies, such as French Noisette Shells on page 220. The pans are made of metal, plain or nonstick, and in an increasing variety of shell sizes.

Bread pans | The most common bread pan sizes are 9×5 inches and $8\frac{1}{2} \times 4\frac{1}{2}$ inches. Read a recipe carefully to check the recommended pan size, as there is a 2-cup capacity difference between the two pans. Bread pans can be made of aluminum, dark metal, or glass and may have a nonstick surface. Reduce the oven temperature by 25°F if using dark metal or glass pans. Mini pans are popular for individual servings and gift loaves.

Specialty pans | Many serious bread bakers often use specialty pans for their rustic loaves. We are ambivalent on the issue—we like people to learn how to bake without molds so they don't feel that they must own special equipment for bread baking. Nonetheless, these pans are worth discussing in case you want to try them out.

Baguette pans have two or three trenches and help the loaves keep their elongated shapes during the final rise and baking. To promote crisping, they usually have a perforated bottom and are made of aluminum or dark metal. A *cloche* is a shallow, round, ceramic pan with a domed lid. The intense top heat from the lid creates loaves with a golden, crackly crust. A *banneton* is a round or oval basket made of wood or wicker, sometimes lined with canvas (unlined bannetons must be lined with kitchen towels before they are filled with dough).

Cooking Pots

GOOD QUALITY, HEAVY-DUTY cookware is an investment that should last a lifetime. Most quality cookware is made of heavy stainless steel or aluminum with an aluminum or copper core. As far as bakers are concerned, the most important feature of a saucepan is a heavy, thick bottom, which helps distribute the heat evenly and prevents scorching of custards and fillings. A small unlined copper pot, which conducts heat well, can be used for caramelizing sugar, but it isn't a must.

The interior of *nonreactive cookware* is lined with materials that prevent the pots from interacting with acidic ingredients like lemon juice and brown sugar. Especially in unlined aluminum pots (which are not easily found in kitchenware shops but are available at restaurant supply stores), these ingredients may pick up a metallic taste and color. Note that a pot can have an aluminum core but be lined with nonreactive stainless steel.

A *double boiler* is useful for cooking custards, but the same effect can be achieved by fitting a metal mixing bowl snugly over a pot of simmering water. While some cooks melt chocolate in a double boiler, our chocolate expert, Alice Medrich, recommends placing a stainless steel bowl in a skillet of shallow simmering water instead, because the sides of a double boiler can heat the sides of the bowl or insert and burn the chocolate.

Bowls

TO THE SERIOUS BAKER, owning many mixing bowls of various sizes is far from a luxury; it is a necessity. There are times when it seems that every bowl in the kitchen is in use. It is useful to have bowls in a variety of sizes. At least one very large bowl is nice to have for mixing breads, cakes, and any large-sized or multiple recipe.

While bowls can be made of glass, plastic, and ceramic, *stainless steel bowls* are by far the most versatile. They are lightweight, can be heated without damage (we use them often to melt chocolate and heat eggs for buttercreams), come in many sizes, and stack inside one another for easy storage. Unless they have wide, flat bottoms, they can wiggle during mixing. Remedy this by placing a wet kitchen towel under the bowl to provide traction.

Glass and ceramic bowls are heavier and will often break if dropped. While they are too thick to use in a double-boiler setup, this same built-in insulation makes them a good choice for fermenting dough. Their heaviness gives them stability when mixing dough and batters. *Plastic bowls* may be lightweight, but they cannot be heated and often retain an oily residue, which will prevent egg whites from whipping properly. An *unlined copper bowl* is sometimes touted as the preferred bowl for beating egg whites (a reaction between the egg and the copper makes the meringue more stable and easier to whip). It may be nice to own, but many of our bakers feel that its egg whipping benefits are overrated.

Measuring Equipment

FOR MEASURING BASICS, SEE "How to Measure" on page 34.
A cook should have at least two sets of measuring spoons, a set of measuring cups

for dry ingredients, and a variety of liquid measuring cups. It is very annoying to have to stop in the middle of a recipe to wash a measuring cup or spoon in order to be able to use it again for a different ingredient.

Dry measuring cups and liquid measuring cups are not interchangeable. When measuring dry ingredients, the goal is a level measurement. In a liquid measuring cup, dry ingredients will always mound slightly. Conversely, when measuring liquids in a measuring cup for dry ingredients, some of the liquid will spill over the edges if it is poured right up to the very top of the cup.

Always buy the sturdiest, best-quality measuring equipment that you can. There is a tendency for kitchenware shops to sell measuring equipment in a huge range of sizes, well beyond the most useful, standard measurements. Do you really need a ⅛ cup or ¾-teaspoon measure? If you buy these extraneous measures, be very careful not to mix them up with the standard ones. Especially when you are hurried, it is extremely easy to grab a ⅔-cup measuring cup instead of a ½-cup, or to confuse a ⅛-teaspoon with a ¼-teaspoon measuring spoon.

Measuring spoons | These should be made of a durable material such as stainless steel or hard plastic. The most useful set of measuring spoons includes ¼ teaspoon, ½ teaspoon, 1 teaspoon, and 1 tablespoon.

Dry-ingredient measuring cups | Made of stainless steel or hard plastic. The standard set provides four cups with ¼-cup, ⅓-cup, ½-cup, and 1-cup capacities. Dry-ingredient cups are designed to have ingredients leveled to an exact measurement.

Liquid measuring cups | Made of Pyrex glass or transparent plastic (which has the advantage of being unbreakable). It is important to be able to see through the cup for accurate measurement of liquids. These measuring cups have a spout for pouring and provide space between the highest measurement and the top of the cup so that liquids don't spill when being poured. Common sizes for liquid measuring cups are 1-cup, 2-cup, and 4-cup. There is also a 2-cup measure that measures not only in cups but in tablespoons, teaspoons, ounces, milliliters, and cubic centimeters. These measurements are convenient when reading recipes with metric measurements and when multiplying recipes, but the smaller cups and spoons are more accurate.

Scales | Preferred in most professional kitchens and in many home kitchens to provide accurate measurements of both wet and dry ingredients by weight rather than volume. To measure by weight allows easy multiplication of recipes and ensures the same results every time a recipe is made. In some cases, to satisfy the preference of the recipe's author, we have provided weights of ingredients as well as volume measurements. Be sure when buying a scale to get one that has adequate capacity. An 11-pound scale will allow you to weigh roasts as well as cups of flour.

How to Measure

Professional bakers always measure by weight. Many cookbook authors have done their best to promote weighing ingredients on a kitchen scale (professionals often call the procedure scaling). The truth remains that most home bakers continue to measure by volume, using measuring cups. With a few exceptions where we give both weight and volume measurements, we side with the volume camp, but hope that a scale becomes a standard item in home kitchens.

The type of measuring cup does make a difference. To measure flour and other dry or semisolid ingredients, always use squat metal or plastic measuring cups. For liquid ingredients, use a liquid measuring cup made of glass or plastic. The two types are not interchangeable. When measuring dry ingredients, it is important that the measure be level, which is impossible in a liquid measuring cup. And liquid will spill if it is poured all the way up to the lip of a dry measuring cup. You need both kinds of measuring cups, and we're not kidding.

Because flour settles, you can get a variety of measurements depending on exactly how the flour was placed in the cup. Was it packed? Was it sifted? Even though we use the volume method, we could not come to an agreement on one best way to measure. Most home cooks measure by the *dip-and-sweep method*, dipping their measuring cup into a bag or bin of flour and leveling it off. This method is fine for most doughs and batters.

But many of our chapter editors argued strongly for an alternate method that is best for delicate cakes and pastries. This manner of measuring is called the *spoon-and-sweep method*, where the flour is spooned into the measuring cup, then leveled off. This makes a lighter pack in the cup and slightly aerates the flour. When a recipe requires this method, we say so in the ingredients list next to the flour.

To measure dry ingredients by the dip-and-sweep method, dip the cup into the bag of flour and scoop it into the cup. Be sure that there are no air pockets in the cup, but don't pack the flour. Using a straight-edged knife or metal spatula, sweep off the excess flour so the flour in the cup is level with the edge of the cup.

To measure flour by the spoon-and-sweep method, stir the flour to loosen it. Lightly spoon the flour into a metal measuring cup, being sure there are no air pockets, and sweep off the excess flour.

For sifted flour, sift a generous amount of flour through a triple sifter onto a large piece of wax paper (or sift the flour three times through a wire sieve). Lightly spoon the sifted flour into a metal measuring cup, being sure there are no air pockets, and sweep off the excess flour to level it.

Ingredients like brown sugar and vegetable shortening should be packed into a metal measuring cup and leveled. Just do a reasonable amount of packing—packing too tightly will create an inaccurate measurement.

To measure a liquid, pour it into a liquid measuring cup placed on a counter. Get down to check at eye level; if you hold it up to your eye, the liquid could waver. Egg whites, which are sometimes given a volume equivalent instead of counted (4 large egg whites do not always equal ½ cup), are measured in a liquid measure, as are thick liquids like molasses. To measure molasses or other sticky liquids, oil the cup first with vegetable oil or coat with nonstick cooking spray—the molasses will pour right out.

Battery-operated digital scales are small, easy to use, and accurate. They can usually toggle between metric and U.S./Imperial weight readings, which can be very useful. These scales are expensive but the way to go if you want a versatile scale that doesn't take up much room.

Spring scales are easier to use, relatively inexpensive, and compact, but less accurate than balance scales. They have a shorter life span than balance scales and need to be calibrated frequently to ensure that weights are accurate. The ingredient to be weighed is placed in the scale's bowl, and the weight is displayed on a calibrated face on the side of the scale.

Thermometers

ONE THING THAT ALL of The Baker's Dozen members agree on is that thermometers are essential for good baking. Marion Cunningham is adamant that glass-enclosed mercury thermometers are the best, but unfortunately, concerns for the environment and personal health have made mercury thermometers scarce on store shelves. Alcohol is the replacement used for mercury in thermometers; it is accurate between −4°F and 392°F (−20°C to 200°C). Most thermometers do not list whether they are made with mercury or alcohol.

Accurate thermometers can be purchased at scientific equipment stores, are expensive, and are probably not necessary for most home cooking. Thermometers purchased at kitchen supply stores or supermarkets are fairly accurate but should be periodically checked and calibrated. Thermometers come with either analog dials or digital faces, which are easier to read. If you buy a battery-operated thermometer, remember to turn it off between uses, and have back-up batteries handy (most use small watch batteries that you may not be able to find in a pinch).

Instant-read thermometers | These are very popular with chefs and home cooks. They are used to take a quick temperature reading while food is cooking or being mixed. This is especially handy for roasting meats, working with yeast mixtures, and baking bread. These thermometers are not made to remain in food while it is baking or cooking but should only be used for quick checks. They can be found with both digital and analog faces. Instant-read thermometers usually display temperatures between 0° and 200°F, but some models have a wider temperature range.

Sugar and deep-frying thermometers | For cooking sugar syrups and heating fat for deep frying, they are designed to clip onto the side of a pan. There is a very useful battery-operated *probe thermometer* that sits on the counter, with a long probe attached to a cord that will extend into the oven or into a pot on the stove. Not only does it give a digital reading, but it signals when the preset temperature is reached. As long as the probe isn't exposed to temperatures above 392°F, it can do the job of any of the other thermometers listed above.

To check the accuracy of a stem thermometer, immerse the probe into a glass of ice water. The temperature should read close to 32° F (0° C). Most thermometers have a screw that can be turned to adjust the reading on the dial if the temperature is off. Some bakers prefer to use boiling water 212°F (100°C) to check their thermometers, but unless you live at sea level, be aware that water boils at different temperatures depending on altitude. This difference in temperature must be taken into consideration. The boiling point of water is lowered by 1.8°F (1°C) for each 1,000 feet above sea level.

Oven thermometers | A must! They are made to stay in the oven to check the accuracy of oven heat.

Freezer or refrigerator thermometers | They will monitor internal temperature in these appliances. If you freeze baked goods or frostings, you will want to be sure the freezer temperature is at the optimum 0°F.

Miscellaneous Small Equipment

ALL COOKS HAVE FAVORITE tools or gadgets that make cooking easier. Some of the most commonly used tools are described below.

Juicers | The job of extracting a large quantity of juice from citrus fruits is quick and easy. They come in many forms and at many prices, from expensive electric and hand models to inexpensive plastic juicers and wooden reamers.

Zester | is a hand tool used to remove only the outer colored skin (zest) from citrus fruits. The Microplane zester, which is modeled after a carpenter's rasp, is now preferred by many bakers. It effortlessly produces billows of very fine zest. A traditional zester has five small holes in its head that cuts the peel into fine strips as it is removed from fruit. However, the strips must be chopped before they are added to a batter. The fine holes on a box grater will also remove the zest from citrus; be sure the holes aren't so coarse that they cut into the pith (the pale bitter layer under the zest). Whenever you zest citrus, do it right over the bowl of batter or dough to catch the released spray of citrus oils.

Peelers | Used to remove the skins of fruits and vegetables. Although they come in many different designs, use one with a sharp blade that swivels on a handle. The swivel allows the blade to better follow the contours of the fruit or vegetable. There is a slit in the center of the blade so that the peelings can go through.

An apple peeler/corer is specifically made to peel apples (although it can also be used for potatoes). It is a metal device (often cast iron) that attaches to the countertop with a hand-cranked handle. An apple is skewered onto the mechanism, and, when the handle is turned, a peeled, sliced, and cored apple is produced. Once you get the hang of it, this tool makes quick work of a pile of apples!

Graters | Available in many varieties, they are used in baking to grate firm fruits and chocolate. The most versatile one is a *box grater*, which comes in four- and six-sided models. Each side has different-sized cutting surfaces. This type of grater is freestanding and easy to use but often difficult to store and clean. Flat graters are easier to store but have only one size cutting surface. A hand-held *rotary grater* allows easy grating of small amounts of chocolate and nuts. For larger amounts, use a standing *nut grater. Nutmeg graters* have a very fine, curved cutting surface and are used for grating whole nutmegs. *Ginger graters*, usually made of porcelain, are imported from Asia and are used to grate fresh ginger into a very fine consistency.

Whisks | Used to incorporate air into egg whites, cream, and other mixtures. They are also used to blend dry and wet ingredients. Most whisks are made of flexible stainless steel wire loops held together by a handle. They come in a variety of sizes. The baker needs at least a few different sizes and shapes of whisks. A large balloon whisk with thin wires is best for whipping egg whites and cream. A medium-sized whisk with medium-thick wires is the whisk to use for mixing liquids or whisking custard sauces to keep lumps from forming. A small whisk is good to have for combining small amounts of ingredients in small bowls.

Spoons | Available in many shapes, sizes, and materials. The most common spoons used for cooking are wooden, metal, plastic, and fiberglass. Wooden spoons can discolor, and plastic can melt in high heat. Both metal and fiberglass spoons can withstand high heats and do not stain. It all boils down to a matter of preference. We all have our favorite spoons that we wouldn't trade. A flat-bottomed wooden spoon (really a spatula) works especially well for scraping the bottom of a saucepan when cooking custard.

Spatulas | These flexible scrapers are made of rubber, plastic, nylon, or silicone, with wooden or plastic handles. They make it easy to scrape a bowl clean and are good for folding and blending light, aerated mixtures. Rubber, nylon, and plastic spatulas will melt if used in hot pans, but silicone spatulas will withstand heat up to 500°F. Spoon-shaped spatulas make it easy to scoop mixtures from one container to another, with the bowl-cleaning power of a regular flat spatula.

Metal icing spatulas | They have a flexible narrow stainless steel blade that is not used for cutting. Straight spatulas are fine, but models with an offset blade make it easier for bakers to spread icing at awkward angles. Large *wide metal spatulas* are very useful for moving cakes and pastries to serving plates. *Triangular spatulas* with serrated blades are perfect for cutting pies and cakes.

Pie weights | Large reusable ceramic or aluminum beads that are placed in the bottom of an unfilled crust during prebaking (blind baking). Their purpose is to prevent the crust from buckling or puffing during baking. Some bakers use uncooked rice or dried beans instead, which can also be reused many times, but they will go rancid in time and need replacing. Whether using weights, rice, or beans, always put parchment or foil between the piecrust and the weights to allow for easy removal after baking.

Scissors | Used for cutting parchment and string, for trimming piecrust and cookie dough.

Ruler | Keep handy for measuring pans and cutting straight, even slices. Buy a plastic ruler that is easy to clean in soap and water.

Pastry brush | A flat natural-bristle brush usually ranging in size from ½ to 2 inches wide. The natural bristles help retain the brush's pliability. It is used to apply glazes, egg washes, chocolate, syrups, or melted butter to cakes and pastries. A feather brush can be used to apply glazes to very delicate dough, such as cream puffs, but it is not essential and it is very difficult to clean.

Serrated knife with a long blade | Very useful in a baker's kitchen for slicing breads and cakes. The serrated blade prevents them from crumbling when cut.

Rolling pins | Long cylinders of smooth hardwood, marble, glass, or metal, made to roll dough into a flat shape. Depending on the finished baked goods, the dough can be rolled relatively thick or very thin. Rolling pins can have a fixed handle, a handle that turns, or no handle at all (which most professional chefs prefer) and can be long or short. All rolling pins should be well floured during use and should not be immersed in water when cleaned, but should be wiped with a damp cloth and allowed to air dry.

Pastry boards | Made of wood, plastic, or marble, they are placed on a table or counter as a work surface when rolling pastry or kneading bread. Boards should be flat, smooth, and free of cracks. Wood boards are usually made of a single piece of wood. Marble boards remain cool, making it easier to work with pastry, and are perfect for certain kinds of candy, such as the Nougatine Sticks on page 96.

Bench scraper | Sometimes called a dough scraper, it comes in handy for dividing yeast dough and scraping your work surface clean of sticky dough. It has a flat 6 × 3-inch stainless steel blade set into a wooden or metal handle.

Baking stone | Ideal for baking pizza and golden, crisp breads. This large flat stone should be preheated in the oven for at least 20 to 30 minutes before using.

Timer | Professional bakers acquire an internal clock that reminds them to check on food that's cooking. Home bakers should rely on a *timer*. There are two types that are particularly helpful, depending on your style of cooking. A portable timer can be handy for people with big living spaces, so you don't need to stay within earshot of the kitchen. Multiple-use timers can time three or four items at the same time. They are small enough to fit into an apron pocket.

Pastry blender | Makes blending fat into a pastry dough an easy, quick, and clean job. This tool comes with either firm or flexible cutters (usually five or six) attached in a U shape into a wooden or metal handle. The blades are pressed through the flour and fat mixture, dispersing the fat in small pieces throughout the flour.

Wire sieve | Strains solids from liquids and can sift fine particles from coarse ones. It can also be used to scatter flour or sugar, and it works well as a sifter. The best sizes for baking are a large sieve with a medium to coarse mesh (for straining custards) and a small sieve with a fine mesh (for straining tiny seeds from berries).

Although a wire sieve will work in a pinch, most bakers insist on a high-quality *sifter*. The task is not just to mix the dry ingredients, but to aerate them. A triple sifter, Flo Braker's preference, sifts the ingredients through three levels of mesh in one sequence; if using a wire sieve, you should really sift the ingredients three times for the proper aeration.

Wire cooling racks | Come in all shapes and sizes but are usually made of metal with a straight-line or grid-patterned surface and feet attached to raise them off the counter for air circulation. Hot baked goods are placed on the rack to cool and keep them from getting soggy. Racks are used when removing a cake from its pan and also are used when glazing a cake or pastry to allow the glaze to drip off onto a pan below. If your kitchen is space-challenged, look for stackable wire cooling racks.

Parchment paper | Makes any pan nonstick. Professional bakers say they simply can't do their jobs well without it. This sturdy paper is used to line cake pans, sheet pans, and cookie sheets and is sometimes placed under loaves as they bake on a hot baking stone. It can be reused if not soiled. You can find it in kitchenware and baking supply stores; it can be purchased in sheets or rolls (which tend to make sheets that curl up and must be adhered to a pan or sheet with a dab of softened butter). Buy a professional-weight paper; some brands are very flimsy and won't stand up to high oven temperatures. Perhaps the best approach is to buy a large stack at a local professional baking supply shop, and split up the batch with other home bakers.

Baking mats | Silicone-coated flexible mats that are absolutely nonstick are manufactured under the French names of Silpat and Exopat. They are washable (just wipe them clean with a hot, wet sponge), reusable (at least two thousand times), and come in sizes to fit both whole and half-sheet pans.

Turntable | Anyone who decorates many cakes will appreciate the convenience of this tool. When centered on the turntable, the cake can be frosted and decorated on all sides without ever being touched by the decorator's hands. Both heavy metal and plastic models are available. Although more expensive, the metal version is much more stable and easier to use.

Pastry bags | Found in every pastry chef's bag of tools, they are used not only to decorate cakes, but also to pipe batter into muffin tins, shape cream puffs, and create elegant cookies. The bags come in many sizes, but larger ones hold more food without needing to be refilled. They were once made only of canvas but now come in plastic-lined fabric, plastic-coated nylon, and disposable clear plastic. Bags should be thoroughly washed in a bowl of hot soapy water with a drop of bleach to remove all traces of food.

To avoid having to refill your pastry bag, choose one that is 12 to 14 inches long. After washing, hang the bag to air dry or suspend over a tall bottle. A separate pastry bag should be reserved for savory application, to avoid transferring flavors.

Pastry tips | Used with pastry bags to create shapes and decorations with the food or frosting being piped. They come in many, many shapes in either metal or plastic. A few plain round and open star tips from ⅛ to ½ inch diameter will cover the needs of most bakers. A more complete set is needed for fancier decorations with frosting, but they are outside the scope of this book. Be sure to wash tips well after use.

High-Altitude Baking

A substantial number of our members live or vacation in mountain areas, so the subject of adjusting recipes for high-altitude baking comes up quite often. This information was contributed by Cynthia Ware.

Unless you are baking from a cookbook specifically for high altitudes, the recipes always assume that the baker is working at sea level. At altitudes higher than 2,500 feet, there is less of the atmospheric pressure that literally presses on baked goods (and everything else). As a result, the baked goods will not only rise more quickly (therefore requiring less leavening), but they will also need assistance in maintaining their structure (by adding more eggs or using a stronger flour with more gluten). If the leavening, flour, and eggs are kept at the amounts appropriate for sea level, cakes and muffins will sag in the center, and cookies will spread excessively. There is no need to adjust the quantities of sugar or other sweeteners. In order to set the structure more quickly, however, the baking temperature should be higher.

To make these adjustments, you will certainly need a calculator and probably a kitchen scale, unless you are a mathematics savant. It can be aggravating to calculate volume measurements. Just try to figure out 8.25 percent of 3¾ cups of flour. But if that same 3¾ cups is calculated at the weight of 14 ounces or 392 grams, the figuring will be much easier.

HIGH-ALTITUDE ADJUSTMENTS FOR BAKING

At all elevations above 3,500 feet, increase the oven temperature by 25°F.

2,500 feet • Leavening: −20%   Flour: no change   Eggs: +3%

3,000 feet • Leavening: −24%   Flour: +3%   Eggs: +4.25%

3,500 feet • Leavening: −28%   Flour: +3.75%   Eggs: +5.5%

4,000 feet • Leavening: −32%   Flour: +4.5%   Eggs: +6.75%

4,500 feet • Leavening: −36%   Flour: +5.25%   Eggs: +8%

5,000 feet • Leavening: −40%   Flour: +6%   Eggs: +9.25%

5,500 feet • Leavening: −44%   Flour: +6.75%   Eggs: +10.50%

6,000 feet • Leavening: −48%   Flour: +7.5%   Eggs: +11.75%

6,500 feet • Leavening: −52%   Flour: +8.25%   Eggs: +13%

7,000 feet • Leavening: −56%   Flour: +9%   Eggs: +14.25%

7,500 feet • Leavening: −60%   Flour: +9.75%   Eggs: +15%

Oven Temperature | Beginning at an elevation of 3,500 feet, increase the baking temperature specified by your recipe by 25°F. That increase remains the same at all higher elevations. The objective is to set the protein structure as soon as rising has taken place and heat is dispersed more toward the interior of your baked goods. Baking times will remain the same.

Leavening Agents | Chemical leavenings, such as baking powder and baking soda, must be reduced in quantity when baking at altitudes above 2,500 feet. Reduce the amount by 20 percent at 2,500 feet, then deduct an additional 4 percent for every 500 additional feet in elevation, up to a maximum reduction of 60 percent at 7,500 feet.

As an example, let's use a muffin recipe that calls for 1 tablespoon baking powder and adjust it for baking at an altitude of 5,000 feet. Since 1 tablespoon equals 3 teaspoons, and the reduction required is 40 percent, the new amount would be 1.8 teaspoons. For practicality, simply round this figure to 1.75, or 1¾ teaspoons. Where a recipe calls for both baking powder and baking soda, reduce both by the same appropriate amount.

Working with yeast is trickier. When yeast is reduced, it affects other ingredients as well, such as salt, which is used in very specific amounts to control yeast growth. Therefore it is best not to adjust the quantity of yeast called for in a recipe. Yeast dough will rise more quickly at high altitudes, so overproofing is always a risk. Choose a cool place for fermenting the dough, even the refrigerator. A slow rise benefits the gluten structure.

It is important to obtain a very well-established gluten structure—knead the dough a bit longer than the recommended kneading time at sea level, but watch out for overkneading. One reliable sign of a strong gluten structure is windowpaning (see page 259). Shoot for a windowpane of dough that could nearly be cleaned with Windex.

If using commercial yeast, replace one-quarter of the flour with a flour of higher gluten content. For example, if the recipe uses 4 cups unbleached flour (with around 11 percent protein), replace 1 cup with bread flour (12.5 percent protein). If the recipe uses bread flour, substitute high-gluten flour with a protein content of 14.5 percent. This flour is available from bakery suppliers and some natural food stores, and is not to be confused with vital wheat gluten, which is used in small amounts as a dough additive. For wet dough, such as Italian Whole Wheat Bread on page 270, add a tablespoon of vital wheat gluten to the flour (2 tablespoons above 4,500 feet), but don't change the mix. For sourdough breads without commercial yeast, do not change the flour mix, but do extend the kneading time. Sourdoughs are by their nature wetter doughs, and adding more flour undermines their essential character.

Flour and Eggs | Flour and eggs provide the structure to a dough—in other words, they hold it up. At higher altitudes, the amounts of both components need to be changed to make a stronger dough or batter that won't fall back on itself as it rises. For an example, let's use a chiffon cake that takes 3¾ cups flour and 8 whole eggs (separated), baked at Lake Tahoe's 6,500 feet.

Beginning at 3,000 feet elevation, add 3 percent more flour. For each additional 500 feet of elevation, add .75 percent more, up to a maximum of 9.75 percent at 7,500 feet. The cake's 3¾ cups flour (14 ounces) would need 8.25 percent more, which is 1.155 (rounded to 1.2), to make a total of 15.6 ounces (about 4 cups and 1 tablespoon). If you do not have a scale, convert the cups to tablespoons. There are 16 tablespoons per cup of flour; 3¾ cups equals 60 tablespoons; 8.25 percent of 60 is 4.95 (rounded to 5 tablespoons). So you would add an extra 5 tablespoons flour, to make 4 cups and 1 tablespoon.

For eggs, begin with adding 3 percent more whole eggs (or whites or yolks, depending upon what the recipe calls for) at 2,500 feet. Then add 1.25 percent more for every additional 500 feet of elevation, to a maximum increase of 15 percent at 7,500 feet. Our chiffon cake with 8 separated eggs would need 13 percent more egg whites and yolks; 13 percent of 8 is 1.04, so, practically speaking, you would separate one additional egg. For odd amounts that require less than a whole egg, weigh the eggs or measure them in a liquid measuring cup, and calculate the amount of eggs by teaspoons or tablespoons (1 cup is 48 teaspoons).

Steam-Leavened Goods | Steam-leavened baked goods, such as angel food cake and cream puffs, contain very small amounts of chemical leavening or none at all.

For angel food cake, simply adjust the quantities of cake flour and egg whites according to the above formulas, and raise the oven temperature by 25°F. Cream puff pastry (*pâte à choux*) is a bit of a challenge at high elevations. The high proportion of egg yolks, which are fatty, shortens the gluten structure of the flour and affects the protein in the egg whites. First strengthen the gluten structure by substituting 25 percent of the flour (usually all-purpose) with bread flour. At elevations over 5,000 feet, you may even want to increase the gluten more by using high-gluten flour or adding a tablespoon of vital wheat gluten. After incorporating the last of the eggs, continue beating the paste well to activate the gluten. Raise the baking temperature by 25°F, and bake about five minutes longer to be sure the puffs are well set.

The Basics of Cake

A slice of tender, even-textured cake is delicious evidence of successful culinary chemistry. What pride we feel when we turn out a perfect cake from scratch! And perfect cakes can be achieved by anyone who is willing to follow recipe directions and who pays attention to details.

What sets a cake apart from other baked goods? The mixing process. A cake always has some kind of leavening, which can be the air beaten into the batter or chemical leavenings like baking soda or baking powder. The goal is to incorporate the tiny bubbles that give the baked cake a perfect texture into the batter. A superior cake is the result of proper mixing.

Cakes are almost endlessly versatile. They are edible building blocks, ready to mix and match with frostings and fillings to make new creations, and that's the approach we've taken with this chapter. Here are the basic cakes, with variations, that every baker needs to know, described in detail. In turn, we expand on these basic cakes to create some of the offerings in "Cakes for Family and Friends." For example, we frost the Rich Chocolate Cake with Creamy Chocolate Frosting to make Triple Chocolate Cake. You can devise your own favorite combinations, mixing and matching as you desire . . . and cakes can prompt many desires.

Flo Braker was the chapter head who created or adapted these recipes. Her committee members, who shared their expertise and tested recipes, included Cynthia Elliot, Lily Gerson, Sally Holland, Eve Kuhlman, Nancy Kux, Toni Lee, Evie Lieb, Patricia Murakami, Patti Murray, Cindy Mushet, Amy Pressman, Maralyn Tabatsky, and Amy Whitelaw.

Ingredients for Cakes

Flour | This subject was the most controversial in our group. Some of us think cake flour, with its low gluten content, makes the best cakes. Others find that it makes a less flavorful cake, and that bleached all-purpose flour is better. With Solomon-like wisdom, rather than choose between the two and state an unequivocal preference, we have decided to use the type of flour that tested best in each particular recipe.

The higher gluten content of unbleached flour makes it a less than perfect ingredient for tender cakes. Some cakes may have enough fat to give a tender result in spite of the gluten content, but in general, we prefer not to experiment, and we keep unbleached flour for other baked goods.

Note: The flour in this chapter was measured by the spoon-and-sweep method (see page 34). If you are using a scale, 1 cup unsifted all-purpose flour should weigh 5 ounces, or 140 grams. One cup sifted cake flour should weigh 3.5 ounces (3.57 ounces if you have a very precise scale), or 100 grams.

Butter | The temperature of the butter is very important. For the classic creaming method, the butter should be at cool room temperature, about 70°F. The texture will be somewhat malleable and plastic, and the surface will look dull, not shiny. Butter at this consistency will allow for the creation of more stable air bubbles during beating.

Of course, the easiest way to soften butter to the proper temperature is to let it stand at room temperature. If you are impatient, there are a number of methods to speed up the process. You can grate the chilled butter into the mixing bowl using the large holes of a box grater, or cut the butter into small cubes. The grated butter will be ready to cream in the time it takes to gather the other ingredients for the batter (5 minutes or so), the cubed butter in about 15 minutes. Do not use the microwave oven to soften butter. Unless you are very careful, you will end up with butter that is too hard in some spots but melted in others, or completely melted.

Eggs | Current culinary wisdom dictates that eggs be at room temperature (about 70°F) when blending whole eggs into a batter or whipping whites. This stands true for most applications, but for the soft meringue required by angel food and chiffon cakes, the whites will beat to their optimum consistency at 60°F, a temperature that is a bit cooler than the typical room. For more information, see "Testing and Tasting . . . Angel Food Cake" on page 72.

To quickly bring refrigerated eggs to room temperature (the temperature needed for blending them into batters), place the eggs in a bowl of very warm tap water for 5 to 10 minutes.

Sugar | Granulated sugar is the primary sweetener for cakes. Confectioners' sugar is often used for decorating a finished cake, but it is sometimes used in a batter to impart a tender crumb. When a recipe calls for brown sugar, you may use either light or dark, depending on the strength of molasses flavor you prefer—dark brown sugar is stronger.

Leavenings | For the best flavor, use a baking powder free of sodium aluminum sulfate (Rumford's is a good brand) and be sure it is fresh and active. From our tastings, we did not see any difference in leavening power among popular brands of baking powder. To thoroughly combine the leavening with the dry ingredients and remove any lumps, always sift the dry ingredients together. Whisking or stirring may not be enough.

Milk and other dairy products | When you are mixing a batter, the ingredients will blend best if they are at room temperature. All refrigerated dairy products other than butter should be allowed to stand at room temperature for about an hour before being used in a batter. While low-fat milk can be substituted for whole milk, remember that cakes are an indulgence, and that the extra bit of fat in the whole milk will only enhance the result. When used in conjunction with baking soda, acid ingredients such as butter-milk, yogurt, and sour cream create carbon dioxide and tenderize the crumb. Measure yogurt and sour cream in a dry measuring cup, leveling off the surface even with the edge of the cup.

Vanilla | Use only pure vanilla extract.

Equipment for Cakes

Cake pans | We are fans of dull, heavy-gauge aluminum pans, which retain heat well and encourage even baking. We don't like nonstick pans. If your pans are made of a black material or coated with a dark nonstick surface, they will absorb and hold the oven heat, creating a tendency toward overbaking, and cause overbrowning of the outside of the cake. Reduce the oven temperature by 25°F to compensate.

For layer cakes, we prefer 9×2-inch round pans. Some recipes call for a 9×3-inch springform pan. A plain (that is, unfluted) tube pan with a removable bottom is used to make angel food, chiffon, and sponge cakes. Many of us remember our mothers cooling an upside-down angel food cake on a tall glass soda pop bottle, the kind that you hardly see anymore. These days most tube pans have little feet on the lip to lift the pan above the work surface, making the bottle unnecessary. Nonetheless, we prefer a tube pan without feet, so the cake can be well clear of the counter and have more air circulation for faster cooling. Tube pans with nonstick surfaces are self-defeating, as these foam-based cakes need the traction of an ungreased surface to climb up the sides of the pan. Hold out for an unlined old-fashioned aluminum pan.

Mixers | Most of the recipes in this chapter were tested with a standing heavy-duty mixer, such as a KitchenAid. This mixer does a terrific job of whipping lots of air into meringues (especially the large amount of egg whites in an angel food cake) and creamed mixtures (nonetheless, scrape the sides and bottom of the bowl a few times during the creaming process). One other caveat: When folding in dry ingredients, use a long-handled rubber spatula to reach down into the very bottom of the bowl, being sure to bring up any ingredients that may have sunk. Use the paddle attachment for creaming and mixing batters, and the whisk attachment for beating egg whites. If you do a lot of cake making, you may want to have a second bowl and whisk for beating egg whites.

You can use a hand-held electric mixer to cream butter and whip egg whites, but use a higher speed and allow extra time to compensate for the smaller beaters and reduced motor power. Because the timings in this chapter are for heavy-duty mixers, go by the visual description of a mixture rather than the timing. A hand mixer is also very convenient for batters that call for separately beaten egg whites.

Utensils | Efficient sifting is a very important part of a successful cake. If unsifted dry ingredients are dumped into a batter, they will clump and you could get little lumps of baking soda throughout the cake. A *triple-mesh sifter* passes the dry ingredients through three tiers of mesh to combine and aerate them thoroughly. However, many of us sift the ingredients up to three times through a standard wire sieve.

Other favorite tools include an *offset metal icing spatula* (which does a fine job of spreading batter in a pan, especially when you have to coax a roulade batter into the corners of a sheet pan); a 12- to 14-inch-long *serrated knife* (for sawing a spongy cake into serving portions and for slicing a tall cake into thin layers); *wire cooling racks* (at least two, so you can reinvert unmolded cakes right side up); *long-handled rubber spatulas* (for reaching down into the bottom of a bowl of batter); an *instant-read thermometer* (for determining the temperature of butter and egg whites); and a *Microplane zester* (for lemons and oranges).

Techniques for Cakes

IN GENERAL, CAKES FALL INTO TWO categories: butter cakes, with a base of butter and sugar, and foam or sponge cakes, with a base of eggs or whites beaten into a foam.

Most layer cakes and pound cakes are butter cakes, characterized by their familiar moist, tender crumb. We prefer the conventional method for making butter cakes, known as the creaming method. This classic technique beats or "creams" the butter and sugar into a light and fluffy mixture, with the other ingredients added to the creamed mixture. The popular "one-bowl" method, where well-softened butter is beaten with all of the ingredients at once, creates a moist, slightly dense cake. Though this method may be easier for some bakers (and we use it for our Rich Chocolate Cake), it is more difficult to aerate the batter, and the cake will not be as high or light. We prefer the creaming method because if done properly, it will produce a fine-grained cake with a velvety crumb every time.

Genoise, sponge, chiffon, and angel food cakes are all foam based, easily recognized by their slightly spongy texture. These cakes start with eggs or whites whipped with sugar into a foamy meringue, with the dry ingredients gently folded in to retain as much air as possible in the batter.

Preliminaries | Preheating the oven and preparing the cake pans for the batter are the first steps of every cake recipe.

Oven temperature is a very important factor in all baking, but especially cake making. The oven temperature must be as precise as possible so the batter can set properly and the leavening can do its work to expand the air bubbles.

While many cookbooks recommend positioning the rack in the center in the oven for cake baking, we have gotten better results when the rack is in the bottom third of the oven. The lower third position allows for proper circulation of the heat around the cake. A rack in the middle of the oven sets up the batter too soon (because the heat rises to the top of the oven) and prevents full expansion of the cake.

Buttering and flouring the cake pan is usually optional because the high proportion of fat in most batters keeps the cake from sticking, and the cake usually shrinks from the sides of the pan before unmolding anyway.

To keep the wide bottom surface of the cake from sticking to the pan, always line the cake pan with a round of parchment or wax paper. Place the pan on the paper, trace with a pencil, and cut out the round. Or fold a piece of parchment (about 12 inches long) into a square. Starting at the closed corner of the paper, fold it two or three times to create a thin triangle (the kind a child makes to cut paper into snowflakes). Place the point of the triangle in the center of the inverted pan. Mark the paper triangle at the curved edge of the pan with your fingernail or scissors. Cut along the curve and unfold the paper, which will be the same size as the bottom of the pan. Do not butter and flour the paper.

Do not butter, flour, or line pans for tall sponge and angel food cakes. These batters need to cling to the sides of the pan to rise to their full height.

As a final preliminary step, sift the dry ingredients together. This way they will be ready when you are to add them to the creamed butter and sugar. In foam-based cakes, a small amount of sugar is sifted with the flour, as the sugar helps distribute the flour better in the batter.

Mixing Butter Cakes

IN THE CLASSIC CREAMING METHOD, the key is to have all the ingredients at room temperature. If one element is much cooler than another, the batter will not blend smoothly.

The first step is creaming the butter and sugar until "light and fluffy," a common baking technique that more than one baker mistakenly takes for granted. Creaming disperses millions of tiny, fat-covered air bubbles throughout the sugar. In the oven, the liquid in the batter is converted into steam through the air bubbles, expanding and leavening the cake. Chemical leavenings will help this process, but remember that baking soda and baking powder do not create additional structure to leaven a batter—they only expand the air bubbles already present.

Start by creaming the butter on medium speed for about a minute with the paddle blade to initiate the aeration. Then gradually beat in the sugar. Continue beating, scraping down the sides and bottom of the bowl about every minute to incorporate every bit of butter and sugar into the creamed mixture. Don't rush this process—it should take 4 to 7 minutes of beating with a heavy-duty mixer.

Next add the eggs, which create more air bubbles. They should be added slowly over a 3- to 4-minute period so they can be gradually absorbed into the creamed mixture. If they are added too quickly, the mixture will look curdled, watery, and separated. If this happens, stop adding the eggs, increase the speed to high, and beat until the mixture looks smooth and homogeneous. In extreme cases, switch to the whisk attachment until the mixture comes together, then go back to the paddle attachment. Continue adding the eggs, but more slowly than before. Continue beating until the mixture is even lighter in color than before, a sign that more air has been beaten into the batter. During the last few seconds of beating, add the flavorings.

The stage is set for the other ingredients, which are added in alternate portions. Alternating the dry and liquid ingredients allows the flour to absorb the liquid gradually and maintain a smooth mixture. With large amounts of batter, the flour is added in four equal portions, alternating with three of the liquids. For smaller amounts of batter, alternate three additions of flour with two of liquid. On low speed, start with the dry ingredients and blend just until they are incorporated. Now add a portion of the liquid, and blend just until absorbed. Scrape down the sides of the bowl to mix in any clumps of unmixed batter. Alternate the remaining additions of the flour and liquid, scraping down the bowl after each liquid addition and again when the batter is completely mixed. Finally fold in any additional ingredients like nuts, raisins, or chocolate chips.

Mixing Foam-Based Cakes

SPONGE, ANGEL FOOD, AND CHIFFON cakes use little or no chemical leavening. The whole eggs or whites alone are beaten with sugar into a fluffy and stable foam (actually a meringue, which classically excludes yolks, but the description fits). Air is the principal leavening of foam-based cakes, and it is the baker's job to whip enough air into the foam. If the foam is not beaten to its optimum consistency, or if the air is knocked out by improper folding or rough handling, your cake will not be the light-textured creation you were looking forward to.

A heavy-duty electric mixer is a great help for mixing sponge cake batters. Its large bowl is the perfect capacity for the eggs (which expand dramatically during beating) and it allows room for folding. And the whisk attachment beats a maximum amount of air into the foam. If you use a hand mixer, allow more time for the foam to reach the right state.

Genoise is made by the warm method, where whole eggs and sugar are heated over simmering water until they are warm to the touch. The warming step gives the mixture an elasticity that incorporates more beaten air than when using cold eggs. Melted butter is folded into the batter for extra flavor and moistness. Sponge cake uses the cold method of mixing. The eggs are separated, then the yolks and whites are each beaten with equal amounts of sugar to make two distinct foams. These foams are folded together, without butter, with the dry ingredients to make the batter. Chiffon cake is a variation on sponge cake but includes vegetable oil to give it a moister texture. Angel food cake has a base of beaten egg whites without any yolks. The whites are beaten to a special consistency. Read "Testing and Tasting . . . Angel Food Cake" on page 72 for the details.

The consistency of the foam is crucial. The egg mixture must be whipped on medium speed with the whisk attachment until tripled in volume and very light in color and texture. For whole eggs (and the yolks in sponge cake), the mixture must be thick enough to form a ribbon; when the whisk is lifted a few inches above the foam, it will form a thick ribbon that falls back on itself and rests on top of the foam for 5 seconds or longer before being absorbed back into the mass. The flavoring is added during the last few seconds of whipping. For the whites in a sponge cake, aim for the classic stiff, not dry, shiny peaks.

After the foam is created, the dry ingredients are carefully and gradually folded in. During folding, remember to use a gentle hand to keep the foam as inflated as possible. It will naturally deflate a bit, but if the foam was beaten correctly, it will retain its fluffiness. In a genoise, melted butter is also added to the batter. To accomplish this, the butter is mixed with a large dollop of batter to lighten it. If it were added directly to the batter, the heavy butter would sink to the bottom of the bowl and make gentle folding difficult.

Baking the Cake

SCRAPE THE BATTER INTO THE prepared pan, and smooth it evenly with a metal icing spatula (the offset model does the best job). Place the pan on the rack in the oven. If you are baking two layers, air circulation around the pans is imperative. Be sure the pans are not touching and that they are at least 2 inches away from the sides of the oven.

To test a cake for doneness, never rely on color alone—it can be deceiving. Always start testing about 5 minutes before the end of the estimated baking time, as such variables as exact oven temperature and the material of the cake pan will affect the exact duration.

For a butter cake, the top should be golden brown, but always use an additional test. The sides of the cake should begin to pull away from the pan, a wooden toothpick inserted in the center of the cake should come out clean, and the top should spring back when lightly pressed with your fingers.

For a foam-based cake, the golden brown top should spring back when pressed in the center, but it should also sound and feel spongy. Sponge cakes do not contract from the pan like butter cakes. The toothpick test is unreliable because it could easily pierce an area with all air bubbles and not batter and still come out clean even if the cake were not yet done.

Cooling the Cake

BUTTER CAKES SHOULD NOT BE allowed to cool completely in their pans, as steam would be trapped underneath and make them soggy. Place the cakes in their pans on a wire cooling rack and let stand for about 10 minutes, long enough to cool slightly and firm the cake for removal without cracking or crumbling. Run a small, sharp knife around the inside of the pan to release any clinging cake from the sides. Place a cooling rack or plate over the pan, hold the pan and rack together, and invert. Remove the pan and carefully pull away the parchment paper. Place the paper liner, sticky side up, on the cake layer (this keeps the cake from sticking to the rack). Reinvert the cake onto another rack, and cool right side up; cool the cake completely, allowing at least 1 hour.

Sponge and chiffon cakes are usually cooled upside down in their pans. Allow at least 3 hours for the cakes to cool. Angel food cake, which is also completely cooled in its pan, has a special cooling method. These cakes are cooled upside down so gravity can set the texture of the cake during cooling. You can rig up any kind of cooling apparatus that works, as long as the cake doesn't touch the counter.

To remove a cooled foam-based cake from the pan, slip a flexible metal spatula carefully down the side of the pan. Slowly trace around the perimeter to release the cake. When the sides are free, push up on the removable bottom to remove the cake from the sides. Tilt the cake and rotate, gently tapping the edge of the bottom of the pan against the counter to loosen the cake from the base and central tube, until the cake appears free. Cover the cake with a serving plate, invert, and remove the bottom of the pan.

Storing Basic Cakes

CAKE LAYERS CAN BE INDIVIDUALLY wrapped in plastic wrap and stored at room temperature for 1 or 2 days (the fresher the better!). To freeze them, remember that cakes are delicately flavored and can easily pick up odors from the freezer. To protect the cakes, wrap in plastic wrap and an overwrap of aluminum foil, and freeze for no more than 2 weeks. Rather than freezing a frosted cake, we think it is best to separately freeze the cake and frosting, then construct the cake from the thawed components the day of serving.

Our Favorite Butter Cake

MAKES TWO 9-INCH LAYERS

Flo Braker

We tested more than 20 butter cakes before choosing this one. Many bakers will recognize it as the ever-popular "1-2-3-4" cake (that is, 1 cup butter, 2 cups sugar, 3 cups flour, and 4 eggs). If there is one recipe to have in your file for making tender, golden celebration cakes, it's this one. Any number of frostings can be used to create your favorite combination. If undecided, go for the classic marriage of butter cake with chocolate frosting, either Chocolate Buttercream Frosting or Creamy Chocolate Frosting on pages 328 and 330.

*The
Baker's
Dozen
Cookbook*

3 cups all-purpose flour (spoon-and-sweep)

1 tablespoon baking powder

¼ teaspoon salt

½ pound (2 sticks) unsalted butter, at room temperature

2 cups sugar

4 large eggs, lightly beaten, at room temperature

1 cup whole milk, at room temperature

1 teaspoon vanilla extract

1. Position a rack in the lower third of the oven and preheat to 350°F. Line the bottoms of two 9 × 2-inch round cake pans with parchment or wax paper.

2. Sift the flour, baking powder, and salt onto a piece of wax paper; set aside.

3. In the bowl of a heavy-duty mixer fitted with the paddle blade, beat the butter on medium speed until it is lighter in color, about 45 seconds. Add the sugar in a steady stream, then stop the machine and scrape down the bowl. Resume beating, stopping occasionally to scrape down the sides of the bowl, until the mixture is very light in color and texture, 4 to 5 minutes.

4. Gradually pour in the eggs, about a tablespoon at a time. (If the mixture looks curdled, stop adding the eggs, increase the speed to high, and beat until it looks smooth and shiny. Return the speed to medium, and add the remaining eggs.) Continue beating until the mixture is ivory-colored. The entire process of adding and beating the eggs should take 3 to 4 minutes.

5. Reduce the mixture speed to low. Add the flour mixture in four additions, alternating with three additions of the milk. After each addition, beat until smooth and scrape down the sides of the bowl. Beat in the vanilla with the final addition of milk. Spread the batter evenly in the prepared pans.

6. Bake until the tops spring back when the cakes are lightly pressed in the centers and a toothpick inserted in the centers comes out clean, about 25 minutes.

7. Transfer the layers to wire cooling racks and cool for 10 minutes. Invert onto the racks or plates and remove the pans. Peel off the paper liners and place them back on the layers, sticky sides up. Invert onto wire racks, right side up, and cool completely on the wax paper. (The cake can be baked 1 day ahead, cooled, and stored, wrapped tightly in plastic wrap. Or freeze, overwrapped with foil, for up to 2 weeks.)

Baker's Notes

WHEN MAKING any butter cake, it is very important to cream the butter and sugar thoroughly. This incorporates air and is the key to producing a high-rising cake. Remember that baking powder or baking soda will not create bubbles in a batter; they will only make the existing bubbles larger. Only thorough creaming can create those all-important bubbles.

Be sure that all of the ingredients are at room temperature to reduce the chances of curdling. Scrape down the sides of the bowl often during the creaming and mixing stages.

Rich Chocolate Cake

MAKES TWO 9-INCH LAYERS

Flo Braker and
Evie Lieb

True, the creaming method consistently makes the lightest cakes, but this alternative one-bowl method also creates a moist cake with a velvety, smooth texture. When you want a great chocolate layer cake, look no further.

3 ounces unsweetened chocolate, finely chopped

2¼ cups all-purpose flour (spoon-and-sweep)

1½ teaspoons baking soda

½ teaspoon salt

2⅓ cups packed light brown sugar

8 tablespoons (1 stick) unsalted butter, at room temperature

1 cup sour cream, at room temperature

3 large eggs, lightly beaten, at room temperature

1 teaspoon vanilla extract

1 cup water

1. Position a rack in the lower third of the oven and preheat to 350°F. Line the bottoms of two 9 × 2-inch round cake pans with parchment or wax paper.

2. In the top part of a double boiler over hot, not simmering, water, or in a microwave oven on medium, melt the chocolate, stirring occasionally, until smooth. Cool until tepid.

3. Sift the flour, baking soda, and salt into the bowl of a heavy-duty electric mixer. Add the brown sugar. Attach to the mixer, fit with the paddle blade, and mix on the lowest speed just to combine the dry ingredients. Add the butter and sour cream and mix on medium-low speed to make a thick batter, about 1 minute. Add the eggs, melted chocolate, and vanilla. Increase the speed to high and beat for 2 minutes. Stop and scrape down the bowl. Resume mixing at medium-high speed, about 5 seconds. Reduce the speed to low and slowly pour in the water just until thoroughly blended. Spoon the batter equally into the prepared pans and spread it evenly.

4. Bake until the tops spring back when pressed lightly in the centers and a toothpick inserted into the centers comes out clean, 30 to 35 minutes.

5. Transfer the layers to wire cooling racks and cool for 10 minutes. Invert onto the racks or plates and remove the pans. Peel off the paper liners and place them back on the layers, sticky sides up. Invert onto wire racks, right side up, and cool completely on the wax paper. (The cake can be baked 1 day ahead, cooled, and stored, wrapped tightly in plastic wrap. Or freeze, over-wrapped with foil, for up to 2 weeks.)

Baker's Note

THE ONE-BOWL BLENDING METHOD mixes the cake batter in a way that discourages the formation of gluten, which is formed from certain proteins in flour when flour is mixed vigorously with liquid. Here the dry ingredients are combined with the butter and sour cream, fats that coat the flour's proteins. *The butter should be quite soft, not cool, or it will not disperse evenly throughout the batter*—it should stand at room temperature for 2 hours. When the liquid is added, the fat-coated proteins can't combine to form a strong gluten structure, so the cake stays tender.

Carrot-Applesauce Layer Cake

MAKES TWO 9-INCH LAYERS

Flo Braker

For a new combination of two old favorites, combine the moist richness of applesauce cake with the golden color of carrot cake.

3 cups all-purpose flour (spoon-and-sweep)

1 teaspoon baking powder

1 teaspoon ground cinnamon

½ teaspoon baking soda

½ teaspoon ground nutmeg

½ teaspoon salt

¼ teaspoon ground cloves

½ pound (2 sticks) unsalted butter, at room temperature

2 cups sugar

2 large eggs, at room temperature

1 teaspoon vanilla extract

1 cup store-bought unsweetened applesauce, at room temperature

⅔ cup golden raisins

⅔ cup finely chopped walnuts

1 cup finely shredded carrots (see Baker's Note)

1. Position a rack in the lower third of the oven and preheat to 350°F. Line the bottoms of two 9 × 2-inch round cake pans with parchment or wax paper.

2. Sift together the flour, baking powder, cinnamon, baking soda, nutmeg, salt, and cloves onto a piece of wax paper; set aside.

3. In the bowl of a heavy-duty mixer fitted with the paddle blade, beat the butter on medium speed until it is lighter in color, about 45 seconds. Add the sugar in a steady stream, then stop the machine and scrape down the bowl. Return to medium speed and beat, stopping occasionally to scrape down the sides of the bowl, until the mixture is very light in color and texture, about 3 minutes. One at a time, beat in the eggs, beating well after each addition, then add the vanilla.

4. Reduce the mixer speed to low. Add the flour mixture in three additions, alternating with two additions of the applesauce. After each addition, beat just until smooth and scrape down the sides of the bowl. Spread the batter evenly in the prepared pans.

5. Bake until the tops spring back when the cakes are lightly pressed in the centers and a toothpick inserted in the centers comes out clean, 25 to 30 minutes.

6. Transfer to wire cooling racks and cool for 10 minutes. Invert onto the racks or plates and remove the pans. Peel off the paper liners and place them back on the layers, sticky sides up. Invert onto wire racks, right side up, and cool completely on the wax paper. (The cake can be baked 1 day ahead, cooled, and stored, wrapped tightly in plastic wrap. Or freeze, overwrapped with foil, for up to 2 weeks.)

Baker's Note

THE CARROTS for this cake should be finely shredded on the small holes of a box grater or the fine shredding disk of a food processor.

Peanut Butter Layer Cake

MAKES TWO 9-INCH LAYERS

Flo Braker

While this cake was created specifically for the Peanut Butter and Strawberry Jam Cake on page 90, it is just as good when frosted with your favorite chocolate frosting.

2¼ cups sifted cake flour (sifted, then measured by spoon-and-sweep)

2 teaspoons baking powder

¼ teaspoon salt

12 tablespoons (1½ sticks) unsalted butter, at room temperature

¼ cup creamy peanut butter

1⅓ cups sugar

3 large eggs, lightly beaten, at room temperature

¾ cup whole milk, at room temperature

1 teaspoon vanilla extract

1. Position a rack in the lower third of the oven and preheat to 350°F. Line the bottoms of two 9 × 2-inch round cake pans with rounds of parchment or wax paper.

2. Sift the flour, baking powder, and salt onto a piece of wax paper; set aside.

3. In the bowl of a heavy-duty mixer fitted with the paddle blade, beat the butter and peanut butter on medium speed until the mixture is lighter in color, about 45 seconds. Add the sugar in a steady stream, then stop the machine and scrape down the bowl. Return to medium speed and beat, stopping occasionally to scrape down the sides of the bowl, until the mixture is very light in color and texture, 4 to 5 minutes.

4. Gradually pour in the eggs, about a tablespoon at a time. (If the mixture looks curdled, stop adding the eggs, increase the speed to high, and beat until it looks smooth and shiny. Return the speed to medium, and add the remaining eggs.) Continue beating until the mixture is ivory-colored. The entire process of adding and beating the eggs should take 3 to 4 minutes.

5. Reduce the mixer speed to low. Add the flour mixture in four additions, alternating with three additions of the milk. After each addition, beat until smooth and scrape down the sides of the bowl. Add the vanilla toward the end of mixing. Spread the batter evenly in the prepared pans.

6. Bake until the tops spring back when the cakes are lightly pressed in the centers and a toothpick inserted in the centers comes out clean, 30 to 35 minutes.

7. Transfer the layers to wire cooling racks and cool for 10 minutes. Invert onto the racks or plates and remove the pans. Peel off the paper liners and place them back on the layers, sticky sides up. Invert onto wire racks, right side up, and cool completely on the wax paper. (The cake can be baked 1 day ahead, cooled, and stored, wrapped tightly in plastic wrap. Or freeze, over-wrapped with foil, for up to 2 weeks.)

Classic Genoise

MAKES ONE 9-INCH CAKE

Flo Braker

Genoise is the classic European sponge cake. (The name may be French, but it seems to have originated in Italy.) It makes a tender but, frankly, dry cake that is usually moistened with a flavored syrup. For all of its popularity, it is not the easiest cake to master. First the eggs must be beaten to light and fluffy heights; then a deft hand must be used to smoothly incorporate the flour and butter. But don't be concerned. Our members have baked countless genoise cakes, and we share tips that can help even the most experienced baker. See "Testing and Tasting . . . Flour for Genoise" on page 62 for the results of our testing.

1 cup sifted cake flour (sifted, then measured by spoon-and-sweep)
½ cup plus 1 tablespoon sugar
⅛ teaspoon salt
4 tablespoons (½ stick) unsalted butter
4 large eggs
1 teaspoon vanilla extract

1. Position a rack in the lower third of the oven and preheat to 350°F. Lightly butter and flour a 9 × 2-inch round cake pan and tap out the excess flour.

2. Sift the flour, 1 tablespoon of the sugar, and the salt onto a sheet of wax paper; set aside.

3. In a small saucepan, melt the butter over low heat. Pour the melted butter into a medium bowl; set aside.

4. In the bowl of a heavy-duty electric mixer, whisk the eggs and the remaining ½ cup sugar to combine. Place in a skillet containing 1 inch of barely simmering water. Stir the egg mixture with a whisk until the mixture is warm to the touch (but not higher than 110°F) and the sugar is dissolved (rub a dab between your fingers to check for grittiness).

5. Attach the bowl to the mixer and fit with the whisk. Beat on high speed until the mixture has tripled in volume and is very light in color and texture, 3 to 4 minutes. To check for consistency, lift up a bit of the mixture with the whisk—if it falls back on itself and remains on the surface for a few seconds, it is thick enough. If it immediately sinks into the mass, keep whipping.

6. One-third at time, sift the flour mixture over the egg mixture. Using a long-handled rubber spatula, fold in the flour just until barely incorporated. Use a light touch to keep the batter as inflated as possible. Add the vanilla with the last addition of flour.

7. Gently pour about 1 cup of the batter into the melted butter and stir with the spatula to combine. Pour this mixture back into the batter and fold again. Be sure that there are no specks of flour in the batter, and that the butter mixture is completely incorporated and not sitting in the bottom of the bowl. Gently pour the batter into the pan, taking care not to deflate the foamy consistency, and smooth the batter.

8. Bake until the top of the cake springs back when gently pressed in the center and the sides begin to contract away from the pan, about 25 minutes.

9. Transfer the cake to a wire cooling rack and cool for 5 to 10 minutes. Run a knife around the inside of the pan to release the cake from the sides. Invert onto the rack and remove the pan. Cool completely. (The cake can be baked 1 day ahead, cooled, and stored, wrapped tightly in plastic wrap. Or freeze, overwrapped with foil, for up to 2 weeks.)

Orange Genoise: Add the finely grated zest of 1 large orange to the batter with the vanilla.

Lemon Genoise: Add the finely grated zest of 2 medium lemons to the batter with the vanilla.

Baker's Notes

IF YOU WANT to make this cake with all-purpose flour, remember that it is denser and heavier than cake flour. One cup of sifted cake flour weighs about 3.5 ounces, but the same volume of sifted all-purpose flour weighs about 4.5 ounces. For the best results, weigh 3.5 ounces sifted all-purpose flour, or measure it by volume (¾ cup plus 1 tablespoon sifted all-purpose flour, measured by the spoon-and-sweep method).

One of the common problems with genoise is improper folding of the flour, resulting in small clumps of flour dotting the cake. Sifting a small amount of sugar with the flour helps disperse the flour granules, making them easier to fold into the batter.

The melted butter must be tepid, not hot, but must remain liquid to be incorporated with the batter. If you wish, melt the butter while the eggs are beating.

Use a long-handled rubber spatula that can really reach down to the bottom of the mixing bowl during folding.

One of our very first comparison tastings was to determine whether all-purpose or cake flour is the best flour for cakes.

Only one person baked the sample cakes, so there wouldn't be variables in flour brands, egg temperature, mixing times, and so on. The flour was weighed, not measured by volume; otherwise, the all-purpose version would be significantly denser and drier, skewing the results. (All-purpose flour is heavier than cake flour, so there is more all-purpose in 1 cup flour.)

Both cakes were good, but there were notable differences. The genoise made with cake flour was tender, fine-grained, and soft; overall, it was a little lighter. Some bakers went so far as to call this cake "wimpy." The cake with all-purpose flour was also tender and evenly grained, but the crumb was slightly coarser, giving the cake a more rustic, homey look. The shocker was that the all-purpose genoise had the better flavor! It had the clear, honest flavor of the wheat in the flour, and the taste of the eggs and the nuance of butter came through.

Using the same recipe but two different flours, the end result is two different genoise cakes for specific applications. The cake-flour cake, with its fine crumb and delicate texture, would be preferred for a fancy European layer cake with liqueur syrup and buttercream frosting, which tend to overwhelm the flavor of the cake anyway. The all-purpose cake would be perfect for a simpler dessert in which the flavor of the cake would be prominent, such as a layer cake with a whipped cream frosting to be served with fresh fruit or custard.

But our comparisons do not always yield a single conclusion. The information's greatest value is often in the complexity of the results. The outcome of a vote is interesting, but it is only part of the story.

Alice Medrich

Our Favorite Chocolate Genoise

6 tablespoons (¾ stick) unsalted butter

½ cup sifted all-purpose flour (sifted, then measured by
    spoon-and-sweep)

½ cup sifted unsweetened cocoa powder, preferably Dutch
    processed (sifted, then measured by spoon-and-sweep)

6 large eggs, at room temperature

1 cup sugar

1 teaspoon vanilla extract

1. Position a rack in the lower third of the oven and preheat to 350°F. Line the bottom of a 9 × 3-inch springform pan with parchment or wax paper.

2. In a small saucepan, bring the butter to a full boil over medium heat. Remove from the heat and let stand while preparing the rest of the batter.

3. Sift the flour and cocoa together three times (or use a triple sifter). Return to the sifter and set aside.

4. In the bowl of a heavy-duty electric mixer, whisk the eggs and sugar together by hand. Place over a saucepan of barely simmering water. Stirring constantly with the whisk (no need to beat air into the eggs at this point), heat the egg mixture until it is hot to the touch and the sugar is dissolved.

5. Remove from the heat, attach to the mixer, and fit with the whisk beater. Beat on high heat until the egg mixture triples in volume and resembles softly whipped cream, about 3 minutes.

6. Skim the foam from the top of the butter. Reheat the butter just until it is hot (the butter must be hot). Pour the butter into a glass measuring cup, leaving the bits of milk solids behind in the pan. You should have ¼ cup melted clarified butter. Pour into a medium bowl (even though it seems too big) and add the vanilla.

7. Sift about one-third of the flour mixture over the whipped eggs. Using a large rubber spatula, fold together, quickly but gently, until nearly combined. Sift in half of the remaining flour mixture and fold again. Repeat with the remaining flour. Scoop about 1 cup of the batter into the hot butter and fold together until well blended. Pour the butter mixture into the batter and fold it in, being sure it is completely incorporated. Pour into the prepared pan and smooth the top.

MAKES ONE 9-INCH CAKE

Lily Gerson

Chocolate genoise is often very dry and desperately needs a thorough drenching with syrup and a generous slathering of buttercream— but not this version. It's so tasty that we challenge you to resist nibbling the trimmings, and any genoise that can be snacked on without frosting is pretty good.

*The Basics
of Cake*

8. Bake until the cake shrinks slightly from the sides of the pan and the top of the cake springs back when pressed in the center with your fingers, 25 to 30 minutes.

9. Transfer to a wire cooling rack. Let stand in the pan until completely cooled. Run a thin knife around the inside of the pan to release the cake. Invert onto the cooling rack and remove the pan bottom and paper. (The cake can be baked 1 day ahead, cooled, and stored, wrapped tightly in plastic wrap. Or freeze, overwrapped with foil, for up to 2 weeks.)

Baker's Notes

GENOISE IS LEAVENED only by the air beaten into the batter. There are a few tricks to guarantee a light, tender cake.

Triple-sift the already sifted flour and cocoa together so they are evenly combined. This well-sifted flour mixture will blend more easily into the batter, too.

Clarifying eliminates excess water in the butter that may cause the cake to sink in the center, so don't be tempted to save time by skipping this step—it only takes a minute or two. In contrast to Classic Genoise, the butter here must be clarified and hot.

A heavy-duty standing mixer is the best choice for beating the eggs, because the large whisk attachment quickly incorporates air into the mixture. If you must use a hand mixer, use a large heatproof bowl and allow plenty of time for whipping the eggs—it could take 15 to 20 minutes if the beaters are especially small. Go by the light, fluffy consistency of the eggs, not by the amount of time.

We prefer to bake the cake in one 2½- to 3-inch-tall springform pan instead of two shorter pans. This cuts down on the amount of trimming needed to remove the tough top skin, and it reduces the amount of dry bottom crust. If you must bake the batter in two 9 × 1½-inch layer pans, allow about 18 minutes baking time.

Either Dutch-processed or natural cocoa works in the batter, but most of us prefer the slightly nuttier, toastier flavor of the former.

Classic Sponge Cake

1 cup sifted cake flour (sifted, then measured by spoon-and-sweep)

1 cup plus 1 tablespoon sugar

⅛ teaspoon salt

6 large eggs, separated, plus about 2 large egg whites to make 1 cup egg whites, at room temperature

1 teaspoon vanilla extract

1 teaspoon cream of tartar

1. Position a rack in the lower third of the oven and preheat to 350°F. Have a 10-inch tube with a removable bottom (and without a nonstick surface) ready.

2. Sift the cake flour, 1 tablespoon of the sugar, and the salt onto a piece of wax paper; set aside.

3. In the bowl of a heavy-duty electric mixer fitted with the whisk attachment, combine the egg yolks, ½ cup sugar, and the vanilla. Beat on medium speed, scraping down the bowl occasionally with a rubber spatula, until the mixture is thickened and pale yellow and forms a thick ribbon that falls back on itself when the whisk is lifted a few inches, about 5 minutes.

4. In a large bowl, using a whisk or a hand-held electric mixer at medium speed, whip the egg whites just until foamy. Add the cream of tartar and continue whipping until the foam has increased but peaks haven't formed yet. Gradually whisk in the remaining ½ cup sugar, 1 tablespoon at a time. Whip until the whites form moist, soft peaks.

5. Using a long-handled rubber spatula, stir about one-fourth of the whites into the yolks to lighten them. Pour the remaining whites over the yolk mixture. While folding, sift the flour mixture over the egg foam, folding until the batter is smooth and combined with no visible specks of flour. Pour into the tube pan and spread evenly.

6. Bake until the top of the cake is golden and springs back when lightly touched, 50 to 55 minutes.

7. Turn the pan upside down, positioning the edges of the pan on cans or inverted glasses of the same height to be sure the cake does not touch the work surface. Cool the cake completely in the pan, 2 to 3 hours.

MAKES ONE 10-INCH TUBE CAKE

Flo Braker

In contrast to the genoise, where the eggs are warmed before whipping, the eggs for this cake are separated and whipped without the benefit of heat. The result is a firmer, spongier cake. Like its cousin, this sponge cake can be flavored in many different ways. It can also be baked in an angel food–type tube pan with a removable bottom (as it is here, to become the base for our Espresso Sponge Cake with Caramel Crunch Topping on page 92), or in layers to be frosted for a celebration cake.

8. To remove the cake from the pan, slip a flexible metal spatula carefully down the side of the pan. Slowly trace around the perimeter to release the cake. When the sides are free, push up on the removable bottom to remove the cake from the sides. Tilt the cake and gently tap the bottom of the pan against the counter to loosen the cake, rotating as you do so, until the cake appears free. Cover the cake with a serving plate, invert, and remove the bottom of the pan. (The cake can be baked 1 day ahead, cooled, and stored, wrapped tightly in plastic wrap. Or freeze, overwrapped with foil, for up to 2 weeks.)

Espresso Sponge Cake: Dissolve 1 teaspoon instant espresso powder in 2 teaspoons hot water. Pour into the egg yolk mixture during the last moments of beating.

Lemon Sponge Cake: Add the finely grated zest of 2 lemons to the egg yolk mixture during the last moments of beating.

Orange Sponge Cake: Add the finely grated zest of 1 large orange to the egg yolk mixture during the last moments of beating.

Sponge Layer Cakes: Use a 9 × 3-inch springform pan. Do not grease the pan. Spread the batter evenly in the pan. Bake in a preheated 350°F oven until the top is golden and springs back when pressed in the center, 35 to 40 minutes. Invert the pan, positioning the edges of the pan on inverted glasses of the same height so the cake does not touch the work surface. Cool the cake completely. Tilt and rotate the pan, tapping it gently on the counter to free the cake from the sides. Remove the sides of the pan. Tilt and rotate the cake, rapping the pan bottom on the counter, until the bottom is released, and lift it off the cake. To create layers, slice the cake horizontally with a long serrated knife.

Baker's Notes

THE EGGS will be easier to separate when they are straight from the refrigerator, but let them stand for about an hour to bring them to about 60°F. Cover the yolks tightly with plastic wrap to prevent a skin from forming. (See page 9 for more about optimum egg-whipping temperature.)

You need 1 cup whites for this cake, which will be 7 to 8 large egg whites. If you have a second bowl for your heavy-duty mixer, use it, whipping the whites with the whisk attachment. Otherwise, use a large bowl and a whisk or hand-held electric mixer.

Do not grease the tube pan. This cake needs traction to climb up the sides of the pan and reach its full height. For the same reason, don't use a pan with a nonstick surface.

A double-check for doneness is to listen to the cake. Remove the cake from the oven, and gently press the top. If it sounds spongy with a slight "swoosh," and it springs back, it is done. The toothpick test is not as effective with this cake.

Meyer Lemon Chiffon Cake

Flo Braker

Springy, fine-textured chiffon cake is one of the most recent additions to the classic cake. It was invented by a Southern California baker and popularized in the late 1920s, and we have enjoyed creating variations. Also based on beaten eggs, chiffon is similar to angel food and genoise, with baking powder for extra assurance of height. Lemon is the traditional flavoring. If you have them, use Meyer lemons, or substitute Eureka lemons, the common supermarket variety.

CAKE

2¼ cups sifted cake flour (sifted, then measured by spoon-and-sweep)
1½ cups sugar
1 tablespoon baking powder
1 teaspoon salt
½ cup vegetable oil
6 large eggs, separated, plus 2 large egg whites
¼ cup fresh lemon juice, preferably Meyer
½ cup water
Grated zest of 4 lemons (about 2 tablespoons)
1 teaspoon vanilla extract
½ teaspoon cream of tartar

GLAZE

2 cups confectioners' sugar
5 teaspoons strained fresh lemon juice, preferably Meyer, or as needed
Grated zest of 1 lemon, preferably Meyer (2 teaspoons)

1. Position a rack in the lower third of the oven and preheat to 350°F. Have an ungreased 10-inch tube pan with a removable bottom (and without a nonstick surface) ready.

2. To make the cake, sift the flour, ¾ cup sugar, the baking powder, and salt into a large bowl.

3. In a small bowl, whisk the oil, egg yolks, lemon juice, water, lemon zest, and vanilla to combine. Add to the flour mixture and whisk until smooth.

4. In the large bowl of a heavy-duty mixer fitted with the whisk attachment, whip the egg whites on medium speed until foamy. Add the cream of tartar and continue whipping until soft peaks form. Gradually beat in the remaining ¾ cup sugar and beat until stiff but not dry, shiny peaks form. Using a long-handled rubber spatula, stir about one-third of the whites into the batter to lighten it. Gently fold in the remaining whites. Spread evenly in the tube pan.

5. Bake until the top of the cake is golden brown and springs back when pressed gently, about 40 minutes.

6. Turn the pan upside down, positioning the edges of the pan on cans or inverted glasses of the same height to be sure the cake does not touch the work surface. Cool the cake completely in the pan, at least 3 hours.

7. To remove the cake from the pan, slip a flexible metal spatula carefully down the side of the pan. Slowly trace around the perimeter to release the cake. When the sides are free, push up on the removable bottom to remove the cake. Tilt the cake and gently tap the edge of the pan against the counter to loosen the cake, rotating as you do so, until the cake appears free. Cover the cake with a serving plate, invert, and remove the bottom of the pan.

8. To make the glaze, sift the confectioners' sugar into a medium bowl. Add the lemon juice and zest and stir until smooth and spreadable. If necessary, add more lemon juice, a teaspoon at a time, to get the desired consistency.

9. Using an offset spatula, spread the glaze over the top of the cake, letting the excess drip down the sides. Let stand until the glaze sets, about 2 hours. (The cake can be baked 1 day ahead, cooled, and stored, wrapped tightly in plastic wrap. Or freeze, overwrapped with foil, for up to 2 weeks.) To serve, slice with a serrated knife, using a sawing motion.

Baker's Notes

EGG WHITES for a chiffon cake are whipped stiffer than for an angel food cake, as they are folded into a heavier mixture. For best results, the egg whites should be cooler than room temperature, about 60°F. Read "Testing and Tasting . . . Angel Food Cake" on page 72.

Salt is important for flavor in a chiffon cake.

A chiffon cake is usually made with unflavored oil, which results in a moist cake with a tender crumb. For a flavor boost, substitute an equal amount of melted and cooled, but still liquid, butter for the oil.

Do not grease the tube pan. This cake needs traction to climb up the sides of the pan and reach its full height. For this same reason, you should not use a pan with a nonstick surface.

Flo's Angel Food Cake

MAKES ONE 10-INCH TUBE
CAKE, 4 INCHES HIGH

Flo Braker

Our angel food cake bake-offs have been some of our most revealing. Light and fluffy angel food cake has been beloved for decades, but in recent years it has found new popularity as a delicious low-fat dessert. Flo Braker worked diligently to perfect this recipe. One of her secrets is the addition of confectioners' sugar to the flour, for an especially delicate, tender, fine-textured cake. The other is the proper whipping of egg whites. These and other tips for making angel food cakes can be found on page 72.

1½ cups (11 to 12 large) egg whites
1½ cups sifted (150 grams) confectioners' sugar
1 cup (100 grams) sifted cake flour
¼ teaspoon salt
1½ teaspoons cream of tartar
1 cup (200 grams) granulated sugar
1 teaspoon vanilla extract

1. About 1 hour before baking the cake, place the cold egg whites in the bowl of a heavy-duty mixer. (This will bring them to about 60°F, slightly below room temperature.) Be organized. This batter goes together very quickly.

2. Position a rack in the lower third of the oven and preheat to 350°F. Have an ungreased 10-inch tube pan with a removable bottom (and without a nonstick surface) ready.

3. Pour the sifted confectioners' sugar, sifted cake flour, and salt into a triple sifter and sift onto a sheet of wax paper.

4. Using the whisk attachment, whip the egg whites on low speed until foamy. Add the cream of tartar and increase the speed to medium. Whip just until soft peaks form. Continue whipping and gradually add the granulated sugar in a steady stream, until the whites thicken and form soft, droopy white peaks. Add the vanilla in the final moments of whipping.

5. Sprinkle one-quarter of the flour mixture over the whites, and with a rubber spatula, fold into the whites. Repeat this process with the remaining flour mixture, folding in only one-quarter at a time. Gently *pour* the batter into the tube pan.

6. Bake until the top is golden and springs back when gently pressed with your fingers, and a toothpick inserted in the center comes out clean, 40 to 45 minutes.

7. Invert the cake pan onto the neck of a bottle or funnel. (If the cake tilts a little, that's fine.) Cool completely in the pan, 2 to 3 hours.

8. To remove the cake from the pan, slip a flexible metal spatula carefully down the side of the pan. Slowly trace around the perimeter to release the cake. When the sides are free, push up on the removable bottom of the pan to remove the cake. Tilt the cake and gently tap the bottom of the pan against the counter to loosen the cake, rotating as you do so, until the cake appears free. Cover the cake with a plate, invert the cake, and gently remove the bottom of the pan. Cool completely. To serve, slice with a serrated knife, using a sawing action.

Five-Spice Angel Food: A popular seasoning in Asian cooking, five-spice powder typically combines ground cinnamon, cloves, Sichuan peppercorns, fennel, and star anise. If you can't find it at an Asian market or your supermarket, you can substitute pumpkin pie spice, or mix up a combination of ground spices that appeals to you. Add 1 teaspoon five-spice powder to the egg whites with the flour.

Tall, short, and middling. Colors ranged from as golden as hay to as dark as café au lait, with every hue between the two. Textures were from fluffy and light to sodden and heavy.

For our first angel food cake bake-off, everyone used the same recipe for the scores of entries. Amazingly, it was difficult to find two cakes that were alike in looks and texture. There was nothing wrong with the recipe. Foremost, the variations were simply testaments to the differences among bakers, their ovens, and their utensils (some bakers bought brand-new nonstick tube pans, only to find that the slick surface thwarted their efforts). But the variety of cakes was evidence that some bakers made their cakes without a full understanding of the process that turns flour, sugar, egg whites, and a bit of salt into one of the most exquisite cakes around.

Egg whites | It's essential to whip the egg whites correctly because they are the sole leavening. The egg white-and-sugar mixture for this cake is whipped differently from any other meringue-based dessert.

Egg whites whip best at cooler than room temperature, about 60°F. With angel food cake, you want whites that are whipped to the optimum, but not necessarily the maximum, capacity. Angel food cake needs a smooth, shiny, and soft meringue that will incorporate easily with the other ingredients, leaving room to expand in the oven. The traditional "stiffly beaten egg whites" are too stiff to be folded efficiently into the other ingredients.

At 60°F, the egg whites are viscous, and the air bubbles that are whipped into the foam are more stable. Many cookbooks recommend room-temperature whites, about 70°F. Whites whipped at this temperature will whip more quickly into a foam, but there is a greater risk of overwhipping. It is better to err on the side of under-whipping rather than the other extreme.

An instant-read thermometer will easily determine the temperature of the whites. Separate the eggs right from the refrigerator (they separate most easily when chilled), and place the whites in the bowl of a heavy-duty electric mixer. Let the whites stand at room temperature for about an hour to warm up. Or place the bowl in a larger bowl of very warm (not hot) water, and stir with the stem of the thermometer until they reach 60°F.

The egg whites are whipped in three stages so they gradually reach their optimum texture. First whip them with the whisk attachment at low speed until they are frothy, and add the cream of tartar. Now increase the speed to medium and whip just until soft peaks form. Finally, still beating at medium speed, gradually add the granulated sugar, about 2 tablespoons at a time, until the whites are shiny but stand in soft, droopy peaks that appear dense and elastic. Stiffly whipped whites cause many problems. They will require extra folding to incorporate the other ingredients, losing precious volume. Also, the overextended air cells are more likely to collapse in the oven, resulting in a tough and chewy cake.

Sugar | Our angel food cake uses both granulated and confectioners' sugars, exploiting the best properties of each. Granulated sugar is gradually added to the whites to form a meringue, because this sugar stabilizes the egg foam, creating better aeration than egg whites alone. If you add too much sugar, or add the sugar too quickly, the whites will be burdened with an extra load. The result? A heavier foam with less air than required for a light and fluffy cake. Confectioners' sugar is not used in this application, because it would dissolve into the foam and make an icing-like mixture. However, confectioners' sugar is sifted with the flour and salt. This helps disperse the flour particles in the meringue, reducing the amount of folding necessary to get a smooth batter. The minuscule granulation of the confectioners' sugar gives the cake a close-grained, tender texture.

Folding the batter | When making angel food cake, you want to combine the dry ingredients gently with the meringue to retain as much aerated volume as possible. The two components are folded, not stirred, which would deflate the air bubbles you have worked so carefully to create.

To make folding efficient, sift the dry ingredients through a triple sifter onto a sheet of wax paper (or sift them through a wire sieve two or three times). The dry ingredients should be well aerated. Sprinkle the flour mixture over the meringue, one-fourth at a time. Don't dump it in, or you will get clumps that deflate the whites. Use a long-handled rubber spatula that reaches all the way down into the batter. Cut straight down into the center of the mixture, pull along the bottom and up the side of the bowl nearest you, and, with a flick of the wrist, lift the mixture up and over itself, letting it fall gently onto the remaining mixture in the bowl. Repeat, turning the bowl a quarter turn every stroke, until the ingredients are almost, but not completely, blended. Your goal is to end up with a smooth batter, but if you fully blend the batter after each addition of flour, you will overmix and deflate the batter. Continue folding in the flour, using no more strokes than necessary, until everything is incorporated into a fluffy, pourable batter. The batter will feel heavier as you add more of the flour, but the mixture should retain its fluffiness.

Oven temperature | In the oven, the sugar interacts to set the whites and the flour proteins. If the oven is too low, this amount of sugar will absorb liquid from the egg whites, turning syrupy and weeping out of the batter, while at the same time pulling down the air cells and decreasing the cake's volume. If the oven is too hot, the cake's outer structure will set before it can fully expand and bake through.

Cakes for Family and Friends

There are times when the occasion calls for a special cake, and nothing but a special cake. What would a birthday be without the glow provided by a frosted layer cake studded with candles? For an intimate chat over coffee with a friend, the forthright sincerity of pound cake seems just right. When you're serving a special dinner to guests, how can you lose with a spectacular chocolate torte? Have you ever heard of someone serving pie at a wedding?

Here is a collection of our favorite cakes. These are not pie-in-the-sky fantasy chef recipes that you will never make, but the ones that we serve to our friends and family, day in and day out. Homey tube cakes, frosted layer cakes, dense chocolate tortes, cupcakes for the kids—they're all here. And we've provided the tips for decorating cakes that we've learned over the years.

Flo Braker was the chapter head who created and adapted these recipes. Her committee members, who shared their expertise and tested recipes, included Cynthia Elliot, Lily Gersen, Sally Holland, Eve Kuhlman, Nancy Kux, Toni Lee, Evie Lieb, Patricia Murakami, Patti Murray, Cindy Mushet, Amy Pressman, Maralyn Tabatsky, and Amy Whitelaw.

Ingredients for Cakes for Family and Friends

SEE "INGREDIENTS FOR CAKES," page 44.

Equipment for Cakes for Family and Friends

THE EQUIPMENT DISCUSSED IN The Basics of Cake on page 46 will also be used here. In addition, a *pastry brush* is needed to brush layer cakes with syrup. A *cake turntable* can be handy when frosting a cake. *Cardboard cake rounds*, available at bakery suppliers and many kitchenware stores, are very helpful to give the cake a sturdy and portable base, but you can cut them out of any strong cardboard. The round should be slightly smaller than the cake layer, making the sides of the cake completely accessible during frosting. If you want to decorate your cake with a few rosettes or swirls, you'll need a *large pastry bag and decorating tips*. Large bags (12 to 14 inches) hold enough frosting for most cakes without refilling. We prefer a simple approach and use only two ½-inch-wide tips in this book, a plain round tip and an open star tip.

Fluted tube pans, based on the classic European *Kugelhupf* design, can turn the simplest batter into a lovely creation. Bakers often call them Bundt pans, but not all fluted tube pans are Bundt pans, a name owned by Nordic Products. Nordic's Bundt pan is quite heavy, molded from cast iron, and coated with a dark nonstick surface. The most common size has a 10-inch diameter and 12-cup capacity. There are other tube pans on the market that are made from aluminum and steel, and they are fine. If you use a dark, heavy Bundt pan, be sure to reduce the oven temperature to 325°F. For the Dried Cherry and Almond Cake on page 88, we use a small tube pan with an 8-inch diameter and 8-cup capacity. For cupcakes, we use a standard 2¾ × 1½-inch *muffin pan* with 12 cups.

Techniques for Cakes for Family and Friends

ALL OF THE CAKES in this chapter fall into either the butter- or foam-based categories discussed on pages 48–50. Butter cakes in this chapter include Sour Cream Pound Cake, Heavenly Hazelnut Cake with Chocolate Rum Glaze, Coconut Cupcakes with Nougatine Sticks, Dried Cherry and Almond Cake, Orange-Ginger Gateau, Carrot-Applesauce Layer Cake with Golden Fluffy Frosting, and Peanut Butter and Strawberry Jam Cake. To familiarize yourself with their mixing techniques, see page 48. For tips on making the foam-based cakes (Pistachio Roulade with White Chocolate Cream and Five-Spice Angel Food Cake with Penuche Glaze), see page 49. Although the textures of the Gateau Victoire, Molten Chocolate, and Queen of Sheba Torte cakes are not supposed to be light and fluffy, they include elements that are discussed in the foam-based cake section, as well.

While most of us do not butter and flour layer cake pans, we do recommend doing so for fluted tube pans, even if they are nonstick. You can use softened butter, solid vegetable shortening, or a nonstick cooking oil spray. Using a paper towel or pastry brush (not your fingers), coat the inside of the pan with an even thin film of the solid fat, or spray lightly with the oil. Add a few tablespoons of all-purpose flour to the pan (don't be stingy), then tilt the pan so the flour clings to the fat. Invert the pan over the sink and tap it well to knock out the excess flour. The pan should look evenly coated, with no heavy streaks or lumps of butter or flour.

Cake Decorating

FROSTING A CAKE is actually culinary construction. Just as in erecting a building, there is a sequence to follow. Our purpose is to cover the basics, not provide instructions for covering a multi-tiered wedding cake with curlicues, swags, and flounces. Here are the basics for decorating a fine cake with a few rosettes of a delicious frosting and a few flowers or chopped nuts. Let the flavor of the cake speak for itself.

Trimming and Splitting the Cake

MOST OF THE CAKES in this book are baked in a single pan, and then split into layers. Splitting cakes is an important technique. (Some egg-rich cake recipes may yield layers that dome; the domes may be trimmed off for even layers.)

If time allows, wrap the cake in plastic and freeze until it is firm (it doesn't have to be frozen solid). This reduces the amount of crumbs that will form when the cake is split or trimmed.

You can cut the cake with a long serrated knife or dental floss. Start by placing the chilled cake on a cardboard round or rimless baking sheet so it is easy to move.

To trim or split a cake with a knife, use a serrated knife that is at least 3 inches longer than the diameter of the cake. If you bake cakes frequently, buy a 12- to 14-inch knife for this purpose. Keeping the blade level and parallel to the work surface at all times, position the knife where you want to trim or split the cake, and make a very shallow cut at this point. Keeping the knife and your hand steady, cut a shallow line by rotating the cake until you have turned the cake in an entire circle. Using a gentle sawing motion, cut through the shallow lines to the center of the cake, gradually working your way around the cake until you have completely cut through it. Ease a cardboard round or rimless baking sheet under the top layer and lift it off.

To split or trim a cake with dental floss, cut a string of unflavored, unwaxed dental floss about 6 inches longer than the diameter of the cake. Using a paring knife, cut a shallow cutting line around the cake at the point where you want to separate or trim the cake. Position the floss tautly around this shallow marked line. Keeping the floss taut and parallel to the work surface, pull the floss through the cake with both hands, using a sawing motion if necessary.

After dividing the cake into layers, it can be frustrating to try to match the top and bottom during reassembly. If you have experienced this problem, there is a remedy. It's called notching, and it's foolproof. Before cutting the cake into layers, cut a small V-shaped groove (or notch) about ¼ inch deep down one side of the cake, running from top to bottom. Then you can realign the notches in the top and bottom layers when you fill the cake. The notch will be unnoticeable after frosting, and the alignment will be perfect.

Frosting the Cake

GOOD CAKES MAKE CRUMBS. That is a baker's fact of life. But too many crumbs in a frosting can ruin its texture, taste, and appearance. Crumbs are created when the cake is trimmed or sliced into layers. They can also be pulled up from the cake during frosting if the frosting is too stiff or if the crumbs are too delicate to remain on the cake's surface. There are ways around these pitfalls to get a frosted cake with a smooth, crumb-free exterior.

Before trimming and slicing the cake into layers, freeze or partially freeze the cake until it is firm, as chilled, firm crumbs are less likely to loosen than room-temperature, tender ones. Always use a dry, clean pastry brush to remove any loose crumbs from the cake layers. And the texture of the frosting should be soft enough to be manipulated easily, similar to the texture of mayonnaise or pudding.

The filled cake (or single cake layer) should be placed on a cardboard cake round (a dab of frosting secures the cake to the round) or its serving platter. Elevate the cake above the work surface so you have easy access to all sides without hunching over in an awkward position. A cake decorating turntable is ideal, but not absolutely necessary. You can stand the cake on an inverted bowl with a wide bottom or a large coffee can. While you are frosting, watch your posture and arm position. Stand up as straight as possible (you will have to lean down occasionally to check that the frosting is level).

To avoid a crumb-flecked frosting, a preliminary crumb coat is essential. This is a very thin layer of frosting applied to the surface of a layer cake, then chilled to seal off loose crumbs. A second, more attractive layer of frosting is smoothed over the crumb coat. Spoon about ½ cup of the frosting onto the center of the top of the cake (if you have frozen the cake, use the cold cake and don't worry about thawing). Using a metal icing spatula, cover the top of the cake by turning, spreading, and flattening the frosting from the center out to the cake edges, using a back-and-forth motion. Move only a couple of tablespoons of the frosting with each motion, keeping the spatula on the frosting—if you lift the spatula, you could pick up crumbs.

When the top is covered, slowly push the frosting down the sides of the cake. Move the spatula an inch or two at a time, getting more frosting from the cake top or as needed.

If you need to use more frosting than the amount on the cake, be very careful not to transfer any crumbs on the spatula to the frosting in the bowl. The goal is to have a very thin layer of frosting completely covering the cake. Discard any frosting left over on the top of the cake from applying the crumb coating, as it contains crumbs. Freeze the cake until the crumb coat is firm, 5 to 10 minutes. If the remaining frosting softens at room temperature, refrigerate it.

Frost the cake with a second, final coat of the remaining frosting. Start with the top. Spoon about one-half of the frosting on top of the cake (always begin with more on the top than you actually need), and sweep it toward the edges, keeping the layer as even as possible. Do not worry about making the frosting completely smooth at this point, or be concerned about the ridge of frosting standing around the circumference of the top of the cake. Now frost the sides of the cake. If you have a turntable, you can smooth the cake by lightly holding the spatula against the frosting and rotating the cake. To smooth the top, sweep the frosting from the edges toward the center of the cake, rotating the cake until you have gone entirely around it.

For smooth sides, dip a metal icing spatula in hot water, quickly wipe dry, and glide it over the sides of the frosted cake, keeping the spatula perpendicular to the turntable. For swirled sides, use the tip of an icing spatula or the back of a spoon that has been dipped in hot water. For ridges, score the frosted cake with a cake comb (available at kitchenware stores) or the tines of a fork for an interesting pattern.

There are times when it is not necessary to crumb coat a cake before frosting it. This is especially true when the frosted sides of the cake will be completely covered or decorated. Chopped or sliced nuts, cookie or cake crumbs, or coconut are great for a quick decoration, and they also hide crumbs in the frosting or any frosting mishaps. They have the added benefit of protecting the sides of a cake that has a distance to travel. Pour the nuts, crumbs, or coconut onto a tray or baking sheet. The finished cake must be on cardboard or its serving plate. Pick up the cake and let it rest in one hand. With your free hand, pick up handfuls of the coating, spreading it out over your taut fingers and the top part of your palm. With the cake over the tray of coating, press the coating onto the sides of the cake. If the frosting is too firm or chilled, the coating will not stick; let the cake stand at room temperature for a few minutes, then try again.

If you wish, add panache to your cake with a slick finish. This technique works with buttercream-frosted cakes. The easiest way is to use a hot metal icing spatula. Rinse the spatula under hot water and quickly wipe it dry. Holding the hot spatula at a 45-degree angle, glide it over the frosted surface, pressing very lightly. Or, refrigerate the cake until the frosting is completely chilled. Place the cake on a turntable. Hold a long, sharp knife or metal icing spatula against the side of the cake at a 45-degree angle, being sure the knife is touching the frosting from top to bottom. Turn the cake and shave off about ⅛ inch of the excess frosting in 2- to 3-inch increments, cleaning the knife after each section. To finish the top, hold the knife so the edge barely touches the frosting from the center to the edge of the cake. Rotate the cake to shave off ⅛ inch or so of the excess frosting.

Using a Pastry Bag

WITH JUST ONE BAG and a couple of well-chosen tips, you can embellish your cake with a few elegant, simple flourishes.

Two indispensable pastry tips allow for a lot of creativity: a ½-inch plain round tip (such as Ateco Number 806) and a ½-inch open star tip (such as Ateco Number 824). The plain tip is used to pipe frosting into round mounds and straight lines, and does double duty as a tool to shape cream puff dough. The open star tip (a closed tip is similar, but it has more points that curve in to make a tighter design) is more versatile, and is usually used to make stars, rosettes, or shells. You won't need a coupler unless you plan on using both tips in your design.

To fill the pastry bag, slip the pastry tip into the bag so it protrudes through the small end (you may have to trim the end of the bag with scissors to widen the opening). Twist the bag a couple of times just behind the tip, then push this twisted section into the tip itself. Fold back the top third of the large end to make a cuff. Stand the bag, tip end down, in a tall container or glass, slipping the cuff over the lip of the container to hold the bag open. Using a rubber spatula, fill the bag with the frosting. Force the frosting toward the tip so there are no large air pockets, leaving enough space at the top to close the bag. Remove the bag from the container and twist it closed.

Hold the bag with the tip about ½ inch above the surface, with one hand near the bottom of the bag to act as a guide and the other hand on top of the twist at the large end of the bag to control the flow of frosting. Squeeze the bag gently from the top to extrude the frosting. As the bag empties, twist the bag as needed to keep it closed, and move your upper hand down to the level of the frosting.

There are three basic piped shapes, all made with an open star tip: the star, the rosette, and the shell. The three designs can be piped freestanding (individual rosettes make nice bases for holding birthday candles) or connected into a chain (which looks great piped around the bottom or top of a cake). Practice first by piping out the designs on a large piece of wax paper. When you're finished and ready to decorate the cake, scrape the frosting back into the bowl with a metal icing spatula. If the frosting has softened, refrigerate it briefly to firm it up a bit.

To make a star, hold the bag directly above the surface and squeeze out a ¼- to ½-inch-wide star, then lift up. If you wish, pipe individual stars next to each other, lifting up after piping out each one, to make a row.

To make a rosette, rotate the bag in a tight circle as you pipe, stopping just before completing the entire circle, lifting the bag up as you finish the rosette. To make a connecting chain of rosettes, don't lift up, but continue moving your hand in a spiral.

To make a shell with a pointed end, move the bag down about 1 inch as you pipe, using slightly more pressure as you begin the shell, then lifting up. To make a connecting chain of shells, pipe the first shell. Move the pastry tip back to cover the bottom quarter of the shell, then pipe another shell, making connecting shells as needed to complete the chain. With practice, you'll be able to perfect a smooth back-and-forth motion to make the chain.

Using a Parchment Cone

THE BIRTHDAY CAKE is frosted, but it looks naked without an inscription. Or you plan to glaze a torte, but you feel it might need a design as a final touch. A handmade parchment cone is an important tool for these decorations. Decorating kits come with small metal tips for writing inscriptions, but they work only with frosting. Chocolate is quick and versatile, but melted chocolate will harden when it comes into contact with the metal tip, clogging the hole. Chocolate won't clog in a paper cone.

You can use melted white, milk, or dark chocolate for these decorations. Melt the chocolate carefully; white and milk chocolate are especially delicate. Or, if you have any leftover chocolate glaze (such as Chocolate Butter Glaze or Peanut Butter and White Chocolate Ganache on pages 333 and 90, they can be melted in a double boiler and substituted for plain chocolate. The melted chocolate or glaze should be warm enough to flow, yet slightly cooled so the flow is easier to control.

Cut an 8- to 10-inch square of parchment or wax paper. Fold in half diagonally, then cut along the fold (cut smoothly, with no rough edges) to make two triangles. Work with one triangle, reserving the other for another time (or to fill with a contrasting chocolate). Hold the triangle with the point facing you and the straight edge across the top. Fold one corner around to the point, and then wrap the other corner around to the other side, so that both outside corners meet the point that is facing you. Adjust the cone so the paper comes to a sharp point at the bottom. At the top of the cone, fold the connecting three points down inside the cone, locking the paper in place.

Pour melted chocolate into the cone, filling it about halfway. Fold down the top of the cone, securing first the sides and then the top edge to seal it. Snip off the very end of the cone with sharp scissors. Test the writing on a piece of parchment or wax paper—if the script is too fine, snip off a bit more of the tip of the cone to widen the opening. You may write directly on the cake.

For a free-form design, place the cake on a baking sheet or a large piece of wax paper. Using a paper cone filled with warm chocolate glaze (white or dark), cut off the tip to the desired width. Applying even pressure to the cone, and using a quick back-and-forth movement with your hand, squeeze the glaze over the cake, being sure to go past the edges of the cake on both sides for a more even look. Be creative—anything goes. You can crisscross the design, or make lots of spirals. Two different chocolates can be used for a layered effect.

The spider web design must be applied while the glaze on the cake is still warm and fluid. Using a paper cone filled with warm chocolate glaze (white on dark, or dark on white), pipe the glaze on the cake in a spiral, starting from the center of the cake and working out to the edge. Working quickly, using a toothpick or the tip of a paring knife, draw through the glaze in eight equal spokes from the center out to the edge of the cake. Wipe the knife or toothpick clean after each spoke is drawn. Using the same technique, but working from the outside edge of the cake to the center, draw eight more lines in between the first set, again being sure to wipe the knife or toothpick clean after each spoke is drawn. Let the glaze set before cutting the cake.

Storing Cakes

FOR SIMPLE UNFROSTED cakes, or those with dry glazes or icings, wrap the cake tightly in plastic wrap and store at room temperature. Cakes with frosting or moist glazes should be covered with a tall cake dome, which will protect the cake without marring the frosting. Cakes with eggs in the frosting should be refrigerated, but the the butter in the batter and frosting will harden when chilled and make the cake unpleasantly tough; remove the cake from the refrigerator at least an hour before serving so the cake can lose its chill and soften. Press pieces of plastic wrap against the cut surfaces of frosted cakes to protect them from drying out.

Triple Chocolate Cake

CHOCOLATE CURLS

4 ounces bittersweet or semisweet chocolate, in one piece

Rich Chocolate Cake (page 54)
Creamy Chocolate Frosting (page 330)

1. To make the chocolate curls, the chocolate should be slightly warmer than room temperature. Place the chocolate under a desk lamp for 10 to 15 minutes, until warm and very slightly softened. Or microwave the chocolate for 20 to 30 seconds at medium power.

2. Line a jelly-roll pan with wax paper. Working over the pan, using a swivel vegetable peeler, shave curls from the chocolate. If the chocolate is too cold, it will crumble and shatter instead of curling; let it warm up for a few more minutes. The harder you press on the chocolate, the thicker the curl. Continue until you have as many curls as you wish. You may not use the entire chunk of chocolate. Do not touch the curls, as the warmth from your hands may melt them. Refrigerate the curls to firm them. (The curls can be prepared up to 1 day ahead, covered loosely with plastic wrap, and refrigerated.)

3. If desired, trim the tops of the cake layers. Place a dab of the frosting in the center of a serving plate or cardboard cake round. Place a cake layer, bottom side up, on the frosting. Using a metal icing spatula, spread with about ⅓ cup frosting, spreading it to the edges of the cake. Top with the second layer, right side up. Spread the top of the cake and then the sides with the remaining frosting. Sprinkle the chocolate curls over the cake. Using a chopstick, press the curls into the frosting to adhere. To keep the curls as intact as possible, press only the bottom part of the curl touching the frosting. (The cake can be stored, covered with a cake dome, at room temperature for up to 2 days.)

MAKES 10 TO 12 SERVINGS

Alice Medrich and Flo Braker

An old-fashioned chocolate layer cake, spread with thick chocolate frosting, and topped off with chocolate curls—a triple treat for chocolate lovers. If you want a simple decoration (although chocolate curls are very easy to make), press mini-chocolate chips or chocolate jimmies onto the sides of the cake.

Cakes for Family and Friends

Sour Cream Pound Cake

MAKES ONE 10-INCH TUBE CAKE

Flo Braker

Pound cake is plain and simple, yes, but one of the most mouthwatering cakes around. While most cakes in the butter cake family are leavened by a combination of air and chemical leavenings, the traditional pound cake (classically made with 1 pound each of butter, sugar, eggs, and flour) gets its lift from air alone. Today, pound cake is defined more by its dense, fine-grained texture and buttery flavor than by any strict adherence to the old formula. This cake needs no frosting and stays moist and fresh for days. Serve it plain or with seasonal fruit.

3¼ cups sifted cake flour (sifted, then measured by spoon-and-sweep)
½ teaspoon salt
¼ teaspoon baking soda
½ pound (2 sticks) unsalted butter, at room temperature
3 cups sugar
6 large eggs, lightly beaten, at room temperature
1 teaspoon vanilla extract
½ teaspoon lemon extract
½ teaspoon almond extract
1 cup sour cream, at room temperature
Confectioners' sugar, for decoration

1. Position a rack on the lower third of the oven and preheat to 350°F. Grease and flour a 10-inch (12-cup) fluted tube pan and tap out the excess flour.

2. Sift the flour, salt, and baking soda together onto a piece of wax paper; set aside.

3. In the bowl of a heavy-duty mixer fitted with the paddle blade, beat the butter on medium speed until it is lighter in color, about 45 seconds. Add the granulated sugar in a steady stream, then stop the machine and scrape down the bowl. Return to medium speed and beat, stopping occasionally to scrape down the sides of the bowl, until the mixture is very light in color and texture, 4 to 5 minutes.

4. Gradually beat in the eggs. (If the mixture looks curdled, stop adding the eggs, increase the speed to high, and beat until it looks smooth and shiny. Return the speed to medium and add the remaining eggs.) Continue beating until the mixture is ivory-colored. The entire process of adding and beating the eggs should take 3 to 4 minutes. Add the vanilla, lemon, and almond extracts.

5. Reduce the mixer speed to low. In three additions, add the flour mixture, alternating with two additions of the sour cream. After each addition, scrape down the sides of the bowl and beat until smooth. Spread the batter evenly in the prepared pan.

6. Bake until the top springs back when pressed lightly and a wooden toothpick inserted in the center of the cake comes out clean, about 1 hour and 20 minutes.

7. Transfer to a wire cooling rack and cool for 10 minutes. Invert onto the rack and remove the pan. Cool completely. (The cake can be stored, wrapped tightly in plastic wrap or in an airtight container, for up to 5 days.)

8. Just before serving, sift confectioners' sugar over the top of the cake. Cut into thin wedges with a sharp knife.

Baker's Notes

T H E   B A K I N G   S O D A in this cake neutralizes the acidity of the sour cream and produces some carbon dioxide that aids in leavening. Nonetheless, thorough creaming is a primary consideration, so beat the butter and sugar well to ensure aeration.

Pound cakes keep well. In fact, most bakers agree that their flavor improves after a day or two of aging at room temperature.

If your cake pan has a dark finish, preheat the oven to 325°F.

Heavenly Hazelnut Cake
with Chocolate Rum Glaze

MAKES ONE 10-INCH TUBE CAKE

Flo Braker

Fragrant ground hazelnuts are combined with flour in this cake to give it extra depth of flavor. The dark chocolate glaze not only is an easy, beautiful finish but also complements the nuts.

CAKE

1 cup (4 ounces) toasted, skinned, and coarsely chopped
  hazelnuts (see page 16)
2¾ cup all-purpose flour (spoon-and-sweep)
1 teaspoon baking powder
½ teaspoon baking soda
½ teaspoon salt
½ pound (2 sticks) unsalted butter, at room temperature
2 cups sugar
4 large eggs, lightly beaten, at room temperature
1 teaspoon vanilla extract
1 cup plain yogurt, whole or low-fat, at room temperature

CHOCOLATE RUM GLAZE

2 tablespoons unsalted butter
1 cup confectioners' sugar
3 tablespoons unsweetened cocoa powder
2 tablespoons hot water, or as needed
1 teaspoon dark rum

1. Position a rack in the lower third of the oven and preheat to 350°F. Grease and flour a 10-inch (12-cup) fluted tube pan and tap out the excess flour.

2. To make the cake, in a food processor fitted with the metal blade, process ¼ cup of the chopped hazelnuts with ¼ cup of the flour until the hazelnuts are very finely ground, almost a powder. Transfer to a medium bowl. Sift the remaining 2½ cups flour with the baking powder, baking soda, and salt into the bowl, and whisk to mix. Set aside.

3. In the bowl of a heavy-duty mixer fitted with the paddle attachment, beat the butter on medium speed until it is lighter in color, about 45 seconds. Add the granulated sugar in a steady stream, then stop the machine and scrape down the bowl. Return to medium speed and beat, stopping occasionally to scrape down the sides of the bowl, until the mixture is very light in color and texture, 4 to 5 minutes.

4. Gradually, about a tablespoon at a time, beat in the eggs. (If the mixture looks curdled, stop adding the eggs, increase the speed to high, and beat until it looks smooth and shiny. Return the speed to medium and add the remaining eggs.) Continue beating until the mixture is ivory-colored. The entire process of adding and beating the eggs should take 3 to 4 minutes. Add the vanilla toward the end of mixing.

5. Reduce the mixer speed to low. In four additions, add the flour mixture, alternating with three additions of the yogurt. After each addition, scrape down the sides of the bowl and beat until smooth. Stir in ½ cup of the remaining hazelnuts. Spread the better evenly in the prepared pan.

6. Bake until the top springs back when pressed lightly and a wooden toothpick inserted in the center comes out clean, 55 to 60 minutes.

7. Transfer the cake to a wire cooling rack and cool for 10 minutes. Invert onto the rack and remove the pan. Place the cake on the rack over a sheet of wax paper.

8. Meanwhile, to make the glaze, melt the butter over low heat in a medium saucepan. Sift together the confectioners' sugar and cocoa onto a piece of wax paper. Add to the saucepan with the water and rum. Mix until the consistency of heavy cream, adding more water as needed. Using a pastry brush, brush the glaze over the warm cake.

9. Coarsely chop the remaining ¼ cup hazelnuts. Sprinkle the hazelnuts over the cake. Cool completely to set the glaze. (The cake can be stored under a cake dome at room temperature for up to 2 days.)

10. Transfer the cake to a serving plate and cut into wedges to serve.

Dried Cherry and Almond Cake

Flo Braker

Each bite of this moist cake is packed with almond flavor and studded with dried cherries. It uses a small 8-cup tube pan, as it is quite rich, and you won't need to serve large portions. It is especially handsome when accompanied by a multicolored compote of fresh Bing, Rainier, and Queen Anne cherries.

Baker's Notes

Many bakers find the almond paste sold in cans to be moister and more flavorful than the kind that comes in a cellophane-wrapped sausage shape.

This recipe may also be made in two 8-inch round cake pans; bake for 30 to 35 minutes.

The Baker's Dozen Cookbook

88

⅓ cup dried cherries, coarsely chopped
1 tablespoon kirsch
1 tablespoon vanilla extract
¾ cup plus 2 tablespoons all-purpose flour (spoon-and-sweep)
1 teaspoon baking powder
¼ teaspoon salt
8 ounces (1 scant cup) canned almond paste, at room temperature
1 cup sugar
½ pound (2 sticks) unsalted butter, at room temperature
5 large eggs, lightly beaten, at room temperature

1. Position a rack in the lower third of the oven and preheat to 350°F. Butter and flour an 8-inch (8-cup) plain-sided or decorative tube pan.

2. Combine the cherries, kirsch, and vanilla in a small bowl. Let stand for 20 minutes.

3. Sift the flour, baking powder, and salt together onto a sheet of wax paper; set aside.

4. In the bowl of a heavy-duty electric mixer fitted with the paddle attachment, beat the almond paste at low speed until it forms small crumbs with no large lumps. Gradually beat in the sugar. One tablespoon at a time, beat in the butter. Increase to medium speed and beat until the mixture is light in color and texture, about 3 minutes.

5. Add the eggs about 1 tablespoon at a time, beating until each addition is absorbed before adding more. Reduce the speed to low. In three additions, beat in the flour mixture, scraping the bowl occasionally, to make a smooth batter. Mix in the cherries and their liquid. Spread evenly in the prepared pan.

6. Bake until the cake springs back when pressed lightly in the center and a wooden toothpick inserted in the center comes out clean, about 45 minutes.

7. Transfer to a wire cooling rack and cool for 10 minutes. Invert onto the rack and remove the pan. Cool completely. (The cake can be stored at room temperature, wrapped tightly in plastic wrap or in an airtight container, for 3 days.)

Carrot-Applesauce Layer Cake with Golden Fluffy Frosting

GOLDEN FLUFFY FROSTING

⅓ cup (about 3 large) egg whites
¼ cup plus 2 tablespoons water
⅔ cup packed light brown sugar
⅛ teaspoon cream of tartar
2 tablespoons sugar
1 teaspoon vanilla extract

Carrot-Applesauce Layer Cake (page 56)

1. To make the frosting, fill a skillet with enough water to come 1 inch up the sides. Over medium heat, bring the water to a simmer. Reduce the heat to low and maintain a bare simmer. In a medium stainless steel bowl, combine the egg whites and 2 tablespoons water. Place in the simmering water and stir with a rubber spatula until the whites are heated to 160°F on an instant-read thermometer. Remove the bowl from the water; set nearby.

2. Place the remaining ¼ cup water in a small (3-cup) saucepan and sprinkle the brown sugar on top. Bring to boil over low heat, stirring until the sugar dissolves. Increase the heat to medium-high and attach a candy thermometer to the pan. Boil, without stirring, until the syrup reaches 235°F. Wash down any sugar crystals sticking to the sides of the pan with a pastry brush that has been dipped in cold water.

3. Meanwhile, when the syrup is close to 235°F, using a hand-held electric mixer on low speed, whip the egg whites until foamy. Add the cream of tartar and increase the speed to medium-high. Whip until soft peaks form. Gradually add the granulated sugar and whip until the whites form stiff, shiny peaks that are elastic, not dry or granular. When the syrup reaches 235°F, pour the syrup over the whipped whites, immediately increase the speed to high, and whip until the mixture is completely cool, thick, and glossy, about 3 minutes. Beat in the vanilla and use immediately.

4. Place a dab of frosting in the center of a serving plate or cardboard cake round. Place a cake layer, bottom side up, on the frosting. Using a metal icing spatula, spread with ⅓ cup frosting, spreading it to the edges. Top with the second layer, right side up. Spread the top of the cake and then the sides with the remaining frosting. The frosting is best the day it is made.

MAKES 10 TO 12 SERVINGS

Flo Braker

The quintessential cake for an autumn celebration— moist with applesauce, chunky with raisins and nuts, and warmly spiced with cinnamon, nutmeg, and cloves. A homey, full-flavored brown sugar meringue frosting pulls it all together.

Peanut Butter and Strawberry Jam Cake

MAKES 10 TO 12 SERVINGS

Flo Braker

For peanut butter and jam fans of all ages, the subtly flavored cake is an adult version of the all-American sandwich classic.

Baker's Note

Be sure that the white chocolate contains cocoa butter fat.

PEANUT BUTTER AND WHITE CHOCOLATE GANACHE

½ cup heavy cream

3 tablespoons creamy peanut butter

6 ounces high-quality white chocolate, finely chopped

Peanut Butter Layer Cake (page 58)

6 tablespoons strawberry jam

2 cups (8 ounces) salted peanuts, finely chopped

6 to 8 strawberries, hulled and cut vertically into ⅛-inch-thick slices

1. To make the ganache, heat the cream in a small saucepan over low heat just until warm. Add the peanut butter and whisk to blend. Place the white chocolate in a medium bowl and pour the warm cream on top. Let stand for 1 minute, then stir until melted and smooth. Let stand at room temperature until cooled, thick, and spreadable, about 1 hour.

2. Using a long serrated knife, cut each cake layer in half horizontally. The tops will become the bottom and top of the cake, and the remaining layers will be the center. Place a dab of the ganache in the center of an 8½-inch cardboard cake round. Place a layer, top side down, on the cardboard. Spread with 3 tablespoons jam, spreading to the edges. Top with another layer and spread with 3 tablespoons ganache, spreading to the edges. Top with the remaining layer and spread with the remaining 3 tablespoons jam. Top with the remaining layer, top side up. Spread the top, then the sides, with the remaining ganache.

3. Place the chopped peanuts in a jelly-roll pan. Hold the cake in one hand directly over the pan and tilt the cake slightly. With the other hand, pick up some of the peanuts and press them into the ganache on the sides. Rotate the cake as you apply the peanuts until the sides are completely covered. Using a clean metal spatula, press the peanuts into the ganache to make them fully adhere. (The cake can be stored at room temperature, under a cake dome, for 1 day.)

4. No more than 1 hour before serving, starting at the edge of the top of the cake, arrange the strawberry slices in concentric circles until the surface is covered.

Orange-Ginger Gateau

ORANGE SYRUP

⅓ **water**

⅔ **cup plus 2 tablespoons sugar**

2 tablespoons orange liqueur, preferably Grand Marnier

Orange Genoise (page 61)

Orange-Ginger Buttercream (page 327)

⅔ **cup finely chopped crystallized ginger**

1. To make the syrup, pour the water into a small saucepan and sprinkle the sugar evenly on top. Bring to a boil over medium heat, swirling the pan by the handle to dissolve the sugar. Remove from the heat and cool completely. Stir in the liqueur. (The syrup can be stored for up to 1 week, tightly covered and refrigerated.)

2. To assemble the cake, using a long serrated knife or dental floss, slice the cake horizontally into 3 equal layers. Place a dab of buttercream in the center of an 8½-inch cardboard cake round. Place the bottom layer, cut side up. Using a pastry brush, moisten the layer with ¼ cup of the syrup. Using a flexible metal icing spatula, spread about ¼ cup buttercream evenly over the cake layer. Sprinkle with ⅓ cup chopped ginger. Center the second layer on top and moisten with more syrup and spread with ¼ cup buttercream. Sprinkle with the remaining ginger. Center the last layer on top, gently press down on it, and moisten with more syrup.

3. Following the instructions on page 78, give the cake a crumb coat of the buttercream. Freeze until the buttercream is firm, about 10 minutes. Spread with more buttercream to make a smooth surface. (You may not use all of the frosting.) If you wish, transfer any remaining frosting to a large pastry bag fitted with a ½-inch open star tip and pipe decorations on top of the cake.

4. Refrigerate until the buttercream is completely firm, about 1 hour. (The cake can be refrigerated, under a cake dome, for up to 2 days.) Remove the cake from the refrigerator 1 hour before serving.

MAKES 8 TO 10 SERVINGS

Flo Braker and Nancy Kux

Fragrant orange and ginger team up in this contemporary version of a French gâteau. *If you have an unsprayed orange tree in your backyard, clip a few blossoms to decorate the top of the cake.*

Cakes for Family and Friends

Espresso Sponge Cake with Caramel Crunch Topping

MAKES 10 TO 12 SERVINGS

Flo Braker

It's not easy to describe the topping for this cake (reminiscent of brittle with a foamy texture that melts in your mouth), but we know you'll love it. The coffee flavor in the cake works beautifully in tandem with the caramel.

CARAMEL CRUNCH TOPPING

Vegetable oil, for oiling the pan
1 tablespoon baking soda
¼ cup water
¼ cup light corn syrup
1½ cups sugar

FROSTING

2 cups heavy cream
2 tablespoons sugar
2 teaspoons vanilla extract

Espresso Sponge Cake (page 66)

1. To make the topping, generously oil a jelly-roll pan or marble slab. Sift the baking soda into a piece of wax paper.

2. In a deep, heavy-bottomed 4-quart saucepan, combine the water and corn syrup, then add the sugar. Bring to a boil over medium heat, stirring often to dissolve the sugar. Attach a candy thermometer to the pan and increase the heat to high. Boil, stirring often toward the end of cooking to prevent scorching, until the syrup reaches 290°F, about 5 minutes total cooking time.

3. Remove from the heat, sprinkle the baking soda into the syrup, and stir it in. Be careful—the mixture will foam furiously and turn golden brown. Don't stir too much, or it will deflate. Immediately pour out on the oiled pan and let the caramel foam spread naturally, without spreading it. Cool completely, at least 1 hour.

4. Remove the crunch from the pan and place between two sheets of wax paper. Tap with a rolling pin to break into irregular pieces. (The crunch can be stored in an airtight container in a cool, dry place for up to 2 days.)

5. To make the frosting, in a chilled large bowl, beat the heavy cream, sugar, and vanilla until soft peaks form.

6. Using a long serrated knife, cut the cake horizontally into 3 equal layers. Place the bottom layer on a serving plate, and spread with a thin layer of the whipped cream. Top with the second layer and more cream, then the third layer. Spread the remaining cream over the top and sides of the cake. Refrigerate uncovered until ready to serve, up to 4 hours.

7. Up to 1 hour before serving, generously sprinkle and press the crunch onto the top and sides of the cake, and return to the refrigerator. To serve, using a serrated knife, slice the cake with a sawing motion.

Baker's Notes

THE SYRUP FOAMS because of the carbon dioxide formed in the reaction between the alkaline baking soda and the acidic sugar syrup. To make sure the baking soda dissolves completely, sift it before using, and sprinkle it over the syrup to avoid lumping.

Some sponge cake batters contain butter, which firms the cake when it is chilled, giving it an unpleasant texture. This recipe does not have butter, so the cake can be frosted with whipped cream and refrigerated, then served chilled.

Chocolate Raspberry Cake

MAKES 10 TO 12 SERVINGS

Alice Medrich

If your idea of heaven includes chocolate and raspberries, this is your cake. Chocolate genoise is splashed with raspberry liqueur, filled with a light whipped ganache and lots of fresh raspberries, then cloaked in bittersweet chocolate. Note that the light chocolate ganache must be well chilled but not whipped before step 2. The dark chocolate glaze should be made in advance to allow it to cool to spreading consistency.

Our Favorite Chocolate Genoise (page 63)
¾ cup sweet raspberry liqueur, such as Chambord
3 containers (6 ounces each) fresh raspberries
Alice's Light Ganache (page 331)
Chocolate Glaze (page 332)
Additional fresh raspberries, for garnish

1. Using a serrated knife, cut the cake horizontally into three equal layers. Place the bottom layer in a 9 × 3-inch springform pan. Brush the cake with about ¼ cup liqueur. Distribute half of the berries over the cake layer, leaving a little space between the berries.

2. Whip the ganache as instructed in step 3, page 331. Dollop about half of the ganache over the berries. Using an offset metal spatula, spread the ganache evenly over the berries, pressing the ganache gently so it surrounds the berries and adheres to the cake.

3. Brush the center cake layer with about 2 tablespoons of the remaining liqueur. Place in the pan, moist side down, and press gently. Brush the top of the layer with another 2 tablespoons of liqueur. Distribute the remaining berries over the cake, then spread with the remaining ganache.

4. Brush the top cake layer with about 2 tablespoons liqueur. Place in the pan, moist side down, and press gently. Brush the top of the cake with the remaining liqueur. Cover with plastic wrap and chill for at least 1 hour before glazing. (The cake can be prepared to this point, covered, and refrigerated up to 36 hours ahead.)

5. Run a thin knife around the inside of the pan and remove the sides. Using an offset metal spatula, spread enough of the thickened glaze in a very thin layer over the cake to smooth the surface and cover any cracks and uneven areas. Transfer the cake, on the pan bottom, to a wire cooling rack set over a jelly-roll pan.

6. Place the remaining glaze in a skillet of very hot water. Stir and warm the glaze just until it reaches 90°F. Pour the warm glaze over the top of the cake. Using a few strokes of the cleaned spatula, spread the glaze evenly over the cake so it flows down the sides. Use the tip of the spatula and the glaze on the jelly-roll pan to patch any unglazed spots. Refrigerate until the glaze sets. Decorate the cake with a cluster of raspberries. (The cake can be refrigerated, under a cake dome, for up to 2 days.)

7. Remove the cake from the refrigerator about 1 hour before serving. Slice with a thin, sharp knife dipped in hot water.

Baker's Notes

GENOISE IS USUALLY moistened with a liqueur-flavored syrup. Alice prefers simply to use a sweet liqueur without the syrup.

Fragile genoise layers, especially those that are moistened with syrup or liqueur, tend to break when lifted. To transfer without breaking, moisten the layer, then slide the bottom of a tart pan, an inverted springform pan bottom, or a rimless cookie sheet under it. Invert the cake onto another pan bottom or cookie sheet. Slide the cake layer, moist side down, where you want it (in this case, into the springform pan), nudging it with a metal spatula if necessary. If the cake layer breaks anyway, just piece it together in the knowledge that no one will know when the cake is filled and glazed.

Coconut Cupcakes with Nougatine Sticks

MAKES 16 CUPCAKES

Flo Braker

Dessert lovers who claim they don't like coconut probably haven't tried these cupcakes. Their diminutive size and playful presentation make them look like little drums with crossed drumsticks—cupcakes with a grown-up sensibility.

CUPCAKES

1½ cups all-purpose flour (spoon-and-sweep)

1 teaspoon baking powder

¼ teaspoon salt

12 tablespoons (1½ sticks) unsalted butter,
    at room temperature

1 cup sugar

3 large eggs, lightly beaten, at room temperature

½ cup canned unsweetened coconut milk (not sweetened
    cream of coconut)

½ teaspoon vanilla extract

1 cup (3 ounces) unsweetened medium-shred coconut

COCONUT NOUGATINE STICKS

Vegetable oil, for coating utensils

1 cup (3 ounces) unsweetened medium-shred coconut

⅓ cup water

¼ cup light corn syrup

1 cup sugar

1. Position a rack in the lower third of the oven and preheat to 350°F. Grease and flour sixteen 2¾-inch muffin cups and tap out the excess flour, or line the cups with paper cupcake liners.

2. To make the cupcakes, sift the flour, baking powder, and salt together onto a piece of wax paper; set aside.

3. In the bowl of a heavy-duty mixer fitted with the paddle attachment, beat the butter on medium speed until it is lighter in color, about 45 seconds. Add the sugar in a steady stream, then stop the machine and scrape down the bowl. Return to medium speed and beat, stopping occasionally to scrape down the sides of the bowl, until the mixture is very light in color and texture, 4 to 5 minutes.

4. About a tablespoon at a time, beat in the eggs. (If the mixture looks curdled, stop adding the eggs, increase the speed to high, and beat until the mixture looks smooth and shiny. Return the speed to medium and add the remaining eggs.) Continue beating until the mixture is ivory-colored.

The entire process of adding and beating the eggs should take 3 to 4 minutes.

5. Reduce the mixer speed to low. In three additions, add the flour mixture, alternating with two additions of the coconut milk. After each addition, scrape down the sides of the bowl and beat until smooth. Beat in the vanilla with the final addition of milk. Using a rubber spatula, fold in the coconut. Spoon the batter into the prepared cups, filling them about two-thirds full (a scant ¼ cup per cupcake).

6. Bake until the tops spring back when pressed lightly and a wooden toothpick inserted in the centers of the cupcakes comes out clean, about 20 minutes.

7. Transfer the pans to a wire cooling rack and cool for 10 minutes. Remove the cupcakes from the cups and cool completely on the rack, top sides up.

8. To make the nougatine sticks, position a rack in the center of the oven and preheat to 350°F. Lightly oil a marble slab or hard plastic cutting board, a rolling pin, a large chef's knife, and a metal pastry scraper.

9. Spread the coconut on a baking sheet. Bake, stirring often, until lightly toasted, about 5 minutes. Remove from the oven and cover with aluminum foil to keep warm.

10. Pour the water, corn syrup, and sugar into a heavy-bottomed medium saucepan. Bring to a boil over low heat, occasionally swirling the pan by the handle to dissolve the sugar. Raise the heat to high and cook, swirling occasionally, until the syrup is light amber in color, about 2½ minutes. Remove from the heat and stir in the coconut.

11. Pour onto the oiled work surface and cool until the outer edges of the nougatine begin to set, about 45 seconds. Using the oiled pastry scraper, fold the nougatine from the edges toward the center. Fold a few times to cool the nougatine slightly. Using the oiled rolling pin, roll the nougatine into a ⅛-inch-thick rectangle. If the nougatine is too hot, it will stick to the rolling pin; if it is too cold, transfer to an oiled baking sheet and place in the warm oven until softened. Before the mass cools and hardens, using the oiled chef's knife, cut the nougatine into 5 × ¼-inch sticks, separating the sticks as you cut them. Cool until firm. (The nougatine sticks can be prepared up to 3 days ahead and stored in an airtight container at room temperature.)

12. Just before serving, poke two nougatine sticks into each cupcake in crisscross fashion.

Baker's Notes

YOU CAN USE a mounded #24 ice cream scoop to portion out the batter.

Medium-shred unsweetened coconut can be found, usually in bulk or bags, in natural food stores and some well-stocked supermarkets.

Pistachio Roulade with White Chocolate Cream

PISTACHIO ROULADE

4 ounces (scant 1 cup) shelled raw pistachios, finely ground in a rotary nut grinder to yield 1⅓ cups

⅛ teaspoon salt

6 large eggs

¾ cup sugar

½ teaspoon pure pistachio or almond extract

WHITE CHOCOLATE CREAM

4 ounces high-quality white chocolate, finely chopped

1 cup heavy cream

Confectioners' sugar, for garnish

1. Position a rack in the lower third of the oven and preheat to 350°F. Line a 15 × 10 × 1-inch jelly-roll pan with aluminum foil, leaving a 2-inch overhang at each short end. Butter and flour the foil in the pan, tapping out the excess flour.

2. To make the cake, stir together the ground pistachios and salt; set nearby. In the bowl of a heavy-duty electric mixer, whisk the eggs and granulated sugar to combine. Place over a saucepan or in a skillet of barely simmering water. Stir with a whisk until the mixture is warm to the touch (no more than 100°F) and the sugar is dissolved (rub a dab between your fingers to check for grittiness).

3. Attach the bowl to the mixer and fit with the whisk attachment. Beat on medium speed until the mixture has tripled in volume and is very light in color and texture, 3 to 4 minutes. To check for consistency, lift up a bit of the mixture with the whisk—if it falls back on itself and remains on the surface, it is thick enough. If it immediately sinks and disappears back into the mass, keep whipping. During the last few seconds of whipping, add the pistachio extract.

4. In two additions, using a long-handled rubber spatula, fold the ground pistachios into the egg mixture just until incorporated. Spread the batter

MAKES 12 SERVINGS

Flo Braker

You may have heard of flourless chocolate cake, but how about a flourless genoise? Actually, the ground pistachios act as a flour of sorts, and give the cake a vibrant green hue that is set off by a creamy white chocolate filling. The nuts must be ground into a fine meal consistency with a rotary nut grinder (available at kitchenware shops).

Cakes for Family and Friends

evenly in the prepared pan, being sure to reach the corners (an offset metal spatula does a good job).

5. Bake until the top of the cake is golden and springs back when pressed gently in the center, 8 to 11 minutes. (The cake will deflate slightly toward the end of baking.)

6. Remove the pan from the oven. Run a thin knife around the edges to loosen the cake. Pull up on the foil overhangs and transfer the roulade on its foil to a large wire cooling rack. Tent a large sheet of foil over the cake, crimping the foil so it doesn't touch the cake. (This retains moisture and prevents the cake from cracking later.) Cool completely, about 1 hour.

7. To make the cream, place the chocolate in a small heatproof bowl that fits snugly over another bowl of hot tap water (the water should not touch the bottom of the bowl). Let stand, stirring occasionally, until melted and smooth. Transfer 2 tablespoons of the hot water from the lower bowl to the chocolate and whisk until smooth. Leave the mixture over the water.

8. In a medium bowl, using a hand-held electric mixer on high speed or a balloon whisk, beat the cream until soft peaks form on the surface but the cream is still somewhat liquid beneath (shake the bowl to check).

9. Remove the chocolate from the water bath. Dip a finger in the chocolate to check the temperature—it should be just body temperature. Add one-third of the softly whipped cream and whisk immediately to combine. Pour this mixture back into the bowl of softly whipped cream and whisk just until incorporated and soft peaks form. Be careful not to overwhip the cream, or it will look curdled. Use immediately.

10. Discard the foil tent and transfer the roulade on its foil to the work surface, with a long side facing you. Using an offset metal spatula, spread the cream mixture evenly over the roulade, stopping 1 inch from the farther long side. Starting from the long side closest to you, and using the ends of the foil as an aid, roll up the cake (the foil lining will release from the cake as you roll). Discard the foil lining. Transfer to a long serving platter, seam side down. Cover with plastic wrap and refrigerate until ready to serve. (The cake can be stored up to 1 day, wrapped in plastic wrap and refrigerated.)

11. Using a serrated knife, trim off the ends of the cake at a diagonal for eye appeal. Sift confectioners' sugar over the cake. Cut into slices at a slight diagonal, and serve chilled.

Baker's Notes

DO NOT GRIND THE pistachios in a food processor—they will not have a consistent fineness and the roulade's texture will be heavy. A rotary nut grater can also be used to grate hard cheese and chocolate.

Shelled pistachios are available at Middle Eastern and Indian grocers and well-stocked health food stores. Store leftover pistachios in the freezer.

Pistachio extract is available at some specialty kitchenware stores.

Adding the warm water to the melted white chocolate for the chocolate cream results in a smooth mixture free of any solid chocolate bits.

Five-Spice Angel Food Cake
with Penuche Glaze

MAKES 10 TO 12 SERVINGS

Flo Braker

Five-spice powder gives good old American angel food cake an exotic kick. The buttery brown sugar glaze complements the spicy flavor.

PENUCHE GLAZE

8 tablespoons (1 stick) unsalted butter, cut into ¼-inch slices
1 cup packed light brown sugar
¼ cup whole milk
About 1½ cups confectioners' sugar
⅛ teaspoon salt

Five-Spice Angel Food Cake (page 71)

1. To make the glaze, bring the butter and sugar to a boil in a heavy-bottomed medium saucepan over medium heat, stirring until the butter is melted. Boil, stirring occasionally, for 2 minutes. Carefully and gradually add the milk (the mixture will bubble up) and stir to combine. Return to a boil and remove from the heat. Pour into a large bowl and let cool until warm, about 30 minutes.

2. Sift the confectioners' sugar into a bowl. Stir 1 cup of the confectioners' sugar and the salt into the brown sugar mixture. Using a rubber spatula, stir vigorously, gradually adding more confectioners' sugar as needed, until the glaze is thickened but still pourable.

3. Place the cake on a serving plate. Slip four 2-inch-wide strips of wax paper just under the edges of the cake to form a square under the cake. Pour most of the glaze over the top of the cake. Spread with a metal icing spatula, letting the excess run down the sides. Apply the remaining glaze to the unglazed areas of the cake. Let stand until the glaze sets, about 1 hour.

4. Carefully remove the wax paper strips from under the cake. To serve, use a serrated knife and a sawing motion to cut the cake into slices. (The cake can be stored at room temperature, covered loosely with plastic wrap, for 1 day.)

Baker's Note

TO TEST THE consistency of the glaze, pour about a tablespoon over a small piece of bread; it should barely seep in. If it is too thin, add additional confectioners' sugar. If it is too thick, warm over a saucepan of very hot water, stirring gently to avoid creating bubbles.

Caramel Ice Cream Roll

MILK SPONGE CAKE

1 cup sifted cake flour (sifted, then measured by spoon-and-sweep)

½ teaspoon baking powder

⅛ teaspoon salt

⅓ cup milk, at room temperature

3 tablespoons unflavored vegetable oil

3 large eggs

1 large egg yolk

⅔ cup sugar

1 teaspoon vanilla extract

2 pints caramel (such as dulce de leche) ice cream

Confectioners' sugar, for garnish

CHOCOLATE-CINNAMON SAUCE

8 ounces bittersweet chocolate, finely chopped

1 cup heavy cream

One 3-inch cinnamon stick

½ cup confectioners' sugar

1 cup sliced almonds, toasted (see page 16)

MAKES ABOUT 12 SERVINGS

Flo Braker

Here's a reworking of the Boston cream pie theme. Instead of the classic layer cake and pastry cream, a sponge cake roulade is filled with store bought caramel ice cream and served with a Mexican-inspired cinnamon-chocolate sauce. Toasted almonds finish it off with a flourish.

1. Position a rack in the lower third of the oven and preheat to 425°F. Line a 15 × 10 × 1-inch jelly-roll pan with aluminum foil, leaving a 2-inch overhang at each short end. Grease and flour the foil in the pan, tapping out the excess flour.

2. To make the cake, sift the flour, baking powder, and salt into a small bowl or onto wax paper. In a glass measuring cup, combine the milk and oil (they will separate).

3. In the bowl of a heavy-duty electric mixer fitted with the whisk attachment, beat the eggs, yolk, and granulated sugar on medium speed until very light and fluffy, about 6 minutes. Beat in the vanilla. Add the flour and milk mixtures alternately in two additions, folding them in with a long-handled rubber spatula. Spread the batter evenly in the pan (an offset metal spatula does a good job).

Cakes for Family and Friends

4. Bake just until the top of the cake is golden and springs back when pressed gently in the center, 8 to 11 minutes. (Do not overbake, or the cake will crack when it is rolled.)

5. Remove the pan from the oven. Run a thin knife around the edges to loosen the cake. Pull up on the foil overhangs and transfer the roulade on its foil to a large wire cooling rack. Tent a large sheet of foil over the cake, crimping the foil so it doesn't touch the cake. (This retains moisture and prevents the cake from cracking later.) Cool completely, about 1 hour.

6. Soften the ice cream in the refrigerator for about 15 minutes. Transfer to a large bowl and mix with a large spoon to combine the soft and firm portions (or transfer to the chilled bowl of a heavy-duty mixer and beat briefly with the paddle attachment).

7. Discard the foil tent and transfer the cake on its foil to the work surface, with a long side facing you. Using an offset metal spatula, spread the cake evenly with the softened ice cream, stopping 1 inch from the farthest long side. Starting from the long side closest to you, and using the ends of the foil as an aid, roll up the cake (the foil lining will release from the cake as you roll). Wrap securely in the aluminum foil. Freeze for 2 hours or longer. (The cake can be frozen up to 1 day.)

8. To make the sauce, place the chocolate in a medium bowl; set aside. Bring the cream to a simmer with the cinnamon stick in a medium saucepan over low heat. Cover, remove from the heat, and let stand for 5 minutes. Remove the cinnamon stick. Pour the hot cream over the chocolate. Let stand for 2 minutes, then whisk until smooth and melted. Keep warm. (The sauce can be prepared up to 1 day ahead, cooled, covered, and refrigerated. Melt and reheat in a heatproof bowl over simmering water.)

9. When ready to serve, remove the dessert from the freezer, unwrap, and place on a long serving platter. Let stand at room temperature for 5 to 10 minutes. Using a serrated knife, cut the roulade on the diagonal. Sift confectioners' sugar lightly over each dessert plate. Transfer each slice to a dessert plate. Spoon the warm sauce next to each serving and sprinkle the toasted almonds on each plate opposite the chocolate sauce. Serve immediately.

Baker's Notes

USING MILK in this batter gives the cake a softer, more tender structure than other sponge cakes. Some recipes call for hot milk, but after testing many times several ways, we have concluded that heating the milk isn't necessary. The milk should be at room temperature, though, so it blends well into the batter.

The foil over the sheet cake holds in moisture during cooling, so the cake will roll without cracking. The tented shape keeps the foil from touching and sticking to the cake.

Gateau Victoire

Julia Cookenboo

We adore this sumptuous, flourless dark chocolate extravaganza, perfected by Julia Cookenboo, pastry chef at Oliveto restaurant in Oakland, California. A little goes a long way.

12 ounces semisweet or bittersweet chocolate (no more than 62 percent cocoa solids), coarsely chopped

⅓ cup plus 1 tablespoon strong brewed coffee

4 large eggs, at room temperature

2 large egg yolks, at room temperature

⅓ cup sugar

Scant ⅛ teaspoon salt

¾ cup heavy cream

Confectioners' sugar, for garnish

Whipped Cream Topping (page 336)

1. Position a rack in the lower third of the oven and preheat to 350°F. Line the bottom of a 9 × 2-inch cake pan (do not use a springform pan) with a round of parchment or wax paper.

2. In a large heatproof bowl placed in a skillet of hot, not simmering, water, melt the chocolate with the coffee, stirring often, until smooth. Remove from the heat and keep the chocolate mixture warm.

3. In the bowl of a heavy-duty mixer, whisk the eggs, yolks, sugar, and salt until combined. Place in a skillet of barely simmering water and stir constantly with the whisk until the eggs are very warm to the touch and the sugar is dissolved, about 2 minutes. Attach the bowl to the mixer and fit with the whisk attachment. Whip on high speed until the egg mixture is cool and very light and fluffy, about 3 minutes.

4. In a medium bowl, whip the cream until it forms soft peaks.

5. Add about one-third of the egg mixture to the chocolate mixture and fold until almost blended. Repeat with half of the remaining eggs, then the remaining eggs. Fold in half of the whipped cream until almost blended, then fold in the remaining cream until the mixture is evenly colored. Spread evenly in the pan. Place in a large roasting pan with at least 1 inch space around the sides of the pan.

6. Place the roasting pan in the oven and add enough hot water to come halfway up the sides of the cake pan. Bake until the top of the cake is crusty and firm to the touch, about 1½ hours.

7. Transfer the cake pan to a wire cooling rack and cool for 20 to 30 minutes. Invert the cake onto a serving platter and peel off the paper. Cool completely. Cover with plastic wrap and refrigerate until chilled, at least 2 hours. (The cake can be made up to 2 days ahead, covered, and refrigerated.)

8. To serve, let the cake stand at room temperature for about 1 hour to remove the chill. Sift confectioners' sugar over the cake as a garnish. Slice the cake with a hot, wet knife, wiping the knife clean between cuts. Serve with a dollop of whipped cream.

Baker's Notes

BECAUSE THE CAKE is baked in a water bath, don't use a springform pan; the water will seep through the crevices.

A heavy-duty standing mixer is the best choice for beating the eggs because the large whisk attachment quickly incorporates air into the mixture. If you must use a hand mixer, use a large heatproof bowl and allow plenty of time for whipping the eggs—it could take 6 minutes or more if the beaters are especially small. Go by the light, fluffy consistency of the eggs, not by the amount of beating time.

Queen of Sheba Torte

Alice Medrich

Different cakes lurk within this one recipe. Known to the French as Reine de Saba, *or* Queen of Sheba, *this moist, rich cake is infinitely versatile. Follow the mixing instructions carefully—if allowed to stand too long, the chocolate mixture may set and be difficult to fold with the egg whites. Whether you substitute other nuts for the almonds, use another liquor instead of brandy, or add soaked dried fruit, this cake is always a hit.*

½ cup whole almonds, natural or blanched

3 tablespoons all-purpose flour

6 ounces semisweet or bittersweet chocolate, finely chopped

10 tablespoons (1¼ stick) unsalted butter, cut up

3 tablespoons brandy or Cognac

⅛ teaspoon almond extract

4 large eggs, separated, at room temperature

⅔ cup plus 2 tablespoons sugar

⅛ teaspoon cream of tartar

Chocolate Butter Glaze (page 333)

⅓ cup sliced blanched almonds, toasted

1. Position a rack in the lower third of the oven and preheat to 350°F. Line an 8 × 3-inch springform pan with parchment or wax paper.

2. In a food processor fitted with the metal blade, process the almonds and flour until the almonds are ground into a very fine meal; set aside.

3. In the top part of a double boiler over hot, not simmering, water, melt the chocolate and butter, stirring often, until smooth. Remove from the heat and stir in the brandy and almond extract.

4. In a large bowl, whisk the egg yolks with ⅔ cup sugar until pale and well blended, about 1 minute. Whisk in the chocolate mixture. Set aside.

5. In a medium bowl, using a hand-held electric mixer at high speed, whip the egg whites and cream of tartar until soft peaks form. Gradually beat in the remaining 2 tablespoons sugar, beating just until the peaks are stiff and shiny (do not overbeat).

6. Stir the almond mixture into the chocolate mixture. Immediately fold about one-quarter of the egg whites into the batter to lighten it. Fold in the remaining whites. Spread evenly in the prepared pan.

7. Bake until a wooden toothpick inserted 1½ inches from the edge comes out clean but the center is still very moist, 35 to 40 minutes. Transfer to a wire cooling rack and cool completely in the pan. The torte will fall as it cools, leaving a slightly higher rim around a sunken center. Don't worry about the cracks in the surface.

8. Run a thin knife around the edges of the pan to release the torte. Press the edges down with your fingers until they are level with the center. Remove the sides of the pan. Invert onto an 8-inch cardboard cake round. Remove the bottom of the pan and the parchment paper. If the cake still appears uneven, press it with the bottom of a cake pan to make it level. (The cake can be prepared up to 3 days ahead, covered, and stored at room temperature. The cake can also be frozen for up to 3 months. Defrost overnight in the refrigerator, and be sure the cake is thoroughly defrosted and at room temperature before glazing.)

9. Place the torte on a cake decorating turntable or platter. Glaze according to the instructions on page 333. Hold up the cake with one hand, and use the other hand to press the sliced almonds onto the sides of the cake. Transfer to a wire cake rack until the glaze sets, about 15 minutes. Serve at room temperature.

Queen of Sheba Torte with Fruit: Toss ¼ cup finely chopped dried cherries, dried cranberries, or raisins with 2 to 3 tablespoons kirsch or brandy and let stand for 30 minutes. Fold into the batter before the egg whites.

Baker's Notes •───────────────────────────────

THE WORD "TORTE" means many things to many bakers. Usually it refers to a dense, moist cake that is made with a minimum of flour, if any. Often ground nuts or bread crumbs substitute for some or all of the flour.

The torte can be served unglazed as a fallen soufflé cake. Before baking, do not line the pan with parchment or wax paper. To serve, do not press the higher edges of the cake down. Sift confectioners' sugar through a wire sieve to highlight the cracks. Serve at room temperature with a dollop of whipped cream.

For more intense chocolate flavor, use a bittersweet chocolate with 70 percent cocoa solids. The baking time will be about 10 minutes less.

Substitute walnuts, pecans, or toasted and peeled hazelnuts for the almonds, and omit the almond extract. Substitute walnut- or hazelnut-flavored liqueur for the brandy.

Or, substitute dark rum, bourbon, kirsch, or framboise for the brandy.

Molten Chocolate Cakes

MAKES 6 SERVINGS

Alice Medrich

Tender and cakelike on the outside, these homely little cakes deliver a gush of bittersweet chocolate sauce from within, thanks to a truffle embedded in the center. As an added bonus, they can be prepared well ahead of baking. Choose your favorite high-quality chocolate and prepare yourself for a major indulgence.

Softened butter and sugar, for the ramekins

8 ounces semisweet or bittersweet chocolate, finely chopped

8 tablespoons (1 stick) unsalted butter, cut into bits

2 tablespoons milk

3 tablespoons unsweetened cocoa powder, natural or Dutch processed

2 large eggs, separated, at room temperature

1 large egg white, at room temperature

⅛ teaspoon cream of tartar

3 tablespoons sugar

Whipped Cream Topping (page 336)

1. Lightly butter the insides of six 6-ounce custard cups, sprinkle with sugar to coat, and tap out the excess.

2. In a medium stainless steel bowl placed in a skillet of hot, not simmering, water, melt the chocolate and butter, stirring often, until smooth. Remove from the heat. Measure 6 tablespoons into a small shallow bowl (a cereal bowl is perfect). Add the milk and stir well. Place in the freezer while preparing the rest of the recipe. Stir the cocoa and egg yolks into the remaining chocolate-butter mixture.

3. In a grease-free medium bowl, whip the egg whites with the cream of tartar until soft peaks form. Gradually beat in the sugar until the peaks are stiff and glossy but not dry. Fold about one-quarter of the egg whites into the cocoa mixture, then fold in the remaining whites. Spoon the batter into the cups, filling them half full. Set the remaining batter aside.

4. Remove the chocolate-butter mixture from the freezer; it should be firm. Using a dessert spoon, scrape up the mixture and roll into 6 truffle-like balls (they do not have to be perfectly round). Embed a truffle into the center of each custard cup, top with equal amounts of the remaining batter, and level the tops. Place the cups on a baking sheet. Cover the cups with plastic wrap and refrigerate for at least 3 hours. (The cakes can be prepared to this point up to 3 days ahead, covered, and refrigerated.)

5. Position a rack in the lower third of the oven and preheat to 400°F.

6. Bake until the cakes are puffed and cracked and a toothpick inserted in the center comes out gooey, indicating that the truffle is melted, about 12 minutes. Let the cakes cool for 3 minutes.

7. Run a thin knife around the inside of each cup to release the cake. Protecting your hands with a towel, invert a cup in the center of a dessert plate to unmold the cake. Repeat with the remaining cakes. Serve immediately with a dollop of whipped cream.

Baker's Note

FOR MORE OF a "restaurant-style" presentation, sift confectioners' sugar over the entire plate and garnish with drizzles of raspberry or caramel sauce.

Sweet and Savory Pies

Even though pie is a British import, it has long been a symbol of our country's baking. How many times have you heard the term "American as apple pie"? A pie, which is really nothing more than a filling in a crust, looks as easy to make as . . . well, pie. The truth is that pie making intimidates many bakers.

Few desserts satisfy like a piece of pie. But how many times have you turned into a diner or truck stop and hungrily ordered an enticing piece of their "baked on the premises" pie, only to be served a slab of tough, dry crust with a gooey canned filling? To use one more homily, when it comes to pie, "There's no place like home." For home-baked masterpieces of the pie baker's art, you don't have to outfit your kitchen with a bunch of fancy equipment—many a great pie has been made from a dough mixed with the baker's fingers, rolled out with a wine bottle instead of a proper rolling pin, and baked in an ordinary pie pan.

Pies seem to celebrate the seasons even more than other baked goods. Pumpkin or pecan pies make Thanksgiving dessert something to look forward to; peach or blueberry pies capture the flavor of summer. They can be served comfortingly warm or refreshingly chilled. We divided pies into four major categories, and we give recipes for each: custard-based pies (those that use eggs for flavor and as a thickener), cream pies (chilled pies with creamy fillings), fruit pies (including, of course, apple), and savory pies (a group that should not be overlooked for hearty brunch or supper dishes).

The more pies you make, the better you'll get at the very techniques that make some bakers nervous. Picture-perfect pies with golden, flaky crusts will become second nature, and you'll feel like a blue-ribbon prizewinner.

The majority of the recipes in this chapter were provided by Carolyn B. Weil, with contributions by Marion Cunningham, Rochelle Huppin-Fleck, Cynthia Elliot, and Letty Flatt.

Ingredients for Pies

TO GET A FLAKY, TENDER, AND tasty piecrust, there are four important considerations:

The fat-to-flour ratio

The type of fat

The temperature of the ingredients (think cold)

Proper handling of the dough (mixing, rolling, and baking)

When flour and water are mixed together, the gluten in the flour develops and strengthens, giving the dough a chewiness that may be desirable in pizza but not in piecrust. To keep the gluten from developing, the flour must be coated with a fat before adding the water. On the other hand, a certain amount of gluten activation is necessary to give structure to the dough. Water binds the dough and creates the steam that lifts the dough into layers, forming the tiny air pockets that make a flaky crust. In essence, a piecrust is a balance between inhibiting the gluten (working in a fat) and developing it (adding water).

Fats for Pie Dough

WHEN CHOOSING A recipe, consider the fat-to-flour ratio. The larger the amount of fat, the more tender the crust. This leads to a frequently asked question: Which fats are best to use in a crust?

There is no one right answer. There are choices to be made. Some bakers prefer butter, as it makes a crisp, distinctly flavorful crust. Others are unwilling to give up the characteristic flakiness of a shortening crust, even though they admit that the trade-off is a lack of flavor. Some cooks take the middle ground and combine the two, although most of our bakers simply prefer one or the other. Here are descriptions of the appropriate fats for piecrust.

Butter | By far, butter is the fat with the best flavor. If the fat-to-flour ratio is high and the dough is kept cold, butter makes a tender and flaky crust.

Vegetable shortening | To make this fat, oil is hydrogenated (a procedure that turns the liquid into a semisolid) and bleached. Because it contains little water, allowing the amount of water added to the dough to be precise, it makes one of the flakiest and most tender crusts. But it doesn't add much flavor to the crust, and some bakers describe that flavor as greasy.

Lard | Old-fashioned piecrusts made with lard (rendered pork fat) are especially tender and flaky because lard contains none of the water that is found in butter (remember, water can activate gluten and toughen the crust). Lard was once a common ingredient, but vegetable shortening muscled in on its territory. Store-bought lard has little flavor and bakes with an unpleasant aftertaste, thanks to its typical lacing of preservatives. For best results, render your own lard from fresh pork fatback (see page 126).

Margarine | Another hydrogenated and bleached oil, but with artificial flavors added. While it may feel similar to shortening, it makes a less flaky crust because it contains a fair amount of water. Low-fat, "lite," and tub margarines, with their high water content, make very tough crusts and should be avoided at all costs.

Oil | This liquid fat soaks into the flour instead of coating it, and makes a very soft, crumbly, non-flaky crust. The dough is soft and sticky and not easy to handle. It is only suggested for pies for people with dietary restrictions.

Flour

ALL-PURPOSE FLOUR, made from a combination of soft and hard wheat that encourages tenderness, is the best for pie dough. Remember that the exact protein content of the flour varies from region to region, and that all-purpose flour in the South (White Lily, for example) will often be softer than brands from the North (such as King Arthur). A soft all-purpose flour will not need any special handling; it will just make a very tender crust.

For these recipes, we used supermarket brands of unbleached all-purpose flour with an average protein content of 10.5 percent. Many of us prefer organic unbleached all-purpose flour for our pie dough; it is available at some gourmet and health food stores. Whole wheat flour, cornmeal, and buckwheat flour can be flavorful additions to pie crusts when combined with all-purpose flour. However, don't substitute other flours for more than one-quarter to one-half of the all-purpose flour, or the crust will be tough.

There are professional bakers who like low-gluten pastry flour for their piecrusts, but it is difficult to find at retail, and most home bakers would find that the small difference in quality would not be worth the effort and expense.

The flour in this chapter was measured by the dip-and-sweep method.

Thickeners for Pie Fillings

THICKENERS ARE USED in juicy fruit pies to give some body to the flavorful juices. Without thickeners, your pie will have baked fruit in a puddle of juice. It is better to have the juices surround the fruit to intensify the flavor. Lemon juice is often used to enhance or balance the flavor of the fruit, but don't overdo it, because acid will break down the starches that thicken the filling. A pinch of salt can also complement the filling's flavor.

Even in a familiar recipe that has worked well in the past, a pie filling is sometimes too runny to suit your tastes. Mother Nature is usually the culprit, as the fruit in today's pie may be more acidic than yesterday's, and acids have a tendency to diminish the effectiveness of some thickeners. If you try to compensate for an acidic fruit with extra sugar, that will also thin the filling. The main thickeners for pie fillings are:

Tapioca | This starch is extracted from the root of the cassava plant. It is a good thickener for fruit fillings, as it adds no flavor of its own and it cooks quickly. Use quick-cooking or instant tapioca granules for pie fillings, not the large-grained pearl variety. When cooked properly, the tapioca granules will be translucent and soft (undercooked granules are gritty), and the fruit juices will be clear. To avoid clumping, mix the tapioca well with the fruit and sugar, and let stand for 5 to 15 minutes to soften the tapioca. Tapioca granules are not recommended for lattice-top or open-crust fruit pies, as they will remain hard if exposed to the hot air of the oven. To solve this problem, some bakers recommend pulverizing the tapioca in the recipe into a flour with a coffee or spice grinder, and then mixing it with the fruit and sugar.

Cornstarch | A popular thickener, cooked cornstarch has no flavor of its own. It tends to remain a bit starchy if undercooked, so always cook cornstarch-based fillings until they are visibly bubbling through the center vent in the crust. The juices will firm into a clear gel, but be careful not to use too much cornstarch, or the filling will be gooey.

Flour | If undercooked, a filling thickened with flour will be gritty or pasty, and even when cooked properly, the set juices will be cloudy. For a clear filling, choose another thickener. Flour is generally used for low-acid fillings with fruits like apples, pears, and peaches.

Gelatin | A pure protein derived from meat products, gelatin is used to set some cream pies. While leaf gelatin is favored in Europe, powdered gelatin is much quicker and easier to use and preferred in American home kitchens. (Many of the professional bakers in our group were trained to use sheets of leaf gelatin, and refuse to switch allegiance.) Powdered gelatin is sprinkled over a small amount of liquid (usually about ¼ cup) and allowed to stand for 5 minutes to soften or "bloom." It is melted over or in simmering water, then incorporated into a warm puree or cream. When melting, the gelatin must be stirred constantly for at least 1 minute to ensure dissolving. While gelatin will set in less time, it really takes a full 24 hours of chilling for it to reach its maximum thickening potential. Freezing does not enhance or speed up this process.

Equipment for Pies

Rolling pins | These come in all shapes and sizes, and every baker has an opinion about which is the perfect pin. The choice remains yours.

Wooden ball-bearing pins | Lengths of 12 to 14 inches are especially helpful because the ball bearings make for smoother rolling. Before buying, check to be sure that your knuckles clear the table when you grab the handles. Some bakers say that the longer and heavier a pin, the better. Length is an advantage when rolling out large batches of dough (the ends of short pins can dig into the dough), and a heavy pin will press the dough to make it spread more easily. Another camp prefers smaller and lighter pins because they are more comfortable to handle.

French-style pins | These look like wooden dowels. They can have plain or tapered ends. These take practice to use properly and can be hard on your palms, but again, personal choice will make the call. Take care to actually roll the dough and not push it out, or the dough will be uneven.

There are a couple of other options, neither of which we have taken to heart. Pie dough wants to be kept as cool as possible, and *marble rolling pins* do stay cooler than wood. However, these pins are very heavy and usually quite expensive. *Metal rolling pins* that can be filled with ice cubes seem like a good idea, but they usually leak and are ultimately a gimmick.

To clean any rolling pin, just scrape off any clinging dough and wipe it with a damp cloth. Never submerge a rolling pin in water; the ball bearings could rust, and the wood will eventually warp.

Pie pans | Pie pans are made from many different materials. Bakers who love to bake pies should have a choice of pie pans, as some are better for certain types of pies than others.

The pie recipes in this book are for 9-inch-diameter pie pans with 1-inch-deep sides, which make 8 good-sized portions.

Metal pans | These conduct heat very well and help ensure a fully cooked bottom crust. High-gauge aluminum (avoid flimsy disposable aluminum pans), stainless steel, and tin are all good. Take care to wash and promptly dry metal pie pans to avoid rusting. A dark coating will help absorb the heat in the oven and further encourage a nicely browned crust. Metal pans are best for double-crusted pies, where a firm, golden brown crust is a must.

Glass (Pyrex) pie pans | Glass pans bake more slowly than metal, but they have the advantage of letting the baker check the browning of the bottom crust. Many bakers prefer to use glass pans for their single-crust pies. If the bottom crust doesn't look quite brown enough, just bake it a few minutes longer, tenting the top of the crust with aluminum foil if it seems to be getting too dark.

Ceramic pie pans | With results similar to glass, many of these pans are 1½ inches deep or more and should be considered deep-dish pie pans. These deep pans really aren't good for many sweet pies, as the crust overbrowns before the filling is cooked through, especially with pumpkin and other custard-based pies. They are best for fruit-filled or savory pies.

Work surfaces | The ideal surface for rolling out pie dough is cool and flat. This means that just about any typical kitchen counter material will do: Wood, marble, stainless steel, granite, and laminate all have their pluses and minuses, but they all work. Avoid tiled surfaces—the grout lines will mark your dough. A large cutting board, made from hard plastic, rubber, or wood, can be placed on the work surface. It also has the advantage of being portable, so it can be moved out of a hot kitchen if the need arises.

Ovens | Pie baking can be done in any oven, as long as the baker is familiar with the oven's individual quirks. Electric ovens tend to cook on the fast side. The top heating element tends to brown top crusts before the filling is cooked through, so pay attention to the pie's progress. If necessary, tent the crust with aluminum foil to slow down the browning. Gas ovens may take a bit longer, but the heat is more even. In either case, an oven thermometer is a must. Convection ovens bake hotter and more quickly.

The position of the oven rack is important. For either oven (except convection, where the circulating hot air makes the rack position a moot point), the rack should be placed in the lower third of the oven, which places it relatively close to the heat source and promotes a thoroughly cooked bottom crust. If you have a baking stone, place it on the rack before preheating the oven. The hot, even surface of the stone will help brown and cook the bottom crust. To keep bubbling juices from spilling over and staining the stone, you can place the pie on a sheet of foil.

The oven must be thoroughly preheated before baking a pie. The temperature must be hot enough to set the piecrust before the fat starts melting out of it. In some cases, the temperature is lowered after a few minutes to avoid overbrowning. We like to start preheating the oven before rolling out the dough, to give it at least 20 to 30 minutes to heat to the desired temperature.

Pie weights | When baking a pie shell, the dough must be weighed down to hold the sides in place and keep the bottom flat. (Blind baking refers to the prebaking process, not the weighting.) There are many different ways to do this. You can purchase ceramic or metal pie weights, or even pie weights connected together in a chain. These pricey, efficient weights are fine if you plan to bake one or two pies at a time, but if you need to bake many pies at once, you may want to go to a less expensive method.

Rice is an inexpensive alternative to pie weights and can be stored between uses in a jar or plastic bag. While rice is odorless to begin with, remember it will eventually go rancid, so give it a sniff before using it. Rice is much better than dried beans, as the beans get an unappetizing aroma after their first baking, and the skins can dry out after a few uses and flake off. Line the dough with a round of parchment paper or aluminum foil and fill with about 2 cups of the weights, being sure to place some of the weights against the sides of the dough.

Mixing the Dough

NO MATTER WHICH method you choose to make pie dough, remember that the fat must be cold when mixed with the dry ingredients. The flour should coat the fat—if the fat is too warm or soft, it will absorb the flour and the dough will be sticky and difficult to handle. Cold ingredients (chilled fat and ice water) also help arrest gluten development. In very warm weather, chill the bowl, utensils, and flour in the refrigerator as well.

In general, the dry ingredients (flour, salt, and sometimes sugar to add a bit of sweetness and promote tenderness and browning) are mixed together; then the fat is incorporated until the mixture looks crumbly. Don't reduce the amount of fat in the recipe, or you'll end up with a tough crust. If the fat seems too soft, just chill the mixture for about 15 minutes, until it firms up. Add only enough cold water to make a dough that holds together when pinched with the thumb and forefinger. The exact amount of water will depend on the humidity of the flour, so add it carefully.

Pie dough has been made by hand for centuries, and it is still the simplest way, requiring just a bowl and your hands. With this method, the fat and dry ingredients are rubbed together with the fingertips until the mixture is crumbly. To keep the fat cool, use the fingertips (the palms are too warm and could melt the fat) and work quickly. If you prefer to use a tool instead of your hands, use a pastry blender, two knives, or even a large serving fork (after you've cut up the pieces well with a knife) to cut the fat into the flour.

A standing heavy-duty electric mixer with the paddle attachment does a fine job of making pie dough. The mixer works quickly and keeps the fat cooler than any other method. When adding the water, take care not to overmix the dough, or the gluten will be activated. Hand-held mixers are not strong enough and are not recommended.

The food processor is an efficient dough-making tool, but only for the step of cutting the fat into the flour. The blade moves so quickly that it can heat the dough and overactivate the gluten. If you want to use a food processor, transfer the crumbly flour-fat mixture to a bowl and stir in the cold water by hand.

Again, when adding the water to the flour-fat mixture, add it carefully. Once you've added too much water, you cannot compensate by adding more flour—the fat-to-flour ratio will be thrown off, and the dough will be tough. When the dough is mixed, it should hold together but not feel wet or sticky. Do not mix the dough until it forms a ball. It may look crumbly, but the clumps should form a mass if pressed together.

Gather up the dough and press it into a thick disk. Disregard old recipes that tell you to make a ball of dough; rolling out a ball of dough is a sure way to end up with a crust that looks like the state of Florida. The dough should be in a flat, thick disk that reminds you of a fat hamburger patty, about 4 inches wide and 2 inches thick.

Wrap the disk in plastic wrap or wax paper. Refrigerate it for at least 20 minutes and up to 1 hour. This allows the gluten in the the dough to relax, and distributes the moisture throughout the dough. (The Butter Pie Dough on page 123 can be used immediately after mixing, if desired.) Pie dough can be chilled overnight, but it will be very hard and difficult to roll out. Be sure to let the dough stand out at room temperature for 10 to 15 minutes, or until it softens enough to roll out without cracking. If necessary, rap the dough all over with your rolling pin to soften it more, but be careful not to activate the gluten. It should be pliable but still chilled.

Rolling Out the Dough

TO THE NOVICE, one of the biggest mysteries of pie making is how to roll out the dough into a round. There is no secret—practice makes perfect. Handle the dough as little as possible during rolling to keep gluten activation to a minimum.

The first step is to prepare the work surface. Sprinkle it lightly with flour, then pass your hand through the flour to distribute it in a thin layer. Experience will be the judge of how much is enough. The flour should be sufficient to keep the dough from sticking to the surface, but if the flour coating is too thick, it could be absorbed into the dough. Some recipes for sweet, sticky dough call for rolling out between wax paper or plastic wrap. While they may keep a dough from sticking to the work surface, they also wrinkle and keep the dough from extending properly.

Sprinkle the top of the dough lightly with flour. Brush the flour over the top of the dough to distribute it into a very light coating, then brush off any excess. The rolling pin should be dusted with flour, too. A fabric rolling pin sleeve sounds like a good idea, but it must be seasoned with flour and doesn't always prevent sticking. If you don't wash the sleeve often, the flour can go rancid and lead to another set of problems (this goes for canvas pastry cloths as well).

The idea is to roll out the disk of dough one quarter at a time, turning it after each roll, until it gradually widens into a thinner round. Starting at the center of the disk, roll out to within ¼ inch of the upper edge of dough, using short strokes and even pressure, releasing the pressure as you reach the edge. Do not roll over the edge, or you'll flatten it and get an uneven thickness. Pick up the dough and rotate it one quarter turn. Roll out the dough, again starting at the center and working to the edge. Continue rolling out the dough and rotating one quarter turn each time, checking to be sure the dough isn't sticking, and dusting the surface and pin with more flour if needed, until the dough is about ⅛ inch thick. As the dough widens, you will not have to turn it as often.

To judge the diameter of dough needed for the pie pan, place the pan in the middle of the dough round. You should have a 1- to 1½-inch-wide border of dough around the circumference of the pan.

Shaping and Baking the Pie

IT IS IN THE nature of pie dough to shrink, bubble, or even collapse during baking. It is the baker's job to discourage the pie dough from doing its thing. Docking (pricking dough with a fork or a strange instrument that looks like a roller with spikes) helps prevent shrinkage and bubbles but can also leave undesirable holes that could allow a wet filling to leak through the crust. It is best to check for bubbling during baking, and carefully prick any bubbles that occur with a cake tester or wooden skewer to make as few holes as possible. If you dock the dough, don't overdo it.

To fit the dough into the pie pan, fold the dough in half. Transfer the dough to the pie pan. Unfold the dough and press it gently into the corners of the pan. Trim away any excess with a sharp knife or scissors to leave ½ inch of dough extending over the edges. Fold the excess dough over so the edge of the dough is flush with the edge of the pan.

The dough is now ready to flute. Fluting provides the pie with a decorative edge and can highlight the baker's personal style. There is no one right way to flute a pie. The simplest method gives the dough a pointed scallop. Using the knuckle of one hand, press the dough at the edge of the pie pan. At the same time, use the thumb and forefinger of the other hand to press against the dough from the other side, forming a pointed scallop. Move around the entire circumference of the dough, spacing the scallops about 1 inch apart. For a smaller, more pointed scallop, use your fingertip.

After the pan has been lined and the dough has been fluted, the pan must be refrigerated or frozen for at least 30 minutes. This relaxes the gluten in the dough (discouraging shrinkage) and firms up the fat (promoting flakiness). Most bakers do not bother to cover the pan with plastic wrap for such a short period, but if the pan will be chilled longer, cover it so it does not pick up any odors from food in the refrigerator.

Single-crust pies are often prebaked to the partially baked or fully baked stage before filling. Baking a pie shell without a filling is called blind baking. Pie shells are partially baked to set the dough so it doesn't become soggy when filled with a wet filling. Fully baked pie shells are used when the pie does not require further baking after filling.

For a partially baked pie shell, line the dough shell with a round of parchment paper or aluminum foil that comes up the sides of the pan, then fill with about 2 cups of pie weights. Cover with plastic wrap and refrigerate for 30 minutes to relax the gluten and discourage shrinkage. Remove the plastic and bake in a preheated 400°F oven until the dough looks set but not browned, about 12 minutes. Remove the pie from the oven and lift up the foil with the weights.

For a fully baked pie shell, bake as above. Remove the foil with the weights, then continue baking until the pie is golden brown, about 12 more minutes. Check occasionally to be sure that the dough isn't bubbling—deflate any bubbles by piercing with the tip of a sharp knife.

For a double-crusted pie, divide the dough equally into two thick disks. Roll out one disk for the bottom crust. Fit into the pie pan (do not flute) and add the filling. Do not over-fill the pie, or too many juices will run out during cooking, not only making a mess in the oven but ruining the look of the pie. Roll out the remaining disk of dough into a ⅛-inch-thick round about 1 inch larger than the pie pan. Center it over the filling, letting the excess dough hang over the edges. Fold the top crust under the edge of the bottom crust to make a double thickness at the edge of the pan. Press the two layers of crust together to seal them tightly (this is called crimping). This step is especially important with juicy fillings. Refrigerate the pie briefly, no longer than 15 minutes, to relax the dough.

For a lattice-top pie, divide the dough into two disks, one slightly larger than the other. Roll out the larger disk into a 12-inch-wide circle about ⅛ inch thick. Fit into the pie pan, letting the excess dough hang over the edges. If necessary, trim the dough to a 1-inch overhang. Add the filling. Roll out the remaining disk of dough into a ⅛-inch-thick round about 1 inch larger than the pie pan. Using a ruler and a pizza wheel (which works better than a knife), cut the dough round into 20 ½- to ¾-inch-wide strips.

For a *simple lattice top*, arrange the strips about ½ inch apart, placing half of them vertically and the other half horizontally.

For a *woven lattice-top*, place 10 of the strips vertically about ½ inch apart over the filling. Do not seal the ends to the bottom crust. Fold back every other strip about 4½ inches (if the strips were numbered, they would be strips 1, 3, 5, 7, and 9). Place one strip over the center of the filling at a right angle to the first strips to make a center cross strip. Replace the folded part of the strips. Now fold back strips 2, 4, 6, 8, and 10 where they touch the center cross strip. Place a second strip parallel to the cross strip and ½ inch away, and replace the folded part of the strips. Repeat, folding alternate strips back and placing cross strips about ½ inch parallel to them, to weave a lattice. Fold over the bottom crust to enclose the strips.

You may now flute the crust as you wish. If you would like a decorative crimping, after pressing the dough layers together, mark the edge of the dough with the tines of a fork. For a double crust pie, cut a vent in the center of the top crust to allow steam to escape. For a pretty effect, cut out a hole using the small end of a large (½-inch-diameter or so) plain pastry tube, or even a small, decoratively shaped canapé cutter.

To judge when a pie is done, don't rely just on the color of the crust, which should be golden brown. For a fruit pie, be sure that the juices are thick and bubbling through the center vent. For an apple pie, insert a knife through the center vent to ensure that the apples are tender.

Serving and Storing

SERVING ANY PIE will be easier if you use a pointed pie server. Any other tool is a compromise.

Fruit pies are best eaten warm, but not hot from the oven, as the filling needs time to cool and set. They should really be served within 24 hours of baking. Most pies can be refrigerated, loosely covered with plastic wrap or foil, for up to 5 days. Try to warm left-over fruit pies before serving—the warmth restores tenderness and flakiness to the crust. Reheat the pie in a 350°F oven, loosely covered with aluminum foil, until warm, 10 to 15 minutes.

Cream or other refrigerated pies are best served at cool room temperature. If served too cold, the butter in the crust will be hard, and your crust will seem tough even if there is nothing wrong with it. For easy serving, first cut the well-chilled pie into pieces with a hot, dry knife, then let it stand at room temperature for 30 minutes to an hour to lose its chill.

Butter Pie Dough

1 cup unbleached all-purpose flour (dip-and-sweep)

2 tablespoons sugar

¼ teaspoon salt

8 tablespoons (1 stick) unsalted butter, chilled and cut into
   ¼-inch cubes

2 tablespoons ice-cold water, or as needed

Mix the flour, sugar, and salt in a medium bowl. Using a pastry blender, cut in the butter until the mixture is crumbly, with a few coarse, pea-sized pieces of butter. Sprinkle in the water and mix with a fork, adding just enough until the mixture is moistened and begins to clump together. Gather up the dough and form into a flat disk. You can use this dough immediately.

Double-Crust Butter Pie Dough: Use 2 cups all-purpose flour, ½ pound (2 sticks) unsalted butter, ¼ cup sugar, ½ teaspoon salt, and about ¼ cup ice-cold water. Divide the dough into 2 equal pieces.

Savory Pie Dough: Use 1 cup all-purpose flour, 1 cup whole wheat flour or yellow cornmeal, ½ teaspoon salt, ½ pound (2 sticks) unsalted butter, and about ¼ cup ice-cold water. If desired, stir ¼ cup shredded sharp Cheddar cheese or 1 tablespoon minced fresh herbs into the crumbly mixture before adding the water. Divide dough into 2 equal pieces. Roll out the dough, place in the pan, and chill for 15 minutes before baking. Makes enough for 10 turnovers.

MAKES ONE 9-INCH PIE SHELL

Carolyn B. Weil

Carolyn B. Weil, The baker whom The Dozen turns to on pie-related matters, loves this pie dough for its rich, buttery flavor. It has a high proportion of fat to flour, ensuring a tender and flaky crust. This dough does not have to be chilled before using. In fact, Carolyn prefers to use it right after mixing, then chill the dough-lined pie pan. But chilling will not hurt the dough, either. Suit yourself.

*Sweet and
Savory Pies*

Shortening Pie Dough

MAKES ONE 9-INCH PIE SHELL

Marion Cunningham

Marion Cunningham, the guiding light of The Baker's Dozen, is a member of the shortening piecrust school. To her, a piecrust is all about flakiness (which shortening provides better than butter), with most of the flavor coming from the filling (many of which include butter anyway).

1½ cups all-purpose flour (dip-and-sweep)
½ teaspoon salt
½ cup vegetable shortening, at room temperature
¼ cup ice-cold water, or as needed

1. Combine the flour and salt in a medium bowl. Using a pastry blender, cut in the shortening until the mixture is crumbly, with a few pea-sized pieces of shortening. Sprinkle in the water and mix with a fork, adding just enough until the mixture is moistened and begins to clump together. Gather up the dough and form into a flat disk. You can use this dough immediately or proceed to the next step.

2. Wrap the dough in wax paper or plastic wrap. Refrigerate for at least 30 minutes or up to overnight. If chilled until hard, let the dough stand at room temperature for about 10 minutes to soften slightly before rolling.

Double-Crust Shortening Pie Dough: Use 2¼ cups all-purpose flour, ¾ teaspoon salt, ¾ cup vegetable shortening, and about 6 tablespoons ice-cold water. Divide the dough into 2 equal pieces.

Cream Cheese Pie Dough

8 tablespoons (1 stick) unsalted butter, chilled,
    thinly sliced
4 ounces cream cheese (not reduced-fat), chilled, cut
    into pieces
½ teaspoon sugar
Pinch of salt
1 cup unbleached all-purpose flour (dip-and-sweep)

1. In the bowl of a heavy-duty mixer fitted with the paddle, beat the butter on medium speed until smooth, about 1 minute. Add the cream cheese and mix until well combined with the butter, about 1 minute. Beat in the sugar and salt. Add the flour and mix on low speed just until the dough holds together. Do not overbeat. Gather up the dough into a thick disk.

2. Wrap the dough in wax paper or plastic wrap. Refrigerate for at least 1 hour or up to overnight. If chilled until hard, let the dough stand at room temperature for about 10 minutes to soften slightly before rolling.

Double-Crust Cream Cheese Pie Dough: Use ½ pound (2 sticks) unsalted butter, 8 ounces cream cheese, 2½ teaspoons sugar, ⅛ teaspoon salt, and 2 cups all-purpose flour. Divide the dough into 2 equal pieces, cover, and chill for 1 hour before using.

MAKES ONE 9-INCH PIE SHELL

Letty Flatt

Many bakers find that a beaten blend of butter and cream cheese makes an especially flaky and flavorful crust. The dough is very tender because it is made without any water other than that found in the butter and cream cheese, and gluten needs water in order to activate and toughen the crust. Also, the blended fats are thoroughly mixed into the flour, and fat also inhibits gluten activity. You'll need a heavy-duty mixer to cream the chilled unsalted butter with the cream cheese.

Baker's Note

FOR THE BEST RESULTS, don't use all-natural cream cheese. Supermarket varieties, such as Philadelphia Brand, work just fine.

Old-fashioned Lard Pie Dough

MAKES ONE 9-INCH PIE SHELL

Carolyn B. Weil

It's not fair to disparage lard piecrust—after all, until the invention of vegetable shortening in the early twentieth century, this was the most popular crust of all. Today's bakers will find that lard makes a very flaky, tender crust with a rich flavor that does well in savory pies. Some may find that they even prefer this golden crust with apple pie—pork and fruit are old acquaintances. Give it a try someday, but make your own lard for the best results and skip hyper-preserved supermarket lard. If you live in the East or South, a butcher or pork store in your neighborhood may make its own lard.

1½ cups unbleached all-purpose flour (dip-and-sweep)
2 tablespoons sugar (optional, for fruit pies)
½ teaspoon salt
½ cup lard, chilled (see Baker's Note)
¼ cup ice-cold water, or as needed

1. Combine the flour, sugar, and salt in a medium bowl. Using a pastry blender, cut in the lard until the mixture is crumbly, with a few pea-sized pieces of lard. Sprinkle in the water and mix with a fork, adding just enough until the mixture is moistened and begins to clump together. Gather up the dough and form into a flat disk.

2. Wrap the dough in wax paper or plastic wrap. Refrigerate for at least 30 minutes or up to overnight. If chilled until hard, let dough stand at room temperature to soften slightly before rolling out.

Double-Crust Lard Pie Dough: Use 2¼ cups all-purpose flour, ¾ teaspoon salt, ¾ cup lard, and about 6 tablespoons ice-cold water. Divide the dough into 2 equal pieces.

Baker's Note

TO MAKE LARD, finely chop 1 pound pork fatback (not salted fatback) in batches in a food processor. Transfer to a large, heavy-bottomed saucepan. Cover and cook over medium heat for 5 minutes. Uncover and reduce the heat to low. Cook at a bare simmer just until the fat is rendered and golden and the solids in the pan are golden brown, about 45 minutes. Strain into a medium bowl, pressing on the residue to extract as much rendered lard as possible, and discard the solids. Transfer the lard to a container with a tight-fitting lid. Refrigerate until the lard is solid, at least 4 hours or overnight, or store for up to 2 months. Makes about 1 cup.

Crumb Crust

1½ cups graham cracker crumbs
6 tablespoons (¾ stick) unsalted
    butter, melted
¼ cup sugar

MAKES ONE 9-INCH PIE SHELL

Carolyn B. Weil

Talk all you want about flaky crusts, but some pies just call out for a crumb crust.

Mix the crumbs, melted butter, and sugar in a medium bowl until well combined. Press firmly and evenly into an unbuttered 9-inch pie pan. Refrigerate until ready to use.

Chocolate Crumb Crust: Substitute chocolate wafer or chocolate graham cracker crumbs for the plain graham cracker crumbs.

Vanilla Crumb Crust: Substitute vanilla wafer crumbs for graham cracker crumbs.

Baker's Note

MAKE THE CRUMBS in a food processor or blender, or place the crackers in a zippered plastic bag and crush with a rolling pin.

Bourbon Pecan Pie

MAKES ONE 9-INCH PIE,
8 SERVINGS

Carolyn B. Weil

Dark corn syrup and a splash of bourbon make this a pecan pie with backbone.

Butter Pie Dough (page 123) or Shortening Pie Dough
(page 124)
½ cup packed light brown sugar
3 large eggs
1 cup dark corn syrup
2 tablespoons unsalted butter, melted
1 tablespoon bourbon
1 teaspoon vanilla extract
Pinch of salt
1½ cups coarsely chopped pecans

1. Following the instructions on page 120, line a 9-inch pie pan with the dough and flute the edges. Cover loosely with plastic wrap and refrigerate for 30 minutes.

2. Position a rack in the bottom third of the oven and preheat to 400°F.

3. Remove the plastic wrap and line the pastry shell with parchment paper or aluminum foil, then fill with pie weights. Bake until the pastry seems set, about 15 minutes. Remove the foil and weights and set the pie shell aside on a baking sheet. Reduce the oven temperature to 350°F.

4. Whisk the brown sugar and eggs in a medium bowl, then whisk in the corn syrup. Add the melted butter, bourbon, vanilla, and salt and whisk to combine. Arrange the pecans in the shell, then pour in the filling.

5. Bake the pie on the baking sheet until the sides of the filling are puffed but the center is still slightly indented, 35 to 45 minutes.

6. Transfer the pie to a wire cooling rack. Let stand until warm, or cool completely. (The pie can be stored, covered, at room temperature for up to 2 days.) Serve at room temperature.

Baker's Notes

THE PECANS SHOULD be coarsely chopped—whole pecans make the pie impossible to cut.

Serve the pecan pie warm with a big scoop of vanilla ice cream alongside, or with a huge dollop of whipped cream.

Toasted Coconut Custard Pie

Butter Pie Dough (page 123), Shortening Pie Dough
(page 124), or Cream Cheese Pie Dough (page 125)
1½ cups sweetened shredded coconut
1½ cups sugar
3 large eggs
1 cup milk
8 tablespoons (1 stick) unsalted butter, melted
1 tablespoon all-purpose flour
2 teaspoons vanilla extract
1 teaspoon cider vinegar or distilled white vinegar

MAKES ONE 9-INCH PIE,
8 SERVINGS

Carolyn B. Weil

Here's an old-fashioned classic that any roadside diner would be proud to serve. The custard goes beyond eggs and milk—melted butter adds richness, vinegar balances the sweetness, and flour gives it a firmer, easier-to-slice texture.

1. Following the instructions on page 120, line a 9-inch pie pan with the dough and flute the edges. Cover loosely with plastic wrap and refrigerate for 30 minutes.

2. Position a rack in the bottom third of the oven and preheat to 400°F.

3. Remove the plastic wrap and line the pastry shell with parchment paper or aluminum foil, then fill with pie weights. Bake until the pastry seems set, about 15 minutes. Remove the foil and weights and set the pie shell aside on a baking sheet. Reduce the oven temperature to 350°F.

4. Spread the coconut on another baking sheet. Bake, stirring occasionally, until toasted light gold, about 12 minutes. Set aside to cool slightly.

5. Whisk the sugar and eggs in a medium bowl. Add the milk, melted butter, flour, vanilla, and vinegar, and whisk well to dissolve the flour. Stir in the coconut. Pour evenly into the pie shell.

6. Bake until the top of the filling is puffed and golden and it looks set in the center when the pie is gently shaken, 45 to 55 minutes.

7. Transfer to a wire cooling rack and cool completely. (The pie can be covered and refrigerated for up to 2 days.) Serve at room temperature.

Baker's Note

CUSTARD PIE RECIPES often suggest testing the filling for doneness by inserting a knife in the center of the pie, but the coconut in this filling prevents the knife from going in smoothly.

*Sweet and
Savory Pies*

Fall Squash Pie

MAKES ONE 9-INCH PIE,
8 SERVINGS

Carolyn B. Weil

For a world-class pie for the Thanksgiving table, skip canned pumpkin and make the filling from fresh squash puree. There are many winter squashes that can do the job. If you want to use pumpkin, do not use the typical jack-o'-lantern variety, but hold out for what are considered eating pumpkins. Examples include sugar or cheese pumpkins, which can be found at farmers' markets during pumpkin-pie season. Or substitute 1 cup mashed cooked yams for a Southern treat.

Butter Pie Dough (page 123)
1 cup packed light brown sugar
3 large eggs
1 teaspoon ground cinnamon
1 teaspoon ground ginger
½ teaspoon freshly grated nutmeg
¼ teaspoon ground cloves
¼ teaspoon salt
1 cup fresh winter squash puree (see Baker's Notes)
1 cup heavy cream
Whipped Cream Topping (page 336)

1. Following the instructions on page 120, line a 9-inch pie pan with the dough and flute the edges. Cover loosely with plastic wrap and refrigerate for 30 minutes.

2. Position a rack in the bottom third of the oven and preheat to 400°F.

3. Remove the plastic wrap and line the pastry shell with parchment paper or aluminum foil, then fill with pie weights. Bake until the pastry seems set, about 15 minutes. Remove the foil and weights and set the pie shell aside on a baking sheet. Reduce the oven temperature to 350°F.

4. In a large bowl, whisk the brown sugar and eggs until smooth. Mix in the cinnamon, ginger, nutmeg, cloves, and salt, then the squash puree and cream. Pour into the pie shell.

5. Bake the pie on the baking sheet until the sides of the filling are slightly risen and the center is firm when jiggled, 35 to 40 minutes.

6. Transfer the pie to a wire cooling rack and let stand until completely cooled. (The pie can be stored, covered and refrigerated, for up to 2 days.) Serve at room temperature with a dollop of whipped cream.

Sweet Potato Pie: Use orange-fleshed yams to make this Southern favorite (true sweet potatoes actually have yellow flesh, even though we use "yam" and "sweet potato" interchangeably). Steam 1 very large (8- to 10-ounce) yam, peeled and cut into 2-inch chunks, until tender, about 25 minutes. Rub through a wire sieve to puree; you should have 1 cup. Substitute the yam puree for the squash in the filling.

Baker's Notes •————————————————————————

HUBBARD, DELICATA, BUTTERNUT, or acorn squash and sugar or cheese pumpkin are all good choices for baking into a pie filling. Buy a large squash, at least 1½ pounds. If you buy a huge squash, you can have a whole season's worth of squash puree. Cut the squash in half and place cut side down in a baking pan. Add about ½ inch of water to the pan. Bake in a preheated 350°F oven until the squash is tender enough to be pierced with the tip of a sharp knife, about 1 hour, depending on the hardness of the squash. Cool completely. Scoop out the seeds and pare and discard the skin. Puree the squash in a food processor fitted with the metal blade. If the squash seems watery (it should be about the same consistency as canned pumpkin), let it drain in a cheesecloth-lined wire sieve over a bowl for an hour or so. Divide the puree into 1-cup portions and freeze in small freezer bags for up to 3 months.

Pumpkin pies always seem to crack when cooled. Don't let it bother you. If you wish, spread whipped cream over the top of the pie as camouflage.

Key Lime Pie

MAKES ONE 9-INCH PIE,
8 SERVINGS

Carolyn B. Weil

Key limes are a small yellow lime often found growing in Florida backyards, with a mild, almost spicy flavor. The commercial crop was wiped out by a frost many years ago and is just being revived. Bottled Key lime juice is available in some gourmet markets, but it is a far cry from the real thing. Use fresh Persian lime juice instead.

Crumb Crust (page 127)

FILLING

4 large egg yolks
1 tablespoon plus 1 teaspoon freshly grated lime zest, preferably Key lime
One 14-ounce can sweetened condensed milk
½ cup fresh lime juice, preferably Key lime (8 to 10 limes)
Pinch of salt

WHIPPED CREAM TOPPING

1 cup heavy cream
1 tablespoon confectioners' sugar
1 teaspoon vanilla extract

1. Make the crumb crust; refrigerate.

2. Position a rack in the center of the oven and preheat to 350°F.

3. In a medium bowl, beat the yolks and lime zest with an electric mixer on high speed until well mixed and slightly thickened, about 1 minute. Add the condensed milk and beat well. Add the lime juice and salt and beat again. Pour into the pie shell.

4. Bake the pie on a baking sheet until the filling looks firm when the pie is gently shaken, 15 to 17 minutes. Transfer the pie to a wire cooling rack and cool completely. If desired, cover loosely with plastic wrap (be careful that the plastic doesn't touch the filling) and refrigerate until chilled, up to 1 day. Remove the pie from the refrigerator 30 minutes before serving.

5. To make the topping, just before serving, beat the cream with the sugar and vanilla with the mixer on high speed until stiff peaks form. If desired, transfer to a pastry bag fitted with a large star tip. Pipe 8 large rosettes or a wide zigzag around the edge of the pie, or spread the whipped cream over the pie. Cut into wedges to serve.

Baker's Note

CONFECTIONERS' sugar contains a small amount of cornstarch, which helps stabilize the whipped cream, and dissolves more easily than granulated sugar.

Cranberry Chess Pie

Butter Pie Dough (page 123), Shortening Pie Dough
    (page 124), or Cream Cheese Pie Dough (page 125)
1½ cups sugar
8 tablespoons (1 stick) unsalted butter, at room temperature
3 large eggs
8 tablespoons all-purpose flour
½ cup buttermilk, whole or low-fat
1½ teaspoons vanilla extract
2 cups fresh or frozen cranberries, pulsed in a food processor
    until coarsely chopped

MAKES ONE 9-INCH PIE,
8 SERVINGS

Carolyn B. Weil

*Chess pies have been a
Southern favorite for
decades—they usually
include buttermilk, and they
are always sweet. This version
cleverly uses tart cranberries
to counteract the sweetness.
No one is sure how chess pie
got its name. Among other
explanations, some people
think the pie originated in
Chester, England; some
believe it's a derivation of
"cheese pie," as the filling is
soft and curdlike; and others
say it's "jes' pie," so that's
what it's called.*

1. Following the instructions on page 120, line a 9-inch pie pan with the dough and flute the edges. Cover loosely with plastic wrap and refrigerate for 30 minutes.

2. Position a rack in the bottom third of the oven and preheat to 400°F.

3. Remove the plastic wrap and line the pastry shell with parchment paper or aluminum foil, then fill with pie weights. Bake until the pastry seems set, about 15 minutes. Remove the foil and weights and set the pie shell aside on a baking sheet. Reduce the oven temperature to 350°F.

4. In a medium bowl, using an electric mixer, beat the sugar and butter until well combined and sandy-textured, about 1 minute. One at a time, beat in the eggs, beating well after each addition. Beat in the flour, then the buttermilk and vanilla. Stir in the cranberries. Pour into the pie shell.

5. Bake the pie on the baking sheet until the top is light gold and domed and the filling seems firm in the center when the pie is gently shaken, about 1 hour.

6. Transfer the pie to a wire cooling rack and cool completely. (The pie can be stored, covered and refrigerated, for up to 2 days.) Serve at room temperature.

Baker's Note

IF USING frozen cranberries, they will chill the filling; allow an extra few minutes' baking time.

*Sweet and
Savory Pies*

Banana Cream Pie

MAKES ONE 9-INCH PIE,
8 SERVINGS

Carolyn B. Weil

A vanilla custard filling is a fine beginning to a banana cream pie. With a few changes, it can be easily transformed into another favorite, coconut cream pie. No matter what route you take, there will be happy pie-eaters in the house.

Butter Pie Dough (page 123), Shortening Pie Dough
   (page 124), or Cream Cheese Pie Dough (page 125)

CUSTARD

2 cups milk
½ cup sugar
4 large egg yolks
¼ cup cornstarch
¼ teaspoon salt
1 teaspoon vanilla extract

3 ripe bananas, peeled and cut into ¼-inch-thick rounds
Whipped Cream Topping (page 336)

1. Follow the instructions on page 120: line a 9-inch pie pan with dough and flute edges. Cover loosely with plastic wrap and refrigerate for 30 minutes.

2. Position a rack in the bottom third of the oven and preheat to 400°F.

3. Remove the plastic wrap and line the pastry shell with parchment paper or aluminum foil, then fill with pie weights. Bake until the pastry seems set, about 15 minutes. Remove the foil and weights and continue baking until the crust is golden brown, about 10 more minutes. Transfer to a wire cooling rack and cool completely.

4. To make the custard, bring the milk to a simmer in a nonreactive medium saucepan over medium heat. In a bowl, whisk the sugar and yolks, then whisk in the cornstarch and salt. Gradually whisk in the hot milk. Pour the mixture into the saucepan. Cook over medium heat, whisking almost constantly, until the mixture thickens and comes to a full boil. Remove from the heat and whisk in the vanilla. Strain the filling through a wire sieve set over a bowl to remove any cooked bits of egg white.

5. Spread the banana slices over the bottom of the pie shell. Pour the warm filling into the shell. Cover with plastic wrap, pressing the wrap directly onto the surface of the filling. Pierce the plastic with the tip of a knife a few times so the steam can escape. Refrigerate until well chilled, at least 2 hours. (The pie can be made up to 1 day ahead, covered, and refrigerated.)

6. About 30 minutes before serving, remove from the refrigerator. Spread or pipe the whipped cream over the top of the pie. Cut into wedges to serve.

Peanut Butter and Fudge Pie

Chocolate Crumb Crust (page 127)

CHOCOLATE FUDGE FILLING

4 ounces bittersweet or semisweet chocolate, finely chopped
½ cup heavy cream
1 tablespoon light corn syrup

PEANUT BUTTER FILLING

1½ cups smooth or chunky peanut butter
1½ cups confectioners' sugar
1 cup heavy cream
1 teaspoon vanilla extract

1. Prepare the crumb crust; refrigerate.

2. To make the chocolate filling, place the chocolate in a small bowl. In a small saucepan, bring the cream and corn syrup to a boil over medium heat. Pour over the chocolate. Let stand to soften; whisk until smooth. Cool until tepid.

3. Transfer ¼ cup of the chocolate mixture to a small plastic bag and set aside at room temperature. Spread the remaining chocolate filling in the crust. Freeze or refrigerate until the chocolate layer is firm, 15 to 30 minutes.

4. To make the peanut butter filling, in a medium bowl, using a hand-held electric mixer on low speed, beat the peanut butter, confectioners' sugar, cream, and vanilla until smooth, then increase the speed to high and beat until fluffy. Spread on the chilled chocolate layer and smooth the top.

5. Squeeze the chocolate in the plastic bag into one corner of the bag and twist the top closed. The chocolate should be warm and fluid. If it has hardened, warm it in your hands or microwave on very low power for a few seconds to soften it. Using scissors, snip off the corner of the bag to make a ⅛-inch opening. Following the instructions on page 81 for making a spider web design, squeeze a close spiral of the chocolate mixture onto the peanut butter layer, then mark it into the design.

6. Refrigerate the pie until well chilled, at least 2 hours. (The pie can be made up to 2 days ahead, covered with a cake dome, and refrigerated.) About 30 minutes before serving, remove the pie from the refrigerator. Serve chilled but not cold.

MAKES ONE 9-INCH PIE, 8 TO 10 SERVINGS

Carolyn B. Weil

Chocolate and peanut butter always go well together, so this is a guaranteed crowd pleaser. The baker will like it too—there aren't many pies that are easier to make. It is topped off with a sophisticated cobweb design that contrasts its "kids' stuff" flavor.

Bittersweet Chocolate Pudding Pie

MAKES ONE 9-INCH PIE,
8 SERVINGS

Carolyn B. Weil

The combination of bittersweet chocolate and cocoa powder gives this pie filling a deep, dark chocolate flavor.

Butter Pie Dough (page 123), Shortening Pie Dough
   (page 124), or Cream Cheese Pie Dough (page 125)
2½ cups milk
½ cup heavy cream
¾ cup sugar
2 large eggs
2 large egg yolks
¼ cup cornstarch
3 tablespoons unsweetened cocoa powder, preferably
   Dutch processed
Pinch of salt
7 ounces bittersweet chocolate, finely chopped
3 tablespoons unsalted butter
1 teaspoon vanilla extract
Whipped Cream Topping (page 336)

1. Following the instructions on page 120, line a 9-inch pie pan with the dough and flute the edges. Cover loosely with plastic wrap and refrigerate for 30 minutes.

2. Position a rack in the bottom third of the oven and preheat to 400°F.

3. Remove the plastic wrap and line the pastry shell with parchment paper or aluminum foil, then fill with pie weights. Bake until the pastry seems set, about 15 minutes. Remove the foil and weights and continue baking until the crust is golden brown, about 10 more minutes. Transfer to a wire cooling rack and cool completely.

4. To make the filling, bring the milk and cream to a simmer in a nonreactive medium saucepan over medium heat. In a medium bowl, whisk the sugar, eggs, and yolks. Add the cornstarch, cocoa, and salt and whisk well. Gradually whisk in the warm milk. Return the mixture to the saucepan.

5. Cook over medium heat, whisking constantly, until the filling comes to a full boil. Remove from the heat and add the chocolate, butter, and vanilla. Let stand for a few minutes, then whisk until the chocolate and butter are melted. Strain through a wire sieve into a medium bowl to remove any bits of egg white.

6. Pour the warm filling into the pie shell. Cover with plastic wrap, pressing the wrap directly onto the surface of the filling. Pierce the plastic with the tip of a knife a few times so the steam can escape. Refrigerate until well chilled, at least 2 hours. (The pie can be made up to 1 day ahead, covered, and refrigerated.)

7. About 30 minutes before serving, remove the pie from the refrigerator. Just before serving, spread or pipe the whipped cream on top of the pie. Cut into wedges to serve. Serve chilled but not cold.

Baker's Notes

GARNISH THE TOP of the pie with chocolate curls (see page 83) or grated chocolate, or with a light dusting of cocoa sprinkled through a wire sieve.

Pie fillings that are thickened with cornstarch must come to a full boil in order for the cornstarch to be fully activated. The cornstarch in the filling will prevent the eggs from curdling.

Remember that brands of bittersweet chocolate vary widely in sweetness. Taste the warm filling; if it seems too bitter, add a little extra sugar if you wish.

Creamy Mocha Pie

MAKES ONE 9-INCH PIE,
8 SERVINGS

Carolyn B. Weil

Although there's no cream to be found in this chocolate-coffee filling, it has a rich and luxurious texture. This recipe used to be made with raw eggs, but we heat them over hot water to kill any harmful bacteria.

Butter Pie Dough (page 123), Shortening Pie Dough
(page 124), or Cream Cheese Pie Dough (page 125)
1¼ cups packed light brown sugar
5 large eggs
5 ounces unsweetened chocolate, finely chopped
1 tablespoon instant coffee dissolved in 1 tablespoon boiling
water
1 teaspoon vanilla extract
½ pound (2 sticks) unsalted butter, at room temperature
Whipped Cream Topping (page 336)

1. Following the instructions on page 120, line a 9-inch pie pan with the dough and flute the edges. Cover loosely with plastic wrap and refrigerate for 30 minutes.

2. Position a rack in the bottom third of the oven and preheat to 400°F.

3. Remove the plastic wrap and line the pastry shell with parchment paper or aluminum foil, then fill with pie weights. Bake until the pastry seems set, about 15 minutes. Remove the foil and weights and continue baking until the crust is golden brown, about 10 more minutes. Transfer to a wire cooling rack and cool completely.

4. In a medium metal bowl set over a saucepan of simmering water or in the top of a double boiler, whisk the brown sugar and eggs. Cook, stirring constantly with a wooden spoon or heatproof rubber spatula, until an instant-read thermometer inserted in the mixture reads 140°F. Maintain the temperature between 140° and 150°F for 5 minutes, adjusting the heat as needed and stirring constantly.

5. Remove from the heat, add the chocolate, and whisk until the chocolate is melted. Stir in the dissolved coffee and the vanilla. Cool until the chocolate mixture is warm but not hot. A few tablespoons at a time, whisk in the butter. Pour into the pie shell and cover loosely with plastic wrap. Refrigerate until the filling is firm, at least 3 hours. (The pie can be made up to 2 days ahead, covered, and refrigerated.)

6. About 30 minutes before serving, remove the pie from the refrigerator. Just before serving, spread or pipe the whipped cream over the top of the pie. Serve chilled but not cold.

Baker's Notes

GARNISH THE TOP of the pie with chocolate curls, grated chocolate, or chocolate-covered espresso beans.

While 160°F will kill salmonella, a temperature of 140° to 150°F for 4 minutes is equally effective.

Lemon Meringue Pie

MAKES ONE 9-INCH PIE,
8 SERVINGS

Carolyn B. Weil and Kathleen Stewart

Old-fashioned lemon meringue pie has now become new-fashioned meringue pie. Thanks to the pioneering work of cookbook authors like Shirley Corriher and Pam Anderson, we have learned to add cornstarch to our meringue to reduce the amount of weeping and shrinkage. Also, the success of a firm filling depends on cooking the bubbling mixture for a full 30 seconds. This filling is richer, firmer, and tangier than most, to make this version a real winner.

The Baker's Dozen Cookbook

140

Butter Pie Dough (page 123), Shortening Pie Dough (page 124), or Cream Cheese Pie Dough (page 125)

FILLING

1¼ cups sugar

3 tablespoons cornstarch

4 large eggs

4 large egg yolks (reserve whites for topping)

1 cup fresh lemon juice (about 7 lemons)

2 tablespoons freshly grated lemon zest (3 lemons)

¼ teaspoon salt

4 tablespoons (½ stick) unsalted butter, thinly sliced

MERINGUE

¼ cup water

½ cup superfine or granulated sugar

1 tablespoon cornstarch

½ teaspoon cream of tartar

½ cup egg whites (about 4 large), at room temperature

1. Following the instructions on page 120, line a 9-inch pie pan with the dough and flute the edges. Cover loosely with plastic wrap and refrigerate for 30 minutes.

2. Position a rack in the bottom third of the oven and preheat to 400°F.

3. Remove the plastic wrap and line the pastry shell with parchment paper or aluminum foil, then fill with pie weights. Bake until the pastry seems set, about 15 minutes. Remove the foil and weights and continue baking until the crust is golden brown, about 10 more minutes. Transfer to a wire cooling rack and cool completely.

4. To make the filling, whisk the sugar and cornstarch in a medium bowl. Add the eggs and yolks and whisk until pale yellow. Whisk in the juice, zest, and salt. Add the butter. Transfer to a medium saucepan.

5. Cook, stirring constantly with a wooden spoon or heatproof rubber spatula, over medium heat until the mixture bubbles, then stir for another 30 seconds to be sure the filling reaches its optimum thickness. Whisk to smooth the filling. Strain through a wire sieve into a medium bowl to remove any bits of cooked egg white.

6. Pour the warm filling into the pie shell. Cover with plastic wrap, pressing the wrap directly onto the surface of the filling. Pierce a few slits in the wrap with the tip of a knife a few times to allow the steam to escape. Refrigerate until completely chilled and set, about 3 hours. Discard the plastic wrap.

7. Position a rack in the middle of the oven and preheat to 375°F.

8. To make the meringue, pour the water into a small saucepan, add the cornstarch, and whisk to dissolve. Whisk over medium-low heat until cooked into a thick, opaque, and gooey paste, about 1 minute. Set aside to cool.

9. In a small bowl, mix the sugar and cream of tartar. In a medium bowl, using a hand-held mixer at low speed, whip the egg whites until foamy. Increase the speed to medium-high. One tablespoon at a time, add the sugar mixture to the egg whites as you whip them to soft peaks. Add the cooled cornstarch mixture and continue whipping to form stiff, shiny peaks.

10. Heap the meringue on the filling, spreading it with a metal icing spatula to touch the crust. Swirl the meringue into peaks, if desired. Bake until evenly colored to a light gold, about 15 minutes. Transfer to a wire rack and let stand until completely cooled. The pie is best served the day of baking.

11. To serve, cut into wedges, using a thin, sharp knife dipped in hot water.

Baker's Note

USE A HAND-HELD mixer to make the meringue, as the amount is too small to be whipped effectively in the large bowl of the typical standing mixer.

Testing and Tasting . . . Meringue

In September 1999, cooking teacher Carolyn B. Weil and bakery owner Kathleen Stewart conducted an extensive workshop on egg whites and, more specifically, meringue for pies.

First consider the age and temperature of the eggs: Fresh egg whites whip into a stronger, more stable meringue. Older and thinner whites whip up more quickly, but are less stable and may collapse when ingredients are folded in. Room-temperature egg whites whip up quickly. There is no ultimate difference in volume between room-temperature and chilled eggs; the latter simply take longer to whip. Whipping in a copper bowl will not increase volume, but the meringue will be more stable, and it will expand better during baking. If not using a copper bowl, an acid such as cream of tartar, vinegar, or lemon juice is a good substitute, using about ⅛ teaspoon for every white.

The point at which the sugar is added to the whipped whites is crucial. The whites should be whipped until the whisk or beater begins to leave a ridge or trail; this is equal to the soft peak stage. While whipping the whites, add heaping tablespoons of the sugar, but don't add them too slowly, or you will overbeat the whites. The meringue should form stiff, shiny peaks (overbeaten whites are dull), and the sugar will not be completely dissolved. If adding flavorings, such as vanilla, add them toward the end of beating. A brown flavoring added with the sugar will tint the sugar crystals and discolor the meringue.

There are three classic methods for making meringue, although new methods of preparing egg whites to kill harmful bacteria have blurred the distinctions. *Swiss (also called warm) meringue* warms the egg whites and sugar to 120°F before whipping. This method was usually reserved for items that would be baked. (This book often uses a version of this method, mixing the whites with a few tablespoons of water to make them more heat tolerant, then heating. *Classic (or cold) meringue* whips the whites without heating, and can be prepared in soft or hard textures. Soft meringue, with about 2 tablespoons sugar per white, is used for pie toppings, mousses, and baked Alaska. Hard meringue uses about ¼ cup sugar for every white, and is slowly baked to dry to a crisp texture. Unless stored airtight, hard meringues will absorb humidity and eventually soften. *Italian meringue* is made by adding a sugar syrup heated to 238° to 248°F to the whites while they are being whipped. This partially cooks the whites, but not enough to kill bacteria. It was the traditional method for buttercreams, meringue toppings that were browned under a broiler, and fruit mousses, but many bakers now prefer to use a method that heats the whites to 160°F.

The topping for American lemon meringue pie is made by the cold meringue method. This topping often shrinks, and tiny beads of moisture will form after a few hours. Controlling these problems is a challenge to most bakers. Carolyn and Kathleen, who have baked thousands of lemon meringue pies at their bakeries, believe that the most important shrinkage preventative is to spread the meringue to actually touch the crust. Contrary to bakers who recommend piling the meringue onto a hot filling, they believe the filling temperature does not affect the success of the meringue. To stabilize the egg whites and make them more heat tolerant (overcooking is the cause of beading), they add a cooked cornstarch paste to the whipped whites. Baking the meringue at a moderately high temperature also cuts down on the chance of overcooking. If possible, don't refrigerate a lemon meringue pie after baking, as the humidity of the refrigerator can also cause beading.

Stephanie A. E. Mulroony

Blood Orange Chiffon Pie with Chocolate Crumb Crust

MAKES ONE 9-INCH PIE,
8 SERVINGS

Rochelle Huppin-Fleck

Here's an updated version of the refreshing chiffon pie, using garnet-red blood orange juice and a chocolate crumb crust. Blood oranges, once an imported crop from the Mediterranean, are now grown in our country, where they are in season during January and February. Navel oranges may be substituted. Chiffon pie recipes used to have beaten raw egg whites for volume, but we substitute whipped cream and cook the egg yolks.

Chocolate Crumb Crust (page 127)
¼ cup water
2¼ teaspoons (1 envelope) unflavored gelatin
1 cup sugar
½ cup fresh blood orange juice
¼ cup fresh lemon juice
4 large egg yolks
1 tablespoon freshly grated blood orange zest
    (1 or 2 oranges)
⅛ teaspoon salt
1¼ cups heavy cream
Whipped Cream Topping (page 336)
Six to eight 3-inch strips of blood orange zest
    (use a channel knife or zester), for garnish

1. Make the crumb crust; refrigerate.

2. Pour the water into a small, heavy-bottomed saucepan. Sprinkle the gelatin over the top and let stand for 5 minutes, or until the gelatin softens. Add ¾ cup sugar with the orange juice, lemon juice, yolks, and orange zest and whisk well.

3. Cook over medium-low heat, stirring constantly with a wooden spatula, until the mixture is thick enough to heavily coat the spatula (an instant-read thermometer inserted in the mixture will read 185°F). Do not allow the mixture to boil, or the yolks will curdle. Strain through a wire sieve into a medium bowl to remove any bits of cooked egg white.

4. Refrigerate uncovered, stirring often, until the mixture is cooled but not set and thick enough to form a small mound when dropped from a spoon, about 45 minutes.

5. In a chilled medium bowl, beat the cream with the remaining ¼ cup sugar just until soft peaks form. Do not overbeat or the cream won't fold smoothly into the lemon mixture. Fold the whipped cream into the orange juice mixture. Pour into the crust and cover with plastic wrap.

6. Refrigerate until the filling is chilled and completely set, at least 2 hours. (The pie can be prepared up to 2 days ahead, covered, and refrigerated.)

7. To serve, place a dollop or pipe large rosettes of whipped cream around the edge of the filling. Tie the orange zest strips into an overhand knot and garnish each dollop with a knot.

Lime or Lemon Chiffon Pie: Substitute ¾ cup fresh lemon or lime juice for the blood orange/lemon juice combination and 1 tablespoon freshly grated lemon or lime zest for the blood orange zest. Garnish with strips of lime or lemon zest. Use a vanilla wafer or graham cracker crust.

Baker's Note

B E S U R E N O T to let the orange mixture set completely when chilling. Frequent stirring helps you keep an eye on its progress.

Apple Mincemeat Pie

MAKES ONE-9-INCH PIE,
8 SERVINGS

Carolyn B. Weil

Traditional mincemeat must age for a few months before serving, and often contains braised beef and suet. But this quick meatless version has all of the classic flavors with none of the fuss, and sports a lovely lattice topping.

Double-Crust Butter Pie Dough (page 123),
    Double-Crust Shortening Pie Dough (page 124), or
    Double-Crust Lard Pie Dough (page 126)
4 large baking apples (such as Pippin, Jonathan,
    Granny Smith, Mutsu, or Golden Delicious),
    peeled, cored, and cut into ¼-inch dice
    (4 cups)
½ cup packed light or dark brown sugar
½ cup golden raisins
½ cup dried currants
½ cup dried cranberries
¼ cup unsulfured molasses
¼ cup dark rum
1 tablespoon all-purpose flour
Grated zest of 1 large orange
Grated zest of 1 large lemon
¼ teaspoon ground allspice
¼ teaspoon ground cinnamon
¼ teaspoon ground cloves
¼ teaspoon ground ginger
¼ teaspoon freshly grated nutmeg

1. Make the pie dough and divide it into 2 disks, one slightly larger than the other. Wrap and refrigerate while making the mincemeat.

2. In a food processor fitted with the metal blade, pulse the apples with all of the remaining ingredients until coarsely chopped and blended together, 8 to 10 pulses.

3. On a lightly floured work surface, roll out the larger disk of dough into a 12-inch round about ⅛ inch thick. Fit the dough into a 9-inch pie pan, letting the dough hang over the edge. Trim the dough to a 1-inch overhang. Spread the mincemeat in the shell.

4. Roll out the remaining dough into a ⅛-inch-thick round about 10 inches in diameter. Following the instructions on page 120, cut out twenty ½-inch-wide strips and arrange the strips in a lattice pattern on the mincemeat. Fold the overhanging dough over to enclose the strips, and flute. Refrigerate for 15 minutes.

5. Meanwhile, position a rack in the bottom third of the oven and preheat to 375°F.

6. Bake the pie for 15 minutes. Reduce the oven temperature to 350°F and continue baking until the top is golden and the filling is bubbling, 50 minutes to 1 hour.

7. Transfer to a wire cooling rack. Let stand until warm, or cool completely. (The pie can be made, covered, and refrigerated for up to 2 days. Reheat before serving, if possible.) Serve warm or at room temperature.

Cinnamon Apple Pie

MAKES ONE 9-INCH PIE,
8 SERVINGS

Carolyn B. Weil

Fall is obviously the best time to make apple pie, with new crops readily available. Apples for pie should be firm, crisp, and flavorful, and should hold their shape after baking. Reliable candidates are Pippin, Jonathan, Granny Smith, Mutsu, and Golden Delicious (although the farmstand variety is better than what the supermarket carries). Pass up eating apples such as McIntosh, Red Delicious, and Fuji. But you never know what treasures your local farmers' market will hold, so ask apple sellers if they have anything new for you to try.

Double-Crust Butter Pie Dough (page 123) or Double-Crust Lard Pie Dough (page 126)
6 medium baking apples, peeled, cored, and cut into ½-inch-thick slices (8 cups)
1 tablespoon fresh lemon juice, optional
½ cup sugar
½ teaspoon ground cinnamon
Pinch of salt
1 tablespoon unsalted butter, cut into small pieces

1. On a lightly floured work surface, roll out one disk of dough into a ⅛-inch-thick round. Fit the dough into a 9-inch pie pan.

2. In a medium bowl, toss the apples with the lemon juice, if using. Add the sugar, cinnamon, and salt and toss.

3. Arrange the apples in the dough in overlapping layers, leaving as little space as possible between them. Dot the apples with the butter. Trim the overhanging dough to ½ inch. Roll out the remaining dough into a ⅛-inch-thick round. Center the dough over the filling. Fold the top crust under the edge of the bottom crust and pinch together firmly to seal. Flute the dough. Cut a few slits in the top crust to allow the steam to escape. Place the pie on a baking sheet and refrigerate for 15 minutes.

4. Meanwhile, position a rack in the bottom third of the oven and preheat to 375°F.

5. Bake for 10 minutes. Reduce the heat to 350°F and continue baking until the top crust is golden brown and the apples are tender when pierced through a slit with the tip of a knife, 50 minutes to 1 hour.

Baker's Note

USE THE lemon juice if you think the apples are a little too sweet.

Vanilla Peach Pie

¾ cup packed light or dark brown sugar

3 tablespoons all-purpose flour

½ teaspoon ground cinnamon

Pinch of salt

One 1-inch piece of vanilla bean, split

7 ripe medium peaches, peeled, pitted, and cut into
   ¼-inch-thick slices

1 tablespoon fresh lemon juice

Double-Crust Butter Pie Dough (page 123) or Double-Crust
   Cream Cheese Pie Dough (page 125)

1 tablespoon unsalted butter

MAKES ONE 9-INCH PIE,
8 SERVINGS

Carolyn B. Weil

A sprinkle of fresh vanilla seeds adds another layer of flavor to peach pie. Brown sugar not only supplies extra flavor but enhances the deep color of the peaches.

1. In a medium bowl, mix the brown sugar, flour, cinnamon, and salt. Using the tip of a knife, scrape in the tiny seeds from the vanilla bean, saving the bean for another purpose. Add the peaches and lemon juice and toss.

2. On a lightly floured work surface, roll out one disk of dough into a ⅛-inch-thick round. Fit the dough into a 9-inch pie pan. Fill the shell with the peach mixture and dot with the butter. Trim the overhanging dough to a ½-inch overhang. Roll out the remaining dough into a ⅛-inch-thick round. Center the dough over the filling. Fold the top crust under the edge of the bottom crust and pinch together firmly to seal. Flute the dough. Cut a few slits in the top crust to allow the steam to escape. Place the pie on a baking sheet and refrigerate for 15 minutes.

3. Meanwhile, position a rack in the bottom third of the oven and preheat to 375°F.

4. Bake the pie for 10 minutes. Reduce the heat to 350°F and continue baking until the top crust is golden brown and the peaches are tender when pierced through a slit with the tip of a knife, 50 minutes to 1 hour.

Baker's Note

TO PEEL PEACHES, drop a few at a time into a pot of boiling water and blanch until the skin loosens, about 30 seconds. (If the peaches aren't perfectly ripe, the skins will take longer to loosen.) Remove them with a slotted spoon and transfer to a bowl of cold water. Drain and peel with a sharp paring knife.

Deep-Dish Summer Pie

MAKES ONE 9-INCH PIE,
8 SERVINGS

Carolyn B. Weil

Berries are usually so juicy that, no matter what tricks the baker uses, the bottom crust remains somewhat underdone. Carolyn Weil accepts that fact; her solution is a deep-dish pie with just a top crust.

1 cup sugar

2 tablespoons cornstarch

2 tablespoons instant tapioca

Pinch of salt

3 pints fresh berries, such as raspberries, blueberries, blackberries, bushberries, or huckleberries, rinsed and spread on paper towels to dry

1 tablespoon fresh lemon juice

1 tablespoon unsalted butter

Butter Pie Dough (page 123) or Cream Cheese Pie Dough (page 125)

1. In a medium bowl, mix the sugar, cornstarch, tapioca, and salt. Add the berries and lemon juice and toss. Pour into a 9-inch pie pan.

2. On a lightly floured work surface, roll the dough into a ⅛-inch-thick round. Place the dough over the filling, letting it hang over the edges of the pan. Trim the dough to a ½-inch overhang. Fold the edge of the dough under the round so it is flush against the inside of the pan, and flute the edges. (Or gently pleat the dough to fit the inside of the pan.) Place on a baking sheet and refrigerate for 15 minutes.

3. Meanwhile, position a rack in the bottom third of the oven and preheat to 375°F.

4. Bake the pie for 10 minutes. Reduce the heat to 350°F and continue baking until the crust is golden brown and the filling is thick and bubbling.

Baker's Notes

JUST ABOUT ANY BERRY will do for this pie except for strawberries, which look washed out when heated, so mix them with other berries.

To make this in a true deep-dish pie pan (about 1½ inches deep), use 1½ cups sugar, 3 tablespoons cornstarch, 3 tablespoons instant tapioca, ⅛ teaspoon salt, 4½ pints berries, 1½ tablespoons lemon juice, and 2 tablespoons unsalted butter.

Raspberry-Rhubarb Pie

1 cup sugar

2 tablespoons cornstarch

2 tablespoons instant tapioca

Pinch of salt

3 cups raspberries

3 medium stalks rhubarb, cut into ½-inch-thick slices
(3 cups)

1 tablespoon unsalted butter

Double-Crust Butter Pie Dough (page 123) or Double-Crust
Cream Cheese Pie Dough (page 125)

MAKES ONE 9-INCH PIE,
8 SERVINGS

Carolyn B. Weil

*The essence of early summer
in a pie.*

1. Mix the sugar, cornstarch, tapioca, and salt in a medium bowl. Add the raspberries and rhubarb and toss well.

2. On a lightly floured work surface, roll out one disk of dough into a ⅛-inch-thick round. Fit the dough into a 9-inch pie pan. Fill the shell with the fruit mixture and dot with the butter. Trim the overhanging dough to ½ inch. Roll out the remaining dough into a ⅛-inch-thick round. Center the dough over the filling. Fold the top crust under the edge of the bottom crust and pinch together firmly to seal. Flute the dough. Cut a few slits in the top crust to allow the steam to escape. Place on a baking sheet and refrigerate for 15 minutes.

3. Meanwhile, position a rack in the bottom third of the oven and preheat to 350°F.

4. Bake until the top crust is golden brown and the juices are bubbling through the slits in the top crust, about 50 minutes.

Baker's Note

RHUBARB FREEZES WELL. Rinse and slice the stalks into ½-inch-wide pieces. Spread the slices on a baking sheet and freeze until solid. Transfer the frozen rhubarb to a zippered plastic bag and freeze for up to nine months.

Spinach, Feta, and Ricotta Pie

MAKES ONE 9-INCH PIE,
8 SERVINGS

Carolyn B. Weil

If you have a pie shell in the freezer, this vegetarian supper dish can be ready for the oven in minutes.

Butter Pie Dough (page 123) made without sugar, Cream Cheese Pie Dough (made without sugar) (page 125), or Savory Pie Dough (page 123)

1 tablespoon olive oil

1 small onion, chopped

1 box (10 ounces) frozen chopped spinach, thawed and drained

8 ounces ricotta cheese

½ cup crumbled feta cheese

2 large eggs

¼ teaspoon salt

¼ teaspoon freshly ground pepper

1 cup sour cream

1. Following the instructions on page 120, line a 9-inch pie pan with the dough and flute the edges. Cover loosely with plastic wrap and refrigerate for 30 minutes.

2. Position a rack in the bottom third of the oven and preheat to 400°F.

3. Remove the plastic wrap and line the pastry shell with parchment paper or aluminum foil, then fill with pie weights. Bake until the pastry looks set, about 15 minutes. Remove the foil and weights and set aside.

4. In a medium skillet, heat the oil over medium heat. Add the onion and cook, stirring often, until translucent and softened, about 4 minutes. Transfer to a large bowl. Add the spinach, ricotta and feta cheeses, eggs, salt, and pepper and mix well. Spread evenly in the pie shell, then spread with the sour cream.

5. Bake until the top is slightly puffed and feels firm when pressed in the center, 45 to 50 minutes. Serve warm.

Artichoke and Potato Turnovers

1 large all-purpose potato, peeled, cut into ½-inch cubes
   (1 cup)
1 cup cooked and coarsely chopped artichoke hearts
   (you can use thawed frozen hearts)
2 Roma or plum tomatoes, seeded and cut into ½-inch dice
2 scallions, white and green parts, thinly sliced
1 garlic clove, finely chopped
2 tablespoons sour cream
2 teaspoons Worcestershire sauce
Salt and freshly ground pepper, to taste
Savory Pie Dough (page 123)

MAKES TEN 4-INCH TURNOVERS

Carolyn B. Weil

These savory turnovers are hearty and light at the same time. Other vegetable combinations will work as well. Use vegetarian chili the next time you have leftovers.

1. Bring a medium saucepan of lightly salted water to a boil over high heat. Add the potato cubes and cook until barely tender, about 12 minutes. Drain and rinse under cold running water until cool.

2. In a bowl, mix the potatoes, artichoke hearts, tomatoes, scallions, garlic, sour cream, and Worcestershire sauce. Season with salt and pepper.

3. On a lightly floured work surface, roll out one disk of dough into a ⅛-inch-thick round. Using a saucer as a template, cut out 6-inch rounds; set the rounds aside. Gather up the scraps, cover, and return to the refrigerator. Repeat with the other disk of dough. Gently knead the scraps together and roll out again to make 10 rounds total.

4. Place a spoonful of the filling on the bottom half of a round, leaving a ½-inch border. Fold over and use the tines of a fork to press and seal the edges closed. Place on a baking sheet. Repeat with the remaining rounds and filling. Cover with plastic wrap and refrigerate while preheating the oven.

5. Position a rack in the center of the oven and preheat to 400°F.

6. Bake the turnovers until they are golden brown and the edges are firm, about 30 minutes. Cool slightly and serve warm.

Baker's Note

Ten turnovers will fit on a half-sheet baking pan. If using two smaller baking sheets, position the racks in the center and top third of the oven. Halfway through baking, switch the positions of the sheets from top to bottom and rotate them from front to back.

Tarts to Tempt

A baker never confuses a tart with a pie. Pies are served from the pan, but a tart is unmolded and free-standing. To keep the sides of a tart standing up, the crust is always made with butter, which results in a crisp, firm shell and imparts rich flavor in the bargain. A tart is always on the shallow side, usually no more than one inch high—there is no such thing as a "mile-high" tart. A tart can be a simple combination of buttery pastry with a thin layer of sugared fruit, or it can be a glorious construction of pastry filled with custard and topped with glazed fruit. However, like a pie, it can be open-faced or double-crusted, and be filled before or after baking. Less hearty than potpies, savory tarts can be served as hors d'oeuvres or main courses. Keep savory tarts in mind when looking for a way to use up leftovers.

If pies are all-American, tarts are one of the marvels of the classic European kitchen, particularly of French cuisine. In fact, the tart doughs we love are straight from the French pastry repertoire: puff pastry (a flaky but streamlined version for today's busy cook, *demi-feuilleté*), short pastry (*pâte sablée*), sweet pastry (*pâte sucrée*), and a basic tart dough that we especially like to use for the free-form tarts called galettes (*pâte brisée*).

Our chapter chairperson was Lindsey Shere, who provided many of the recipes in this chapter, with assistance from Carol Field, Letty Flatt, Lily Gerson, Karen Holmes, and Shari Saunders.

Ingredients for Tarts

Flour | For best flavor, use unbleached all-purpose flour for pastry dough. These doughs have a high proportion of butter, which will inhibit gluten activity and make the pastry tender. The flour in this chapter is measured by the spoon-and-sweep method.

Butter | Unsalted butter is our preference. If you must use salted butter, reduce the salt in the recipe by ¼ teaspoon.

Equipment for Tarts

Tart pans | A true tart is always served freestanding. To get the tart out of the pan, it must be baked in a pan with removable bottom. Tarts made in solid ceramic pans must be served directly from the pans, but the slices may break.

Tart pans should be made from sturdy, light-colored metal. Dark-colored pans tend to absorb the oven's heat and almost guarantee an overbrowned, if not burned, crust. If you buy tartlet pans, they usually have permanent bottoms; buy ones with nonstick linings so the baked tartlets are easier to remove.

Tart pans come in a variety of diameters (we use a standard 9-inch-wide pan for most of these recipes), as well as rectangles, squares, and even hearts. They are reasonably inexpensive, so you can have a lot of different shapes without spending a lot of money. You will have to experiment with the amounts of dough and filling when you use a pan that is a different size from the one in the recipe. (The rule of thumb is one ounce of dough for every inch of the pan's diameter.) It's best to err on the generous side, because it is easier to discard leftover dough or filling than it is to make a new batch because you've run out. And you can always make leftover short pastry into cookies or roll out scraps and make cut-out designs for the tops of tarts.

Rolling pins | The best tool for rolling out the dough is a large, heavy, ball-bearing pin, at least 14 inches long and about 2½ inches in diameter. The weight makes rolling the pastry much easier. Some people like "French" rolling pins, tapered or plain but always without handles; it is really just a matter of personal preference. Lindsey Shere says she has even used a wine bottle in a pinch when she had no pin, and it worked perfectly well. Never wash your rolling pin in soapy water; just wipe it clean with a damp cloth.

Pie weights | These little balls, made from metal or ceramic, are used to support the sides of the pastry and keep it from falling during baking. You can also use dry beans, rice, or even pennies.

Baking stone | Most bakers use these ceramic or tile slabs for their breads and pizzas. However, they are great for tarts because they supply concentrated heat to the bottom of the pastry shell, helping it to cook quickly before the juices from the cooking fruit get the chance to soften it. To protect the stone from spills, place a piece of aluminum foil under the tart pan. Allow at least 30 minutes of preheating to heat the stone thoroughly.

Mixing the Dough

HERE'S ONE AREA where bakers often disagree. When it comes to mixing tart dough, Lindsey Shere, whose recipes we use here, disagrees with her colleagues who use machines to make their dough at home (although she certainly condones the use of machines in a bakery). She much prefers using fingertips or a pastry blender because it gives the baker more control over the process. If you want to use a machine, see the recommendations for pie dough on page 118.

When making tart dough, as with pie dough, the butter should be chilled and firm. This allows the fat to become coated with flour and interfere with gluten development, allowing the butter to melt and make a flaky crust. A pastry blender really works best. If you use your hands to rub the butter into the dough, use only your fingertips, as your palms are too warm and could melt the butter. Some bakers go so far as to dip their fingers into ice water to chill them, but a light touch is all you need. In general, combine the flour and butter until the mixture looks like coarse cornmeal with pea-sized bits of butter. The higher the proportion of pea-sized butter bits, the flakier the pastry. If the mixture is blended into a mixture of fine crumbs without bits, it will be tender but not flaky.

The liquid (usually water, but sometimes an egg is added) should be ice-cold, but remove any ice cubes before measuring. Mixing the flour-butter mixture with a fork, add just enough of the liquid to make the dough hold together. Press a little of it between your fingers to see if it holds together in a pliable mass. Often it will still look crumbly even though it is moist enough. Do not overmix. Gather up the dough and press it together into a thick disk. Wrap the dough in plastic wrap and refrigerate for at least 30 minutes to relax the gluten. You can refrigerate the dough for up to 2 days. If you wish to freeze it, overwrap it with aluminum foil and freeze it for up to 2 months. Defrost the frozen dough overnight in the refrigerator, not at room temperature.

Rolling Out the Dough

AS YOU ROLL OUT the dough, you may need to add more flour to the work surface or the top of the dough to discourage sticking, but use as little flour as possible. If you add too much flour, the pastry could be tough.

If the dough is well chilled and hard, it will be difficult to roll out and it will crack. It must be slightly softened but still retain its chill. Let the wrapped refrigerated dough stand at room temperature for about 10 minutes. Then pound the dough all over with the rolling pin until it is pliable.

Place the dough on a lightly floured work surface and sprinkle the top with a little flour. Roll from the center outward. Each time you lift your rolling pin, give the dough a quarter turn and dust the area under the dough with a little flour. For a 9-inch shell, roll out the dough into an 11-inch circle about ⅛ inch thick. Be sure the dough is the same thickness all around. If the dough sticks to the pin, sprinkle a little flour on the pin and rub to distribute the flour evenly over the pin. Often all you will need to do is dip the palm of your hand in flour to lightly coat it, and run it over the dough.

To lift the dough, place the rolling pin on one edge of the dough and gently lift the edge onto the pin. Roll the pin so the dough scrolls up onto it. Holding the pin over one edge of the tart pan, reverse the motion, and the dough will unroll into place over the top of the pan. Ease the dough to fit naturally into the corners of the pan, being careful not to stretch or pull it, always pushing it gently toward the center of the pan. If it should tear in the process, just press it back together with your fingers.

Usually the dough is trimmed flush with the edge of the pan. For doughs that have a tendency to shrink, the excess is trimmed to a 1-inch overhang that is folded over to meet the corner of the dough-lined pan, making a double thickness at the sides. In either case, press the dough around the side of the pan so the top of the dough rises slightly over the edge of the pan. Press it down slightly so that it bends over the top edge of the pan. This will help keep the sides from sliding down during baking. Freeze the pan for at least 30 minutes, again to relax the gluten and firm the dough. There is no need to wrap the pan in plastic wrap unless you plan to freeze the dough for longer than 1 hour. In that case, you should double-wrap the tart shell; it can be frozen in the pan for up to 2 months.

Baking the Pastry

PREHEAT THE OVEN thoroughly before baking, allowing about 30 minutes for it to reach the optimum temperature. If you have a baking stone in your oven, there is no need to remove it when baking tarts. The rack should be in the center of the oven, a position that allows for even baking without overbrowning of the top of the tart.

To blind bake the pastry (that is, to bake it without a filling), prick the bottom of the chilled shell with a fork and line the crust tightly with foil. Fill the pan with about 2 cups of pie weights. The dough is now ready to be baked according to the recipe. If you are filling the tart with a loose custard filling, check the baked shell carefully for any holes or cracks. If any cracks appear in the shell after baking, they must be patched. Use left-over scraps of dough that have been completely softened by the warmth of your hands. If you have no dough, just make a little paste of flour and softened butter and gently press it into the holes, feathering it out over the edge of the hole. Bake the patched shell for 5 minutes or so, until the patches look set and dry. Then proceed with the filling and any further baking.

Storing Tarts

TARTS ARE BEST WHEN served a few hours after baking, but no one complains about leftovers, which should be served within 24 hours. Tarts that contain eggs or any dairy product should be refrigerated within 2 hours of baking. Other tarts can be stored overnight in a cool place for the next day.

Basic Tart Dough (Pâte Brisée)

1 cup unbleached all-purpose flour (spoon-and-sweep)

¼ teaspoon fine sea salt

6 tablespoons (¾ stick) unsalted butter, chilled, cut into
   ¼-inch slices

¼ cup cold water, or as needed

MAKES ENOUGH DOUGH FOR
ONE 9-INCH TART OR 10-INCH
GALETTE

Lindsey Shere

The French term for this dough is pâte brisée, *which means "broken dough," a nod to its melt-in-your-mouth tenderness. This versatile dough is the most austere of the classic pastry doughs, without any sugar or enriching egg, and can be used for just about any sweet or savory tart or galette.*

1. Combine the flour and salt in a bowl. Cut in half the butter with a pastry blender (or rub it between your fingertips) until the mixture resembles coarse cornmeal. Cut in the remaining butter until it is in pea-sized bits.

2. Sprinkle the water in evenly, tossing the flour mixture with a fork as you do so, adding just enough water so that the mixture is completely moistened and holds together when pressed between your fingers. Gather up the dough and press into a ½-inch-thick disk. Wrap tightly in plastic wrap.

3. Refrigerate for at least 30 minutes. (The dough can be prepared up to 2 days ahead, wrapped, and refrigerated. It can also be frozen, overwrapped with aluminum foil, for up to 2 months. Defrost the frozen dough overnight in the refrigerator, not at room temperature. If the dough is very hard and well chilled, let it stand at room temperature for about 10 minutes. Then pound the dough, vertically and horizontally, with the rolling pin until it is pliable but still cold.)

Rye Pastry Dough: Rye gives this dough a slightly more hearty flavor that is perfect with savory tarts. Substitute ½ cup rye flour for ½ cup of the all-purpose flour, and use 6 to 8 tablespoons cold water. The rye flour, which absorbs water differently from wheat flour, will make the dough feel slightly sticky and damp. Add only enough water to the dough to make it hold together.

Baker's Note

THE TWO-STEP process of cutting in the butter has a double purpose. The small butter "crumbs" waterproof the gluten in the flour, keeping it from forming the invisible strands that will toughen the dough. The larger pieces of butter separate the dough into layers as it bakes and provide flakiness.

Short Pastry Dough (Pâte Sablée)

1 cup unbleached all-purpose flour (spoon-and-sweep)
1 tablespoon sugar
¼ teaspoon grated lemon zest
¼ teaspoon fine sea salt
8 tablespoons (1 stick) unsalted butter, cool but not chilled,
    cut into ¼-inch-thick slices
1 tablespoon cold water
½ teaspoon vanilla extract

MAKES ENOUGH DOUGH FOR
ONE 9-INCH TART

Lindsey Shere

When you want a slightly sweet dough with hints of vanilla and lemon zest to complement the tart filling, turn to this dough. When English-speaking cooks refer to a crumbly, tender pastry, we call it a short dough, but the French call it pâte sablée, *or "sandy dough."*

1. Combine the flour, sugar, lemon zest, and salt in a medium bowl. Cut in the butter with a pastry blender (or rub it between your fingertips) until the mixture resembles coarse cornmeal.

2. Mix the water and vanilla and sprinkle all at once over the flour mixture, then toss together quickly until the dough begins to hold together. Gather up the dough and press into a flat ½-inch-thick disk.

3. Refrigerate for at least 30 minutes. (The dough can be prepared up to a day ahead, wrapped, and refrigerated. It can also be frozen, overwrapped with aluminum foil, for up to 2 months. Defrost the frozen dough overnight in the refrigerator, not at room temperature. If the dough is very hard and well chilled, let it stand at room temperature for about 10 minutes. Then pound the dough, vertically and horizontally, with the rolling pin until it is pliable but still cold.)

Baker's Note

THE BUTTER FOR this dough should be cool and malleable, but not shiny or in any way squishy. This slightly softer butter will absorb into the flour, waterproofing the gluten and keeping the dough tender.

Sweet Tart Pastry (Pâte Sucrée)

6 tablespoons (¾ stick) unsalted butter, cool but not chilled,
   cut into ½-inch cubes
2½ tablespoons sugar
1 large egg, at room temperature
¼ teaspoon vanilla extract
Pinch of fine sea salt
1 cup unbleached all-purpose flour (spoon-and-sweep)

1. In a medium bowl, using a hand-held electric mixer on medium-high speed, cream the butter and sugar until light in color and texture, about 2 minutes. Break the egg into a cup, mix it thoroughly with a fork, and measure 2½ tablespoons; discard the remainder. Beat it in with the vanilla and salt just until blended. Scrape down the bowl. On low speed, add the flour all at once and mix just until the ingredients are moistened. Do not overmix.

2. Turn the dough out onto an unfloured work surface. Quickly finish combining the ingredients by smearing small amounts away from you. Using a bench knife or plastic scraper, scrape up the dough and gather it together. Form into a flat disk about ½ inch thick. Wrap in plastic wrap. Refrigerate until firm, at least 1 hour. (The dough can be prepared up to a day ahead, wrapped, and refrigerated. It can also be frozen, overwrapped with aluminum foil, for up to 2 months. Defrost the frozen dough overnight in the refrigerator, not at room temperature. If the dough is very hard and well chilled, let it stand at room temperature for about 10 minutes. Then pound the dough, vertically and horizontally, with the rolling pin until it is pliable but still cold.)

MAKES ENOUGH DOUGH FOR
ONE 9-INCH TART

Lindsey Shere

Here is a crisp and buttery pastry that is just a shade away from being a cookie— the butter and sugar are creamed, and no additional water is used. The dough gets an extra mixing step with the French method called fraisage, *in which the dough is smeared on a work surface for a final combining. Sugar not only adds sweetness but acts as a tenderizer, which can make the dough delicate to handle. If it breaks during transfer to the tart pan, just press it back together.*

Baker's Note

WHEN ROLLING OUT this dough, work quickly so it doesn't soften.

Tartlet Dough

MAKES ENOUGH DOUGH FOR
NINE 4-INCH TARTLETS

Lindsey Shere

Tartlets present their own set of challenges to the baker. The dough must be sturdy so it can be easily removed from the tartlet pans (not all of which have removable bottoms), but that doesn't mean compromising its flavor. If the dough doesn't have to be lined with foil and weighted when blind baked, so much the better. This buttery, sweet dough has all of these attributes.

12 tablespoons (1½ sticks) unsalted butter, at room temperature
6½ tablespoons sugar
¼ teaspoon vanilla extract
¼ teaspoon salt
2 cups unbleached all-purpose flour (spoon-and-sweep)
1½ teaspoons cold water

1. In a medium bowl, using a hand-held electric mixer at high speed, cream the butter until light in color and texture, about 1½ minutes. Add the sugar, vanilla, and salt and beat until very light, about 1½ minutes. On low speed, beat in the flour. Add the water and mix just until the flour is moistened and the mixture forms pea-sized bits. Gather into a thick disk and wrap in plastic wrap.

2. Refrigerate just until firm, about 1 hour. (The dough is easiest to work with if not chilled until rock hard.)

Quick Puff Pastry

1 pound unsalted butter, chilled

2 cups unbleached all-purpose flour (spoon-and-sweep)

⅔ cup bread flour

1 cup ice-cold water

1 teaspoon fresh lemon juice

1 teaspoon fine sea salt

MAKES ABOUT 2 POUNDS

Lindsey Shere

Traditional puff pastry is the classic example of artfully layering fat and flour to get flaky results. It is undeniably delicious and tender, but it is also time-consuming. This method is much quicker and virtually foolproof. Lindsey Shere says it is so reliable that it became her puff pastry of choice when she was the pastry chef at Chez Panisse— high praise indeed. You can use this dough whenever you have a recipe that calls for puff pastry. It makes a generous amount; you will probably freeze the leftovers for another time. Do not try to reduce the quantity; the results will not be the same.

1. Cut the butter into ½-inch cubes, spread on a baking sheet, and freeze until very cold, about 15 minutes.

2. Combine the flours in the bowl of a heavy-duty standing mixer fitted with the paddle blade. Add the frozen butter and toss to coat the cubes. With the machine on low, mix until cubes are two-thirds their original size.

3. In a glass measuring cup, stir the water, lemon juice, and salt to dissolve the salt. With the machine running, add to the flour mixture and mix just until the dough holds together. Gather up the dough. It will look very rough at this point but will smooth out during rolling.

4. Place the dough on a floured work surface and pat into a thick rectangle. Dust the top of the dough with flour. Roll out into a 16 × 5-inch rectangle, with a long edge of the dough running vertically. Using a pastry brush, brush the flour off the surface of the dough. Fold the dough into thirds, folding the top third of the dough down, then the bottom third up to cover it, like a business letter. This is called a turn. Rotate the dough so the open sides are on the right and the fold is on the left. Repeat the rolling and folding procedure three more times, being sure to brush off all flour from the surface of the dough before folding, and keeping the open side of the dough packet on the right, for a total of four turns. (To keep track of the number of turns, press the back of a knife into the dough to make a shallow mark after each turn.) Wrap in plastic wrap and refrigerate for at least 30 minutes.

5. Roll and fold the dough two more times for a total of six turns. Wrap and refrigerate for at least 30 minutes. (The dough can be prepared up to 2 days ahead, wrapped, and refrigerated. It can also be frozen, overwrapped with aluminum foil, for up to 2 months. Defrost the frozen dough overnight in the refrigerator. If the dough is very hard and well chilled, let it stand at room temperature for about 10 minutes. Then pound the dough, vertically and horizontally, with the rolling pin until it is pliable but still cold.)

6. If you divide the dough into portions, use a large knife to cut it. Always cut straight down in one push; never saw through the dough.

Warm Pear Tart

MAKES ONE 9-INCH TART,
8 SERVINGS

Lindsey Shere

*True, apple tarts are
considered one of the great
comfort foods, but don't forget
about pears, which can also
be a sublime filling. There are
a few tricks to making this
tart. Be flexible with the
baking time so that the pears
are tender and the pastry is
cooked through and golden
brown. Bake the tart on a
baking stone to give the
bottom an even source of heat
and encourage even browning.*

11 ounces Quick Puff Pastry (page 163), about ⅓ batch

Approximately 2 pounds ripe Bosc or Winter Nelis pears

2 tablespoons sugar, or to taste

**1 tablespoon kirsch, dark rum, or brandy, or more to taste,
optional**

2 tablespoons unsalted butter, melted

**Vanilla ice cream or Whipped Cream Topping (page 336),
for serving**

1. On a lightly floured work surface, roll out the dough into a 13-inch circle about ⅛ inch thick. Work quickly so the dough doesn't soften. Make straight cuts around the edge of the circle to trim it into a rough octagon. Line a large pizza pan or rimless baking sheet with parchment paper. Move the pastry to the pan. Brush the edges of the dough with water. Fold about 1½ inches of the dough inward to make a border, pinching it down at intervals to secure it to the bottom of the crust. Prick the bottom well with a fork. Freeze for 30 minutes.

2. Position a rack in the center of the oven. If you have one, place a baking stone on the rack, and preheat to 400°F.

3. Peel and core the pears, then cut them lengthwise into ¼- to ½-inch-thick slices. You should have 6 cups. Toss them with the sugar and the liquor, if using, tasting to check for sweetness. Arrange the pears in overlapping concentric circles over the pastry, right up to the inner edge (this will allow the pastry on the sides to puff into a border that will contain the juices). Brush the pears with the butter.

4. Bake for 10 minutes. Turn the oven temperature down to 375°F and continue baking until the pears are tender and the crust is golden brown, 30 to 50 minutes, depending on the firmness of the pears. Using a kitchen towel to protect your hands, carefully lift the edge of the tart from the pan with a spatula to check the sides and bottom for doneness. If the pastry and pears are browning before they are done, loosely cover the tart with a sheet of aluminum foil.

5. Transfer the tart to a wire cooling rack and let stand until slightly cooled. Serve warm with the ice cream or whipped cream.

Baker's Note

FOR A LESS formal look, instead of arranging the pears in circles, evenly spread them over the bottom of the pastry.

Simple Nectarine Galette

MAKES ONE 12-INCH GALETTE,
8 TO 10 SERVINGS

Lindsey Shere

A galette is a free-form tart that may remind you of a fruit-covered pizza. You'll want to keep this easy galette in mind for other seasonal fruits, too. See the suggestions in Baker's Notes on adjusting the recipe for different fruits.

Basic Tart Dough (page 159)
2 tablespoons unbleached all-purpose flour
7 tablespoons sugar
8 medium ripe nectarines (about 1 dry quart), unpeeled,
    pitted and cut into ⅓- to ½-inch-wide slices

1. Position a rack in the center of the oven. If you have one, place a baking stone on the rack, and preheat to 400°F. Line a large pizza pan or rimless baking sheet with parchment paper.

2. On a lightly floured work surface, roll out the dough into a very thin (no more than $1/16$ inch thick) 14-inch-diameter round. Roll out the edges a bit thinner than the center so that when the edges are folded over to make a border, it won't be too thick. Transfer to the pizza pan.

3. In a small bowl, combine the flour and 2 tablespoons of the sugar with your fingers and sprinkle over the dough, leaving a 2-inch border. Arrange the nectarines in concentric circles on top on the sugar, leaving a border. Sprinkle the fruit with 4 tablespoons of the remaining sugar. Fold the border of dough over onto the nectarines. Lightly brush the dough with a little water and sprinkle with the remaining 1 tablespoon sugar.

4. Bake until the edges and bottom of the pastry are quite brown (lift up an edge of the galette with a spatula to check), 50 minutes to 1 hour.

5. Immediately slide the galette off the pan onto a large wire cooling rack. Let stand for 5 minutes. If the nectarines have given off syrupy juices that have collected in the galette, brush them over the fruit to make an instant glaze. Let the galette stand for at least 10 more minutes, and serve warm or at room temperature.

Flo's Angel Food Cake
page 70

*Chocolate Raspberry Cake
(page 94) made with Our
Favorite Chocolate Genoise
(page 63), Alice's Light
Ganache (page 331), and
Chocolate Glaze (page 332)*

Our Favorite Chocolate Genoise
page 63

FACING PAGE:

Blood Orange Chiffon Pie (page 144)
with Chocolate Crumb Crust (page 127)
and Whipped Cream Topping (page 336)

*Caramel Ice Cream
Roll with Chocolate-
Cinnamon Sauce*
page 103

*Tomato and Cheese Galette
(page 178) made with
Basic Tart Dough (page 159)*

Almond and Chocolate Sandwich Cookies
page 202

Summer Pudding
(page 192) *made with*
White Sandwich Bread
(page 264)
and Raspberry Sauce
(page 339)

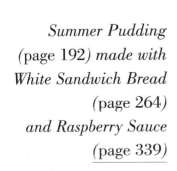

*Orange-Rum Sweet Bread
(Crescia Cingolana)*
page 288

Buttery Dinner Rolls
page 292

Spicy Cornmeal Crackers
page 298

Focaccia di Recco
page 300

Chocolate Budini

page 311

TRIPLING EGGS IN VOLUME

Once the eggs and sugar have been whisked together, place the bowl in a skillet with 1 inch of barely simmering water. Whisk until the mixture is warm to the touch (no more than 110°F) and the sugar is dissolved. The mixture will look frothy. Attach the bowl to the mixer and fit with a whisk.

Beat on high speed until the mixture has tripled in volume and is pale in color and light in texture. This will take 3 to 4 minutes.

WHIPPING EGG WHITES

In the bowl of a mixer fitted with the whisk attachment, beat the egg whites on medium speed until foamy. Add the cream of tartar and continue beating until soft peaks form.

Gradually add the remaining sugar and beat until stiff but not dry, until shiny peaks form.

MAKING PIE AND TART DOUGH BY HAND

Mix the flour, sugar (if using), and salt in a bowl. Using a fork or pastry blender, cut butter/shortening/lard in, until the mixture is crumbly with a few coarse, pea-sized pieces.

Sprinkle in the water and mix with a fork, adding just enough until the mixture is moistened and begins to clump together. Gather up the dough and form into a flat disk.

CREAMING BUTTER AND SUGAR

Cut the butter into small pieces and place in the bowl with the sugar. Start creaming the butter on medium speed for about a minute to initiate the aeration, then gradually beat in the sugar. Continue beating, scraping down the sides and bottom of the bowl every minute or so to incorporate every bit of butter and sugar into the creamed mixture. This will take 4 to 7 minutes with a heavy-duty mixer. When thoroughly creamed, the mixture will look like this.

TO MAKE THIS galette with sweet and juicy fruits, such as cherries, peaches, or summer pears, use a moderate amount of sugar, about ¼ cup. For tart and juicy fruits, such as plums, sour cherries, or apricots, you may need up to ½ cup or more.

To make the galette with not-very-juicy fruits, such as apples or winter pears, brush the top of the arranged fruit with about 2 tablespoons melted unsalted butter, and sprinkle with 1 to 2 tablespoons sugar.

If you have any doubts about the sweetness of the fruit for the galette filling, cook a few slices in a small saucepan over low heat with a bit of water until they are tender (cooked fruit tastes different from uncooked). Cool and taste for sweetness, and add sugar accordingly.

Plum-Frangipane Tart

MAKES ONE 9-INCH TART,
6 TO 8 SERVINGS

Lily Gerson and Lindsey Shere

Frangipane is an almond filling for tarts that goes well with sweet-tart plums.

Sweet Tart Pastry (page 161)

FRANGIPANE

½ cup (2 ounces) sliced natural almonds
¼ cup sugar
6 tablespoons (¾ stick) unsalted butter, at room
    temperature
1 large egg
½ teaspoon almond extract

7 ripe Santa Rosa or other tart plums (about 12 ounces)
1 to 2 tablespoons granulated sugar
Confectioners' sugar, for garnish
Whipped Cream Topping (page 336), optional

1. On a lightly floured work surface, roll out the dough into an 11½-inch circle about ⅛ inch thick. Gently lift the dough and center it in a 9-inch fluted tart pan with removable bottom. Ease the dough into the corners and press it gently into the pan. Trim the dough flush with the top of the pan. Press the dough against the sides of the pan so it barely rises over the edge. Prick the bottom well with a fork. Freeze until firm, at least 30 minutes or up to 2 hours.

2. Position a rack in the center of the oven and preheat to 375°F.

3. Line the crust tightly with aluminum foil. Fill the shell with about 2 cups pie weights. Bake until the edges of the pastry are set and dry, about 15 minutes. Remove the foil and weights. Reduce the oven temperature to 350°F. Continue baking the pastry until golden, about 10 more minutes. If the dough bubbles up at any time, pierce the bubble with the tip of a fork. Transfer the tart to a wire cooling rack and cool completely.

4. To make the frangipane, in a food processor fitted with the chopping blade, process the almonds with 2 tablespoons sugar until they are ground to powder. In a small mixing bowl, using a hand-held mixer on high speed or a wooden spoon, beat the butter with the remaining 2 tablespoons sugar until light in color, about 1 minute. Beat in the almond mixture with the egg and almond extract. Spread the frangipane in the cooled pastry.

The Baker's Dozen Cookbook

5. Cut the plums in half and discard the pits. Cut each half lengthwise in half again. Arrange the plum quarters skin side down in a pattern over the frangipane (use any pattern you like, but a spoke pattern is pretty). The plums will not completely cover the filling. Sprinkle with the granulated sugar.

6. Bake until the frangipane is puffed and golden and the plums are tender when pierced with the tip of a knife, about 40 minutes. If the tart browns too quickly, cover the top loosely with aluminum foil and continue baking until the plums are tender.

7. Transfer to a wire cooling rack and cool completely. Dust the top of the tart with confectioners' sugar sifted through a wire sieve. Serve with a dollop of whipped cream, if you like.

Baker's Notes

THIS TART IS EQUALLY good made with other stone fruits, such as apricots, peaches, and nectarines, or with tender pears like Bartlett or Comice. If you use apricots, they are quite tart, so use 3 to 4 tablespoons sugar for the topping.

If you have a rotary nut grinder, use it to grind the almonds. In that case, use whole almonds and beat all of the sugar with the butter.

When rolling out this dough, work quickly so it doesn't soften. If it breaks, simply press it into the pan.

The frangipane can be baked in the shell without the fruit until it is golden brown. Arrange poached fruit (peaches, pears, nectarines, or apricots) on top. Glaze with a little warmed apricot jam, red currant jelly, or whatever preserves would taste good with the fruit.

Raspberry-Lemon Tart

MAKES ONE 9-INCH TART,
6 TO 8 SERVINGS

Lindsey Shere

What baker wouldn't be proud to serve this canary yellow tart with red orbs of raspberries peeking through? Blueberries, blackberries, boysenberries, or any berry of your choice can be used instead of the raspberries. Don't use too many berries, or they could give off juices that would dilute the curd. This is a dessert for those who prefer their sweets on the not-too-sweet side.

Sweet Tart Pastry (page 161)

FILLING

5 large egg yolks
⅓ cup fresh lemon juice
Grated zest of 1 lemon
½ cup sugar
4 tablespoons (½ stick) unsalted butter, chilled, cut into
    ½-inch cubes
1 cup raspberries or blueberries

1. To make the tart shell, on a lightly floured work surface, roll out the dough into an 11½-inch circle about ⅛ inch thick. Gently lift the dough and center it in a 9-inch fluted tart pan with a removable bottom. Ease the dough into the corners and press it gently into the pan. Trim the dough flush with the top of the pan. Press the dough against the sides of the pan so it barely rises over the edge. Prick the bottom well with a fork. Freeze until firm, at least 30 minutes or up to 2 hours.

2. Position a rack in the center of the oven and preheat to 375°F.

3. Line the crust tightly with aluminum foil. Fill the shell with about 2 cups pie weights. Bake until the edges of the pastry are set and dry, about 15 minutes. Remove the foil and weights. Reduce the oven temperature to 350°F. Continue baking the pastry until it is golden brown, about 10 more minutes. If the dough bubbles up at any time, pierce the bubble with the tip of a fork. Transfer the tart to a wire cooling rack and cool completely. (Leave the oven on.)

4. To make the filling, in the top part of a double boiler or a small stainless steel bowl, whisk the yolks, lemon juice, zest, and sugar. Add the butter. Place over simmering water and cook, stirring constantly with a wooden or heatproof rubber spatula, until the mixture is thick enough to coat the spatula lightly (if you run your finger through the curd, it will cut a swath), 5 to 10 minutes. Transfer to a small bowl.

5. Cover the filling with a piece of plastic wrap pressed directly onto the surface. Poke a few holes in the plastic to let the steam escape. Refrigerate until chilled, about 2 hours. (The filling can be prepared up to 1 week ahead, covered tightly, and refrigerated. It can also be frozen for up to 2 months. Defrost in the refrigerator overnight, not at room temperature.)

6. Spread the lemon filling evenly in the pastry shell. Sprinkle the berries on top and gently press them into the filling. Bake until the filling seems set when you gently shake the pan, 20 to 30 minutes.

7. Transfer to a wire cooling rack and cool completely.

Baker's Notes •————————————

FOR A LEMON-BERRY meringue tart, make a half batch of the meringue from Lemon Meringue Pie on page 140. When the tart is baked, reduce the oven temperature to 375°F. Spread or pipe the meringue in designs over the hot tart, return to the oven, and continue baking until the meringue is lightly browned, about 10 minutes.

As a less tart alternative with a delightfully floral fragrance, make the filling with Meyer lemons, available during their short winter season at specialty grocers and produce stores, as well as from California backyards and farmers' markets.

Double-Crusted Apple-Polenta Tart

MAKES ONE 9-INCH TART,
6 TO 8 SERVINGS

Carol Field and Lindsey Shere

At first, apples and corn may seem an unusual combination, but the inherent sweetness of corn makes a good match for many fruits. Use stone-ground yellow cornmeal from a natural food store, or a medium-grind polenta (available at specialty food stores and Italian grocers). This creation of Lindsey Shere uses a pastry that was contributed by Carol Field.

PASTRY

6 tablespoons (¾ stick) plus 1 teaspoon unsalted butter, at room temperature
½ cup sugar
2 large egg yolks
1 cup unbleached all-purpose flour (spoon-and-sweep)
⅓ cup stone-ground yellow cornmeal or medium-grind polenta
½ teaspoon salt

FILLING

5 flavorful medium apples (such as McIntosh, Sierra Beauty, or Empire), peeled, cored, and cut into ¼-inch-thick slices (6 cups)
1 tablespoon sugar, or more to taste
1 teaspoon unbleached all-purpose flour
2 tablespoons stone-ground yellow cornmeal or medium-grind polenta

2 tablespoons heavy cream
1 large egg yolk
1 to 2 tablespoons sanding (coarse) or granulated sugar

1. To make the pastry, in a medium bowl, using a hand-held electric mixer at high speed, cream the butter and sugar until light in color and texture, about 2 minutes. Beat in the yolks one at a time.

2. Combine the flour, cornmeal, and salt in a small bowl. Add to the butter mixture and stir just until a soft dough forms. Divide the dough into 2 thick disks, one slightly larger than the other. Wrap in plastic wrap and refrigerate for 30 minutes to relax the dough.

3. Lightly butter the bottom of a 9-inch tart pan. On a lightly floured work surface, roll out the larger piece of dough into an 11½-inch circle about ⅛ inch thick. Ease into the pan, fitting it carefully into the corners without tearing. Trim off the excess dough flush with the top of the pan. Cover with plastic wrap and refrigerate until chilled, about 30 minutes.

4. Position a rack in the center of the oven and preheat to 375°F. (No need to line this dough with foil and weights.) Bake until the pastry is light golden brown, 25 to 30 minutes. Remove from the oven and cool slightly.

5. To make the filling, toss the apples with the sugar and flour. Sprinkle the polenta over the bottom of the shell and spread the apple mixture in the shell. On a lightly floured work surface, roll out the remaining disk of dough into a 9½-inch circle about ⅛ inch thick. Center the dough over the apples and press the edges of the two layers of pastry together, rubbing off any excess pastry. In a small bowl, mix the cream and egg yolk. Brush some of the cream mixture over the top of the tart and sprinkle with the coarse sugar. Using the tip of a sharp knife, cut a slit in the center of the crust.

6. Bake on a baking sheet until the crust is golden brown and the apples are tender when pierced with a knife through the slit in the crust, about 1 hour. Transfer to a wire cooling rack. Serve warm or at room temperature.

Quince and Apple-Polenta Tart: Quinces are one of the best cool-weather fruits; look for them in specialty grocers and farmers' markets. They have a lovely rose color when cooked. To make this fragrant tart, substitute 2 quinces, peeled, cored, and thinly sliced, for 2 of the apples.

Chocolate Tartlets

MAKES 9 TARTLETS

Lindsey Shere

The filling for these miniature tarts depends completely on the quality of the chocolate, so use the best you can find. Chocolate is the star, but the auxiliary flavor is up to you—chopped toasted nuts, a drizzle of melted white chocolate, or candied violets or rose petals. For the creamiest texture, don't refrigerate the tartlets; just let them stand at room temperature until the filling is completely cooled and set.

Tartlet Dough (page 162)

FILLING

8 ounces bittersweet chocolate, finely chopped

1 cup heavy cream

1 to 2 tablespoons Cognac, kirsch, or any liquor or liqueur of your choice

Chopped nuts, melted white chocolate, or candied violets or rose petals, for garnish

Whipped Cream Topping (page 336), for serving

1. Position a rack in the center of the oven and preheat to 375°F. Thoroughly butter the insides of nine 4-inch tartlet pans with slightly sloping sides (4 inches across the top and 3 inches across the bottom), or use nonstick pans.

2. On a lightly floured surface, roll out the dough to ⅛-inch thickness. Using a 5-inch-wide saucer as a template, cut out rounds of dough. Lay a round of pastry over a tartlet pan. Ease the pastry into the corner of the pan without stretching and press it in evenly. If the pastry breaks (and it probably will), just press it back together. Rub off the excess dough around the edge, and run the back of a knife over the top to make a neat edge. Repeat with the remaining dough. Gather up the scraps of dough and roll out again to make 9 tartlets.

3. Arrange the tartlet pans on a baking sheet. Freeze or refrigerate until the dough is firm, 15 to 30 minutes.

4. Prick the bottoms of the tartlets with a fork. Bake, checking occasionally to be sure the pastry is not puffing (and pricking it with a fork if it does), until golden, about 15 minutes. Transfer the shells to a wire cooling rack and cool completely.

5. Remove the tartlet shells by flexing each pan lightly, squeezing from opposite sides of the rims. If a shell is stubborn, gently slip the tip of a paring knife about ¼ inch down the side to release it. Handle the shells carefully.

6. To make the filling, place the chocolate in a medium bowl. In a small saucepan, heat the cream over medium heat just until scalded (a light skin will form on top). Pour over the chocolate and let stand until softened, about 5 minutes. Add the Cognac and stir until smooth. The mixture should be pourable. If necessary, heat in a skillet of simmering water until warmed and liquid. Tranfer to a liquid measuring cup.

7. Pour the filling into the tartlet shells. Cool until the filling is set, about 30 minutes. (The tartlets can be prepared up to 4 hours ahead and kept at room temperature.)

8. Garnish as desired. Serve at room temperature, with whipped cream passed on the side.

Summer Berry Tart

MAKES ONE 9-INCH TART,
6 TO 8 SERVINGS

Lindsey Shere

This is the classic berry tart, filled with pastry cream and topped with juicy summer berries. It should be made at the height of the local berry season for the most flavorful results. The tart is best served as soon as possible after it's made so there is an interplay of crisp pastry, smooth creamy filling, and juicy berries. But the tart shell and pastry cream can be prepared well ahead of serving, and assembly only takes a few minutes.

Short Pastry Dough (page 160) or Sweet Tart Pastry (page 161)
Pastry Cream (page 334)
2 pints strawberries, rinsed, dried, and hulled, or 1 pint raspberries, blackberries, or boysenberries, or a combination of berries
½ cup raspberry or strawberry jam or jelly or red currant jelly

1. On a lightly floured work surface, roll out the dough into an 11½-inch circle about ⅛ inch thick. Gently lift the dough and center it in a 9-inch fluted tart pan with removable bottom. Ease the dough into the corners and press it gently into the pan. Trim the dough flush with the top of the pan. Press the dough against the sides of the pan so it barely rises over the edge. Prick the bottom well with a fork. Freeze until firm, at least 30 minutes or up to 2 hours.

2. Position a rack in the center of the oven and preheat to 375°F.

3. Line the crust tightly with aluminum foil. Fill the shell with about 2 cups pie weights. Bake until the edges of the pastry are set and dry, about 15 minutes. Remove the foil and weights. Reduce the oven temperature to 350°F. Continue baking the pastry until it is golden brown, about 10 more minutes. If the dough bubbles up at any time, pierce the bubble with the tip of a fork. Transfer the tart to a wire cooling rack and cool completely.

4. Spread the pastry cream in the cooled shell. (If the pastry cream seems thick, whisk or stir it briskly to thin it.) Top with the berries, arranged in any way that suits you. Strawberries can be sliced and placed in overlapping concentric circles or left whole, or arrange the berries in different-colored rings.

5. Heat the jam until simmering in a small saucepan. Strain to remove the solids. Brush the berries with the warm jam. Serve immediately or within a few hours.

Potato and Mushroom Tart

1 Rye Pastry Dough (page 159)

2 tablespoons extra virgin olive oil, plus additional for
    brushing the pastry

1¼ pounds mushrooms, cleaned and sliced ¼ inch thick

1 pound all-purpose potatoes

Salt and freshly ground pepper to taste

1 shallot (1 ounce)

Leaves from three 3-inch sprigs fresh marjoram

Leaves from two 3-inch sprigs fresh tarragon

Leaves from two 3-inch sprigs fresh thyme

1. Position a rack in the bottom third of the oven. If you have one, place a baking stone on the rack, and preheat to 400°F.

2. On a lightly floured work surface, roll out the dough to a very thin (no more than ¹⁄₁₆ inch) 14-inch circle. Transfer the dough to a large pizza pan or baking sheet and freeze while preparing the filling.

3. In a large skillet, heat 1 tablespoon oil over medium-high heat. Add the mushrooms and cook uncovered, stirring often, until their juices evaporate and the mushrooms are barely browned, about 8 minutes (although chanterelles, oyster mushrooms, and some other mushrooms could take much longer). Transfer to a large bowl and cool slightly.

4. Peel the potatoes and slice as thin as possible (a mandoline or the thin slicing blade of a food processor will give you more uniform slices than cutting by hand). Toss the potatoes with the mushrooms and season well with salt and pepper.

5. Spread the potato and mushroom mixture over the pastry, leaving a 1½-inch-wide border. Bring the uncovered border up over the filling, pleating it as needed. Drizzle the remaining 1 tablespoon oil over the filling. Lightly brush the exposed border of pastry with additional olive oil.

6. Bake until the pastry is golden on top and bottom (lift up the bottom of the tart with a spatula to check) and the potatoes are tender, 40 to 45 minutes. If the crust begins to brown too much and the potatoes and mushrooms look dry, cover loosely with a square of aluminum foil while the tart finishes baking.

7. Transfer the tart to a wire cooling rack and cool slightly. While the tart is cooling, chop the shallot, marjoram, tarragon, and thyme together. Sprinkle over the tart. Serve warm.

MAKES ONE 10-INCH TART,
2 MAIN-COURSE OR 4
FIRST-COURSE SERVINGS

Lindsey Shere

This light tart with a hearty flavor would be a welcome winter dish. Use any mushrooms you like, but wild mushrooms make an extraordinary tart. Different mushrooms have various cooking times; be sure to cook them until their liquid has evaporated entirely, or they will make the tart soggy. Use any potato you like— red-skinned, Burbank, russet, and Yukon Gold all work. The fresh relish of chopped shallot and herbs really makes the tart sparkle.

Tomato and Cheese Galette

MAKES ONE 10-INCH GALETTE,
2 MAIN-COURSE OR 4
FIRST-COURSE SERVINGS

Lindsey Shere

*When you have some
perfectly ripe tomatoes on
hand, make this savory tart.
The grated cheeses will
moistureproof the dough from
the tomato juices. Use
whatever fresh herb you have
handy. Or, if you have capers,
sprinkle a couple of
tablespoons on the cheese
before adding the tomatoes
and onions. This tart is light,
so in spite of the ingredients,
don't expect it to be as filling
as pizza.*

Basic Tart Dough (page 159)

½ cup plus 2 tablespoons freshly grated Parmesan cheese
½ cup shredded Gruyère
½ medium onion
1 large ripe tomato, weighing at least 6 ounces, or 2 smaller
   tomatoes
Salt and freshly ground pepper to taste
Extra virgin olive oil, as needed
1 to 2 tablespoons chopped fresh herbs (tarragon, marjoram,
   parsley, basil, or your favorite, but a combination is best)

1. Position a rack in the bottom third of the oven. If you have one, place a baking stone on the rack, and preheat to 400°F.

2. On a lightly floured work surface, roll out the dough to a very thin (no more than ¹⁄₁₆ inch) 14-inch circle. Transfer the dough to a large pizza pan or baking sheet and freeze while preparing the filling.

3. Mix ½ cup of the Parmesan cheese and the Gruyère. Slice the onion and tomato into very thin rounds. Sprinkle ½ cup of the cheese mixture over the pastry, leaving a 1½-inch-wide border. Scatter the onion rings over the cheese, then top with the tomato slices. Season with salt and pepper, sprinkle with the remaining ½ cup cheese mixture, and drizzle with a teaspoon or two of olive oil. Bring the uncovered border up over the filling, pleating it as needed. Lightly brush the exposed border of pastry with olive oil and sprinkle with the remaining 2 tablespoons Parmesan cheese.

4. Bake until the pastry is golden on top and bottom (lift up the bottom of the tart with a spatula to check) and the onions are tender, 35 to 40 minutes. If the tart begins to brown too much before the vegetables are tender, lay a square of aluminum foil loosely over it until it's done. Sprinkle with the herbs and serve warm.

Baker's Notes

THIS MEDITERRANEAN-INSPIRED TART illustrates some of the basic premises of the savory tart family. The tomatoes and onions must be sliced very thin so they are thoroughly cooked by the time the crust browns. And be sure to include an ingredient that will either moistureproof the crust (like the cheese we use here) or else soak up juices (such as potatoes).

Allow at least 30 minutes to thoroughly preheat the baking stone. Bake the tart in the lower third of the oven to encourage a browned, thoroughly cooked bottom crust.

If the bottom of the tart bubbles up, pierce it with the tip of a knife, and it should deflate.

A Harvest of Fruit Desserts

One of our members' favorite pastimes is strolling through the stands at our local farmers' markets. During the peak of the summer season, you'll see one baker directing another toward the farmer with the best berries, perfect for turning into cobbler, or the stand with the ripest, most fragrant peaches. But summer isn't the only time when fruit "speaks" to bakers. In the winter, we can be found huddled over the bins of multicolored apples, discussing which ones are best for pies and crisps.

Why do we love farmers' markets so much? Because the fruit there has an unadorned, old-fashioned fullness of flavor that you can't find in many supermarket varieties. With few exceptions (bananas and pineapples come to mind), the closer the fruit remains to the farm, the better tasting it is (and tropical fruit is surely more delicious at its source).

If you don't have a farmers' market nearby, there are other places where you can find great fruit for your baking. Natural food stores and many supermarkets now carry organic produce, most of which is more flavorful than the mass-produced varieties. Even better, if you have a backyard, grow a dwarf tree or two, or you may have neighbors who have trees with more fruit than they can use.

Most of the desserts in this chapter have been around for centuries. Crisps, cobblers, grunts, and pandowdies were favorite desserts of American frontier cooks, and they are no less delicious today. We love these recipes for their simplicity and flavor. Although they were once the property of home cooks, pastry chefs now appreciate the pleasure these homey desserts bring to their guests, and you can find apple crisp on many an upscale restaurant dessert menu.

The recipes in this chapter were contributed by Lindsey Shere and Carolyn B. Weil.

Ingredients for Fruit Desserts

Fruits | Remember, your fruit desserts will only be as good as the fruit itself. When you locate a store that sells flavorful, high-quality fruits, give it your business—your desserts will thank you for it. This is not to say that you can't make good desserts with supermarket fruit. Just be selective, and spurn mealy apples, fragrance-free pears or peaches, and sour berries, and hold out for better specimens. The season certainly plays a part in the picture. While you can find jet-transported berries in the market in January for a cobbler, that doesn't mean it will be as good as the cobbler you make in July with local fruit.

Part of the fun of cooking these desserts is substituting one fruit for another. Peach, plum, or nectarine is just as tempting as pear or apple crisp, and cherries make a fine cobbler. Of course, a certain amount of common sense must be applied. Taste the sweetened fruit, and if it seems to need a bit more sugar or a few tablespoons of lemon juice to balance the flavor, add them. Here are some measurements of the most common fruits.

Apples:	8 small, 6 medium, or 5 large = 6 cups peeled, cored, and sliced
Apricots:	12 medium = 6 cups pitted and sliced
Blackberries:	3 pint baskets = 6 cups
Blueberries:	3 pint baskets = 6 cups
Cherries:	2 pounds = 6 cups pitted
Pears:	6 large = 6 cups peeled, cored, and sliced
Raspberries:	6 ½-pint baskets = 6 cups
Rhubarb:	7 medium stalks = 6 cups sliced
Strawberries:	4 pint baskets = 6 cups hulled and sliced

Heavy cream | These desserts need little adornment but a drizzle of heavy cream or a scoop of ice cream. If you go the heavy cream route, search out a pasteurized (not ultrapasteurized) brand at a natural food store or dairy; it has an unsurpassable old-fashioned flavor.

Equipment for Fruit Desserts

AS MOST OF THESE desserts are served directly from their baking dishes, use attractive ceramic, porcelain, or Pyrex. An 11½ × 8-inch baking dish or any casserole with a 2-quart capacity is perfect for cobblers, crisps, and other warm fruit desserts. Place the pan on a baking sheet to catch any drips from the bubbling fruit. The dessert can also be baked on a baking stone to cook the fruit more thoroughly and quickly.

Techniques for Fruit Desserts

THE TOPPINGS FOR cobblers and grunts are really quick breads (see "Techniques for Quick Breads," page 225). The most important thing to remember when mixing these doughs is: Don't overmix.

At a glance, topped baked fruit desserts (like cobblers and crisps) look like simplified pies. But there is one major distinction: Because there is no need for the filling to be firm enough to slice, the fruit is unthickened. Serve these baked goods warm from the oven, spooned into bowls to catch the free-running juices.

Storing Fruit Desserts

BAKED FRUIT DESSERTS WITH TOPPINGS are really best served within an hour after baking. Leftovers, cooled, covered, and refrigerated, will be fine, but certainly not as delicious as they were when fresh from the oven. You can reheat leftovers, loosely covered with foil, in a preheated 350°F oven for 10 to 15 minutes to warm through. Don't reheat them in a microwave oven, or the toppings will get rubbery. Baked fruits, like stuffed apples and baked pears, are also best served a few hours after serving (set them aside at room temperature), but they will keep in the refrigerator for a couple of days. Remove them from the refrigerator an hour before serving so they can lose their chill.

A Cobbler by Any Other Name . . .

Old-fashioned American fruit desserts often have amusing names that are reflections of what they look like.

Cobbler | The thick, bumpy crust of a cobbler covering chunks of fruit can often look like a cobbled street. Or perhaps the word comes from another definition of "cobble," meaning to patch up, because a cobbler can be quickly patched together from fruit and a topping. The topping is a matter of controversy. Some bakers use biscuit or sweet scone toppings, while others prefer a pie dough, in which case the cobbler resembles a deep-dish pie.

Crisp | Also known as a crumble, this is baked fruit with a crisp, crumbly topping. Oatmeal, brown sugar, and cinnamon are common ingredients in this warming classic.

Betty | One of the quickest of all fruit desserts to prepare, an apple brown Betty is sliced, spiced apples layered with buttered bread crumbs. The origin of the word "Betty" is obscure. The dessert seems to go back to Colonial times, when Betty was a common name, but it doesn't show up in cookbooks until the late nineteenth century.

Pandowdy | An apple pie with a characteristic broken-crust top. Some people think the name reflects the dessert's homely appearance, but there was an old English custard called *pandoude*.

Grunt | This dessert of stewed fruit with dumplings steamed on top is sometimes called a slump. The fruit is said to grunt while it simmers, and the dumplings do have a bit of a slump to their shape.

Pear Crisp

MAKES 8 SERVINGS

Carolyn B. Weil

Tender fruit under a crumbly oat topping, a crisp is one of the ultimate comfort foods. While it can be made with just about any fruit under the sun (okay, not citrus . . .), there's something especially satisfying about a pear crisp, which is reminiscent of the familiar apple version, yet winning in its own way.

TOPPING

1 cup old-fashioned rolled oats
½ cup unbleached all-purpose flour
½ cup packed light brown sugar
½ teaspoon ground cinnamon
¼ teaspoon salt
8 tablespoons (1 stick) unsalted butter, chilled and cut into ½-inch cubes

6 large ripe pears, such as Comice or Anjou, peeled, cored, and cut into 1-inch chunks (6 cups)
¼ cup sugar
1 tablespoon cornstarch
¼ teaspoon freshly grated nutmeg
Ice cream, for serving

1. Position a rack in the center of the oven and preheat to 350°F. Lightly butter an 11½ × 8-inch (2-quart) baking dish.

2. To make the topping, mix the oats, flour, brown sugar, cinnamon, and salt in a medium bowl. Add the butter and rub between your fingers until the mixture is well combined and crumbly.

3. Toss the fruit, sugar, cornstarch, and nutmeg in a large bowl. Spread in the prepared dish and top evenly with the oat mixture. Place the dish on a baking sheet.

4. Bake until the top is crisp and golden brown, the pears are tender, and the juices are bubbling, about 35 minutes.

5. Cool the crisp for 10 minutes. Serve warm, spooned into shallow bowls and topped with ice cream.

Mixed Berry Cobbler

FILLING

1 cup sugar

2 tablespoons cornstarch

2 tablespoons instant tapioca, ground to a powder in a coffee grinder

8 cups mixed berries (hulled and sliced strawberries, blueberries, raspberries, and blackberries in any combination, but no more than half strawberries)

1 tablespoon fresh lemon juice

Grated zest of 1 lemon

TOPPING

2 cups unbleached all-purpose flour

¼ cup plus 2 tablespoons sugar

1 tablespoon baking powder

8 tablespoons (1 stick) unsalted butter, chilled and cut into ½-inch cubes

¾ cup heavy cream

½ teaspoon ground cinnamon

Whipped Cream Topping (page 336), optional

1. Position a rack in the center of the oven and preheat to 350°F. Lightly butter an 11½ × 8-inch (2-quart) baking dish.

2. To make the filling, mix the sugar, cornstarch, and powdered tapioca in a bowl. In a large bowl, toss the fruit with the lemon juice and zest. Sprinkle with the sugar mixture and toss to combine. Pour into the prepared dish and set aside.

3. To make the topping, whisk the flour, ¼ cup of the sugar, and the baking powder in another large bowl. Using a pastry blender, cut in the butter until the mixture resembles coarse meal with a few pea-sized pieces of butter. Stirring with a fork, add the cream and mix just until a soft dough forms. Drop 8 spoonfuls of the dough over the top of the fruit. In a small bowl, mix the remaining 2 tablespoons sugar and the cinnamon. Sprinkle equal amounts of the cinnamon sugar over each portion of dough.

4. Bake until the juices are bubbling and the topping is firm and golden brown, about 45 minutes.

5. Cool the cobbler for 10 minutes. Serve warm, spooned into shallow bowls and topped with whipped cream, if desired.

MAKES 8 SERVINGS

Carolyn B. Weil

Cobbler lovers are divided into two camps—biscuit topping or pastry topping. For us there is no argument, for we believe that a cobbler is always made with biscuits and it is a deep-dish pie that is topped with pastry. Here's a summertime favorite with a collection of berries. Strawberries lose their color when baked, but they will get a lift from the vibrant juices of the other berries. Just don't use too many strawberries or the filling will look pale.

Apple Brown Betty

MAKES 4 TO 6 SERVINGS

Carolyn B. Weil

An old-fashioned dessert that deserves a comeback, apple brown Betty depends on the quality of its two main ingredients, apples and bread crumbs. The apples can be any flavorful, tart variety (Granny Smith is readily available, but look to your farmers' market for more unusual ones). Make the bread crumbs from firm white sandwich bread with the crusts removed. A blender or food processor makes very short work of this job.

2 cups fresh bread crumbs
1 cup packed light brown sugar
¼ teaspoon ground cinnamon
¼ teaspoon ground nutmeg
4 large tart apples, such as Pippin, Granny Smith, or Golden
   Delicious, peeled, cored, and cut into ⅛-inch wedges
8 tablespoons (1 stick) unsalted butter, chilled and cut into
   ½-inch cubes
Heavy cream, for serving, optional

1. Position a rack in the center of the oven and preheat to 375°F. Lightly butter a 6- to 8-cup soufflé dish.

2. Spread the bread crumbs on a baking sheet and bake, stirring occasionally, until very lightly toasted, about 10 minutes. Do not overbrown. Set aside.

3. Combine the brown sugar, cinnamon, and nutmeg in a large bowl. Add the apples and toss well. Spread half the apples in the prepared dish, sprinkle with half the bread crumbs, and dot with half the butter. Repeat with the remaining apples, bread crumbs, and butter.

4. Bake until the topping is golden brown and the apples are tender, about 45 minutes.

5. Cool the Betty for 10 minutes. Spoon into shallow bowls and serve warm, with heavy cream passed on the side, if desired.

Blueberry Grunt

FILLING

2 pints blueberries, rinsed
½ cup water
⅓ cup sugar
⅓ cup unsulfured molasses
2 tablespoons fresh lemon juice
Grated zest of 1 lemon
¼ teaspoon freshly grated nutmeg
¼ teaspoon ground cloves

DUMPLINGS

1½ cups unbleached all-purpose flour
1 tablespoon sugar
2 teaspoons baking powder
¼ teaspoon salt
3 tablespoons unsalted butter, chilled, cut into
½-inch cubes
¾ cup milk

Heavy cream, for serving

1. To make the filling, mix the blueberries, water, sugar, molasses, lemon juice and zest, nutmeg, and cloves in a large nonreactive skillet. Bring to a boil over medium heat, stirring occasionally. Reduce the heat to low and simmer for 10 minutes.

2. Meanwhile, make the dumplings. In a medium bowl, whisk the flour, sugar, baking powder, and salt to combine. Cut in the butter with a pastry blender until the mixture resembles coarse crumbs with a few pea-sized pieces. Stir in the milk to make a soft dough.

3. Drop 8 large spoonfuls of the dough over the simmering berries. Cover tightly and simmer until the dumplings are firm and cooked through, about 15 minutes.

4. Serve hot, spooned into shallow bowls with the cream passed on the side.

MAKES 6 SERVINGS

Carolyn B. Weil

Blueberry grunt is an unpleasant name for a very pleasing dessert of simmered fruit with sweet dumplings. Blueberries give off lots of juices that make them a good choice for this warming dish, which is perfect for a summer's night when there's a bit of a chill in the air.

Don't use a cast-iron skillet, as the metal would react with the berries and turn the juices gray. The filling should cook for no more than 10 minutes. If there is a delay in making the dumplings, turn off the heat under the filling until the dumpling dough is ready.

Apple-Raisin Pandowdy

MAKES 8 SERVINGS

Carolyn B. Weil

A pandowdy starts off as a deep-dish pie, but the crust is pushed into the filling halfway through baking to give an entirely different result. As this "pie" isn't cut into slices, don't concern yourself with using tart apples that hold their shape after baking. In fact, pandowdy may be at its best when the filling has a collection of apples with different flavors and textures, some firm and tart, others soft and spicy.

6 medium to large apples (in any combination, but include 2 tart apples such as Empire or Winesap), peeled, cored, and cut into ¼-inch wedges (6 cups)

1 cup plus 2 tablespoons sugar

½ cup raisins or currants

2 tablespoons unsulfured molasses

¾ teaspoon ground cinnamon

¼ teaspoon freshly grated nutmeg

Pinch of salt

2 tablespoons fresh lemon juice

2 tablespoons unsalted butter, cut into pieces

Butter Pie Dough (page 123)

1. Position a rack in the center of the oven and preheat to 375°F.

2. To make the filling, toss together the apples, 1 cup sugar, raisins, molasses, ½ teaspoon cinnamon, the nutmeg, and salt. Toss with the lemon juice. Pour into a 10-inch deep-dish pie pan and dot with the butter.

3. On a lightly floured work surface, roll out the dough to a 12-inch circle. Place over the pan, letting the excess dough hang over the sides. Fold 1 inch of the dough back, then flute this thick border onto the edge of the pie pan. Place the pan on a baking sheet.

4. Bake for 10 minutes. Reduce the oven temperature to 350°F and continue baking until the crust is lightly browned, about 30 minutes. Remove the pan from the oven. Using a wide metal spatula (such as a pancake turner) or sharp knife, cut the top into 1-inch squares, being sure not to cut all the way to the edges of the crust. Using a large spoon, press the pastry squares into the apples, using the spoon to gather up the juices and baste the pastry. Mix the remaining 2 tablespoons sugar and ¼ teaspoon cinnamon and sprinkle over the pastry squares and filling. Return to the oven and bake until the topping is golden brown and the apples are tender, about 30 minutes.

5. Remove from the oven and cool for 10 minutes. Serve warm, spooned into shallow bowls.

Warm Pineapple in Puff Pastry with Pineapple Caramel Sauce

PASTRIES

½ recipe Quick Puff Pastry (page 163), about 1 pound
1 tablespoon heavy cream
1 large egg yolk

FILLING

½ cup heavy cream
1 teaspoon kirsch
1 cup Pastry Cream (page 334)

PINEAPPLE CARAMEL SAUCE

⅓ cup plus 1 tablespoon water
1½ cups sugar
1½ cups unsweetened pineapple juice

1 small ripe pineapple

MAKES 8 SERVINGS

Lindsey Shere

As familiar as pineapple has become, it still has a wonderfully exotic flavor that deserves to be showcased in more sweets. The different components of this sophisticated dessert can be made ahead of serving, leaving just a quick warming of the pineapple in the caramel sauce before assembly.

1. To make the pastries, on a lightly floured work surface, roll out the puff pastry into a 13 × 9-inch rectangle about ³⁄₁₆ inch thick. Using a pastry wheel or a sharp knife, trim into a 12 × 8-inch rectangle, then cut into eight 4 × 3-inch rectangles. Arrange 1 inch apart on an ungreased baking sheet and cover loosely with plastic wrap. Freeze until thoroughly chilled, about 30 minutes.

2. Meanwhile, position a rack in the center of the oven and preheat to 400°F.

3. In a small bowl, beat the cream and yolk. Brush the tops of the pastries lightly with some of the cream mixture; do not let the glaze drip down the sides of the pastries or they will not rise properly. Using the tip of a small, sharp knife, score a ¹⁄₁₆-inch-deep pattern of your choice into the tops of the rectangles.

4. Bake the pastries for 10 minutes. Reduce the heat to 350°F and bake until the pastries are puffed, golden brown, and baked through, about 15 minutes. To check for doneness, slit one pastry from the side into the center and force it open to see that the pastry looks dry inside. If not, bake for a few more minutes. Transfer to a cooling rack and cool completely. (The pastries can be prepared up to 8 hours ahead and stored uncovered at room temperature.)

A Harvest of Fruit Desserts

5. To make the filling, beat the cream with the kirsch in a chilled medium bowl until stiff peaks form. Place the pastry cream in another medium bowl and fold in the whipped cream. (The filling can be prepared up to 4 hours ahead, covered, and refrigerated.)

6. To make the caramel sauce, place a small plate in the freezer to chill. Pour the water into a heavy-bottomed medium saucepan and add the sugar. Do not stir. Bring to a boil over medium-high heat and cook without stirring, washing down any sugar crystals on the side of the pan with a pastry brush dipped in cold water, until the syrup caramelizes to a dark golden brown.

7. Carefully add the pineapple juice (it will bubble up). Continue cooking until a few drops poured onto the chilled plate makes a slightly thickened syrup, about 5 minutes. (The sauce can be prepared up to 4 hours ahead and stored uncovered at room temperature.)

8. Using a large, sharp knife, cut off the pineapple crown. Slice the peel from the pineapple. Using the tip of a swivel-bladed vegetable peeler, remove the eyes from the pineapple. Cut the pineapple into eight ¼-inch-thick rounds, reserving the remaining pineapple for another use. Halve each round and cut out the center core, then cut the pineapple into small wedges. Cover and chill until ready to serve.

9. To serve, cook the pineapple wedges with 2 to 3 tablespoons caramel sauce in a large nonstick skillet over medium heat just until the pineapple is heated through. Keep warm.

10. Using a serrated knife, cut each pastry in half horizontally. Place the bottoms on serving plates. Spread with equal amounts of the cream mixture, then spoon the warm pineapple on top. Place the tops on the pastries. Spoon the caramel sauce next to the pastries and serve immediately.

Baker's Notes

THE PUFF PASTRY can be cut into any shape you like. For rounds, use a very sharp cookie cutter. If the cutter is dull, it will press the pastry layers together and reduce the amount of puffing.

Save any dough trimmings to decorate the tops of the pastries. Use tiny truffle or canapé cutters to punch out shapes, place on the glazed rectangles, and glaze the decorations, but very lightly.

When making the caramel sauce, choose a tall saucepan to avoid the risk of boiling over when the juice is added.

If your supermarket carries it, buy fresh peeled and trimmed pineapple to save time.

Summer Pudding

MAKES 9 SERVINGS

Lindsey Shere

At midsummer, our produce stores and farmers' markets offer a huge assortment of berries, including red currants during their short, but welcome, season. This summer pudding makes full use of the bounty, but it should be made with the "soft" berries mentioned in the ingredients. Blueberries or huckleberries will give the fruit juices a dark tint (and you want a pleasing shade of magenta), and strawberries aren't quite juicy enough. If you can't find currants, just use more raspberries. You can make our White Sandwich Bread, but if it's too hot to bake bread, a good commercial loaf will do.

About 8 ounces White Sandwich Bread (page 264), crusts trimmed, cut into ¼-inch-thick slices

3 pints fresh berries (such as red, golden, or black raspberries, blackberries, or boysenberries, in any combination), sorted for any bruised or moldy fruit

½ pint red currants, stemmed

1 cup sugar

1 tablespoon kirsch

Whipped Cream Topping (page 336)

Raspberry Sauce (page 339), optional

1. Line an 8- to 9-inch square baking dish with plastic wrap, leaving enough overhang to cover the top of the pudding. Line the bottom of the prepared pan with a tight-fitting layer of bread, trimming to fit.

2. In a large nonreactive skillet, heat the berries and currants with the sugar over medium heat just until they give off their juices. Sprinkle with the kirsch. Spoon one-third of the berry mixture over the bread. Top with a second layer of bread, then half of the remaining berry mixture. Repeat with another layer of bread, the remaining berry mixture, and a final layer of bread. Cover with the overhanging plastic wrap. Place another baking dish of the same size on top of the pudding, and weight with a few heavy cans. Place on a baking sheet to catch any juices, and refrigerate overnight.

3. Unwrap the top of the pudding. Invert the pudding onto a serving platter (with a lip to hold the juices) and unmold, pulling off the plastic wrap. Cut into 9 squares and transfer to dessert plates. Serve with a dollop of whipped cream and a drizzle of the sauce, if desired.

Baker's Notes

THE TART FLAVOR of fresh red currants is prized by bakers. The currants have a very short season, so when you see them, don't pass them up—they may not be there the next time you look. You can, however, freeze them to use later.

Summer pudding needs a firm-textured white bread with a tight crumb. Buy an unsliced loaf at a bakery and trim and slice it yourself, or use thick-sliced sandwich bread from the supermarket (as long as it isn't the fluffy, spongy kind). Crusty breads with an open crumb do not make good summer pudding.

Baked Apples with Walnut-Orange Stuffing

MAKES 6 SERVINGS

Lindsey Shere

The baker has a wide choice of apples that are suited for stuffing and baking. Depending on your location and what is available, choose from Cortland, Idared, Jonagold, Jonathan, Northern Spy, Rome, Sierra Beauty, or other local varieties like Spitzenberg. McIntoshes work well if you watch them carefully and remove them from the oven the moment they are tender. And use whatever sweet wine is available—late-harvest Riesling, ice wine, Beaumes-de-Venise, Muscat, or Sauternes. Serve these warm, with a cool glass of the wine alongside.

6 medium baking apples (about 7 ounces each)
½ cup sugar
5 tablespoons unsalted butter, at room temperature
Grated zest of 1 small orange
6 tablespoons lightly toasted, coarsely chopped walnuts
¾ cup late-harvest Riesling or other sweet wine
Heavy cream, for serving

1. Position a rack in the center of the oven and preheat to 325°F.

2. Starting at the stem, peel the top third of each apple. With a paring knife, cut out a triangle around each stem and discard. Using a melon baller or small spoon, scoop out the core from each apple, being sure not to go through the bottom. If necessary, trim thin slices from the bottoms of the apples so they stand up straight. Arrange in a baking dish just large enough to hold the apples.

3. In a medium bowl, using a rubber spatula, work the sugar, butter, and zest until combined, then work in the walnuts. Stuff the apples with the walnut filling, leveling the filling even with the tops of the apples, reserving any extra filling. Pour the wine around the apples.

4. Bake, basting every 10 minutes or so with the juices and adding the reserved filling to the cores as the filling level reduces, until the apples are tender when pierced with the tip of a knife, 45 minutes to 1 hour, depending on the size of the apples. Watch carefully toward the end of the cooking time to be sure the apples don't burst.

5. Remove from the oven and cool for 15 minutes. Using a slotted spoon, transfer to shallow bowls, and pour the juices around the apples. Serve warm, with the heavy cream passed on the side.

Pears Baked in Beaumes-de-Venise and Honey

4 ripe medium pears (about 7 ounces each), rinsed
    but unpeeled
¼ cup mild-flavored honey (such as clover, orange blossom,
    or thistle)
1 cup Beaumes-de-Venise or other sweet wine
Heavy cream, for serving, optional

1. Position a rack in the center of the oven and preheat to 375°F.

2. Stand the pears in a baking dish that is just large enough to hold them upright. Drizzle with the honey and pour the wine over them.

3. Bake, basting the pears with the cooking juices every 15 minutes, until they are slightly golden and tender when the thickest part is pierced with a knife, about 45 minutes, depending on the firmness of the pears. Firm Bosc pears, which will be very golden and slightly shriveled but appetizingly beautiful, may take up to 2 hours.

4. Using a slotted spoon, transfer the pears to shallow bowls. If the cooking juices are not syrupy, pour them into a medium saucepan and cook over medium heat until they thicken. Pour the juices over the pears. Serve warm, with the cream passed on the side, if you wish.

MAKES 4 SERVINGS

Lindsey Shere

With only three ingredients, these pears have a deceptively complex flavor that you would expect from a much more intricate recipe. Beaumes-de-Venise is a lovely, gold-colored sweet wine, but there are other possibilities (see Baker's Notes for suggestions). You can use any variety of pear that holds its shape after cooking, such as Anjou, Bartlett, Bosc, or Comice—just adjust the baking time as needed until the pears are tender.

Baker's Note

BEAUMES-DE-VENISE is a sweet fortified wine made in northern Provence from Muscat grapes. It is an excellent apéritif or dessert wine, with many layers of floral and fruity flavors. An excellent substitute from California is Quady Elysium, but any sweet Muscat wine will do, or even a late-harvest Riesling.

*A Harvest
of Fruit
Desserts*

The Cookie Collection

Baking cookies is fun, easy, and rewarding. Techniques used in most cookie recipes are simple, making cookie baking ideal for less experienced bakers, especially kids. Cookies are also perfect for those of us with limited time, as most doughs go together quickly and can be refrigerated or frozen, and baked later. Cookies are the most portable of baked goods, perfect for picnics, potlucks, and sack lunches. They are easy to share with friends and family.

Cookies do have a few requirements for success. It's important to use good ingredients and high-quality baking sheets. Select the correct oven temperature, watch them closely while baking, and store them properly.

Every one of us has a story to tell about how cookies played a role in our professional and personal lives. One of our bakers says the seeds of his career were planted in the seventh grade, when he realized that if he learned how to bake, he could make more cookies than his busy mom could supply by herself. He baked so many cookies that his mother used to joke that he was born with a cookie in his mouth. Another baker tells how she and her sister would bake mountains of holiday cookies, only to guard them carefully until they decided it was just the right time to serve them. Their father would loudly complain, "I don't know why you make all of these cookies if you don't let us eat them!"

The simple cookie, loved by all in its many forms, is a good thing for us bakers: With a little effort, we get big rewards.

This chapter was chaired by Robert Morocco and Julia Cookenboo. The committee members were Yolanda Fletcher, Tami Jewett, Judith Maguire, Patti Murray, and Berry North Todd.

Ingredients for Cookies

AS WE BAKED and nibbled our way through hundreds of cookies, we realized that, even more than with other baked goods, there is no substitute for quality when it comes to cookies. Whether the dough is dropped from a spoon or rolled and cut out, it is usually a simple mixture whose flavors are very pronounced. Use inferior butter, cheap imitation flavorings, or inexpensive chocolate made from flavored vegetable fats instead of fine bittersweet chocolate, and you'll have cookies, but they won't be *great* cookies.

Butter | High-quality unsalted butter is a cookie's best friend. Unless a recipe specifically calls for another fat, such as vegetable shortening or margarine (which will give some cookies a softer crumb), always use butter. It is easier to tell the freshness of unsalted butter, as the salt can mask an off taste or unpleasant aroma. Unsalted butter contains less water than salted, so it is more pliable and better for creaming. Finally, using unsalted butter allows the cook to control the amount of salt in the recipe (a stick of salted butter can contain up to ½ teaspoon salt).

When a recipe calls for softened butter, it must be at the proper temperature—if it is too soft, it will not incorporate air properly, and air acts as a natural leavening. The butter should stand at room temperature until it is slightly softened and malleable, but not squishy and shiny. See page 45 in the The Basics of Cake chapter for tips on softening butter.

Flour | Use bleached all-purpose flour for the most tender cookies. Cake flour has a low gluten content and doesn't give the dough enough structure for proper rising.

When mixing flour with other dry ingredients, especially baking powder, baking soda, or spices, sifting is recommended. Some cooks simply whisk the ingredients together, but they run the risk of not properly distributing the leavening (baking soda can be lumpy, and little white bits of bicarbonate of soda in your cookie aren't very tasty).

We measure our flour by the dip-and-sweep method (see page 34).

Eggs | We used large grade A eggs in testing these recipes. Don't use any other size, or the amount of liquid in the recipe will not be correct.

Flavorings | Use natural flavorings, and insist on pure vanilla extract.

Equipment for Cookies

Oven | Bake a batch of cookies, and you'll get to know your oven's idiosyncrasies very quickly.

Do the cookies spread too much before they set, or do they burn quickly? Then your oven is probably running hot. (Get in the habit of using an oven thermometer to double-check the temperature.) Do some of the cookies brown before others are done? In that case, the oven has hot spots.

Whether your oven is temperamental or not, whenever baking cookies, rotate the cookie sheets. Halfway during the baking period, switch the position of the cookie sheets from the top to the center rack and vice versa, and rotate the sheets from front to back. It's best to place the racks in the center and top third of the oven, as baking sheets placed too close to the heat source at the bottom of the oven will get too hot and burn the cookies. Also, as heat rises, your cookies will brown better.

A convection oven will solve some of the cookie baker's most common problems. Cookies baked in a convection oven will brown more evenly, and you won't have to worry about rack positions. If you have a convection oven, reduce the oven temperature 25°F and expect the cookies to be done in about two-thirds of the suggested baking time. It is best to do a sample batch on a single baking sheet to be sure.

In either type of oven, check the cookies often toward the end of the baking time. Don't linger when checking, as an open oven door will allow heat to escape. Remember that you can always add more baking time, but you can't subtract it. Once a batch of cookies gets too brown, there's no turning back.

Cookie sheets | If you want to bake great cookies and have fun doing it, invest in good-quality cookie sheets! Here's an item where you definitely get what you pay for.

Some bakers make a distinction between cookie sheets (rimless) and baking sheets (with short rims). One camp prefers the rimless sheets, because they believe the sides block the free passage of air over the cookies. However, we tested a wide range of cookie sheets, and the easy winner was the heavy aluminum "half-sheet pan." This rimmed baking sheet is the one used by professional bakers and chefs, and for good reason. It measures about 17 × 12 inches and holds a good number of cookies, cutting down on the batches you need to bake. The thick-gauge aluminum encourages evenly baked cookies, and the shiny surface discourages burned bottoms.

It may be tempting to buy inexpensive lightweight cookie sheets, but we can't recommend them. Cookies baked on lightweight sheets usually burn on the bottom before they are baked through. These pans also bend and warp easily.

For further comparison, we baked cookies on nonstick, black steel, and double-thick insulated cookie sheets. The dark surfaces of the first two pans also browned the cookie bottoms too quickly. If you wish to use these types of pans, experiment with lowering the oven temperature by 25°F or even more to avoid burning the cookies. Double-layer cookie sheets, somewhat new to the marketplace, seem like a good idea because they insulate the baking surface and cut down on burned bottoms. However, this type of cookie sheet can change the cooking time and the character of the cookie. While they worked fine for soft cookies, it was difficult to bake the "snap" into crisp cookies. If you decide to use them, experiment—you may need to increase the cooking time and/or the temperature slightly.

Parchment paper and nonstick pads | The least favorite part of baking cookies is buttering and flouring the cookie sheets for those recipes requiring this chore. And the dirty cookie sheets must be washed and dried before using them for another batch. But now there are solutions to this drudgery.

Professional bakers love parchment paper. It's a time-saver when it comes to cleanup—just toss away the used paper. (Be sure to let the cookie sheet cool between batches, as a warm sheet will melt the dough before it has a chance to bake properly.) When it comes time to move the cookies onto a rack for cooling, let the cookies cool on the sheet for 3 to 5 minutes, then slide the cookies, still on the paper, onto the rack. Rolls of parchment paper are available at kitchenware shops, but they vary in sturdiness and can be difficult to lay flat. Dab a bit of butter under the paper in the corners of the baking sheet to get the furled paper to adhere. Sheets of high-quality commercial-grade paper can be purchased at restaurant supply shops and by mail order (see Sources, page 343). Even if you have to buy more than you think you need, you will probably end up baking more often because the parchment paper is such a help.

Nonstick baking pads are equally successful in the fight against dirty baking sheets and stuck cookies. Often sold under the brand names Expat and Silpat, these flexible silicone sheets act as a reusable nonstick liner for baking sheets. They may seem pricey, but they are actually great value, as you can use them hundreds (some say thousands) of times before they wear out.

Making Cookies

WITH MOST COOKIE DOUGHS, the first step is creaming the butter and sugar together into a homogeneous paste. This is a crucial technique, as it beats air into the dough, lightening the texture of the baked cookie. When the butter and sugar are creamed properly, the mixture will be pale ivory, an indication that the air has been incorporated. If the butter and sugar are insufficiently creamed, cookies that should be plump and light will turn out flat and crisp. But keep in mind that some recipes deliberately reduce the creaming to control the texture of the cookies.

As grandmas of yesteryear (and today's hands-on cooks) can attest, cookie doughs can certainly be made by hand in a big bowl with a sturdy wooden spoon. Provide plenty of elbow grease and allow at least 5 minutes to cream the sugar and butter.

A heavy-duty electric mixer is our favorite mixing machine because it makes fast work out of creaming. Using the paddle blade at medium speed, cream the mixture for at least 3 minutes. Be sure to stop the mixer and scrape down the sides and bottom of the mixer bowl at least twice during the creaming period, as a bit of butter and sugar always remains stubbornly nestled in the bottom of the bowl.

Electric hand mixers are strong enough to cream the butter and sugar and incorporate the eggs and flavorings, but only the highest-wattage models can handle mixing dry ingredients into a stiff dough without burning out. You'll have no trouble creaming the butter and sugar and adding eggs, but when it comes to adding the flour or other dry ingredients, it is best to switch to a wooden spoon and gradually stir them into the creamed mixture.

Food processors are not good for most cookie doughs because they don't beat air into the butter and sugar mixture. Save them for other kitchen jobs, such as chopping nuts for the dough.

Among their many positive qualities, cookies are more forgiving than other baked goods. You can double, triple, or even quadruple these recipes without ill effects. Your only limitation is the size of the bowl.

Some doughs must be refrigerated to make them easier to handle. Don't try to reduce the chilling time by placing the dough in the freezer. It will freeze hard around the edges before chilling in the center, and you will find it even more difficult to work with. If you're strapped for time, shape the dough into neat logs, then refrigerate. Logs chill more quickly than a large mass of dough.

Here's how professional bakers form dough into logs. Place a 16 × 12-inch piece of parchment paper (wax paper works too, but it tears more easily) on the work surface, with a long side facing you. Spoon the dough into a rough log about 11 inches long across the center of the paper. Fold the parchment toward you over the dough to cover it. Firmly press the edge of a sturdy baking sheet or a ruler against the length of the dough. Pull the bottom of the parchment so the paper tightens and the baking sheet compresses the dough into an evenly shaped log. You may have to wiggle the pan a bit to get the right grip. Twist the ends of the paper to close them, then refrigerate as directed.

Most cookie doughs can be made ahead and frozen for use whenever it's convenient, a real boon to the holiday cookie baker. Shape the dough into logs, wrap in plastic wrap, and then overwrap in aluminum foil. Freeze the dough for up to 2 months. When ready to freeze, defrost the logs at room temperature until malleable, then slice and bake.

Storage

COOKIE JARS ARE CUTE, but unfortunately they aren't very good for storing cookies. Most cookies are best stored in an airtight metal container. Buy them whenever you see them—thrift shops can be a rich trove. Be aware that the lids of many metal containers do not fit tightly. Gaps will let in air and maybe even insects. To solve this problem, place a piece of wax paper on top of the cookie tin, making sure that it hangs over the edges the container, and then put on the lid.

Plastic containers are easy to buy at kitchenware shops, but they work best for soft cookies, as they soften crisp ones. Most cookies will remain fresh, if properly stored, for approximately 1 week. Some types of hard cookies, such as biscotti, will last longer.

Baked cookies can also be successfully frozen. How long will they keep in the freezer? The time varies with different types of cookies. A month in the freezer is a good conservative rule to follow when freezing cookies, but members of the cookie editorial board had varying experiences. The temperature obviously plays a big part—use a freezer thermometer to be sure your freezer is 0°F or below. Most of today's freezers are self-defrosting, which is another factor to take into account, as the freezer temperature rises and falls and could thaw small cookies. To insulate the cookies as much as possible, always double-wrap in plastic and aluminum foil, or store them in double-bagged freezer bags or an airtight plastic container.

When it comes time for defrosting, take out a few or a whole batch and leave them at room temperature. Most cookies take less than an hour to thaw in a reasonably warm kitchen.

Almond and Chocolate Sandwich Cookies

MAKES 40 COOKIES

Julia Cookenboo

These crisp cookies are a fine accompaniment to ice cream. We bet they'll remind you of a popular and very expensive supermarket cookie (that will go unnamed). Allow time for the dough to chill.

1 cup whole natural almonds, toasted and cooled (see page 16)
¾ cup plus 3 tablespoons sugar
¾ cup all-purpose flour
1 teaspoon baking powder
⅛ teaspoon salt
8 tablespoons (1 stick) unsalted butter, softened
1 large egg
¼ teaspoon almond extract
4 ounces semisweet or bittersweet chocolate, finely chopped

1. In a food processor fitted with the chopping blade, process the almonds with 3 tablespoons of the sugar until the almonds are finely ground. Set aside.

2. Sift the flour, baking powder, and salt onto a sheet of wax paper or into a bowl. Set aside.

3. In the bowl of a heavy-duty stand mixer fitted with the paddle attachment, beat the butter with the remaining ¾ cup sugar on medium speed until the mixture is light in color and texture, at least 3 minutes. Beat in the egg and almond extract, then the almond mixture, blending just until smooth. On low speed, gradually beat in the flour mixture just until smooth.

4. Cover the dough tightly with plastic wrap. Refrigerate until the dough is thoroughly chilled, at least 2 hours or up to 5 days.

5. Position racks in the center and top third of the oven and preheat to 350°F. Line two large baking sheets with parchment paper or lightly butter them.

6. Using 1 teaspoon for each, portion the dough into 80 pieces. Put 2 pieces of dough into one hand and roll between your palms into 2 balls. (This may seem a bit odd at first, but it works, and cuts the work time in half.) Place the balls about 1½ inches apart on the prepared baking sheets. Do not crowd them, as they will spread during baking. (You will probably have to bake these cookies on three sheets.)

7. Bake, switching the position of the sheets from top to bottom and front to back halfway through baking, until the cookies are lightly browned all over, 10 to 12 minutes.

8. Let the cookies cool on the sheets for 3 minutes. Carefully transfer to wire cooling racks and cool completely.

9. In the top part of a double boiler over hot, not simmering, water, melt the chocolate. Using a small icing spatula, spread about ½ teaspoon on the underside of a cookie, then sandwich with another cookie, placing them back to back. Alternatively, fill a parchment cone (see page 81) halfway with the melted chocolate. Pipe the chocolate onto one cookie, then place another on top and press together lightly. Refrigerate briefly to set the chocolate. (The cookies can be stored at room temperature in an airtight container for up to 5 days.)

Baker's Note

FOR A FANCIER-LOOKING cookie, lightly brush the top of each cookie with an egg glaze (beat 1 egg with 1 teaspoon water) and top with a few sliced almonds before baking. Even without the chocolate filling, these are excellent wafer-type cookies.

Pistachio–Golden Raisin Biscotti

MAKES ABOUT 4 DOZEN
COOKIES

Julia Cookenboo

There are many varieties of double-baked biscotti, but they aren't limited to Italy—what are mandelbrot or rusks but biscotti? Many biscotti are baked rock hard because it is expected that they will be dipped into wine, coffee, or tea. This elegant version is crisp, yet soft enough to eat without dunking.

2½ cups all-purpose flour

1½ teaspoons baking powder

½ teaspoon salt

8 tablespoons (1 stick) cold unsalted butter

1¼ cups sugar

2 large eggs

⅔ cup (about 4 ounces) coarsely chopped pistachios

⅓ cup plus 1 tablespoon golden raisins

1. Position racks in the center and top third of the oven and preheat to 300°F. Line two large baking sheets with parchment paper or lightly butter them.

2. Sift the flour, baking powder, and salt into a medium bowl; set aside.

3. In the bowl of a heavy-duty stand mixer fitted with the paddle attachment, beat the butter and sugar on low speed just until combined, about 1 minute. Do not overbeat. One at a time, beat in the eggs. Add the flour mixture and blend just until almost combined. Add the pistachios and golden raisins and mix until combined, using your hands if necessary to be sure that they are evenly distributed throughout the dough.

4. Divide the dough in half. On a lightly floured work surface, roll each piece of dough under your hands to form a thick log about 14 inches long. Place one log on each baking sheet.

5. Bake, switching the baking sheets from top to bottom and front to back after 45 minutes, until the logs are firm to the touch, approximately 1½ hours. Watch the bottoms of the logs, as many ovens will brown them too quickly. If this happens, put another cookie sheet under each sheet (double panning).

6. Remove the sheets from the oven. Slide the parchment paper with the logs onto a cutting board. While still hot, use a serrated knife to carefully cut the cookies into ½-inch-thick slices. Arrange the cookies on the baking sheets, laying them flat.

7. Bake until the biscotti are golden brown, about 10 minutes. Transfer to wire cooling racks and cool completely. (The cookies can be stored at room temperature in an airtight container for up to 2 weeks.)

Chocolate-Hazelnut Biscotti: Substitute ⅔ cup toasted, peeled, and coarsely chopped hazelnuts and ⅓ cup chopped bittersweet chocolate for the raisins and pistachios.

Pine Nut–Orange Biscotti: Substitute ⅓ cup toasted pine nuts and ⅓ cup chopped candied orange peel for the raisins and pistachios.

Classic Almond–Anise Biscotti: Substitute 1 cup coarsely chopped toasted almonds and 1 tablespoon aniseed for the raisins and pistachios.

Baker's Note

DO NOT CREAM the butter and sugar too long or you will incorporate too much air into the dough. Biscotti should be dense and crisp.

Brown Sugar Thins

MAKES ABOUT 7 DOZEN
COOKIES

Julia Cookenboo

Ideal for making cut-out cookies with children (the dough is so forgiving that it can be rolled out repeatedly), this is an easy recipe with a rich brown sugar flavor. Because it contains more molasses, you'll get more pronounced flavor with dark brown sugar, but you can use light brown if you wish.

2¼ cups all-purpose flour
¼ teaspoon salt
½ pound (2 sticks) unsalted butter, softened
1 cup packed dark brown sugar
1 teaspoon vanilla extract

1. Position racks in the center and top third of the oven and preheat to 300°F. Line two large baking sheets with parchment paper or lightly butter them.

2. Sift the flour and salt into a medium bowl; set aside.

3. In the bowl of a heavy-duty stand mixer fitted with the paddle attachment, beat the butter, brown sugar, and vanilla on medium speed until the mixture is light in color and texture, about 3 minutes. Reduce the speed to low and gradually add the flour mixture to make a smooth dough. Gather the dough into a smooth, flat disk.

4. Working with about one-fourth of the dough at a time, roll it out on a lightly floured work surface until ⅛ inch thick. Do not use too much flour. Occasionally turn the dough or slide a long metal spatula under it to be sure that it isn't sticking. Using a soft pastry brush, brush off any excess flour from the surface of the dough.

5. Using a cookie cutter dipped in flour, cut out the cookies, starting at the edges of the rolled-out dough and working your way into the center (this minimizes waste). Arrange the cookies about 1 inch apart on the prepared sheets. Gather up the scraps and briefly knead together. Let stand for about 5 minutes before rolling out again.

6. Bake, switching the position of the sheets from top to bottom and front to back halfway through baking, until the cookies are a shade deeper brown than the raw dough, about 15 minutes. Cool on the sheets for 3 minutes, then transfer to wire cooling racks and cool completely. (The cookies can be stored at room temperature in an airtight container for up to 5 days.)

Baker's Notes

THE DOUGH CAN be prepared, tightly wrapped in plastic wrap, and refrigerated for up to 5 days. Let it come to room temperature before rolling out. If the dough cracks during rolling, it is too cold; let it stand for a few more minutes, then try again.

Dipping the cookie cutter in flour every time you cut out a cookie helps release the dough from the cutter.

Be sure to brush excess flour off the dough before cutting. Use a soft brush, as stiff bristles could scrape the dough.

Coconut-Pecan Macaroons

MAKES ABOUT 5 DOZEN
COOKIES

Robert Morocco

Macaroon lovers have very strong feelings on the perfect specimen. This recipe, with its unusual addition of pecans, may raise a few eyebrows, but it always gets great reviews.

4 cups (10 ounces) unsweetened desiccated coconut

1¼ cups (5 ounces) pecans, coarsely chopped

1½ cups sugar

¾ cup plus 2 tablespoons egg whites (about 6 large)

3 tablespoons light corn syrup

1 teaspoon vanilla extract

¼ teaspoon salt

1. Position racks in the center and top third of the oven and preheat to 350°F. Line two large baking sheets with parchment paper or lightly butter the sheets.

2. Combine the coconut and pecans in a large bowl and set aside.

3. Combine the sugar, egg whites, corn syrup, vanilla, and salt in a heavy-bottomed small saucepan. Stirring constantly, heat over low heat just until hot to the touch (dip in your finger to check). Pour over the coconut and pecans and mix well.

4. Drop by rounded tablespoons onto the prepared sheets, spacing them about 2 inches apart. Bake, switching the position of the sheets from top to bottom and front to back halfway through baking, until golden brown, about 17 minutes. Transfer to wire cooling racks and cool completely. (The cookies can be stored at room temperature in airtight containers for up to 1 week.)

Double Chocolate Brownies

1 cup walnut halves or pieces

5 ounces semisweet chocolate, finely chopped

2 ounces unsweetened chocolate, finely chopped

8 tablespoons (1 stick) unsalted butter, cut into bits

1 cup sugar

1 teaspoon vanilla extract

½ teaspoon salt

2 large eggs, at room temperature

7 tablespoons all-purpose flour

MAKES 16 BROWNIES

Robert Morocco

A brownie that is plenty chocolaty (but not bitter) will have broad appeal to chocolate lovers young and old. For added flavor, try to make the time to toast the walnuts.

1. Position a rack in the lower third of the oven and preheat to 325°F. Line a 9-inch square baking pan with foil, letting the excess hang over the sides. Do not butter and flour the pan.

2. Spread the walnuts on a baking sheet. Bake, stirring occasionally, until lightly toasted and fragrant, 7 to 10 minutes. Cool completely and coarsely chop if desired.

3. Melt the semisweet chocolate, unsweetened chocolate, and butter in a medium stainless steel bowl set in a skillet of hot, not simmering, water, stirring frequently until the mixture is smooth. Remove from the heat. Using a wooden spoon, stir in the sugar, vanilla, and salt. One at a time, beat in the eggs, mixing well after each addition. Add the flour and stir briskly for 1 minute, or until the batter is smooth and shiny. Stir in the walnuts. Spread evenly in the pan.

4. Bake until the top is slightly puffed, shiny, and cracked and a toothpick inserted in the center comes out with a few moist crumbs, about 40 minutes.

5. Transfer to a wire cooling rack and cool completely in the pan. For the neatest cuts, freeze for 1 hour. Lift up the foil to loosen from the pan, and invert onto a work surface. Peel off the foil. Turn the uncut brownie right side up. Using a sharp knife, cut into 16 squares, wiping the knife clean between cuts. (The brownies can be stored in an airtight container for up to 3 days.)

Chocolate-Hazelnut Meringue Cookies

MAKES ABOUT 40 COOKIES

Julia Cookenboo

Utterly simple and utterly irresistible, these cookies melt in your mouth.

1½ cups (8 ounces) hazelnuts, toasted

8 ounces bittersweet chocolate, coarsely chopped (1⅓ cups)

1 cup sugar

3 large egg whites

¼ teaspoon salt

1 teaspoon vanilla extract

1. Position racks in the center and upper third of the oven and preheat to 250°F. Line two large baking sheets with parchment paper.

2. In a food processor fitted with the metal blade, pulse the hazelnuts, chocolate, and 2 tablespoons of the sugar until chopped into ¼-inch pieces. Set aside.

3. In the bowl of a heavy-duty stand mixer fitted with the whisk attachment, whip the whites on low speed until foamy. Add the salt, increase the speed to medium-high, and whip just until soft peaks form. With the machine running, slowly add the remaining sugar, beating until the peaks are stiff and shiny. Remove the bowl from the mixer. Using a rubber spatula, fold in the hazelnut mixture and the vanilla.

4. Using a dessert spoon, drop 1½-inch-wide mounds of the meringue onto the prepared sheets, spacing them about 1 inch apart. Bake until the cookies are firm but not browned, about 45 minutes. Cool completely on the baking sheets. (The cookies can be stored at room temperature in airtight containers for up to 5 days.)

Baker's Note

THE KEY TO these cookies is low oven temperature. If the cookies are browning, the oven is too hot and should be turned down.

The Best Chocolate Chip Cookies

2 cups all-purpose flour

1 teaspoon baking soda

1 teaspoon salt

12 tablespoons (1½ sticks) unsalted butter, softened

1 cup packed light or dark brown sugar

¾ cup granulated sugar

2 large eggs, at room temperature

1 teaspoons vanilla extract

1¼ cups semisweet chocolate chips

¾ cup (3 ounces) coarsely chopped toasted nuts
    (your favorite), optional

MAKES ABOUT 6 DOZEN
COOKIES

Tami Jewett

Here is the winner of our chocolate chip cookie tasting, originating from Beth, the sister of member Tami Jewett. They are crisp around the edges and chewy in the center.

1. Position racks in the center and top third of the oven and preheat to 350°F. Line two large baking sheets with parchment paper.

2. Sift the flour, baking soda, and salt into a medium bowl. Set aside.

3. In the bowl of a heavy-duty stand mixer fitted with the paddle attachment, cream the butter, brown sugar, and granulated sugar on medium speed until well blended, about 2 minutes; scrape down the bowl.

4. Beat the eggs and vanilla in a small bowl. Add to the butter mixture and blend well; scrape the bowl again. On low speed, add the flour mixture and beat until just mixed; scrape down the bowl. Add the chocolate and optional nuts and mix until incorporated into the dough.

5. Drop rounded tablespoons of the dough onto the prepared sheets, spacing them about 2 inches apart. Bake, switching the position of the sheets from top to bottom and front to back halfway through baking, until the cookies are golden brown but the centers seem slightly underdone, about 13 minutes. Do not overbake or the cookies will be crisp throughout instead of chewy. Cool for a few minutes on the baking sheets, then transfer to wire cooling racks to cool completely. The cookies will crinkle as they cool. (Store at room temperature in airtight containers for up to 1 week.)

Baker's Note

THESE COOKIES ALLOW for many variations. Dark brown sugar will give a deeper flavor. Use any favorite nut—walnuts, hazelnuts, or almonds all are delicious. Use the best chocolate chips you can find. Coarsely chopped semisweet or bittersweet dark chocolate or white chocolate makes a great alternative to the semisweet chips.

*The Cookie
Collection*

Crispy Oatmeal Wafers

**MAKES ABOUT 4 DOZEN
COOKIES**

Julia Cookenboo

Another cookie that is fun to make with kids—they'll love flattening the dough with a glass. Be sure to use quick oats, rather than the old-fashioned variety; the latter will not produce the right texture.

1½ cups all-purpose flour
1 teaspoon baking soda
1 teaspoon ground cinnamon
½ teaspoon salt
½ pound (2 sticks) unsalted butter, softened, plus additional
  for buttering the glass
1 cup granulated sugar, plus additional for forming the
  cookies
½ cup packed dark brown sugar
1 large egg
1 teaspoon vanilla extract
1½ cups quick-cooking oats
¾ cup (3 ounces) finely chopped walnuts or pecans

1. Sift the flour, baking soda, cinnamon, and salt into a medium bowl. Set aside.

2. In the bowl of a heavy-duty stand mixer fitted with the paddle attachment, cream the butter, granulated sugar, and brown sugar on medium-high speed until light and fluffy, about 3 minutes. Beat in the egg and vanilla. On low speed, gradually beat in the flour mixture. Add the oats and nuts and mix until combined. Cover the bowl with plastic wrap and refrigerate for 1 hour.

3. Position racks in the center and top third of the oven and preheat to 350°F. Line two large baking sheets with parchment paper.

4. Roll pieces of dough between your palms into walnut-sized pieces. Arrange about 2 inches apart on the prepared sheets. Butter the bottom of a wide-bottomed drinking glass. Place about ⅓ cup granulated sugar in a small bowl. Dip the bottom of the glass into the sugar and flatten each cookie into a 1½- to 2-inch-wide disk, sugaring the glass each time and buttering the bottom as needed.

5. Bake, switching the positions of the cookie sheets from top to bottom and front to back halfway during baking time, until the cookies are evenly browned, 18 to 20 minutes. Cool briefly on the sheets, then transfer to wire cooling racks to cool completely. (The cookies can be stored at room temperature in airtight containers for up to 1 week.)

Diamonds

12 tablespoons (1½ sticks) unsalted butter, softened

½ cup granulated sugar

½ teaspoon vanilla extract

1 large egg, separated

1¾ cups all-purpose flour

⅛ teaspoon salt

½ cup pearl sugar, approximately, for rolling cookies

1. In the bowl of a heavy-duty stand mixer fitted with the paddle attachment, beat the butter, granulated sugar, and vanilla on low speed just until blended, about 1 minute. Beat in the egg yolk (reserve the white for brushing over the dough). Add the flour and salt and beat just until the dough is very smooth, no longer than 2 minutes. Do not overbeat. Cover the bowl with plastic wrap and refrigerate for 30 minutes.

2. Divide the dough in half. Roll each portion of dough into a 7- to 8-inch log about 1¼ inches in diameter. Wrap each log in plastic wrap and refrigerate until completely chilled.

3. Position racks in the center and top third of the oven and preheat to 350°F. Line two large baking sheets with parchment paper or lightly butter them.

4. Beat the egg white in a small bowl until foamy. Unwrap the logs and brush lightly with the beaten white. Spread the pearl sugar in a shallow dish. Roll each log in the dish to cover with the pearl sugar, lightly pressing the dough into the sugar so it adheres.

5. Using a thin, sharp knife, slice the dough into ½-inch-thick rounds. Arrange the rounds about 1 inch apart on the prepared sheets. Bake until the cookies are lightly browned around the edges, about 13 minutes.

6. Transfer to wire cooling racks to cool completely. (The cookies can be stored at room temperature in airtight containers for up to 5 days.)

MAKES ABOUT 3 DOZEN COOKIES

Julia Cookenboo

These cookies come from France, where they are called diamants *(diamonds), as the pearl sugar coating looks like precious stones. Pearl sugar, which has large round crystals that won't dissolve during baking, can be purchased at stores that cater to specialty bakers and by mail-order (see Sources, page 343). If you can't find it, use rock candy, coarsely crushed under a rolling pin.*

Baker's Note

THIS IS ANOTHER dough that must not be overbeaten. If the butter and sugar are creamed until light and fluffy, the logs will crumble when sliced and will spread too much during baking.

The Cookie Collection

Apricot Streusel Bars

MAKES THREE DOZEN BARS

Patti Murray

Patti Murray contributed this recipe for her favorite fruit-filled bars. You get a lot of cookies with very little effort—they can be in the oven in no time. They are very versatile, too, as the variations at the end of the recipe attest.

1 cup dried apricots, coarsely chopped

1 cup granulated sugar

1½ cups water

2 cups all-purpose flour

2 cups old-fashioned or quick-cooking oats

1 cup packed dark brown sugar

1 teaspoon baking soda

½ pound (2 sticks) unsalted butter, melted

1 teaspoon vanilla extract

Confectioners' sugar, for garnish

1. In a medium saucepan, bring the apricots, granulated sugar, and water to boil over medium-high heat, stirring often. Reduce the heat to medium-low and simmer, uncovered, stirring often, until the fruit has softened and thickened into a puree, 20 to 30 minutes. Remove from the heat and cool completely.

2. Position a rack in the center of the oven and preheat to 350°F. Lightly butter a 13 × 9-inch baking pan. Line the bottom and short sides of the pan with a 14-inch-long sheet of aluminum foil, folding the excess foil back to make handles. Butter and flour the foil and the long sides of the pan, tapping out the excess flour.

3. In a large bowl, thoroughly mix the flour, oats, brown sugar, and baking soda. Add the melted butter and vanilla and stir well. The mixture will be crumbly. Press half of the oat mixture evenly into the prepared pan and spread with the cooled apricot mixture. Crumble the remaining oat mixture on top and gently pat into the filling.

4. Bake until the streusel is golden brown and looks set in the center, about 30 minutes.

5. Transfer to a wire cooling rack and cool completely (allow a couple of hours for this). Lifting by the foil handles, remove from the pan. Peel back the foil. Cut into 3 × 1-inch bars. Sift confectioners' sugar over the tops of the bars. (The cookies can be stored at room temperature in airtight containers for up to 1 week.)

Date Streusel Bars: Substitute 1 cup coarsely chopped dates for the apricots.

Prune Streusel Bars: Substitute 1 cup coarsely chopped pitted prunes for the apricots.

Baker's Note ●

TO CHOP THE apricots, snip them into pieces using lightly oiled kitchen shears or a large chef's knife. Don't try to do this job in a food processor.

Fresh Ginger-Spice Cookies

MAKES ABOUT 4 DOZEN
COOKIES

Barbara Mooradian

Not your grandmother's gingerbread cookie, these are made extra flavorful with such additional ingredients as brewed coffee, fresh ginger, and ground white pepper. Thanks to Baker's Dozen member Barbara Mooradian of Hawaii for this sensational recipe, which bakes into crisp rounds. Allow 4 hours for the dough to chill.

2½ cups all-purpose flour

1 teaspoon baking soda

1 teaspoon ground ginger

1 teaspoon ground cinnamon

½ teaspoon ground cloves

½ teaspoon ground allspice

¼ teaspoon ground white pepper

⅛ teaspoon ground cardamom

¼ teaspoon salt

2 tablespoons cool brewed strong coffee

⅓ cup unsulfured molasses

1 tablespoon minced peeled fresh ginger

¾ cup plus ½ cup sugar

12 tablespoons (1½ sticks) unsalted butter, softened

1. Sift the flour, baking soda, ground ginger, cinnamon, cloves, allspice, white pepper, cardamom, and salt into a medium bowl; set aside. In a glass measuring cup, whisk the coffee, molasses, and fresh ginger; set aside.

2. In the bowl of a heavy-duty stand mixer fitted with the paddle attachment, beat ¾ cup sugar with the butter on medium speed until well combined, about 1 minute. Scrape down the sides and bottom of the bowl with a rubber spatula. In thirds, starting with the flour mixture, alternately add the flour and coffee mixtures, occasionally scraping the bottom and sides of the bowl. Scrape the dough onto a 16 × 12-inch piece of parchment. Following the instructions on page 200, use a ruler to compress the dough into an evenly shaped 11- to 12-inch-long log. Chill the dough until very firm, at least 4 hours or overnight.

3. Position racks in the center and top third of the oven and preheat to 350°F. Line two large baking sheets with parchment paper (these cookies bake best on parchment paper) or butter and flour the baking sheets.

4. Place the remaining ½ cup sugar in a small bowl. Unwrap the dough and cut into ¼-inch-thick rounds. Gently dip both sides of each cookie in the sugar. Arrange the cookies about 2 inches apart on the prepared sheets. Bake, switching the position of the sheets from top to bottom and front to back halfway during baking, until the edges of the cookies are barely browned, about 14 minutes.

5. Cool on the sheets for 2 minutes, then transfer to wire cooling racks and cool completely. (The cookies can be stored at room temperature in airtight containers for up to 1 week.)

Baker's Notes

SCRAPE THE MIXING bowl well and often when making the dough. The dough can be refrigerated for up to 2 days before cutting and baking.

To store fresh ginger, peel and slice the leftover knob. Place in a small jar, add enough vodka to cover, and close tightly. Refrigerated, the ginger will keep for about 8 weeks.

If the molasses is sluggish and difficult to pour, remove the lid and microwave for about 15 seconds on high power.

Lemon Stars

MAKES ABOUT 3½ DOZEN
3-INCH COOKIES

Julia Cookenboo

Looking for a great sugar cookie? Try this one, which gets added flavor from lemon zest and juice.

½ pound (2 sticks) unsalted butter, softened

½ cup granulated sugar

1 large egg yolk

1 tablespoon grated lemon zest

½ teaspoon vanilla extract

1¾ cups plus 2 tablespoons all-purpose flour

¼ teaspoon salt

ICING

1 cup confectioners' sugar, sifted

1 tablespoon milk, or as needed

1½ teaspoons fresh lemon juice

Yellow sanding sugar, for decorating

1. To make the dough, in the bowl of a heavy-duty stand mixer fitted with the paddle attachment, beat the butter and granulated sugar on medium speed until light in color, about 3 minutes. Beat in the yolk, lemon zest, and vanilla. Scrape the bottom and sides of the bowl.

2. In a small bowl, whisk the flour and salt to combine. On low speed, gradually add the flour mixture to the creamed mixture and mix just until smooth.

3. Turn the dough out onto a large piece of plastic wrap. Shape into a thick, flat disk and wrap in the plastic. Refrigerate until the dough is chilled and firm, about 2 hours or overnight. (If the dough is chilled longer than 2 hours, let stand at room temperature for about 10 minutes before rolling.)

4. Position racks in the center and top third of the oven and preheat to 350°F. Line two large baking sheets with parchment paper or lightly butter the sheets.

5. Unwrap the disk and place on a lightly floured work surface. Dust the top of the dough with flour and roll out until the dough is a little more than ⅛ inch thick. If the dough cracks, it is too cold; let stand for a few minutes and try again. Occasionally turn the dough and slide a metal icing spatula underneath it to be sure it isn't sticking. Using a 3-inch-wide star-shaped cookie cutter, cut out the cookies. Arrange them about 1 inch apart on the prepared sheets. Gather up the scraps, knead briefly, roll, and cut out more cookies. Repeat until all of the dough is used.

6. Bake, switching the positions of the sheets from top to bottom and front to back halfway during baking, until the cookies are lightly browned around the edges, about 15 minutes. Cool on the sheets for 2 minutes, then transfer to wire cooling racks to cool completely.

7. To make the icing, whisk the confectioners' sugar, milk, and lemon juice in a small bowl until smooth.

8. Thinly spread the icing on the cooled cookies. Sprinkle with the sanding sugar before the icing sets. Let stand until the icing is set. (The cookies can be stored in an airtight container for up to 1 week.)

Baker's Notes

FOR CLASSIC SUGAR cookies, omit the lemon zest. For the icing, use a bit more milk instead of the lemon juice.

This is a great dough for doubling to make a mountain of cut-out cookies.

For a fast, professional way to ice the cookies, thin the icing with additional lemon juice until it is the consistency of heavy cream. One at a time, dip the cookies face side down in the icing. Lift the cookie out of the icing and draw it along the lip of the bowl to remove excess icing. Ice a few cookies at a time, then sprinkle with sugar before the icing sets.

French Noisette Shells

MAKES ABOUT 3 DOZEN COOKIES

Robert Morocco

The secret to this recipe is browned butter, which adds a distinctive nuttiness to complement the almonds. The batter must be chilled before filling the molds, so allow time (it will keep for up to 4 days). You'll need madeleine molds to make these cookies. If you don't have them already, they're worth the investment, as they create gorgeous shell-shaped cookies that are sure to get applause.

½ pound (2 sticks) unsalted butter
¾ cup all-purpose flour
½ cup whole natural almonds
1¼ cups sugar
¾ cup plus 2 tablespoons egg whites (about 6 large)
Melted butter and all-purpose flour, for the pans

1. In a heavy-bottomed medium saucepan, bring the butter to boil over medium heat. When the foam rises to the top, stir the butter. Continue cooking until the foam rises again. Stir again. There should be tiny browned bits of milk solids at the bottom of the butter. If not, continue cooking until they form. Carefully pour the hot butter through a fine wire strainer into a medium bowl.

2. In a food processor fitted with the metal blade, process the flour and almonds until the almonds are finely ground.

3. In the bowl of a heavy-duty stand mixer fitted with the paddle attachment, mix the almond mixture, sugar, and egg whites on low speed just until blended. Pour in the warm butter and mix on low speed just until well blended; do not overmix. Cover the bowl with plastic wrap and refrigerate until the batter is completely cooled, at least 30 minutes, or up to 4 days.

4. Position a rack in the center of the oven and preheat to 350°F. Brush the molds in a 12-mold madeleine pan with melted butter and thoroughly dust with flour. Turn the pan upside down and tap to remove all excess flour, but be sure each mold is completely covered with a fine film of butter and flour.

5. Fill each mold almost full with the cold batter. Bake until the cookies are lightly browned, about 15 minutes. Immediately invert the cookies to unmold them, then cool completely on wire cooling racks. Cool the mold, and repeat with the remaining batter. (The cookies can be stored in an airtight container for up to 5 days.)

Chocolate Noisette Shells: Line a baking sheet with wax paper. Melt and quick-temper 6 ounces semisweet chocolate (see page 000). Tilt the bowl so the chocolate collects in a deep pool. Dip each cookie at a diagonal so the chocolate reaches about halfway up the side. Scrape off any excess chocolate on the lip of the bowl. Place the cookies on the wax paper and refrigerate briefly until the chocolate sets.

Chocolate Noisette Sandwiches: In a small saucepan, heat ¼ cup heavy cream to simmering. Remove from the heat and add 2 ounces finely chopped bittersweet chocolate. Pour into a bowl and let the ganache stand until cooled and thickened, about 1 hour. Sandwich 2 noisette shells back to back, using the ganache as a filling.

Baker's Notes ●

MADELEINE MOLDS CAN be purchased at well-stocked kitchenware stores or by mail-order (see Sources, page 343). They are often made of heavy black steel, but plain steel and nonstick versions exist. The most common pan has 12 shell-shaped molds. They are pricey, so we assume that you will own only one pan.

If you use dark pans, place them in the preheated 350°F oven, then immediately reduce the oven temperature to 325°F.

Do not wash steel madeleine pans without a nonstick surface with soap and water; just rinse them off under hot water and blot them dry with paper towels. Each time you use the pan, the butter will season it and make subsequent batches of cookies less likely to stick.

When grinding nuts for a recipe, process them with flour or sugar, which acts as a buffer to keep the nuts from releasing too much oil.

Lemon–Poppy Seed Shortbread

MAKES 40 COOKIES

Julia Cookenboo

Even a classic cookie like shortbread can use a makeover every now and then. Poppy seeds and lemon make these into extraordinary cookies to enjoy with your favorite hot beverage. Purists will love the Classic Scottish Shortbread variation.

½ pound (2 sticks) unsalted butter, at room temperature
½ cup sugar
Grated zest of 2 lemons
¼ teaspoon salt
2 cups all-purpose flour
3 tablespoons poppy seeds

1. Position racks in the center and top third of the oven and preheat to 300°F. Line two baking sheets with parchment paper or lightly butter them.

2. In the bowl of a heavy-duty stand mixer fitted with the paddle attachment, beat the butter, sugar, lemon zest, and salt until the mixture is very light in color and texture, about 5 minutes. Reduce the speed to low. Add the flour and poppy seeds and mix until incorporated.

3. Turn out the dough onto a lightly floured work surface and divide it into 4 pieces. Gently form each piece of dough into a flat ½-inch-thick round. Arrange the rounds on the baking sheets and slightly flatten each one.

4. Bake, switching the positions of the sheets from top to bottom and front to back halfway through baking, until the rounds are firm in the middle, about 50 minutes. Remove from the oven and cut each round into 10 wedges. Separate the wedges and spread them out on the baking sheets. Return to the oven and bake until the tips of the cookies are firm, about 10 minutes.

5. Transfer to wire cooling racks and cool completely. (The cookies can be stored at room temperature in airtight containers for up to 1 week.)

Classic Scottish Shortbread: Omit the lemon zest and poppy seeds. Substitute ½ cup white rice flour (available at Asian markets and natural food stores) or cornstarch for an equal amount of the flour.

Baker's Note

THE ONLY LEAVENING in shortbread comes from beating air into the butter and sugar during creaming. Do not skimp on the creaming time; cream the mixture until it is quite pale.

Muffins, Popovers, Easy Quick Breads, and Doughnuts

Here are the Old Faithfuls of the baking world, the homespun recipes that bakers turn to again and again, not just because they're reliably delicious but because they're simple to make. Muffins, biscuits, scones, and popovers can be on the table in less than an hour after you think of making them, and you don't even have to take out the electric mixer. Sweet quick breads, such as banana bread, may take time in the oven, but they sure beat the clock when it comes to mixing time. Granted, doughnuts may require a bit more advance planning. But think of it this way: If the freshly made doughnuts at the local shop are tempting, imagine how much better your homemade dunkers will be!

In contrast to slow-rising yeast-leavened breads, most quick breads get their lift from baking powder, baking soda, or both (an exception being yeast-leavened doughnuts, which cook quickly in oil, and popovers, which get a boost from eggs). They can be mixed with a big spoon, without the strenuous kneading required by yeast breads. Sure, their flavor and texture are different from those of yeast breads, but in its own way, their tender sweetness is just as good.

John Phillip Carroll was the chapter chairperson and contributed most of the recipes, with additional recipes by Carolyn B. Weil.

Ingredients for Quick Breads

Flour | These recipes use all-purpose flour, measured by the dip-and-sweep method. For quick breads, flour is rarely sifted. However, sifting does combine the ingredients better than stirring. Sifting also aerates the dry ingredients, making quick breads that are a little lighter and more finely textured.

Eggs | Use large eggs, at room temperature. If the eggs are cold, they can stiffen the butter in the batter and make it difficult to blend with the other ingredients.

Fats | Many bakers have a preference for butter in all baked goods, but some quick breads in this book call for shortening or even vegetable oil. This is because shortening has less water than butter and makes quick breads with the finest crumb and lightest texture.

Butter is good in quick breads where the wonderful buttery taste is important. As far as the texture of the bread is concerned, you can use salted or unsalted butter, but if you use salted, reduce any salt in the recipe by ¼ teaspoon. What does matter is that your butter tastes good and fresh, because the stale flavor of butter that has languished in the refrigerator will ruin your quick bread. Whenever you have a high proportion of a single ingredient (and quick breads usually have plenty of butter), you can't hide its flavor, good or bad.

Vegetable shortening adds little flavor of its own—if you use shortening, it is for the texture it lends to the finished baked good. And its soft consistency at room temperature makes it easy to use anytime. In breads that are strongly flavored, where the taste of butter would be masked by other ingredients (such as the Kona Inn Banana Bread on page 240, shortening is actually preferred. It also makes great biscuits.

Vegetable oil can be found in some quick bread recipes. If a recipe uses too much, it can produce a heavy, greasy final product. Use a flavorless, light-bodied oil, such as corn oil, and not peanut or olive oil.

Sweeteners | Sugar sweetens quick breads and helps makes them tender. Like salt, it also acts to bring other flavors into balance. Most quick breads, especially loaves and muffins, are sweet—that is their nature. Do not arbitrarily cut back on the amount of sugar in a recipe, or you could end up with a dry, compact quick bread.

Leavenings | Don't make the typical mistake of thinking that there isn't much difference between baking powder and baking soda. About all they have in common is the word "baking," so do not substitute one for the other or omit one from a recipe that uses both. For more information on baking powder and baking soda, see page 000.

Equipment for Quick Breads

Muffin pans | A muffin pan (sometimes called by its older term, muffin tin) used to mean just one thing: the standard pan with six to 12 cups, each 2¾ inches wide by 1½ inches deep, molded from a single metal plaque. Now there are jumbo muffin pans, mini muffin pans, and muffin pans that bake the batter into wide, thin rounds to simulate a crusty muffin top (to many, the best part of the muffin). The recipes in this book are for the standard pan.

Muffins pans are made from a variety of metals. We prefer the shiny, fairly light-weight aluminum pans—they give the muffins a thin outer crust. Heavier pans, often made of steel with a nonstick coating, are also reliable. Passionate home bakers may want to try the flexible silicone muffin pans that are available at specialty kitchenware and restaurant supply stores. They're expensive, but lightweight and very sturdy. Keep in mind that dark pans (gray or black) hold more heat than light-colored ones, so reduce the oven temperature by 25°F as soon as the muffins go in the oven, or your crust may get overbrowned.

Loaf pans | The two most common sizes of loaf pans are 8½ × 4½ × 2½ inches (6-cup capacity) and 9 × 5 × 3 inches (8-cup capacity). With only ½ inch difference in each dimension, it is surprising to find that there is a 2-cup difference in the capacities of the two pans. Do not substitute one for the other, or your cakes will not rise properly. Shiny heavy-gauge aluminum pans are the best bet—aluminum foil pans are too thin for regular use, but they can stand in during the busy holiday baking season. Some bakers like Pyrex loaf pans. If using Pyrex or dark metal pans, the oven temperature should be reduced by 25°F as soon as the pans go into the oven.

Popover pans | Some recipes for popovers simply call for muffin pans, but the cups need to be well separated to allow the air circulation that helps the popovers puff. Look for sturdy metal popover pans with a ½-cup capacity, about 2¼ inches deep and 2 inches across.

Baking sheets | Heavy, shiny metal baking sheets are always the best choice. We are partial to 17 × 12-inch half-sheet pans, along with parchment paper or silicone baking mats to eliminate sticking.

Techniques for Quick Breads

IF THERE IS ONE RULE for mixing all quick breads, it is to avoid overmixing. Remember that the more flour is mixed with liquid, the stronger the gluten structure, and the stronger the gluten, the less tender the bread.

Muffins,
Popovers,
Easy Quick
Breads, and
Doughnuts

225

Preparing the Pans

In almost every quick bread and muffin recipe, the pan is greased before adding the batter. You can use butter or shortening as long as you apply a thin film of the fat. The butter should be well softened, but not melted. A pastry brush (one with a cylinder-shaped cluster of bristles works best), a wad of paper towel, or even your fingers can be used to apply the fat. If you wish, use nonstick vegetable oil cooking spray (especially dandy for greasing muffin tins), but use restraint. Again, you want a light film.

Mixing Muffins

When making muffin batter, stir just until the ingredients are evenly moistened. There shouldn't be any unblended streaks of flour or puddles of liquid. It is okay if the batter looks a bit lumpy, because the little lumps will disappear in baking. Remember, a muffin is not a fine-textured cake; a muffin is coarser but tender. "Pebbly" is a word sometimes used to describe a muffin's texture and appearance, conveying the message that a muffin isn't supposed to look polished. Tiny irregular cracks in the top aren't a flaw—it's the nature of many quick breads to crack a little (or a lot) on top.

Muffin cups can vary in size, wreaking havoc with the yield of the recipe. For standard cupcake-sized muffins, the cups should be filled no more than two-thirds full. If you prefer heftier muffins with tall crowns, fill the cups to the top, and be sure to coat the surfaces between the cups with cooking oil or nonstick spray, as the batter will overflow and will stick if they aren't greased. Any empty muffin cups should be filled with a couple of tablespoons of water to ensure even baking—empty cups will overheat and burn the adjacent muffins. On the other hand, if you have leftover batter, it can stand at room temperature while the first batch is baking.

To transfer the batter into the pan, the preferred tool of most bakers is an ice cream scoop, which makes neat, slightly heaped spheres that bake into muffins with a gentle dome. You can also use a dry-volume measuring cup to get the sticky batter neatly into the pan, or a large spoon.

Mixing Biscuits and Scones

These two quick breads share a technique with pie and tart dough: cutting fat into the flour before adding the liquid. A pastry blender is the quickest, but by no means the only, way to accomplish this easy task. Just remember, as with pastry dough, the idea is to keep the fat particles separate and coated with flour, not melted and absorbed into the flour.

To blend the fat and flour with a pastry blender, plunge the pastry blender into the bowl and through the ingredients. Make a series of circular, downward motions around the sides and bottom of the bowl so the pastry blender works or cuts the fat into the flour.

Use the blender to scrape around the sides of the bowl occasionally, and if the mixture masses on the wires, scrape them off with your fingers and back into the bowl. Continue plunging the pastry blender through the flour and all around the bowl so that the bits of fat get worked into the flour.

To blend the fat and flour with your fingers, plunge your fingers into the bowl, right into the ingredients. Rub the fingers of each hand against their respective thumbs, as if you were snapping all of your fingers at once. Work quickly with the snapping motion, and lift your hands often, thus rubbing the fat into the flour between your fingers, then letting it fall back into the bowl. Use a light touch. Have your fingers and hands lift the flour and fat so you do most of the rubbing above the mixture, and let the particles fall back as they are combined.

To blend the fat and flour with two knives, hold a table knife in each hand, grasping them firmly by the handles, blade side down and at about a 45-degree angle. Plunge the knives into the flour and fat and rapidly pull them through the mixture and past one another so the blades scrape together as they pass in the bowl. Quickly cut the knives through the mixture until you reach the desired consistency.

For biscuits, when you have blended enough, there will be no visible pieces of shortening and the mixture will look dry and crumbly, with small irregular pieces about the size of coarse bread crumbs. For scones, the mixture will look mostly crumbly, with a fair amount of pea-sized bits of butter.

Add the liquid all at once, and stir just until the ingredients have formed a soft, shaggy dough. Do not overmix. Turn the dough out onto a lightly floured work surface. It will seem very sticky, but don't add too much flour, or the finished product will be tough. Flour your hands and pat out the dough into the dimensions directed in the recipe.

Mixing Sweet Quick Breads

When talking about sweet quick breads, perhaps the term "mixing" is misleading. They are really just stirred to barely combine the ingredients. These loaves are not supposed to be light and fluffy like cakes that are made from a base of creamed butter and sugar. However, they include enough fat and sugar to keep them moist and tender, if dense.

Storing Quick Breads

MUFFINS, BISCUITS, AND corn bread don't keep long; in fact, biscuits and corn bread are at their best warm from the oven. Popovers must be eaten right from the oven, before they fall (they still taste good after falling; they just don't look as nice). Wrapped in plastic wrap, muffins will keep for a day and sweet quick breads for up to 3 days. After that, they should be wrapped in an overwrap of aluminum foil, placed in a zip-lock bag, and frozen for up to 2 months. They will defrost in a few hours at room temperature.

Muffins,
Popovers,
Easy Quick
Breads, and
Doughnuts

227

Blueberry Muffins

MAKES ABOUT 12 MUFFINS

John Phillip Carroll

These are all that a blueberry muffin should be: sweet, fine-textured, and buttery. Fresh blueberries are best, but if you only have frozen, stir the solid, unthawed berries into the batter—defrosted blueberries will turn the batter purple. If the berries are covered with ice crystals, place them in a colander, run them briefly under cold running water to remove the ice, and pat them dry with paper towels.

2 cups all-purpose flour
¾ cup plus 1 teaspoon sugar
2½ teaspoons baking powder
1 teaspoon freshly grated nutmeg
1 teaspoon baking soda
½ teaspoon salt
¼ teaspoon ground cinnamon
1 cup buttermilk, at room temperature
8 tablespoons (1 stick) unsalted butter, melted
2 large eggs, at room temperature
½ teaspoon vanilla extract
1 cup fresh or unthawed frozen blueberries

1. Position a rack in the center of the oven and preheat to 400°F. Lightly spray twelve 2¾ × 1½-inch muffin cups with cooking spray.

2. Sift the flour, ¾ cup sugar, baking powder, nutmeg, baking soda, and salt through a wire sieve into a large bowl. In a small bowl, combine the remaining 1 teaspoon sugar and the cinnamon and set aside for the topping.

3. In a medium bowl, whisk the buttermilk, melted butter, eggs, and vanilla until you don't see any unblended egg. Add all at once to the flour mixture and stir just until combined. Scrape the bowl with a rubber spatula and stir just a couple of more times; don't overmix the batter. Gently fold in the blueberries.

4. Using a large spoon or ice cream scoop, divide the batter among the cups. Sprinkle the top of each muffin with the cinnamon sugar.

5. Bake until a wooden toothpick inserted into the centers of the muffins comes out clean and the tops spring back when pressed with your fingers, 15 to 20 minutes.

6. Transfer to a wire cooling rack or a heatproof surface and cool the muffins in the pan for 5 minutes. Remove the muffins from the pan. Serve warm or cooled to room temperature.

Apple or Pear Muffins: Substitute 1 cup peeled and diced (½-inch) tart cooking apples or Bosc pears for the blueberries.

Baker's Notes

COLD EGGS and milk would congeal the melted butter, so be sure that they are at room temperature to make a smooth batter that yields a light-textured muffin.

Start testing the muffins after 15 minutes, especially if they are baked in a dark muffin tin, which absorbs the heat and makes them bake more quickly.

Muffins don't really need to cool on a wire rack—any heatproof surface is fine. But do let the muffins cool for about 5 minutes in the pan, as they are very delicate when hot, and could break when removed from the pan. And remove the muffins after 5 or 10 minutes in the pan, or condensation will build up and make them soggy. The muffins can cool completely on paper towels if you don't want to use a cooling rack.

If you use frozen blueberries, they will chill the dough; bake for an additional few minutes.

Muffins,
Popovers,
Easy Quick
Breads, and
Doughnuts

229

Raisin-Bran Muffins

MAKES ABOUT 12 MUFFINS

John Phillip Carroll

Bran muffins can be heavy and dense. These are moist, tender, and pleasantly sweet, yet with a good dose of bran. Unlike other muffins, they remain fresh for several days.

1 cup whole wheat flour

1 teaspoon baking soda

½ teaspoon salt

1½ cups wheat bran, available at natural food stores and many supermarkets

1¼ cups buttermilk, whole or low-fat

2 large eggs, at room temperature

3 tablespoons vegetable or corn oil

¼ cup unsulfured molasses

¼ cup packed light brown sugar

½ cup raisins

1. Position a rack in the center of the oven and preheat to 400°F. Lightly spray twelve 2¾ × 1½-inch muffin cups with cooking spray.

2. Sift the flour, baking soda, and salt into a large bowl. Add the bran and whisk to combine well.

3. Whisk the buttermilk, eggs, oil, molasses, and brown sugar in a medium bowl until thoroughly blended. Pour into the bran mixture and stir just until moistened. Scrape down the bowl with a rubber spatula and fold in the raisins. The batter will be moist and fairly liquid. Spoon the batter into the prepared cups, filling them almost full.

4. Bake until a wooden toothpick inserted in the centers of the muffins comes out clean, 15 to 18 minutes.

5. Transfer to a wire cooling rack or a heatproof surface and cool the muffins in the pan for 5 minutes. Remove the muffins from the pan. Serve warm or cooled to room temperature.

Baker's Notes

SOME BRANDS of whole wheat flour are ground more coarsely than others. If bits of flour remain in the sifter, just add them to the flour in the bowl.

These muffins tend to stick to paper muffin liners, especially when warm.

Other dried fruits are good in bran muffins—try dried cranberries or blueberries.

Buttermilk Biscuits

2½ cups all-purpose flour
2 tablespoons sugar
2½ teaspoons baking powder
½ teaspoon baking soda
1 teaspoon salt
½ cup vegetable shortening
1 cup buttermilk, whole or low-fat

1. Position a rack in the center of the oven and preheat to 425°F.

2. Sift the flour, sugar, baking powder, baking soda, and salt into a large bowl. Cut in the shortening with a pastry blender until there are no visible pieces of shortening and the mixture looks dry and crumbly, with the consistency of coarse bread crumbs. Add the buttermilk all at once and stir briskly with a fork to make a moist, sticky, ragged-looking dough.

3. Turn the dough out onto a well-floured work surface. Dust your hands with flour and knead the dough gently about 15 times, adding enough flour to keep the dough from feeling too sticky, just until it looks smooth and feels soft.

4. Pat the dough into a 12 × 6-inch rectangle about ½ inch thick. As you flatten the dough, lift it up occasionally to be sure it isn't sticking; dust under the dough with additional flour as needed.

5. *To cut square biscuits,* which are practical because there are no scraps, cut the dough into eighteen 2-inch squares. *To cut round biscuits,* use a 2-inch cookie cutter. When cutting, press straight down and do not twist the cutter. Gather up the scraps and gently knead and press them together just until smooth. Pat out the dough again to ½-inch thickness. Cut out more biscuits and place on the baking sheet. If you wish, gather up the remaining scraps and flatten to cut out a final few biscuits, but these won't look as nice or rise as high as the first two batches. *For soft, fluffy biscuits,* place them just touching each other in three or four rows in the center of the baking sheet. *For crustier, drier biscuits,* arrange them about 1 inch apart on the baking sheet.

6. Bake until the biscuits are almost doubled in height and lightly browned, 12 to 14 minutes. Transfer to a napkin-lined basket and serve immediately. (The biscuits can be baked up to 8 hours ahead, cooled, wrapped in aluminum foil, and kept at room temperature. Reheat in a pre-

MAKES 12 TO 18 BISCUITS

John Phillip Carroll

In spite of the variety of refrigerated biscuit doughs and "brown 'n' serve" biscuits available, take one bite of these and you'll know that nothing beats the homemade variety. The secret? A very gentle touch when mixing the dough.

*Muffins,
Popovers,
Easy Quick
Breads, and
Doughnuts*

231

heated 325°F oven for about 10 minutes. They can also be frozen, double-wrapped in foil, for up to 2 months. Reheat the frozen biscuits in a pre-heated 350°F oven for about 15 minutes.)

Baker's Notes

BUTTERMILK BISCUITS are tender and fine-textured, with a bit of a tang. Regular milk makes a biscuit that will look the same as the buttermilk variety, but it seems sweeter because it lacks the sour buttermilk flavor. If you want to use regular milk, substitute an additional ½ teaspoon baking powder for the baking soda.

This amount of buttermilk makes a soft, sticky dough, so expect to use a fair amount of flour on your hands and work surface to keep the dough manageable. It's better to work with a damp dough than a dry, crumbly one.

The brief kneading smooths out the dough while activating the gluten just enough to give the biscuits strength to rise. That's why drop biscuits (which aren't kneaded but simply dropped in heaping blobs onto the baking sheet) are squat, with a ragged look and coarse texture. We like to cut out our biscuits.

Forget the advice to use a drinking glass for cutting out round biscuits—the blunt edges compress the dough, keeping it from rising into flaky layers. The cutter should have sharp edges, so a standard cookie cutter is ideal. In a pinch, you can use an empty can (a large tomato paste can is the right size).

To bake the biscuits, a shiny, heavy-gauge metal baking pan is a must. If the pan is flimsy or discolored, you can end up with burned biscuit bottoms.

Biscuit dough should be cut out and baked immediately after mixing. However, to save time, the crumbly flour mixture can be prepared up to 12 hours ahead, covered tightly, and refrigerated. When ready to bake, just stir in the buttermilk.

Testing and Tasting . . . Biscuits

There is a myth that you must use a low-gluten, soft flour to make biscuits. This kind of flour (White Lily is a well-known brand) is readily available in the Southern states, where biscuits are the daily bread for many cooks. If you wish, try mixing half cake flour and half all-purpose flour to simulate soft flour. Your biscuits will be very tender indeed.

But in our testing, we found that we liked bleached all-purpose flour just as much as unbleached flour. In fact, the difference in quality between the two was negligible. Biscuit dough made with bleached flour was whiter and stickier than the dough made with unbleached flour (you may have to use more flour on the work surface to keep the dough from sticking). Unbleached flour absorbs liquid at a different rate than bleached (hence the stickiness of the all-purpose–flour dough), and the increased gluten makes the biscuits rise a bit higher, but only about ¼ inch more or so.

We tested the same biscuit recipe with two different fats, butter and shortening. The hands-down winner was shortening, which made the lightest, highest biscuits with a perfect texture. Biscuits made with butter were shorter, heavier, and not as ethereal. And, as almost every biscuit ever made has butter slathered on it before eating, why be concerned about having a buttery flavor in the biscuit, too?

When you want biscuits first thing in the morning, it may be tempting to mix up the biscuit dough the night before. Don't do it. As a test, we placed cut-out biscuits on a baking sheet, covered them with plastic wrap, and refrigerated them overnight before baking. They rose only half as much as the freshly made biscuits, and they were dense, heavy, and hockey puck–like.

The bottom line with biscuits seems to be that it isn't so much the kind of flour you use, but the kind of fat and how you handle the dough.

Muffins,
Popovers,
Easy Quick
Breads, and
Doughnuts

233

Buttermilk Currant Scones

MAKES 16 SCONES

John Phillip Carroll

Although they are similar in ingredients and technique, scones are sweeter and richer than biscuits, with a crisp exterior and a tender, creamy crumb. They are traditionally served with tea and accompanied by an array of jams and preserves.

3 cups all-purpose flour

½ cup plus 2 tablespoons sugar

2½ teaspoons baking powder

½ teaspoon baking soda

1 teaspoon salt

12 tablespoons (1½ sticks) unsalted butter, at room temperature

1 cup buttermilk

2 teaspoons vanilla extract

1 cup currants

1. Position a rack in the center of the oven and preheat the oven to 425°F.

2. Combine the flour, ½ cup sugar, baking powder, baking soda, and salt and sift them together into a large bowl. Cut the butter into tablespoon-sized pieces and add the flour mixture. Using a pastry blender or your fingertips, cut the butter into the dry ingredients until the mixture is the size of small bread crumbs.

3. Stir the buttermilk and vanilla together, then add all at once to the dry ingredients. Stir the mixture briskly with a fork just until a sticky, shaggy dough forms. Stir in the currants.

4. This is quite a soft dough, so flour your work surface generously and turn the dough out onto it. Flour your hands and knead the dough gently about a dozen times. Divide the dough in half, then, flouring your work surface and your hands as needed to keep the dough from sticking, pat each half into a circle about 8 inches across and ½ inch thick. Sprinkle each circle with 1 tablespoon of sugar and, using the flat of your hand, press the sugar gently into the surface of the dough. With a long, sharp knife, cut each round into 8 wedges. Transfer the wedges to a large ungreased baking sheet, placing them about ½ inch apart.

5. Bake until the scones are light brown and puffy, 15 to 18 minutes Remove from the oven and cool about 5 minutes on the baking sheet. Serve the scones warm.

Chocolate Scones: Substitute ⅓ cup mini chocolate chips for the currants.

Baker's Note

EXPECT A very soft, sticky dough. Add just enough flour to the work surface and your hands to keep the dough from sticking.

Muffins,
Popovers,
Easy Quick
Breads, and
Doughnuts

235

Popovers

John Phillip Carroll

For a bit of quick-bread drama, you can't beat popovers, puffed above their baking cups like little hot air balloons. You can serve them as a side dish with soups, salads, and roasts, or make them for breakfast to enjoy with butter and jam. They are easy to mix, and you can have the batter ready in just a couple of minutes. The only caveat is using the right pan. If you have one, a popover pan is, of course, ideal. But there are alternatives, so don't let the lack of a pan stop you from bringing these delicate puffs of pastry into your life.

1½ cups milk
3 large eggs
3 tablespoons vegetable or olive oil
1 teaspoon salt
½ teaspoon vanilla extract
1½ cups all-purpose flour

1. Position a rack in the center of the oven and preheat to 425°F. Spray the inside and top of 8 cups of a popover pan with nonstick cooking spray, even if the cups are nonstick. Don't fill the empty cups with water.

2. In a 2-quart glass measuring cup (the best choice because it makes the batter easy to pour into the cups) or a medium bowl, place the milk, eggs, oil, salt, vanilla, and flour in that order. Whisk just until blended and almost smooth, with a few tiny lumps. Scrape down the sides of the cup with a rubber spatula and whisk until the batter is completely smooth.

3. Pour the batter into the prepared cups, filling them a little more than half full. Place the pan on a shiny metal baking sheet (dark baking sheets will make the popover bottoms too dark).

4. Bake until the popovers are golden brown with dry surfaces and dramatically puffed, 25 to 30 minutes. Do not open the oven door during the first 20 minutes of baking, but begin to check for doneness after 25 minutes.

5. Remove from the cups, place in a napkin-lined basket, and serve immediately. They will keep their puff for a few minutes.

Baker's Notes

THE EGGS and milk can be chilled or at room temperature; use unbleached or all-purpose flour. These variables won't make any difference in the popovers.

The length of baking time will affect the texture of the popovers. If the popovers are baked just until golden, they will be soft and moist inside. If you prefer drier popovers, bake them for about 35 minutes. For even crisper popovers, pierce each one with the tip of a sharp knife (this releases the steam inside the popovers), return to the turned-off oven, and let them dry out for 5 to 10 minutes. Just be aware that the softer they are, the sooner they will deflate.

If you don't have a popover pan, you can bake them in individual 4- to 6-ounce ramekins placed a few inches apart on a baking sheet. Or pour the batter into the outside cups of two 12-cup muffin pans (popovers in the inner cups won't bake evenly), and fill the empty cups with a few tablespoons of water (this encourages even baking). Place on baking sheets and bake as directed. If both sheets won't fit on one rack in your oven, bake them on the center and bottom third racks.

Leftover popovers should be stored in a plastic bag and refrigerated. Reheat them on a baking sheet in a 350°F oven for about 7 minutes. They may reinflate a bit, but don't expect much.

Muffins,
Popovers,
Easy Quick
Breads, and
Doughnuts

237

Melt-in-Your-Mouth Corn Bread

MAKES 9 SERVINGS

John Phillip Carroll

Here's a good, basic corn bread that is soft, light, and slightly sweet. Corn bread styles vary from north to south—many southerners prefer a coarser, unsweetened version. But after trying numerous recipes, this one was our favorite.

1¼ cups all-purpose flour
1¼ cups finely ground yellow cornmeal
¼ cup sugar
2½ teaspoons baking powder
1 teaspoon salt
2 large eggs
1¼ cups milk
3 tablespoons corn or vegetable oil
3 tablespoons unsalted butter, melted

1. Position a rack in the center of the oven and preheat to 400°F. Lightly butter an 8-inch square metal baking pan.

2. Sift the flour, cornmeal, sugar, baking powder, and salt onto a piece of wax paper.

3. In a large bowl, whisk the eggs just until broken up. Add the milk, oil, and melted butter and whisk again until blended. Add the flour mixture and stir with a wooden spoon just until moistened. Scrape down the sides of the bowl with a rubber spatula and stir again just until blended. Don't worry about any small lumps in the batter. Scrape the batter into the prepared pan and smooth the top.

4. Bake until the top of the bread looks dry and slightly cracked and the center springs back when pressed gently with your fingers, 25 to 30 minutes.

5. Transfer to a wire cooling rack and let stand for 5 minutes. Cut the corn bread into squares and lift out of the pan with a metal spatula. Serve warm. (The corn bread is best the day it is made. Reheat leftovers, wrapped in foil, in a 350°F oven until heated through, about 10 minutes.)

Baker's Notes

CORNMEAL COMES IN different textures. This recipe was tested with a supermarket brand of finely ground yellow cornmeal. If you prefer a coarser corn bread, use a medium- or coarse-grind cornmeal.

For an especially dark crust, bake the batter in a 9-inch round cast-iron skillet. Grease the skillet well with vegetable shortening (not butter). Heat the skillet in the oven while making the batter. Pour the batter into the skillet—it should sizzle when it hits the hot iron surface—and bake for 20 minutes.

Muffins,
Popovers,
Easy Quick
Breads, and
Doughnuts

239

Kona Inn Banana Bread

MAKES 2 LOAVES,
8 SERVINGS EACH

John Phillip Carroll

This moist, dark banana bread came decades ago to PTA mothers via Ethel Baumgardner, a retired elementary school teacher who knows banana bread as well as she knows long division. The recipe originally comes from the Kona Inn in Hawaii, and it gets an A+ for easy preparation, keeping qualities, and, of course, flavor.

6 very ripe and soft medium bananas

2½ cups all-purpose flour

2 teaspoons baking soda

1 teaspoon salt

2 cups sugar

1 cup vegetable shortening

4 large eggs, at room temperature

1 cup coarsely chopped walnuts, optional

1. Position a rack in the center of the oven and preheat to 350°F. Lightly butter and flour two 8½ × 4½-inch loaf pans, tapping out the excess flour.

2. Mash the bananas in a medium bowl with a potato masher or fork until smooth, with a few pea-sized lumps. You should have about 2 cups.

3. Sift the flour, baking soda, and salt into a medium bowl.

4. In a large bowl, using a rubber spatula, mix the sugar and shortening well to make a stiff, gritty paste, about 1 minute. One at a time, beat in the eggs, mixing well after each addition until the egg is absorbed. Mix in the mashed bananas until well combined. Stir in the walnuts, if using. (Don't worry if the mixture looks curdled.) Add the flour mixture and stir just until blended. Don't overmix or be concerned about a few small lumps. Spread the batter evenly in the prepared pans.

5. Bake until a long wooden skewer comes out clean and the batter in the cracks on top of the breads looks cooked, about 1 hour.

6. Transfer to a wire cooling rack and cool in the pans for 15 minutes. Run a knife around the inside of the pans to loosen the loaves. Protecting your hands with a kitchen towel, hold a pan in one hand and invert the loaf out into the palm of your other hand. Place right side up on the rack. Repeat with the other loaf and cool completely. (The breads can be baked up to 3 days ahead, cooled completely, wrapped in plastic wrap, and stored at room temperature.)

Baker's Note

CHECK THE PAN size—the loaves won't bake as nicely in larger 9 × 5-inch pans. If you want a single larger loaf, bake the bread in a 10-inch round tube (angel food) pan for about 50 minutes.

Applesauce Gingerbread

CAKE

2 cups all-purpose flour

1 teaspoon baking soda

1 teaspoon ground ginger

½ teaspoon ground cinnamon

½ teaspoon ground cloves

½ teaspoon freshly grated nutmeg

½ teaspoon salt

1 cup packed light brown sugar

½ cup vegetable oil

1 large egg, at room temperature

½ cup applesauce

½ cup water

3 tablespoons finely chopped crystallized ginger

GLAZE

1 cup confectioners' sugar

2 tablespoons fresh orange juice, or as needed

MAKES ABOUT 10 SERVINGS

Carolyn B. Weil

Applesauce gives this spicy gingerbread its moist texture. If you wish, add ½ cup dried cranberries or raisins to the batter. Note that the cake doesn't rise much; it is the height of a single layer cake.

1. Position a rack in the center of the oven and preheat to 350°F. Lightly spray a 10-inch tube (angel food) pan with nonstick spray.

2. To make the cake, sift the flour, baking soda, ginger, cinnamon, cloves, nutmeg, and salt into a large bowl.

3. In another large bowl, whisk the brown sugar, oil, and egg until well combined, then whisk in the applesauce and water. Add the dry ingredients and stir well. Fold in the ginger. Spread evenly in the prepared pan.

4. Bake until the top is firm and springs back when pressed with your fingers, about 35 minutes.

5. Transfer to a wire cooling rack and cool completely in the pan. Remove the cake from the pan.

6. To make the glaze, sift the confectioners' sugar into a small bowl. Stir in enough of the orange juice to make a glaze about the consistency of heavy cream. Drizzle the glaze over the top of the cake, letting the excess drip down the sides. Let stand to set the glaze. (The cake can be stored at room temperature for up to 3 days, wrapped in plastic wrap.)

Muffins, Popovers, Easy Quick Breads, and Doughnuts

Pumpkin Bread with Dates and Walnuts

MAKES 2 LOAVES,

8 SERVINGS EACH

John Phillip Carroll

Pumpkin bread is moist, dark, spicy, and packed with pumpkin flavor. It is good with coffee or tea, of course, and it is dandy for breakfast or brunch, spread with cream cheese. On a more savory note, it makes good open-faced sandwiches, cut in strips and topped with a dab of cranberry sauce and a small slice of turkey or chicken.

3 cups all-purpose flour

2½ teaspoons baking soda

2 teaspoons ground cinnamon

1 teaspoon freshly grated nutmeg

1 teaspoon salt

½ teaspoon ground allspice

1¼ cups granulated sugar

1 cup packed light brown sugar

3 large eggs, at room temperature

⅔ cup corn oil

2⅓ cups cooked, pureed pumpkin (see page 131) or canned
   solid-pack pumpkin

1½ cups chopped walnuts

1½ cups coarsely chopped dates

1. Position a rack in the center of the oven and preheat to 350°F. Lightly butter and flour two 8½ × 4½-inch loaf pans.

2. Sift the flour, baking soda, cinnamon, nutmeg, salt, and allspice together into a large bowl.

3. In another large bowl, whisk the granulated sugar, brown sugar, eggs, and oil until they are completely mixed. Add the pumpkin and whisk until blended. Using a rubber spatula or wooden spoon, stir in the walnuts and dates.

4. Add the pumpkin mixture to the dry ingredients and stir just until the batter is blended and there are no streaks of flour visible.

5. Spread the batter evenly in the prepared pans. Bake until a long wooden skewer inserted in the loaves comes out clean, 65 to 70 minutes.

6. Transfer to a wire cooling rack. Cool in the pans for 15 minutes. Give each pan a sharp downward jerk to loosen the bread, then invert the loaves onto the rack. Turn right side up, and cool completely. (The bread can be baked up to 3 days ahead, wrapped in plastic wrap or a plastic bag, and stored at room temperature. It can also be frozen, double-wrapped in aluminum foil, for up to 3 months.)

Maple Bars

MAKES 16 BARS

BARS

1 envelope (2¼ teaspoons) active dry yeast

⅔ cup warm (105° to 110°F) milk

6 tablespoons (¾ stick) unsalted butter, at
    room temperature

2 large eggs, at room temperature

½ cup granulated sugar

1½ teaspoons vanilla extract

1 teaspoon salt

½ teaspoon freshly grated nutmeg

3¼ to 3¾ cups all-purpose flour,
    or as needed

Vegetable oil, for deep-frying

MAPLE GLAZE

2 cups confectioners' sugar

½ cup maple syrup, at room temperature, plus
    more as needed

Pinch of salt

John Phillip Carroll

Maple bars are the star attraction of many a doughnut shop. Once you've tasted these rectangles of sweet yeast bread topped with a maple-syrup glaze, you'll understand their popularity.

1. To make the bars, sprinkle the yeast over the milk in a large bowl. Let stand for 5 minutes to soften, then whisk until yeast is dissolved. Add the butter, eggs, sugar, vanilla, salt, and nutmeg and beat with a hand-held electric mixer on low speed until blended (the butter will be in small lumps). Stir in 2 cups flour to make a smooth, thick batter. Beat in enough of the remaining flour to make a soft, manageable dough.

2. Turn the dough out onto a lightly floured work surface. Dust your hands with flour and knead the dough for 2 minutes, until it is relatively smooth. Cover the dough with plastic wrap and let stand on the work surface for 10 minutes.

3. Knead the dough for a few more minutes, adding just enough flour to the work surface and your hands to keep it from sticking, until the dough is smooth and supple. Transfer the dough to a buttered large bowl and turn to coat with butter. Cover the bowl with plastic wrap and let stand in a warm place until the dough is doubled in volume, about 1½ hours.

4. Line two large baking sheets with wax paper. Punch the dough down and transfer to a lightly floured work surface. Pat out the dough (or use a rolling

*Muffins,
Popovers,
Easy Quick
Breads, and
Doughnuts*

pin, if you wish) into a 16 × 8-inch rectangle about ½ inch thick, keeping the corners as square as possible. If the dough retracts, cover it with a large sheet of plastic wrap, let stand to relax for 5 minutes, then try again. Cut in half lengthwise, then crosswise into 2-inch-wide rectangles to make sixteen 4 × 2-inch bars.

5. Transfer the bars to the baking sheets, leaving about 2 inches between them. Cover loosely with clean kitchen towels and let stand in a warm place until almost doubled in size, 30 to 40 minutes.

6. About 10 minutes before frying, add enough oil to a large, heavy saucepan to come 2 inches up the sides, and heat to 350° to 375°F over medium-high heat.

7. In batches without crowding, fry the bars, turning them occasionally, until golden brown, 2½ to 3 minutes. Using a skimmer or slotted spoon, transfer them to paper towels or brown paper bags to drain.

8. While the bars are still warm, make the glaze. Sift the confectioners' sugar into a medium bowl and stir in the maple syrup and salt to make a smooth, spreadable glaze. If the glaze is too thick, add more syrup a few drops at a time.

9. Spread a scant tablespoon of the glaze over each bar. Cool completely. (The bars are best served the day they are made.)

Baker's Notes

GRADE A MAPLE syrup has a mild flavor that really shines when poured over pancakes or other breakfast treats. For cooking, look for Grade B amber syrup, which is slightly stronger, but either syrup will work with this glaze.

To make maple bars for breakfast without getting up at the crack of dawn like a professional doughnut maker, refrigerate the dough overnight to rise (it will keep for up to 2 days in the refrigerator). Roll the refrigerated dough and cut into bars. The chilled bars will take longer to rise, up to 2 hours.

Buttermilk Spice Doughnuts

DOUGHNUTS

**¾ cup plus 2 tablespoons buttermilk, whole or
low-fat, at room temperature**

½ cup sugar

¼ cup vegetable shortening, melted

2 large eggs, at room temperature

1 teaspoon vanilla extract

2 cups all-purpose flour

1¾ cups cake flour

2 teaspoons baking powder

1 teaspoon baking soda

1 teaspoon ground cinnamon

1 teaspoon freshly grated nutmeg

1 teaspoon salt

Vegetable oil, for deep-frying

SUGAR GLAZE

2 cups confectioners' sugar

3 tablespoons water, or as needed

1 teaspoon vanilla extract

Pinch of salt

MAKES ABOUT 20 DOUGHNUTS
AND HOLES

John Phillip Carroll

From their New England beginnings, doughnuts became so much a part of American history that World War I infantrymen, who received a steady supply of them from Salvation Army workers, became known as doughboys. Homemade doughnuts are a labor of love, but nothing can beat their flavor and substance.

1. To make the doughnuts, in a large bowl, combine the buttermilk, sugar, and shortening, then add the eggs and vanilla. Whisk well until evenly blended.

2. Sift 1¾ cups all-purpose flour, the cake flour, baking powder, baking soda, cinnamon, nutmeg, and salt onto a piece of wax paper. Add to the buttermilk mixture and stir just until a soft dough forms.

3. Sprinkle 2 tablespoons of the remaining flour onto a work surface. Scrape the dough onto the flour and sprinkle with the remaining 2 tablespoons flour. Knead gently just until the dough is smooth and no longer ragged looking. Push and pat the dough into a 12 × 8-inch rectangle about ½ inch thick.

4. Line a large baking sheet with parchment or wax paper. Using a floured 2½-inch doughnut cutter, cut out about 15 doughnuts and transfer the doughnuts and holes to the wax paper. If the dough seems sticky, dust it

*Muffins,
Popovers,
Easy Quick
Breads, and
Doughnuts*

with a bit more flour. Gently knead the scraps together, pat out to ½-inch thickness, and cut out more doughnuts. (If you want more doughnuts and fewer holes, just add the holes to the scraps.)

5. Meanwhile, about 10 minutes before frying, add enough oil to a large, heavy saucepan to come 2 inches up the sides, and heat to 350° to 375°F over medium-high heat.

6. Line another large baking sheet with paper towels. In batches of 3 or 4, add the doughnuts and their holes to the hot oil. They will sink, then rise to the surface. Using a wire skimmer or slotted spoon, turn them as soon as they rise to the top. Deep-fry, turning occasionally, until golden brown, 2 to 3 minutes. (The holes don't really need to be turned, just nudged so they cook evenly, and they may be done before the doughnuts.) Transfer the doughnuts to the paper towels to drain.

7. To make the glaze, sift the confectioners' sugar into a small bowl wide enough to hold a doughnut. Add 3 tablespoons water, the vanilla, and salt and mix with a fork until blended. Don't worry about any small lumps of sugar. Cover with plastic wrap and let stand for 5 to 10 minutes to dissolve the lumps. Stir again. The glaze should be quite thick but should fall slowly from the tines of the fork. If it is too stiff, beat in additional water ½ teaspoon at a time.

8. Place a wire cooling rack over a baking sheet. Place a doughnut in the glaze and let stand undisturbed for 30 seconds. Lift the doughnut out of the glaze and place glazed side up on the rack. Glaze the holes in the same manner. Let stand until the glaze sets. (The doughnuts are best when served within a few hours. Leftovers can be frozen, wrapped in plastic wrap and an overwrap of aluminum foil, for up to 2 months. If you know you are going to freeze the doughnuts, leave them unglazed and freeze within a few hours of making. To reheat, place the unwrapped frozen doughnuts in a single layer on a baking sheet and bake in a preheated 350°F oven for about 10 minutes. Glaze the warm doughnuts just before serving.)

Buttermilk Bars: These golden, glazed bars are a specialty of California doughnut shops. Each bar has a crevice down the middle, with lots of nooks and crannies to collect more glaze. Increase the buttermilk to 1 cup. Omit the cinnamon and add 1 tablespoon grated lemon zest (from

2 lemons) to the liquid ingredients. Mix the dough and turn out onto a floured surface. Knead the dough with a minimum of additional flour—it should stay quite soft. Pat and press the dough into a 12 × 8-inch rectangle about ½ inch thick. Cut in half lengthwise, then cut crosswise at 1½-inch intervals to make 16 bars. Using a small, sharp knife, cut a shallow slit 2 to 3 inches long down the center of each bar. (This slit will splay open during frying.) Deep-fry the bars in batches for about 3 minutes, or until golden brown. Glaze as directed. Makes 16 bars.

Cinnamon-Sugar Doughnuts: Omit the glaze. In a large bowl, whisk 2 cups sugar and 2 teaspoons cinnamon until well combined. Put 3 or 4 warm doughnuts and holes at a time in the sugar and toss with your hands until evenly coated.

Baker's Notes

DOUGHNUTS REQUIRE A number of easy steps: mixing the dough, cutting out the doughnuts, frying, draining, and glazing or coating. Get organized and think through each step before you proceed. This is good advice for any kind of baking, but especially with a recipe that may be unfamiliar.

If you don't have a doughnut cutter, use biscuit cutters. You'll need a 2½-inch round cutter for the doughnuts, and a 1-inch round cutter for the holes.

We learned the glazing procedure from a professional doughnut maker, who taught us that this method ensures a smooth coat that doesn't drip down the sides. To speed up the procedure, make a double batch of glaze and pour into a shallow dish large enough to hold two doughnuts at a time.

Muffins,
Popovers,
Easy Quick
Breads, and
Doughnuts

247

Doughnut Dos and Don'ts

Good doughnuts require good deep-frying skills. Here are a few tips:

Use any light-bodied vegetable oil you prefer; it should be pleasant and almost neutral in flavor and aroma, with no disagreeable taste or smell. Canola oil is a good choice. Price does not necessarily indicate quality, and you can't really judge an oil without tasting it first. Peanut oil is too strongly flavored for doughnuts. Vegetable shortening is another option, but it can be unwieldy to use in such large amounts.

Do not even think about making doughnuts without a deep-frying thermometer.

Be sure to use enough oil. The doughnuts should "swim" in the oil. If you skimp on the oil, the doughnuts will soak up the oil and turn out sodden. You can use a large saucepan or a deep skillet. The depth of the oil is more important than the amount you use. Estimate at least 1½ quarts oil, regardless of the cooking vessel.

The oil temperature will drop during frying. Keep the heat constant at medium-high so the temperature doesn't drop too much, and allow the oil to return to the proper frying temperature (at least 350°F) between batches.

Do not reuse doughnut-frying oil. Cool the oil completely and discard it. Reheated oil will often have residual or off flavors and ruin your doughnuts.

Rum Raisin Zucchini Bread

1 cup raisins

⅓ cup rum

3 cups all-purpose flour

2 teaspoons cinnamon

½ teaspoon cloves

1½ teaspoons baking soda

1 teaspoon baking powder

1 teaspoon salt

2 cups dark brown or light brown sugar

1 cup corn oil or vegetable oil

2 teaspoons vanilla

2 cups (3 small, or about 12 ounces total) grated zucchini

1 cup chopped walnuts

1. Place the raisins and rum in a screw-top jar. Cap tightly and shake vigorously. Let sit for at least 1 hour—or for several hours, or more—shaking occasionally.

2. Position a rack in the center of the oven. Preheat to 350°F. Grease and flour two 8½ × 4½ × 2½-inch loaf pans.

3. Combine the flour, cinnamon, cloves, baking soda, baking powder, and salt and sift them together into a medium bowl. Set aside. In a large bowl, whisk together until smooth the sugar, oil, and vanilla. Add the zucchini and stir to combine. Add the combined dry ingredients and stir just until the batter is evenly mixed and there are no unblended drifts of flour. Stir in the walnuts and the raisins, along with any remaining rum. Divide the batter evenly between the prepared pans, filling each one about half full.

4. Bake about 50 minutes, or until a wooden skewer inserted into the center of a loaf comes out clean.

5. Remove from the oven and cool in the pans for about 10 minutes. Remove from the pans and place the loaves, top side up, on a rack to cool completely. The bread can be stored, tightly wrapped in plastic, for up to 3 days. Freeze for longer storage.

MAKES 2 MEDIUM LOAVES,
8 SERVINGS EACH

John Phillip Carroll

Full of rum-soaked raisins, this moist and spicy zucchini bread has an adult sophistication. It keeps well for several days, and can be made with shredded carrot instead of zucchini. Either way, it is delicious sliced and spread with softened cream cheese.

Muffins,
Popovers,
Easy Quick
Breads, and
Doughnuts

Baker's Note

THERE IS NO surefire way to prevent additions from sinking, but you can temper the tendency if you keep this in mind: A thin batter will hold small or finely chopped pieces better than it will hold large pieces; a thick batter, on the other hand, has the stiffness to hold larger pieces.

Yeast Breads and Flatbreads

Bread dough is a living organism, and therein lie the rewards and excitement that accompany bread baking. Ironically, it's also this characteristic that makes some people afraid of baking bread. Bakers who don't understand baking with yeast tend to concentrate on its pitfalls instead of its joys. But bread dough is friendly, capable of withstanding a fair amount of abuse and still producing a good loaf. With a little help from the baker, the yeast will do a lot of work.

There has been a renewed interest in bread among American bakers and consumers, partially driven by a lively interest in health and the role that grain plays in a healthy diet. The kinds of breads that people want have changed, too. Instead of flavorless mass-produced white bread, you can find character-rich European-style loaves in almost every supermarket. To meet this need, as well as define it, small bakeries focusing on healthy, hearty breads have opened throughout the country.

There have always been people who love to bake bread at home. In addition to the resurgence of passion for hearth-baked breads, the bread machine has encouraged more people to make bread. The bread machine, however, remains controversial with many home bakers. Some people like how it easily provides a loaf of bread and fills the kitchen with yeasty aroma. Others (including two writers of this chapter) believe that it promotes less-than-perfect bread. To narrow the scope of this chapter and to avoid adding to the controversy, we concentrate on handmade, oven-baked breads. Those bakers who want to know details about bread machines can learn about them in one of the many books on the subject.

Once the basics of bread baking are understood, the baker can move from simple, straightforward breads made with commercial yeast to the more complex breads leavened with starters (mixtures of flour and water that are fermented by wild yeasts in the air). The recipes that follow demonstrate the range in the world of breads, including crackers, focaccia, sweet and savory rolls, pretzels, and some that don't use yeast at all.

The three editors for this chapter were Carol Field, Fran Gage, and Peter Reinhart. Committee members who offered expertise, tested and wrote recipes, and did research were Charlie Brown, Dorothy Calamaris,

Elizabeth Feinberg, Letty Flatt, Danielle Forestier, Cathie Guntli, Baird Lloyd, Karen Mitchell, Joe Ortiz, Craig Ponsford, Monica Spiller, Cynthia Ware, Sue Ann Wercinski, and Lillian Wong.

Ingredients for Bread

FLOUR, LIQUID, SALT, and leavening. So simple, so complex. Mix them together, knead, let rise, and bake, and you can produce loaves that range from soft sandwich bread to crusty, chewy sourdough. By changing the ratio of the basic ingredients, adding other ingredients such as eggs, fats, fruit, nuts, and nonwheat grains to the dough, or fermenting part of the mixture before making the final dough, the texture and flavor of the bread can be almost endlessly altered.

Flour | Most bread dough is made with unbleached or high-gluten flour, which gives the dough enough strength to withstand kneading and rising. When flour is moistened and mixed, the gluten is activated and forms an invisible web in the dough. But what is gluten?

As dough is kneaded, two protein fragments in the flour, gliadin and glutenin (which are more abundant in wheat than in any other grain) are hydrated by the liquid in the dough. They then expand and bond with each other, creating a longer molecule called gluten, which gives bread its strength and invisible skeletal structure. In bread dough, the gluten structure must be strong to withstand the rising process, caused by the carbon dioxide trapped in the bread as the yeast develops. A bread dough is purposely kneaded to strengthen the gluten in the dough, whereas a pastry dough is handled lightly to keep the gluten development at a minimum. Although rye has a small amount of gluten, wheat is the only grain with enough gluten to really affect dough, so nonwheat grains are always mixed with wheat flour to improve the structure of the bread.

We prefer unbleached flours for bread making. Unbleached flours contain more protein than bleached flours, as the bleaching process (which happens naturally as flour ages but is typically done with chemicals) reduces the strength of the gluten. *Bread flour* has a higher protein content than unbleached all-purpose flour and is preferred for some recipes.

There has been much discussion in our group over organic versus commercially milled flours. Some bakers think breads baked with organic flours can have a discernibly fuller flavor than those made with their commercial counterparts, and the lack of chemical processing encourages a healthy environment for wild yeast growth. But many of the professional bakers in the group have found organic flour to be frustrating to work with on a day-to-day basis. One batch can have different properties from another, although improvements have been made to standardize organic flours. If you want to use organic flour, know that it absorbs liquid quickly, and you will probably have to increase the amount of liquid (or use slightly less flour) to compensate.

There are many variables involved when measuring flour. The two most important are how the flour is scooped into the cup (did you dip the cup into the container or spoon it into the cup before leveling?) and the ambient humidity (the flour can soak up extra moisture and weigh more even if the volume remains the same). We strongly recommend weighing the flour on a kitchen scale, a method that is always constant. Of course, since not everyone has a kitchen scale, we provide both volume and weight measures. If you use a measuring cup, aerate the flour by stirring it and then use the dip-and-sweep method, and you'll come closest to our scaled measurement.

Salt | Every bread dough needs salt. It's more than an indispensable seasoning; use too little salt, and your bread will taste dull. Salt makes the fermentation proceed evenly throughout the dough, slows staling of the baked bread, increases the dough's elasticity, and fosters browning of the crust. We used a common fine sea salt from a natural food store (not bulk sea salt, which is heavier) in testing these recipes.

Liquid | The type of liquid used to moisten the dough plays a large part in the finished bread. Water provides a crisp crust and a chewy texture. Some bakers are passionate about the water used and insist on spring water. This isn't necessary as long as you live in an area with water that tastes good and isn't heavily chlorinated. Milk tenderizes the crumb, and its natural sugars promote a browned crust without using high temperatures. The acids in buttermilk do an especially efficient job of tenderizing the gluten in the flour to make light-textured breads and rolls. Egg yolks add color and enrich the bread.

For the best breads, the temperature of the liquid is carefully manipulated so the dough is at the optimum temperature. Most yeasts dissolve best in a small amount of warm (105° to 115°F) water, but the dough will develop the best flavor if the rest of the liquid in the recipe is cooler. (See "Making the Dough," page 256, for more details.)

Yeast

ALL TRADITIONAL BREADS are leavened with commercial or wild yeast. Quick breads are a separate category, as their rise comes from chemical leavenings like baking powder or baking soda. Breads leavened by commercial yeast (*Saccharomyces cerevisiae*) are often called yeasted breads. Sourdough and other breads don't contain commercial yeast but are raised by the wild yeast (*Saccharomyces exiguus*) present in the air. Many bakers refer to them as leavened breads.

Both types of yeast have their place in the bread baker's kitchen. Either yeast feeds on the sugars in the dough (if sugar isn't added, it is found naturally in the flour), creating carbon dioxide and ethanol as by-products. Carbon dioxide is the carbonic gas that raises the dough, and the ethanol dissipates in the oven.

Commercial yeast is very aggressive and ferments the dough so rapidly that it is usually ready for baking within a few hours after mixing. In fact, dough made with commercial yeast can sustain only two or three risings before it overferments. At this point, the yeast begins to die and loses its leavening power, and the bread will have an unpleasant sour flavor.

Wild yeasts live everywhere. The baker's job is to capture these organisms in a medium, such as a dough or starter, and cultivate their flavor and texture contributions in the finished loaf. This is done by *building a dough* gradually, through intermediate steps, allowing the flavor to develop. Some doughs made from wild starters may take up to three days to ferment; this is slow-rise baking at its finest. Slow rising also allows the dough to develop more lactobacillus organisms, which give the dough complexity and acidity. Sourdough breads, leavened with wild yeast, develop their unique flavor not from the yeast but from these organisms.

Commercial yeast can be purchased in three forms: active dry, instant, and fresh (also called compressed).

Active dry yeast | Most readily available in strips of three ¼-ounce packages, but you can also buy it in 4-ounce jars or in bulk. It creates its carbon dioxide more slowly than the other yeast, but no matter: We use it in these recipes because it is usually easy to find in supermarkets.

Instant yeast | Packed in strips of three ¼-ounce envelopes and in 4-ounce boxes or jars, it is encroaching on active dry yeast's territory and is sometimes the only yeast you can find in the supermarket. It is also labeled European yeast, "yeast for bread machines," or with the trademarked name RapidRise. It looks like active dry yeast, but there are important differences. This yeast can be added to dough without dissolving, a convenience that some bakers like. Instant yeast is very strong and shouldn't be substituted in equal amounts for regular active dry yeast, even though it is often misleadingly packaged in the same ¼-ounce envelopes.

So-called fast-rising yeast is just another name for instant yeast. Most manufacturers recommend using the same amount of instant yeast as regular active dry yeast; but the resulting speed comes at the expense of taste, as a long fermentation increases flavor. However, if smaller amounts of instant yeast are used (about one-quarter less than active dry yeast), it can be a fine leavening. Instant yeast manufacturers usually recommend hot tap water to make the dough, a step that encourages an even faster rise. Ignore that advice and simply rehydrate the yeast in lukewarm water, even if the package says to mix it with the flour. It is especially important to dissolve instant yeast in water when making sweet dough, as the sugar and eggs can inhibit proper distribution.

Fresh yeast | Comes in 0.6-ounce and 2-ounce foil-wrapped cubes. Most professional bakers prefer it for its easy mixing (it doesn't require warm water for dissolving) and price in bulk. But it isn't available in every market, and it has a short shelf life. Fresh yeast must be kept refrigerated. It should be an even buff color and break cleanly. If it has any dry spots, discard it.

Here is a handy chart for substituting one kind of yeast for another. Note that the fresh yeast measurement uses a small 0.6-ounce cube, not the large 2-ounce cube.

Active dry yeast	Fresh yeast	Instant yeast
(One ¼-ounce envelope = 2¼ teaspoons)	(One small cube = 0.6 ounce)	(One ¼-ounce envelope = 2¼ teaspoons)
½ teaspoon	⅕ cube	¼ plus ⅛ teaspoon
¾ teaspoon	¼ cube	½ plus ⅛ teaspoon
1 teaspoon	⅓ cube	¾ teaspoon
1½ teaspoons	½ cube	scant 1¼ teaspoons
2 teaspoons	⅘ cube	1½ teaspoons
2¼ teaspoons	1 cube	scant 1¾ teaspoons
1 tablespoon	1¼ cubes	2¼ teaspoons

When purchasing any yeast, always keep the expiration date on the package in mind—yeast quickly loses its potency after that date. Health food stores and wholesale clubs carry bulk yeast and sell it by the pound, although few stores provide an expiration date. The difference in price is substantial and will be appreciated by a frequent baker. While the savings are tempting, be sure that you don't buy more than you will be likely to use by the expiration date. Store all yeast in an airtight container in the refrigerator. Freezing does not extend the life of yeast—in fact, some sources say that it will kill some of the yeast.

Using yeast | While yeast manufacturers insist that the yeast must be dissolved in warm (100° to 110°F) liquid in order to activate the spores, we find that you can use cool water. Yeast is killed at temperatures above 140°F, so take care when heating the liquid and, if necessary, use an instant-read thermometer to check. Yeast has become standardized, and if stored properly, it will activate easily. The proofing step (letting the yeast stand in warm liquid with sugar until the yeast softens, activates, and makes the mixture foamy) is a convenience to the baker who is insecure about the yeast's potency, and is not essential. The small amount of sugar (a large pinch will suffice) in the proofing water will certainly speed up the activation, but it isn't necessary. In fact, most European-style or rustic breads are made without any added sugar.

One question that often arose during this chapter's meetings was how much yeast to use when a recipe is doubled or tripled. Some bakers think it's best to decrease the amount of yeast when doubling a recipe to only one and a half times the original amount. This is because the smaller amount of yeast is really sufficient to raise a larger mass of dough regardless of the amount of flour (up to a point). Others rely on proportions, using yeast in the ratio of 2 percent of the weight of flour.

Yeasted and leavened breads can both be made by many techniques. The actual process of making the dough is sometimes called "building a dough." The baker's art is understanding how to match the methods of leavening and fermentation to produce breads with the desired qualities. For this you need two things: knowledge (which we will share with you) and practice, lots of practice (which you must provide).

Eggs | Besides their nutritional value, when you add eggs to a dough, you accomplish several things. The lipids in the egg yolks emulsify, producing a softer, golden crumb and a crust that browns more quickly. The fat in the yolks will increase the bread's shelf life.

Fats and oils | The addition of any fat to a dough will act as a tenderizer, softening the texture of the crumb and the crust. The bread will be more moist and will keep longer. Fats help carry flavors through the dough, enhancing the flavor of added ingredients and generally enriching the dough. When a fat is creamed, rolled, or flaked into a dough, it releases steam during baking that contributes to the flakiness of the baked good.

Making the Dough

BREAD MAKING IS ONE of the most tactile of the kitchen arts—the baker actually touches the dough, and the sense of touch signals the quality of the dough better than sight alone. This does not mean that you have to bring out a bowl and a spoon to mix the dough. In fact, in these recipes we use a heavy-duty standing electric mixer with a 5-quart bowl. Making dough by hand is a wonderfully sensual experience, but making dough in a mixer is much, much easier. If the dough-making process is made easy, more people will return to baking their own bread, and we're all for that!

When dough is made by mixing all the ingredients together at once, it is called *the straight method* (also called the direct or yeast method). But the dough can also be made by fermenting part of the dough before the final mixing and kneading. This gives more flavor to the bread because organic acids develop during the longer fermentation. Breads made with a *pre-ferment* have a less yeasty flavor, a chewy texture, an irregular crumb, and a crust with a richer appearance and taste. Some examples of pre-ferments include sponge, biga, poolish, and *pâte fermentée*, which are discussed in the individual recipes that use them.

Electric mixer method | Be sure to use a heavy-duty standing mixer with a strong motor. Some smaller electric mixers come with bread-making attachments, but they may not be up to the job. The mixer bowl should be at least 4½-quart capacity (5-quart works best to avoid spills and splashes). You will also need a paddle attachment and a dough hook.

The procedure for mixing the dough is pretty standard. Combine the liquid ingredients and dissolved yeast in the bowl. On low speed, using the paddle attachment, gradually mix in the flour to make the dough. Once the dough has come together, switch to the dough hook. Knead the dough on medium speed until it has reached the consistency described in the recipe (not all doughs are kneaded until smooth and elastic).

Hand method | Surely there are still many bakers who love to make bread by hand. If you have a large bowl and a sturdy wooden spoon, you can make bread the old-fashioned way.

Mix all of the liquid ingredients and the dissolved yeast in a large bowl with at least a 4-quart capacity. Thick ceramic bowls are best because they insulate the dough well, but stainless steel will work, too. About 1 cup at time, stir in the dry ingredients, mixing to make a shaggy dough that is too stiff to stir. Turn the dough out onto a floured work surface. The dough is ready to knead.

To knead by hand, take the top portion of the dough, fold it down to meet the center, and use the heel of your hand to press away from you at this junction in the center of the dough. Rotate the dough one quarter turn and repeat the procedure. Continue, turning the dough one quarter turn each time, turning and pressing until the dough is smooth, about 10 minutes.

Food processor method | This method has its followers, but there are cautions. Because the blade of a food processor creates friction that heats the dough, it is important to use cold liquid (the yeast can be dissolved in warm water). Also, you must use a large-capacity food processor. If your processor isn't large enough, process two half batches of the dough, then knead them together.

Combine the dry ingredients in a food processor fitted with the metal blade. Mix the liquid ingredients (except the dissolved yeast) in a glass measuring cup. With the machine running, add the dissolved yeast. Gradually pour in enough of the liquid to make a ball of dough that rides on top of the blade. (The machine may need to run for about 30 seconds before the ball forms.) If the dough is too wet or too dry, it will not form a ball. Feel the dough, and if it is sticky and wet, add flour 2 tablespoons at a time, processing after each addition, until the dough forms a ball. If the dough is crumbly and dry, follow the same procedure, but add water 1 tablespoon at a time. Since the dough will probably be warm at this point, let it stand in the work bowl, covered with the lid, with the feed tube insert in place for about 20 minutes to cool. To knead, process the ball of dough for 45 seconds—no longer.

About Dough Temperatures

PROFESSIONAL BAKERS CAREFULLY calculate the temperatures of their ingredients and workplaces to reach the best temperature for fermentation of each particular dough. Granted, most home bakers don't follow these calculations, but they could and should. The procedure is easy to follow and will help make better bread, especially during warm weather.

For the optimum fermentation of most doughs, the temperature at the end of kneading should be about 75°F. The four factors influencing this goal are the temperatures of the flour, the room, and the water and how much the dough heats up during the kneading process. Dough kneaded by machine may rise as much as 1°F per minute, hand-kneaded dough not as much.

Because the temperatures of the flour and the room are hard to adjust, the temperature of the water is manipulated. On hot days, cooler water should be used, and on cold days, warmer water. Just check the temperature of the kneaded dough with an instant-read thermometer. If the temperature is higher than 75°F, let it rise in a cool place, or even refrigerate it. If the dough is too cool, put it in a warm place to rise.

You can easily calculate the temperature of the water to be more exact. To check the room temperature, just look at the temperature of your instant-read thermometer. Ideally, the flour, room, and water should be at 75°F, so the sum of these temperatures is 225°F. On a hot summer day, the room and the flour are more likely to be near 80°F, so the water temperature must be cooler. To determine the water temperature, add the flour and room temperatures and subtract the total from the ideal of 225. In this example, 225 − (80 + 80) = 65. The correct water temperature is 65°F. Manipulate the water temperature by adding ice to tap water. To be even more precise, subtract a few more degrees to compensate for the heat rise generated by machine kneading (and even more if you use a food processor).

Kneading the Dough

ALTHOUGH A FEW BREADS (such as downright gloppy ciabatta dough) have mixing rules unto themselves, most breads are kneaded just until the gluten develops. Types of wheat differ in their ability to develop gluten. Some require only a few minutes of kneading, and others take longer. Millers have special machines, such as farinagraphs and alveometers, that test the strength and development of gluten. At home, it is safe to say that most typical breads require about 10 minutes of kneading by hand or machine.

Overkneading is the result of kneading the dough too hard or too long, causing friction that increases the temperature of the dough. When this happens, the gluten molecules begin to break apart and the dough becomes irretrievable. This is hard to do when kneading by hand (we usually wear out before the gluten does), but it isn't hard to overknead dough in an electric mixer or food processor. Overkneaded dough is stretchy like taffy and sticks to your hands like bubble gum on a warm day, no matter how much flour you add. Don't confuse this with merely wet dough.

"Windowpaning" is the best way to check for gluten development. Here's how to do it: After kneading for 6 to 8 minutes, or when the dough feels supple and stretchy, take a small piece of the dough. Slowly stretch it, turning it as you do so and pulling in all directions, attempting to stretch the dough into a thin, translucent membrane. If it tears easily before reaching this "windowpane" state, it probably requires a few more minutes of kneading. (If the dough feels stiff and dry, add water.) If the dough doesn't "windowpane" after 10 or 15 minutes of kneading, there may be another problem, such as an incorrect amount of water. After you have tried this procedure a few times, it will be easy to do and will become part of your bread-making routine.

The First Rise

YEAST DOUGHS HAVE TWO RISINGS. During the first rise, which starts after the dough has been kneaded, it usually doubles in volume. Sometimes a dough is punched down after the first rise and allowed to rise a second time before it is shaped. How can you tell if the dough has doubled? Poke your finger ½ inch into the dough and take it out. If your finger leaves a deep impression, the dough has risen enough.

Dough is usually allowed to rise in a lightly oiled or buttered bowl. Thick ceramic bowls are best because they insulate the dough well. Coat the bowl with a very light film of oil—you don't want to use so much oil that it soaks into the dough. Place the dough in the bowl and turn to coat it very lightly with the oil. Cover the bowl tightly with plastic wrap or a moist kitchen towel. A straight-sided plastic storage container with a tight-fitting lid (3 to 5 quarts) is a good substitute for an oiled bowl. Its airtight environment is perfect for the fermenting dough, and it doesn't need to be oiled. Also, you can mark the volume of the unfermented dough on the side of the container, making it easy to see when the dough has doubled in size.

The temperature of the room is very important to the rise of the dough. If the room is too warm, the dough will rise too quickly and the flavor will be compromised. A cool room is usually not a problem (we prefer a longer, cooler rise), as long as the baker has the time for a longer rise. By room temperature we mean about 75°F, the optimum rising temperature for most dough. In a few cases we ask for a warm place for rising, such as an oven that has been heated to its lowest setting for a few minutes. (See "About Dough Temperatures," page 258.)

Bread making can adjust to the baker's schedule instead of dictating it. The dough's development need not progress from start to finish without interruption. Chilling the dough in the refrigerator is a valuable aid to the baker: It slows the dough's fermentation and allows for a more flexible baking schedule. A slow first rise in the refrigerator can improve the taste of the bread by enhancing the development of organic acids. Bread risen like this will not taste yeasty after baking, and the full flavor of the wheat will come through. The exact length of the rise depends on the recipe.

If the dough has risen in the refrigerator, let it come to room temperature before shaping. This could take 2 to 5 hours, depending on the volume and type of dough; heavier doughs and sourdoughs will need more time. If the dough has not doubled in volume in the refrigerator, be sure it reaches this point as it stands at room temperature. Observing the dough is more important than watching the clock.

If by chance a dough has overrisen beyond the doubled stage, all is not lost. Just punch it down, knead it a few turns, and allow it to rise again. It will take less time than usual to double in volume because the fermentation is already well under way. Watch it closely and proceed to the next step as soon as it is ready.

The dough can also be frozen, either directly after kneading or after the first rise. The best candidates for freezing are plain or egg-and-butter-enriched doughs made with commercial yeast, as some of the wild yeast in sourdoughs can be killed by freezing. Put the dough in a plastic bag. Close it tightly with a twist tie, allowing a little room for expansion. Freeze immediately. The maximum freezing time is 1 month. Defrost in the refrigerator, allowing at least 8 hours, or at room temperature. Make sure that the dough doubles in volume and will hold a finger imprint before shaping it for the second rise.

Dividing and Shaping the Dough

WHEN THE DOUGH HAS FINISHED the first rise, turn it out onto a lightly floured work surface. A wooden surface is probably the easiest to work on, as it gives the dough plenty of traction, but metal, marble, or even Formica will suffice. To cut the dough into pieces, use a bench scraper or a large, sharp knife. Professional bakers weigh each piece of dough to assure consistency; it's a good habit for home bakers to get into if they want uniform loaves or rolls.

Form each piece of dough into a taut ball. To do this, place a piece of dough on an unfloured work surface. Cup your hands slightly and place them on either side of the dough. Tuck the sides of the dough to meet underneath the mass, stretching the surface of the dough taut. Rotate the dough a quarter turn and repeat the procedure, tucking and stretching the dough. After a few rotations, the dough will be shaped into a taut ball. At this point, most recipes ask you to rest the dough so the gluten has a chance to relax. Cover the balls of dough with plastic wrap or kitchen towels and let stand for about 10 minutes (sourdough loaves need more time). If the dough resists shaping, it hasn't rested long enough. Just round up the dough again, cover, and let it rest for a few more minutes.

The Second Rise

AFTER THE DOUGH HAS been shaped, it is usually allowed to double in bulk again before it goes into the oven. Many of the breads in this book rise in loaf pans, on baking sheets, or on baker's peels that have been sprinkled with cornmeal or lined with parchment paper. Be sure the parchment paper is professional grade, as some supermarket brands can't withstand the high heat of the oven and will burn. Recipes for more advanced breads in other books call for floured cloth-lined baskets or special woven baskets that leave their design on the surface of the bread.

We like to let shaped loaves rise on parchment paper, as it makes large, free form loaves easy to transport to the oven and it keeps wet and sticky dough from clinging to the surface. Excess parchment can be cut away from the loaves, which can then be placed right on a baking stone in the oven. Be sure that no paper overhangs the stone, or it will burn. If you wish, when the crust has set, after 20 minutes or so, slide the paper out from under the loaf. Or the loaf can be inverted off the paper onto a stone that has been sprinkled with cornmeal or semolina. In any case, your fingers won't get entangled with dough.

Rising loaves are always covered to keep a skin from forming on the surface, which would hamper the expansion. The most common way to keep air from drying the surface of the loaves is to cover them with plastic wrap or damp kitchen towels (preferred for damp doughs that could stick to plastic wrap).

Professional bakers often use a proof box, a sealed closet with temperature and humidity controls. You can devise a proof "box" at home by slipping the loaves, on a parchment-lined baking sheet, into a tall kitchen-sized plastic bag and sealing it well. To keep the plastic from sticking to the loaves, inflate the bag by giving it a few shakes to introduce air, then tie the two corners of the bag together to close.

The loaves are ready for the oven when they double in volume and hold a finger imprint (the hole will fill in as the loaf bakes). If a loaf overrises (it will look alarmingly large, or deflated and saggy), just punch it down, knead briefly, and reshape for another rise.

If a dough doesn't rise in the time specified in the recipe, don't give up hope. Let it stand longer and check it later. Possible causes are the temperature, the amount or type of yeast, or the addition of wine or liquor (which slows the fermentation). Sourdoughs always take longer than doughs made with commercial yeast.

Sometimes a glaze or egg wash is brushed on the loaves before they go into the oven. These are more common on sweet breads, brioche, and breads filled with fruit and nuts. Egg whites, lightly beaten, give a clear, glossy glaze. Egg yolks beaten with a little water create a rich, golden finish. Whole eggs make a smooth, thick glaze. Rustic loaves are never glazed.

Many doughs are slashed just before going into the oven. This lets the carbon dioxide escape uniformly during the final rise, which occurs when the dough comes into contact with the oven heat. Without these cuts the dough might tear haphazardly. Every baker has a favorite tool for this, even though the traditional tool is the baker's lame, which looks like an old-fashioned barber's razor with a long blade on a handle. Other tools include single-edged razor blades, serrated knives, X-Acto blades, window scrapers, even food processor blades (which have built-in handles!). Whatever you use, just be sure it's sharp. It must cut the dough cleanly and not catch, drag, or rip it.

Baking the Bread

DIFFERENT BREADS BAKE AT different temperatures. Rustic, lean doughs without fat or eggs need a hot oven (425° to 450°F) to develop a dark crust. Doughs rich in fat or eggs must bake at a lower temperature, 350° to 375°F, so that the interior is baked through without the crust becoming too brown. The size and shape of the bread affects the baking time, too. Thin baguettes will bake in 25 minutes, while 2-pound rounds may take an hour or more.

Baking stones mimic the stone floors of wood-fired ovens. The stones supply an additional heat source. The dough is placed directly on the stone, efficiently transferring the heat to the loaf, allowing the final fermentation (known as "oven spring") to occur more quickly, and promoting a crisp crust. Baking stones can be purchased at many cookware stores. A less expensive way of outfitting your oven is buying unglazed quarry tiles at a building supply store. Measure your oven first and buy American-made tiles, as imported tiles may include lead. There's no need to remove the heavy stone from the oven if you aren't making a rustic loaf—it can remain on the rack at all times.

Always allow a sufficient preheating period, especially when baking at high temperatures. With most ovens, estimate at least 45 minutes for the unit to reach the proper temperature. If you are using a baking stone, put it in the oven before preheating, so the stone is good and hot when you bake the bread.

Steam in the oven is vital to attain crisp, crackling crusts on rustic breads. But some loaves, such as sweet breads, don't need a hard crust, so the type of bread determines whether or not to add steam.

If steam is used, it should make the oven moist only during the beginning phase of the baking, then dissipate so the oven is dry toward the end. When a loaf goes into the oven, the heat that gives the oven spring creates additional carbon dioxide, and the expanding gas cells push the loaf to its full expansion. The steam keeps the crust soft so this can happen. It also keeps the crust from drying out too fast, which in turn fosters complex chemical reactions on the loaf's surface. These changes make the crust brown and give the bread flavor. There are many ways to get steam into a home oven. Some bakers use a spray bottle to mist the bread, and others toss ice cubes directly onto the oven floor. Neither of these methods is ideal.

Our favorite technique isn't fussy and gives a good blast of steam. Before preheating the oven, place a metal baking pan on a rack lower than where the bread will bake. The bread bakes on the center rack, so place the pan on the lowest rack of the oven, or even directly on the floor of a gas oven. Preheat the pan along with the oven. Immediately after putting the bread in the oven, pour 2 cups hot water into the pan and close the oven door. The immediate burst of steam will dissipate before the end of the baking period.

The classic method of knowing when a loaf is done is to thump it on the bottom. If it sounds hollow, it can be removed from the oven to cool on a rack. (For loaf pans, protect your hands with a towel, and slip the loaf out of the pan to give it a thump.) The color of the crust can also be an indication. Baked rustic breads are quite brown, even dark brown. If you aren't sure, take the bread's temperature with an instant-read thermometer. Insert the probe in the bottom of the bread so it won't show, and be sure to reach the middle of the loaf. It should read 200°F.

Storing Bread

THE MOMENT A LOAF of bread cools, it starts to become stale. The crust absorbs moisture, becoming soft and rubbery, and the interior dries out. Bread can be stored in plastic or paper. Both have advantages and disadvantages. An airtight plastic bag will maintain maximum freshness, but it will soften the crust, which is especially damaging to rustic breads. A crisp crust will fare better in a paper bag, but the interior of the loaf will stale faster. Sourdough breads don't stale as quickly. Reheating a loaf in the oven will liven it up. Toasting slices of old bread will also give them new life.

If bread is frozen, it must be wrapped airtight to seal in moisture and keep out other flavors. Some bakers wrap the loaf in plastic wrap or aluminum foil. Others wrap it twice, first in foil or paper, then in plastic. There is a difference of opinion on whether or not to defrost a frozen loaf before reheating. There are also differing opinions on the best oven temperature for reheating, from 350° to 400°F. In other words, do what works best for you.

White Sandwich Bread

MAKES 2 LOAVES, 24 ROLLS,
OR 12 HAMBURGER BUNS

Baird Lloyd

This is an easy yeast bread that is almost foolproof and quite versatile. It is perfect for the baking novice, as well as for seasoned bakers who want a fine white loaf. When thinly sliced, it is ideal for Summer Pudding (page 192).

1¾ cups milk, whole or 2 percent, heated to 100° to 110°F

1 tablespoon active dry yeast

2 tablespoons sugar

3 tablespoons plus 1 teaspoon vegetable oil

4¾ cups (1 pound, 8 ounces) bread flour, or as needed

2¼ teaspoons fine sea salt

1. Pour the warm milk into the bowl of a heavy-duty stand mixer. Add the yeast and sugar, then the oil, and stir to combine. Let stand until the yeast dissolves and the mixture begins to bubble, about 5 minutes.

2. Attach the bowl to the mixer and fit with the paddle attachment. With the mixer on low speed, add 1 cup flour and the salt. Gradually add enough of the remaining flour to make a soft, supple dough that cleans the sides of the bowl. Switch to the dough hook and knead on medium speed until the dough is smooth and elastic, about 5 minutes.

3. Lightly oil a large bowl. Turn the dough out onto a work surface and shape into a ball. Place in the bowl and turn to coat with oil. Cover tightly with plastic wrap. Let stand in a warm, draft-free place until doubled in volume, about 1 hour.

4. Lightly oil two 8½ × 4½-inch loaf pans. Turn the dough out onto a lightly floured surface. Cut the dough into 2 equal pieces. Form each piece into a rectangle about 8 × 4 inches. One at a time, starting at a long end, roll up tightly and pinch the seam closed. Place seam side down in the prepared pans. Loosely cover each loaf with a damp kitchen towel and let stand until the dough reaches the top of the pans, about 45 minutes.

5. Meanwhile, position a rack in the center of the oven and preheat to 400°F.

6. Bake the breads until the tops are golden brown and the loaves sound hollow when tapped on the bottom (remove the loaves from the pans to check), 30 to 40 minutes.

7. Remove the loaves from the pans, place on wire cooling racks, and cool completely.

Dinner Rolls: Position a rack in the center of the oven and preheat to 375°F. Cut the dough into 24 equal pieces. (For evenly shaped rolls, cut and weigh the dough into 2-ounce portions.) Shape each piece of dough into a ball. The best way to do this is to place the dough on an unfloured work surface. Cup your hand over the dough, touching the dough with the palm of your hand. Rotate your hand in small, quick circles, pressing the dough gently to form a ball. Line a large baking sheet with parchment paper. Arrange the rolls about 1½ inches apart on the baking sheet. Put the baking sheet in a large plastic bag. Give the top of the bag a few shakes to introduce air, then tie the ends together to close. Let stand until the rolls are almost doubled in size, about 15 minutes, or longer if it's a chilly day. Bake until the rolls are golden brown and sound hollow when tapped on the bottoms, about 15 minutes. Serve warm.

Hamburger Buns: Position racks in the center and top of the oven and preheat to 375°F. Cut the dough into 12 equal pieces. (For evenly shaped buns, cut and weigh the dough into 4-ounce portions.) Form each piece into a ball, cover loosely with plastic wrap, and let rest for 5 minutes. Using a rolling pin, roll each ball into a round about 3½ inches wide. Line two baking sheets with parchment paper. Arrange the buns about 1½ inches apart on the sheets. Put each baking sheet in a large plastic bag. Give the top of the bag a few shakes to introduce air, then tie the ends together to close. Let stand until the buns are almost doubled in size, about 15 minutes. Bake the buns until lightly browned, about 10 minutes. Transfer to wire cooling racks and cool completely. Slice in half crosswise with a serrated knife before toasting in a toaster or over coals in a grill.

Baker's Notes

DON'T LET THE milk get too hot—if you aren't sure of the temperature, use an instant-read thermometer. Be sure to let the milk cool if it overheats. If the milk is over 140°F, it will kill the yeast.

For a bread with a light, thin crust, use shiny aluminum or Pyrex pans. Dark, heavy pans will give the bread a thick, darker crust.

The shaped rolls and buns can be frozen, then baked another day. To freeze, shape the rolls and place on a baking sheet, then in a plastic bag. To defrost, leave at room temperature for about 1 hour, or until they double in size.

Testing and Tasting . . . White Bread

"Beautiful golden loaves," "brown bread sunken in the middle," "slices white as clouds," and "slices dry and crumbly . . ." were just some of the comments at a Baker's Dozen tasting of white sandwich bread.

We used a simple recipe, an easy yeast bread recipe that can be used to make bread, rolls, and hamburger buns. The recipe was followed to a T, and most loaves were baked in loaf pans in home ovens. The results were different from one another. The most striking difference was the variation in color. Because ovens tend to bake differently, the degrees of "golden brown" spanned the spectrum, even though all the loaves were baked through.

The wide differences resulted from the types of flour and fat used in the dough. Bread flour produced the best texture and the finest crumb. All-purpose unbleached flour worked, making an unreliably shaped loaf with a drier texture (in some cases crumbly). Different oils also had an impact. A heavily flavored oil, such as cottonseed, gave an oily, heavy taste to the bread. Neutral oil, such as corn oil, didn't interfere with the bread's natural taste.

While inconsistencies in oven temperatures and the types of milk added to the variations, flour and oil seemed to be the most important factors. The tasting again proved the baker's mantra: "For the best baked goods, use the best ingredients."

Jeff Sherman

Raisin Brioche

11 tablespoons (1 stick plus 3 tablespoons) unsalted butter,
   chilled and cut into thin slices

⅓ cup whole milk, heated to 100° to 110°F

2½ teaspoons active dry yeast

4 large eggs, at room temperature

½ cup sugar

3 cups (15 ounces) unbleached all-purpose flour,
   or as needed

1½ teaspoons fine sea salt

1 cup (9 ounces) raisins

2 large egg yolks beaten with 1 tablespoon water,
   for glazing

MAKES 2 LARGE BRIOCHE

Fran Gage

Enriched with eggs and butter, this French classic is a real breakfast treat. While the bread can be embellished with a dollop of preserves, there's no need to spread it with butter (it's already in the dough). The finished dough must be refrigerated at least 12 hours, overnight, so make it the day before baking. If you want to bake it in the traditional fluted shape, use two 7-inch-diameter brioche tins.

1. Beat the butter in the large bowl of a heavy-duty stand mixer with the paddle attachment until it is a soft mass, but still cool. Transfer to another bowl and wash the mixing bowl.

2. Pour the milk into the washed bowl and sprinkle in the yeast. Let stand until the yeast dissolves, about 5 minutes.

3. Attach the bowl to the mixer and fit with the paddle attachment. Add the eggs and sugar and mix on low speed until combined. Mix in 1 cup flour and the salt. Gradually mix in enough of the remaining flour to make a soft dough. Change to the dough hook and knead on medium-low speed, adding more flour if necessary to make a soft, smooth dough that cleans the sides but not the bottom of the bowl, about 6 minutes.

4. With the machine running, add about 3 tablespoons butter and let the dough absorb it, adding a little flour if the dough seems overly sticky. (Remember that rich sweet doughs will always be stickier than unsweetened doughs, so don't add too much flour.) Add the rest of the butter in three portions, letting each addition absorb into the dough and adding flour as needed. Mix until the dough forms a soft, loose ball on the hook that doesn't clean the bottom of the bowl. Add the raisins and mix just until they are incorporated into the dough.

5. Lightly butter a large bowl. Add the dough and turn to coat with the butter. Cover tightly with plastic wrap. Let stand in a warm place until almost doubled in volume, about 2 hours.

6. Transfer the bowl to the refrigerator. Chill for 12 hours or overnight.

*Yeast Breads
and
Flatbreads*

7. About 30 minutes before shaping, remove the bowl from the refrigerator. Let stand at room temperature until the dough loses its chill but is firm and easy to handle.

8. Generously butter two 3-cup (7-inch-diameter) brioche tins or two 8½ × 4½ × 2½-inch loaf pans. Turn the dough out onto a work surface and cut into 2 equal portions.

9. *To fill the brioche pans,* working with one portion of dough at a time, lightly dust the dough with flour. Cut off one quarter of the dough, form into a ball, and then elongate into a teardrop shape. Form the larger piece of dough into a ball, then work a hole into the center to form a ring. Fit the ring into a prepared pan; then fit the teardrop, pointed end down, into the hole. Brush lightly with some of the egg glaze.

To form loaves, pat and stretch each piece of dough into a 9 × 6-inch rectangle. Roll up tightly from a long end, then pinch the seam closed. Fit each loaf into a prepared loaf pan, seam side down. Brush lightly with the egg glaze.

Cover and refrigerate the remaining egg glaze.

10. Place each mold or loaf pan into a large plastic bag and close the bag, but do not let the plastic touch the dough (if necessary, place a tall glass inside each bag to lift the plastic). Let stand in a warm place until the dough doubles in volume, about 2½ hours.

11. Meanwhile, position a rack in the center of the oven and preheat to 375°F.

12. Remove the pans from the bags and brush the dough again with the egg glaze. Bake until the brioches are well browned, about 35 minutes.

13. Cool on wire racks for 10 minutes. Unmold onto the racks and cool completely.

Individual Brioche Molds: Generously butter twelve 4-inch-diameter brioche molds. Cut the dough into 12 pieces. Following the instructions for the larger brioche, cut off a quarter of each portion of dough and form into a teardrop. Form the larger piece of dough into a ball, then a doughnut shape, and fit into the mold. Add the smaller piece of dough, pointed end down. Brush with egg glaze, place on the work counter in large plastic bags, and let rise until doubled in volume, 45 minutes to 1 hour. Glaze again and bake until deep golden brown, about 20 minutes.

THE FINISHED DOUGH, like all sweet bread doughs, should be soft and somewhat sticky. The butter in this dough will harden under refrigeration, making the chilled dough easier to handle than unchilled. Also, the slow, cool rise will add flavor to the bread.

The dough must be kneaded to develop the gluten structure before adding the butter. If such a large amount of butter were added to the dough before mixing, the fat would coat the gluten and hinder development.

The raisins are added to the dough after mixing. If added too early, they will break up and discolor the dough. If you wish, you can knead them in by hand.

The egg wash serves a dual purpose. It helps keep the dough from drying as it rises, and it colors the crust during baking.

Brioche needs a lower oven temperature than other breads because the dough is enriched with eggs, sugar, and butter—all ingredients that encourage browning of the crust. If the oven is too hot, the crust will overbrown before the interior is baked. Reduce the oven heat slightly, if necessary, to avoid a dark crust.

Italian Whole Wheat Bread
(Pane Integrale)

MAKES 2 LARGE LOAVES

Carol Field

This is the quintessential Italian loaf. Made with a thick, doughlike starter (biga in Italian), it is well fermented, chewy, and flavorful from whole wheat. It is a good example of a moist dough, a wet, sticky blob that may seem difficult to handle. For this reason, this dough is best made in a heavy-duty stand mixer and not by hand. The biga must be made at least 6 and up to 24 hours before making the dough.

BIGA

½ teaspoon active dry yeast
¼ cup warm (100° to 110°F) water
1¼ cups plus 2 teaspoons water, at room temperature
3½ cups (1 pound, 1¾ ounces) unbleached
   all-purpose flour

DOUGH

¼ cup warm (110° to 115°F) water
1¼ teaspoons active dry yeast
2½ cups water, at room temperature
1 cup (8½ ounces) biga (see Baker's Notes)
4½ cups (1 pound, 5½ ounces) unbleached
   all-purpose flour
1 cup plus 2 tablespoons (5½ ounces) whole
   wheat flour, preferably an organically grown,
   stone-ground brand (dip-and-sweep)
1 tablespoon fine sea salt

1. The day before making the bread, prepare the biga. In a medium bowl, sprinkle the yeast over the warm water and let stand until creamy, about 5 minutes. Whisk to dissolve the yeast. Add the room-temperature water. Using a wooden spoon, stir in the flour about 1 cup at a time. Stir for 3 to 4 minutes. (You can also mix the biga in a heavy-duty stand mixer fitted with the paddle attachment for 2 minutes on low speed.)

2. Transfer the biga to a lightly oiled medium bowl. Cover tightly with plastic wrap. Let stand at cool (no higher than 78°F) room temperature for at least 6 and up to 24 hours. The biga will triple in volume and may deflate; it will be wet and sticky. Refrigerate until ready to use, up to 5 days. (The biga will get more sour as it ages. If the biga is chilled, remove it from the refrigerator about 1½ hours before using. The biga can also be frozen in an airtight container for up to 3 months. Defrost for 3 hours at room temperature before using.)

3. To make the dough, pour the warm water into the bowl of a heavy-duty stand mixer and sprinkle the yeast on top. Let stand until creamy, about 5 minutes. Add the room-temperature water and the measured amount of

The Baker's Dozen Cookbook

biga. Attach the bowl to the mixer and fit with the paddle attachment. Mix on low speed until the water is chalky white and the biga is broken into small pieces. Mix the flour, whole wheat flour, and salt. Gradually add enough of the flour mixture to the biga mixture to form a dough (it will still stick to the bottom of the bowl). Switch to the dough hook. Knead on medium speed until the dough is smooth but still quite moist and sticky and clings to the bottom of the bowl, 5 to 7 minutes. Add no more than 2 to 3 tablespoons additional flour—at this stage the wetness of the dough is crucial to the bread's texture.

4. Lightly oil a large bowl. Transfer the dough to the bowl and cover tightly with plastic wrap. Let stand at room temperature until the dough triples in volume, about 3 hours. Do not punch the dough down.

5. Carefully turn the dough out onto a well-floured surface, taking care not to deflate the dough too much—you want to retain the air bubbles. Cut the dough into 2 equal portions. Working with one portion, using moistened cupped hands, pull tight on the sides of the dough, rotating your hands around the edges, until it forms a taut ball. Place the ball on a well-floured piece of parchment paper, rough side up. Repeat with the other piece of dough.

6. Cover each ball with a dampened towel. Let stand at room temperature until the balls have almost doubled in volume, with lots of air bubbles visible under the skin of the dough, about 1 hour.

7. Meanwhile, position a rack in the center of the oven. Place baking stones on the rack and preheat for at least 45 minutes to 450°F. Just before baking, sprinkle the stones with cornmeal.

8. Gently invert one loaf onto a rimless baking sheet or baker's peel that has been generously sprinkled with cornmeal. Using a few well-aimed shakes, slide the loaf off the baking sheet onto the far corner of the stones. Repeat with the other loaf, placing it as far away from the first loaf as possible. (If your oven will bake only one loaf at a time, refrigerate the second loaf while baking the first.)

9. Bake until the loaves are golden brown and sound hollow when tapped on the bottom, 35 to 45 minutes. Cool completely on wire racks.

Durum Bread: Substitute durum flour for the whole wheat flour. Durum is a very hard, high-gluten wheat. When it is used to make pasta, it is called semolina and is ground to a sandy texture. For bread making it is milled to a finer golden flour that must be kneaded a longer time than unbleached or bleached all-purpose wheat flour. If you can't find durum flour, you can make your own golden durum flour by grinding 1 cup semolina with 1 cup unbleached all-purpose flour in a food processor or blender until processed to a powder.

Baker's Notes

AS THE VOLUME of the biga will be different at various stages of rising, it is best to weigh the biga on a kitchen scale. If necessary, measure in a measuring cup.

To refresh the remaining biga, add 1¼ cups unbleached flour and ½ cup water and mix well until smooth. Cover tightly with plastic wrap and let stand at room temperature for 6 hours. Refrigerate or freeze. To keep the biga alive, it needs to be refreshed every 5 days: Use or discard 1 cup biga, then stir in 1¼ cups flour and ½ cup water, cover, and let stand for 6 hours. Refrigerate or freeze.

Most recipes instruct the baker to punch the dough down before shaping, but not this one. The air pockets that have developed during the first rise contribute to the irregular interior of this bread. Punching down would deflate too many of these bubbles.

Some bakers are used to adding steam to the oven to get a crusty loaf, but it's unnecessary with this wet dough. In fact, most Italian bakers rely on the radiant heat from their brick ovens (the baking stone is a fine substitute) as well as the stickiness of the dough to produce a good crust.

The bread may look deflated when you slip it into the oven, but it will eventually puff up like a pillow. Be patient, and don't open the oven door too often—you'll let out the heat.

Multigrain Bread

MAKES 1 LARGE LOAF OR
12 DINNER ROLLS

SPONGE

1¼ cups water, at room temperature

1 tablespoon active dry yeast

1 tablespoon honey

3 cups (15 ounces) bread flour

DOUGH

¼ cup buttermilk or water

3 tablespoons honey

1½ teaspoons fine sea salt

1 cup (5 ounces) total of any combination of the following:
    uncooked rolled oats; uncooked coarse cornmeal
    (or polenta, but not fine cornmeal); cooked brown or
    wild rice; oat or wheat bran; uncooked millet, amaranth,
    or quinoa; rye or kamut flour; triticale, rye, or
    wheat flakes

1 cup bread flour, or as needed

1 large egg beaten with 2 teaspoons water, for glazing,
    optional

1 tablespoon uncooked rolled oats, optional

1. To make the sponge, combine the water, yeast, and honey in the bowl of a heavy-duty stand mixer. Let stand until the yeast is creamy, about 5 minutes. Add the flour and stir well, about 100 strokes (or mix on low speed with the paddle attachment for 1 minute). Scrape the bowl down and cover tightly with plastic wrap. Let stand at room temperature until the sponge is bubbling vigorously (it may collapse, which is fine), about 2 hours.

2. To make the dough, add the buttermilk, 3 tablespoons honey, and the salt to the sponge. Attach to the mixer and fit with the paddle attachment. On low speed, add the grains and mix to form a dough. The amount of dry ingredients and liquid will depend on the grains used. If the dough is too dry, add water 1 tablespoon at a time. If too moist, add more flour as needed; it could take up to a cup, depending on the multigrain blend you use.

3. Switch to the dough hook and knead on medium-low speed until the dough is supple, about 10 minutes. The dough will feel tacky but not sticky, and neutral in temperature, neither cold nor warm.

Peter Reinhart

The challenge in making multigrain breads is providing enough gluten to enable the dough to rise. Since no other grains provide as much gluten as wheat, the addition of other grains dilutes the overall amount of gluten. This recipe uses a ratio that balances the unique flavors and textures of nonwheat grains but provides enough gluten to produce a light loaf with nice webbing in the crumb. Just about any grain can be used, as long as you use three-quarters bread flour with one-quarter other grains. Use the sponge method to make the bread—it will bring out the maximum potential of the gluten with the minimum amount of kneading. It also uses less yeast, as the yeast will multiply during the first stage.

4. Lightly butter or oil a large bowl. Form the dough into a ball, place in the bowl, and turn to coat with the butter. Cover tightly with plastic wrap. Let stand at room temperature (not necessarily in a warm place) until doubled in volume, about 1½ hours.

5. Lightly grease an 8½ × 4½ × 2½-inch loaf pan with vegetable shortening. Pat the dough into a 9 × 6-inch rectangle. Starting at a long end, roll up tightly and pinch the seam closed. Place seam side down in the prepared pan. Cover loosely with a damp kitchen towel and let stand at room temperature until doubled in volume, about 60 to 90 minutes.

6. Meanwhile, position a rack in the center of the oven and preheat to 350°F.

7. If desired, lightly brush the top of the loaf with some of the egg glaze and sprinkle with the oats. Bake until the loaf sounds hollow when tapped on the bottom (remove the loaf from the pan to check), 50 minutes to 1 hour. Cool on a wire rack for 10 minutes. Remove from the pan and cool.

Dinner Rolls: After the dough has risen for 1½ hours, cut it into 12 equal pieces. Shape each piece into a ball (see page 260). Arrange 2 inches apart on a large baking sheet. Put the baking sheet in a large plastic bag. Give the top of the bag a few shakes to introduce air, then tie the ends together to close. Let stand until the rolls are almost doubled in size, about 15 minutes. Brush with egg glaze and sprinkle with oats, if desired. Bake until golden brown, 20 to 30 minutes.

Baker's Notes

THERE ARE TWO keys to making this bread. Remember that the amounts of water and grains are variable—add just enough to make a ball of dough. Also, use room-temperature water to encourage the optimum fermentation temperature of 75° to 80°F.

A sponge is made by mixing a large part of the water and flour plus some (or all) of the yeast that will go into the final dough. Less yeast is used than in straight-method doughs. Generally, the longer the sponge is allowed to ferment, the less yeast is needed. A sponge has a batterlike texture and can rise and bubble dramatically if a large portion of yeast is used, or rise more slowly if less yeast is used. Depending on the recipe, a sponge can ferment for 2 to 12 or more hours before the final dough is mixed.

French Baguettes

MAKES 4 BAGUETTES

Craig Ponsford

Here's a classic recipe for long, crusty loaves, but with a few alterations. The dough is made with a spongelike poolish. This allows the baker to use less yeast, resulting in a long fermentation and a better-tasting loaf that keeps fresh longer. Start the poolish the night before making the dough.

POOLISH

Pinch of active dry yeast
7 tablespoons water, at room temperature
¾ cup (3½ ounces) bread flour

DOUGH

1⅓ cups water, calculated to make a dough of 77°F
    (see page 258)
2 teaspoons active dry yeast
2¼ teaspoons fine sea salt
4 cups (1 pound, 4 ounces) bread flour, or as needed

1. The night before making the bread, make the poolish. In a medium bowl, sprinkle the yeast over the water and let stand until the yeast is creamy, about 5 minutes. Add the flour and stir well to make a smooth batter. Cover tightly with plastic wrap and let stand at 70°F until the batter bubbles, rises, and then collapses. (If your kitchen is warmer than 70°F refrigerate the poolish for a couple of hours whenever it is convenient.)

2. To make the dough, combine the water and yeast in the bowl of a heavy-duty stand mixer. Let stand until creamy, about 5 minutes. Scrape in all of the poolish. Attach the bowl to the mixer and fit with the paddle attachment. Mix on low speed until the poolish breaks up. Add the salt and enough of the flour to form a rough dough. Change to the dough hook. Knead on low speed until the dough comes away from the sides of the bowl, about 3 minutes. Increase the speed to medium-high and knead until the dough is smooth, shiny, and elastic. The dough should be 77°F at the end of the kneading.

3. Lightly oil a large bowl. Transfer the dough to the bowl and cover tightly with plastic wrap. Let stand at room temperature for 1 hour. Punch the dough down, cover again, and let rise until it almost doubles in volume, about 1 hour.

4. Turn the dough out onto a lightly floured work surface and cut into 4 equal pieces. Gently shape each piece into a thick cylinder. Place on the floured surface and cover with damp towels. Let rest for 30 minutes.

5. Working with one piece of dough at a time, form into baguettes. Gently press the dough into a rectangle, being careful not to expel too much gas. Fold the edge nearest you to the center, then fold the top edge to the center.

T HIS RECIPE ILLUSTRATES how temperature affects the flavor of the dough and, subsequently, the bread. Allow the poolish to ferment at cool room temperature, then calculate the temperature of the water in the dough to reach the desired 77°F. Soon you will apply the principles of proper temperature to all of your bread baking—and your bread will be the better for it.

Forming the dough into cylinders (instead of balls) before resting makes it easier to elongate the dough into baguettes. As baguettes are stretched more than typical rounds or loaves, they will need a longer resting period before shaping to allow the gluten to relax. If shaped too soon, the dough will be too elastic for shaping.

The size of your baking stone dictates the length of the baguettes. Most stones measure 16½ × 14½ inches, so you can't make loaves longer than 16 inches (and a 16-inch loaf will shrink a bit as well).

Baguettes require steam in the oven to give them a crisp crust. There are many ways to incorporate steam in the oven, but the hot-pan method described in this recipe is the most efficient of all the methods we've tried.

The parchment paper must be of professional quality—a lesser grade will burn in the very hot oven. If you wish, instead of lining the baking sheets with cornmeal, sprinkle them with a generous amount of flour, which will allow the baguettes to slide easily off the sheets onto the baking stone.

Next fold the dough in half lengthwise. Using the side of your hand, pinch the dough closed at the long seam. (This gives the dough a taut, smooth surface.) Put the dough seam side down on the work surface. Place your hands at the center of the dough. Gently rock it back and forth while gradually working your hands toward the end of the dough. When the dough begins to spring back, cover it with a damp towel and let it relax for a few minutes while making baguettes with the other pieces of dough. Return to each baguette and elongate again until the dough is about 16 inches long.

6. Line two large rimless baking sheets (or inverted half-sheet pans) with parchment paper. Arranging them about 1½ inches apart, place two baguettes on each sheet. Place the baking sheets in a large plastic bag and give the top of the bag a few quick shakes to introduce air, then tie the ends together to close. Let stand at warm room temperature until the loaves are doubled in volume, about 2 hours.

7. Position a rack in the center and bottom third of the oven. Place a baking stone on the center rack and a 13 × 9-inch metal baking pan on the bottom rack. Preheat the oven to 500°F for at least 45 minutes.

8. Bake the loaves in two batches. If the second batch is rising too quickly, refrigerate the baking sheet while baking the first two loaves. Using a baker's lame or sharp serrated knife, score the top of each loaf with 4 or 5 parallel slashes—each cut should be at a 45-degree angle and about ½ inch deep. Slide the parchment paper with the first two loaves onto the baking stone. Pour 2 cups hot water into the heated pan. Bake until the bread is golden brown and sounds hollow when rapped on the bottom, about 20 minutes. Cool completely on wire cooling racks. Repeat with the remaining loaves.

Sourdough Bread

SPONGE STARTER

DAY ONE

1 cup raisins, preferably organic
2 cups warm water
1 teaspoon honey
1 cup (4¾ ounces) whole wheat flour

DAY TWO

¾ cup cool tap water
1 cup (5 ounces) bread flour

DAY THREE

1½ cups cool tap water
2 cups (10 ounces) bread flour

DAY FOUR

3 cups cool tap water
4 cups (1 pound, 4 ounces) bread flour

INTERMEDIATE STARTER

1⅓ cups (10½ ounces) sponge starter
¼ cup cool tap water
1¼ cups (6¼ ounces) bread flour

DOUGH

All of the intermediate starter
1⅓ cups cool tap water
4 cups (1 pound, 4 ounces) bread flour, or as needed
2½ teaspoons fine sea salt

1. To make the starter, begin at least 5 days before baking the bread. In a small bowl, soak the raisins in the warm water for 15 minutes. Drain the raisins, reserving 1 cup of the soaking water. Discard the raisins.

2. Mix the reserved soaking water and the honey in a medium ceramic or glass bowl. Add the flour and stir well to make a thick batter. Cover tightly with plastic wrap and let stand at room temperature (70°F is ideal) for 24 hours.

MAKES 2 LARGE LOAVES

Peter Reinhart

One of the joys of making sourdough bread is the opportunity to create and cultivate your own starter.

There are many ways to make sourdough starters and breads, and every bakery has its own method. But all contain wild yeast and bacteria that ferment the dough and make it rise. The consistency of starters ranges from loose batters to firm doughs. Here a batterlike sponge is mixed into a firmer starter before being mixed into the final dough. The raisins are a lively gathering place for wild yeast and help start the fermentation. Organic raisins are preferred, as other raisins may be sprayed with pesticides that discourage bacterial growth.

The initial starter takes 5 days to make. Once ready, it can be kept alive in the refrigerator with occasional feedings of water and flour, ready to be used again.

*Yeast Breads
and
Flatbreads*

3. On Day Two, there will be little or no sign of fermentation in the starter. Mix the water and then the flour into the batter, cover tightly with plastic wrap, and let stand at room temperature for 24 hours.

4. On Day Three, the fermentation will be minimal, but there will be some bubbles on the surface of the sponge. If the ingredients in the sponge have separated, mix them together. Add the water and then the flour and stir vigorously. Cover tightly with plastic wrap and let stand at room temperature for another 24 hours.

5. On Day Four, there should be active bubbling on the surface of the sponge and a faint aroma of vinegar. Stir the water and then the flour into the sponge as on the previous days, cover, and let stand at room temperature for a final 24 hours, or until the mixture becomes very foamy. The final time is determined by temperature variations and the amount of yeast and bacteria present in the dough. When the sponge is very foamy, it will be able to leaven bread. (The sponge can be refrigerated for up to 3 days. Bring to room temperature before going on to the next step.)

6. To make the intermediate starter, measure the sponge. In the bowl of a heavy-duty stand mixer, combine the sponge, water, and flour. Attach to the mixer and fit with the paddle attachment. Mix on low speed until there are no lumps of sponge visible and the mixture is firm and tacky. Remove the paddle and cover the bowl tightly with plastic wrap. Let stand at room temperature until doubled in size, 4 to 6 hours, maybe longer. Be sure the starter has doubled before proceeding. (The starter can be refrigerated overnight. Bring to room temperature and be sure it has doubled before going on to the next step.)

7. To make the final dough, add the water to the intermediate starter in the mixing bowl. Attach to the mixer and fit with the paddle attachment. Mix on low speed until the starter dissolves. Add 2 cups flour and the salt. Gradually add enough of the remaining flour to make a ball of dough. Switch to the dough hook and knead on medium-low speed until the dough is smooth but tacky, about 5 minutes.

8. Cover the bowl tightly with plastic wrap. Let stand at room temperature until doubled in size, about 4 hours.

9. Turn the dough out onto a lightly floured work surface and cut into 2 equal pieces. Shape one piece of dough into a round and place on a piece of parchment paper. Cover with a damp kitchen towel. Repeat with the other piece of dough. Let stand at room temperature until doubled in size, about 4 hours. If the towels threaten to dry out, mist them well with water or redampen them.

10. About 45 minutes before baking, position a rack in the center of the oven and place a baking stone on the rack. Position another rack on the lowest rung of the oven and place a metal baking pan on it. Preheat the oven to 450°F.

11. Cut away the excess parchment paper from under each round. Lift a round, still on the paper, onto a baker's peel or rimless baking sheet. Using a baker's lame or sharp serrated knife, slash the top with a shallow cross. Slide the loaf onto the far corner of the baking stone. Repeat with the other loaf, positioning it away from the first loaf. Pour 2 cups hot water into the heated pan and immediately close the oven door.

12. Bake until the loaves are well browned and sound hollow when tapped on the bottom, 20 to 25 minutes. Cool on a wire rack before serving.

Baker's Notes

USING A SOURDOUGH starter is just another way of fermenting dough. Sourdough starters are not the same as pre-ferments made with commercial yeast; they are composed of different organisms. Instead of commercial yeast (*Saccharomyces cerevisiae*), these sourdough starters contain *Saccharomyces exiguus*, a different strain, which occurs naturally. Sourdoughs also contain a bacterium, *lactobacillus*, that produces acetic and lactic acids, giving the bread its distinctive sour flavor. These two organisms, the yeast and the bacteria, coexist in a very stable environment, where the yeast tolerates the acidity contributed by the bacteria, and the bacteria ferments maltose, a sugar that the yeast can't use.

The initial sponge starter is potent enough to keep for 3 days, tightly covered and refrigerated. After that it needs to be refreshed once a week. To refresh the sponge after using 1⅓ cups in this recipe, stir 1½ cups water and 2 cups bread flour into the remaining sponge. Cover and let stand at room temperature until bubbly, 4 to 6 hours, then refrigerate until ready to use, up to 1 week. For best flavor, refrigerate the sponge overnight after refreshing, but allow it to come to room temperature before making the intermediate starter.

If you haven't used the sponge for a week or longer, it will need to be refreshed and strengthened over a 2- to 3-day period. Discard about half of the sponge. Each day, add 2 cups bread flour and 1½ cups water; let the sponge stand at room temperature for 4 to 6 hours, then refrigerate overnight. When the starter is bubbly, it is potent enough to act as a leavening.

The potent sponge can be frozen for up to 6 months. Before using, defrost the sponge and refresh and strengthen over a 3-day period, as described above.

If at any time the starter develops mold or turns green or red, discard it and start again.

Classic Rye Bread

PRE-FERMENTED DOUGH

¾ cup water, at room temperature

1 teaspoon active dry yeast

1¾ cups plus 2 tablespoons (9½ ounces) unbleached
all-purpose flour

1 teaspoon fine sea salt

FINAL DOUGH

2 cups water, at room temperature

2 teaspoons active dry yeast

2 tablespoons vegetable oil

¼ cup unsulfured molasses

2 tablespoons caraway seeds

2 teaspoons diastatic malt powder
(see Baker's Notes) or brown sugar

2 teaspoons fine sea salt

1⅔ cups (8 ounces) medium rye flour

3¼ cups (1 pound) bread flour, or as needed

MAKES 2 LOAVES

Peter Reinhart

This slightly acidified rye bread is a top contender for your sandwiches. It is made from a firm, pre-fermented dough (pâte fermentée in French), a process that gives plenty of additional character to the loaf. Medium rye flour is the most common type; it is probably available at your natural food store and maybe even your supermarket. Make the pre-fermented dough at least 2½ hours before you want to make the bread, or refrigerate it overnight.

1. At least 2½ hours ahead of making the final dough, make the pre-fermented dough. Pour the water into the bowl of a heavy-duty stand mixer and sprinkle the yeast on top. Let stand until creamy, about 5 minutes. Attach the bowl to the mixer and fit with the paddle attachment. On low speed, gradually add the flour and salt and mix to form a dough. Change to the dough hook and mix on medium speed until the dough forms a ball. Reduce the speed to medium-low and knead for 8 minutes.

2. Detach the hook and remove the bowl from the mixer. Cover the bowl tightly with plastic wrap. Let the dough stand at room temperature until doubled in volume, about 2½ hours. If you wish, refrigerate the dough for up to 12 hours. (If you have refrigerated the dough, let it stand at room temperature for at least 2 hours to lose its chill. Be sure the dough has doubled before proceeding.)

3. To make the final dough, pour the water into a medium bowl and sprinkle the yeast on top. Let stand until creamy, about 5 minutes. Pour the yeasted water into the mixer bowl with the dough. Using your hands, squeeze the pre-fermented dough to break it up in the liquid. Add the oil, then the molasses, caraway seeds, malt powder, and salt. Return the bowl to the mixer and fit with the paddle blade. On low speed, add the rye flour.

*Yeast Breads
and
Flatbreads*

Gradually add enough of the bread flour to make a rough dough. Change to the dough hook and knead until the dough is smooth and supple, about 6 minutes. The dough should feel somewhat tacky—don't add too much flour.

4. Detach the dough hook and remove the bowl from the mixer. Cover tightly with plastic wrap. Let stand at room temperature until the dough doubles in volume, about 1½ hours.

5. Lightly oil two 9 × 5 × 3-inch loaf pans. Turn the dough out onto a floured work surface and cut into 2 equal portions. Shape one piece of dough into a 9 × 5-inch rectangle. Starting at a long end, roll up and pinch the long seam closed. Seam side down, fit into a prepared pan. Repeat with the other piece of dough. Place the pans on a baking sheet. Slip the sheet into a large plastic bag and close the bag tightly. Let stand at room temperature until the loaves barely dome over the tops of the pans, 45 minutes to 1 hour.

6. Position racks in the center and bottom third of the oven. Place a 13 × 9-inch metal baking pan on the bottom rack. Preheat the oven to 400°F.

7. Remove the loaves from the plastic bag. Place on the center oven rack and immediately pour 2 cups hot water into the heated pan. Bake until the bread sounds hollow when tapped on the bottom (remove from the pans to check), about 35 minutes.

8. Cool for 10 minutes on wire cooling racks. Remove the loaves from the pans and cool completely on the racks.

Round Rye Loaves: Line a large rimless baking sheet or inverted half-sheet pan with professional-grade parchment paper. Cut the dough into 2 equal portions. Form one portion into a round loaf (see page 260). Place, rounded side up, on the prepared baking sheet. Form the remaining dough into an identical round and place it well apart from the other loaf. Slip the baking sheet into a plastic bag, close tightly, and let rise until almost doubled, about 1 hour. The loaves will spread as well as rise. Place a baking stone in the oven and preheat to 400°F, allowing at least 45 minutes. When ready to bake, cut away the excess paper from around the loaves. Cut 3 shallow slashes in the top of each loaf. Slide the loaves onto the baking stone and add the hot water to the heated pan. Bake until the loaves sound hollow when tapped on the bottoms, about 35 minutes.

Baker's Notes ●————————————————————

THE GLUTEN FOUND in rye is somewhat weaker than wheat gluten, so the dough acts differently. Here are a few things to look for in rye doughs:

- The dough will not be as elastic as one made with wheat, so don't overknead, especially in a heavy-duty stand mixer.
- The dough is stickier than wheat-based doughs, so don't be fooled into adding too much wheat flour.
- The formed loaves won't rise as much or as quickly as wheat doughs. If making free-form loaves, expect them to spread out as well as rise.

Malt powder is produced from grains (usually barley, although there is wheat malt) that are allowed to sprout, then dried and ground into a powder or flour. The sprouting produces diastase enzymes and natural maltose sugars that contribute to the dough fermentation and add color to the baked bread. Diastatic malt powder (the diastase enzymes are still active) is a valuable supplement for whole-grain breads or others that may have sluggish fermentation. In fact, a small amount of malted barley flour is routinely added to most commercial flours. Non-diastatic malt powder is used mainly for flavoring, for the enzymes have been killed by roasting. For either type of malt powder, you may substitute light or dark brown sugar, which simulates the sweetness of malt but lacks its fermentation-enhancing qualities. As the type of malt powder is not often included on the label, it may be best to order it specifically through a reliable mail-order source, such as The Baker's Catalogue (see Sources, page 343).

Pita Breads

MAKES TWELVE 6-INCH
PITA BREADS

Fran Gage

Pita breads, those puffy breads that can be split and filled with countless combinations, can actually be made from many different doughs. The technique is to bake the dough after a brief second rise on a baking stone in a very hot oven.

2¼ cups warm water

2½ teaspoons active dry yeast

1½ cups (7½ ounces) whole wheat flour

2¾ teaspoons fine sea salt

4½ cups (1 pound, 6½ ounces) unbleached all-purpose flour, or as needed

1. Pour the water into the bowl of a heavy-duty stand mixer and sprinkle in the yeast. Let stand until creamy, about 5 minutes.

2. Attach the bowl to the mixer and fit with the paddle attachment. On low speed, add the whole wheat flour and salt. Gradually add enough of the unbleached flour to make a ball of dough. Change to the dough hook. Knead on medium-low speed until the dough is smooth and elastic, about 10 minutes.

3. Detach the dough hook and remove the bowl from the mixer. Cover the bowl tightly with plastic wrap. Let stand at room temperature until the dough has doubled in volume, 2½ to 3 hours.

4. Meanwhile, position a rack in the center of the oven. Place a baking stone on the rack. Preheat the oven to 500°F, allowing at least 45 minutes.

5. Turn the dough out onto a lightly floured surface. Cut it into 12 equal pieces. Round each into a ball, then roll out each piece into a thick disk. Set aside, covered with plastic wrap (you can overlap the rounds to save space). Let the rounds of dough relax for 5 minutes. Going in sequence, starting with the rounds of dough that were rolled out first, roll out each round into a thin disk between 6 and 7 inches in diameter. Set aside and cover with plastic wrap. Let the disks of dough relax for another 5 minutes.

6. Lightly dust a baker's peel or rimless baking sheet with flour. Place 2 or 3 disks on the peel. Slide the disks off the peel onto the hot baking stone. Bake until the breads are puffed and the tops are very lightly browned but still soft, about 3 minutes. Do not let the breads get too brown, or they will be brittle when cooled. Remove the breads from the oven and cool on a work surface. Repeat with the remaining dough. (To keep the pita breads soft, store the cooled breads in plastic bags.)

Baker's Note

TO ROLL THE rounds of pita dough into evenly shaped thin disks, use the same technique that pastry bakers use for rolling out pie or tart dough. Place the round of dough on a lightly floured work surface. With the rolling pin at the center of the disk, roll to the top of the dough. Rotate the dough a quarter turn and repeat rolling out from the center to the top. Repeat, turning the dough a quarter turn each time, until the dough is formed into an evenly round, thin disk.

Orange-Rum Sweet Bread (Crescia Cingolana)

MAKES 1 LARGE LOAF

Carol Field

Reminiscent of panettone in shape and texture, this bread is aromatic with orange zest. Crescia refers to the dough's cresting over the top of the mold, and Cingolana refers to Cingoli, the town in Le Marche from which it comes. It goes equally well with morning coffee or a glass of Vin Santo.

SPONGE

½ cup whole milk, heated to lukewarm (100° to 110°F)
2½ teaspoons active dry yeast
⅔ cup (3½ ounces) unbleached all-purpose flour

DOUGH

¼ cup dark rum
3¼ cups (1 pound) unbleached all-purpose flour, or as needed
1 teaspoon fine sea salt
3 large eggs, at room temperature
⅓ cup sugar
Zest of 2 oranges (see step 2)
¼ cup olive oil (not extra virgin)

1 large egg white beaten with 2 teaspoons water, for the glaze

1. To make the sponge, pour the milk into the bowl of a heavy-duty stand mixer and sprinkle the yeast on top. Let stand until the yeast dissolves, about 5 minutes. Add the flour and stir vigorously with a wooden spoon to form a thick batter. Cover tightly with plastic wrap. Let stand at room temperature until the sponge is bubbly and doubles in volume, 30 to 45 minutes.

2. To make the dough, add the rum to the sponge in the bowl. Attach the bowl to the mixer and fit with the paddle attachment. On low speed, add 1 cup flour and the salt and mix until smooth. Add 2 eggs and another 1 cup flour and mix until smooth. Beat in the remaining egg, then the remaining 1¼ cups flour, along with the sugar and zest (grate the orange zest right into the bowl, removing the bowl from the stand if necessary). With the mixer on low speed, add the olive oil in a slow, steady stream, then mix for 3 minutes. Switch to the dough hook and knead on medium-low speed until the dough is firm, elastic, and velvety with a barely sticky surface, about 3 minutes. If the dough seems too firm, beat in an additional tablespoon or so of milk; if too wet, add flour 1 tablespoon at a time.

The Baker's Dozen Cookbook

3. Detach the dough hook and remove the bowl from the stand. Cover the bowl tightly with plastic wrap. Let stand until the dough is doubled in volume, about 3 hours.

4. Lightly oil a 2-quart round soufflé dish or charlotte mold. Turn the dough onto a floured work surface and shape it into a round. Fit, rounded side up, into the prepared dish. Cover with a moistened towel. Let stand at room temperature until the dough has risen to the top of the dish, about 2 hours.

5. Position a rack in the center of the oven and preheat to 400°F.

6. Brush the top of the dough with some of the egg white glaze. Bake for 15 minutes. Reduce the oven temperature to 350°F and bake until the bread is golden and sounds hollow when the bottom is tapped, about 20 minutes.

7. Transfer to a wire cooling rack and cool for 30 minutes. Unmold onto the rack and cool completely.

Baker's Notes

THE USE OF a starter in this bread gives it a long fermentation. The sugar in sweet breads often makes the dough ferment too quickly.

The type of olive oil used will change the flavor of the bread, so choose it carefully. Use a high-quality golden olive oil (formerly called pure olive oil, but now sold without any designation) with an almost neutral flavor. A mild virgin olive oil would be ideal. Assertively flavored, dark-green extra virgin olive oil would overpower the loaf.

When zesting any citrus fruit, grate it right over the mixing bowl to catch the essential oils in the zest.

Morning Buns

MAKES 12 ROLLS

Fran Gage

Cinnamon and caramelized sugar are an irresistible combination. To give the buns their special flaky texture and buttery flavor, the dough is spread with butter and folded like a classic Danish pastry, so allow almost 8 hours to complete the procedure, which includes two 2-hour chilling periods. If you want these buns freshly baked for breakfast, make the dough the night before. Divide it among the buttered muffin cups and let stand at room temperature just until it rises ¼ inch above the top of the cups. Cover the muffin pan with plastic wrap and refrigerate. The next morning, let the dough stand at room temperature for 1 hour to lose its chill, then bake.

*The
Baker's
Dozen
Cookbook*

DOUGH

1½ cups whole milk, heated to lukewarm (100° to 110°F)

1 tablespoon active dry yeast

¼ cup granulated sugar

1 large egg, at room temperature

1 teaspoon vanilla extract

**4 cups (1 pound, 4 ounces) unbleached all-purpose flour
    or as needed**

1¾ teaspoons fine sea salt

**14 tablespoons (1¾ sticks) unsalted butter, softened
    to cool room temperature**

FILLING

1½ cups packed light brown sugar

1½ teaspoons ground cinnamon

1. Pour the milk into a large bowl and sprinkle the yeast on top. Let stand until the yeast dissolves, about 5 minutes. Add the granulated sugar, egg, and vanilla and mix well. Stir in 2 cups flour, then the salt. Gradually stir in the remaining flour to make a soft, shaggy dough. Turn out onto a floured surface and knead by hand a few times, just until it holds together. The dough will look rough.

2. Wipe out any excess dough from the bowl. Return the dough to the bowl. Cover tightly and let stand at room temperature until doubled in volume, about 2½ hours.

3. Turn the dough out onto a lightly floured surface and pat into a rectangle. Using a rolling pin, roll out the dough into a 17 × 11-inch rectangle. Brush off excess flour. (If the dough retracts, cover it with plastic wrap and let stand a few minutes, then try again.)

4. In a small bowl, work the butter with a rubber spatula until it is smooth and malleable but still cool—the butter should be as pliable as the dough. Starting at a short end, spread the butter evenly over two-thirds of the dough. Fold the dough into thirds like a business letter: Fold the unbuttered third of the dough over to cover one-third of the buttered section, then fold the exposed third over to complete the procedure. Roll out the dough again into a 17 × 11-inch rectangle. Repeat the folding procedure. Slip the dough into a large plastic bag or wrap in plastic wrap. Refrigerate for 2 hours.

5. Remove the dough from the plastic. Roll again into a rectangle, then fold into thirds. Repeat the procedure. Return to the plastic bag and refrigerate for another 2 hours.

6. To make the filling, mix the brown sugar and cinnamon in a small bowl. Set aside.

7. Butter the insides of twelve 2¾-inch-wide muffin cups. Remove the dough from the plastic. On a lightly floured surface, roll out the dough into an 18 × 9-inch rectangle. Sprinkle the cinnamon sugar over the dough, leaving a ½-inch border at one long side, and brush the border with water. Starting at the other long side, roll up the dough into a cylinder and pinch the seam closed. Using a sharp knife, cut crosswise into twelve 1½-inch-thick slices. Place each slice into a muffin cup, cut side down, pressing it into the bottom of the cup. Slip the muffin pan into the plastic bag and close tightly. Let stand at room temperature until the rolls have almost doubled in volume, about 1 hour.

8. Position a rack in the center of the oven and preheat to 400°F.

9. Remove the muffin pan from the bag. Bake until the rolls are well browned and the sugar is bubbling, 20 to 25 minutes.

10. Line a large baking sheet with parchment paper. Carefully invert the hot rolls onto the paper. Serve warm or cooled to room temperature.

Baker's Notes

THE DOUGH IS purposely mixed only to a rough state so it won't be overworked when rolled out and folded with the butter.

The temperature of the butter is important. If too soft, it will squeeze out of the dough when rolled. If too hard, it will break through the dough. If you have an instant-read thermometer, the proper temperature is about 65°F.

A trick for cutting uniform pieces from a cylinder of dough: Place a yardstick beside the dough and mark it at 1½-inch intervals before cutting.

Be careful when removing the rolls from the pan—hot sugar can cause serious burns.

Buttery Dinner Rolls

MAKES 12 ROLLS

Peter Reinhart

If you want soft, buttery rolls (as opposed to crusty, chewy ones), the key is to tenderize the gluten proteins with milk (buttermilk in this case), fat (such as butter, but some very good rolls use vegetable shortening), and sugar. This enriched dough must be baked at a moderate temperature to prevent the rolls from overbrowning before the insides are cooked through.

1⅔ cups buttermilk

4 tablespoons (½ stick) unsalted butter, cut into small pieces

1 tablespoon active dry yeast

2½ tablespoons sugar

3¾ cups (18 ounces) unbleached all-purpose flour

1¾ teaspoons fine sea salt

1 large egg, well beaten, for the glaze

2 teaspoons poppy or sesame seeds, optional

1. In a small saucepan, heat the buttermilk and butter over low heat just until the butter melts. The buttermilk may curdle when it is heated. Pour into the bowl of a heavy-duty stand mixer and let stand until lukewarm (100° to 110°F).

2. Sprinkle the yeast over the buttermilk mixture and let stand until softened, about 5 minutes. Stir in the sugar. Attach the bowl to the mixer and fit with the paddle attachment. On low speed, add 1 cup flour, then the salt. Gradually add enough of the remaining flour to make a soft dough (it may not form a ball). Switch to the dough hook and knead on medium-low speed until the dough is supple with a slightly tacky surface, about 8 minutes.

3. Detach the dough hook and remove the bowl from the mixer. Cover the bowl tightly with plastic wrap. Let stand at cool room temperature (70°F is ideal) until the dough doubles in volume, about 1½ hours.

4. Line a large baking sheet with parchment paper. Turn the dough out onto a lightly floured work surface. Cut into 12 equal pieces. Wipe the work surface with a damp cloth. Place a piece of dough on the barely damp work surface and cover with your cupped hand. Moving your hand in a quick circular motion, gently press the dough to the work surface—after about 10 rotations, it will form a ball. With practice, you may be able to do two balls at a time, one in each hand. Transfer the ball to the baking sheet. Repeat with the remaining dough.

5. Place the sheet in a large plastic bag. Stand a tall glass of hot water on the sheet to keep the bag from touching the rolls. Give the bag a few shakes to introduce air, then tie the two corners together to close. Let stand at cool room temperature until the dough has almost doubled in volume, about 1 hour.

6. Meanwhile, position a rack in the center of the oven and preheat to 375°F.

7. Uncover the rolls. Lightly brush the tops with some of the beaten egg, then sprinkle with the seeds, if desired. Bake until the rolls are golden brown (check the bottom of a roll to be sure), about 15 minutes. Cool for at least 15 minutes, then serve warm or at room temperature.

Baker's Notes

KEEP THIS DOUGH nice and soft and don't be surprised by its slightly tacky texture.

If you wish, make other shapes with the dough. *To make cloverleaf rolls*, cut each portion of dough into thirds, then roll each piece of dough into a small ball. Place the three balls next to each other in a buttered muffin cup. *To make knots*, roll each piece of dough into a 6- to 7-inch-long rope. Loosely tie each rope into a knot, positioning the knot in the middle. Transfer to the baking sheet. With either shape, cover with plastic wrap and let rise until doubled. Glaze and add seeds, if desired. Bake until golden, about 15 minutes.

Double Fig Focaccia

MAKES 1 RECTANGLE, ABOUT
6 GENEROUS SERVINGS

Fran Gage

Dried figs in the dough add sweetness, while fresh figs on top keep the focaccia moist. This makes a lovely breakfast bread, by itself or with a little soft cheese spread on top.

3 ounces dried figs, coarsely chopped

⅔ cup warm tap water

2 teaspoons active dry yeast

2 tablespoons granulated sugar

1¾ cups plus 2 tablespoons (9 ounces) unbleached all-purpose flour, or as needed

¾ teaspoon fine sea salt

5 ripe figs, cut lengthwise into ¼-inch-thick slices

1 tablespoon large-grained (sanding or pearl) sugar or additional granulated sugar

1. Combine the dried figs and warm water in a small bowl. Let stand until the water cools, about 10 minutes. Drain the figs, reserving the soaking liquid. Add enough warm tap water to the soaking liquid to measure ⅔ cup and pour into the bowl of a heavy-duty stand mixer. Set the soaked figs aside.

2. Sprinkle the yeast over the liquid in the bowl. Let stand until creamy, about 5 minutes. Stir in the granulated sugar. Attach the bowl to the mixer and fit with the paddle attachment. On low speed, add 1 cup flour, then the salt. Gradually add enough of the remaining flour to make a dough. Switch to the dough hook. Knead until the dough is smooth and elastic, about 10 minutes.

3. Detach the hook and remove the bowl from the mixer. Cover the bowl tightly with plastic wrap. Let stand at cool room temperature (70°F is ideal) until the dough has doubled in volume, about 2½ hours.

4. Line a baking sheet with parchment paper. Turn the dough out onto a lightly floured work surface. Pat and stretch into a 15 × 10-inch rectangle. Sprinkle evenly with half of the soaked figs. Roll up the dough. Repeat the procedure with the remaining figs. (If the dough retracts, cover loosely with plastic wrap and let stand for a few minutes, then try again.) Pat the dough into a 9½ × 8-inch rectangle (again, letting the dough relax if it resists stretching). Transfer to the baking sheet. Slip the sheet into a large plastic bag and close the bag. Let stand at cool room temperature until the dough has almost doubled, about 1 hour.

5. Meanwhile, position a rack in the center of the oven. Place a baking stone on the rack. Preheat the oven to 425°F, allowing at least 45 minutes.

6. Remove the baking sheet from the bag. Using your fingertips, make indentations all over the dough. Brush the dough with water and arrange the sliced figs over the top. Sprinkle with the large-grained sugar.

7. Bake until the focaccia is golden brown, about 20 minutes. Transfer the baking sheet to a wire cooling rack and cool the focaccia before serving.

Baker's Notes

DON'T BE TEMPTED to add the soaked figs to the dough at the end of the kneading time. They will break apart and discolor the dough. Also, they will add their residual sugars to the dough and make it rise too quickly.

As a dough is manipulated by patting out or stretching, the gluten is activated, which can make the dough retract and resist the shaping. Just be patient—cover the dough and let it rest for 5 minutes or so to relax the overactive gluten, then try again.

Soft Pretzels

MAKES 14 LARGE PRETZELS

Peter Reinhart

Crisp on the outside and chewy inside, these familiar street-vendor snacks are fun to make at home. Instead of coarse salt, sprinkle your custom-made pretzels with cumin, caraway, sesame, or poppy seeds (or even a combination).

DOUGH

1½ cups water, at room temperature

3¾ teaspoons active dry yeast

4 tablespoons (½ stick) unsalted butter, melted

½ cup (2½ ounces) whole wheat flour

1¾ teaspoons fine sea salt

3¼ cups (1 pound) bread flour, or as needed

Semolina or cornmeal, for the pans

Olive oil, for spraying the pretzels

2 quarts water

3 tablespoons baking soda

1 large egg yolk mixed with 2 teaspoons water, for the glaze

Kosher or other coarse salt, for topping

Cumin, sesame, or poppy seeds, for topping, optional

1. To make the dough, pour the water into the bowl of a heavy-duty stand mixer and sprinkle in the yeast. Set aside until creamy, about 5 minutes. Stir in the butter, then the whole wheat flour and salt.

2. Attach the bowl to the mixer and fit with the paddle blade. On low speed, gradually add enough of the bread flour to make a dough that cleans the bowl. Change to the dough hook. Knead on medium-low speed until the dough is smooth and a finger pushed ½ inch into the dough leaves an impression, about 6 minutes.

3. Detach the dough hook and remove the bowl from the mixer. Cover the bowl tightly with plastic wrap. Let stand at room temperature for 30 minutes (the dough will not perceptibly rise).

4. Turn the dough out onto a lightly floured work surface and cut it into 14 equal portions. On an unfloured surface, roll the dough back and forth under your hands, moving your hands apart as you roll, to form a 16-inch-long rope that is thick in the middle, with tapered ends. Set the rope aside and cover with plastic wrap. Repeat with the remaining dough. Let the ropes relax for 5 minutes.

5. Line two large baking sheets with parchment paper and sprinkle with semolina or cornmeal. Starting with the rope that was rolled first, reroll each rope into a 16-inch length and shape into a pretzel: Cross the two ends, about 1 inch from each tip, to create a large, roundish loop. Give the loop an additional twist to further entwine the ends. With the looped dough lying on the counter, grab each of the tips, one with each hand, and lift them simultaneously up to the widest part of the loop, resting each tip so it just overhangs the loop by a nub. (Some people prefer to loop the dough once, then lift the tips with their arms crossed, thus adding the extra entwinement while they uncross their arms and simultaneously place the tips on the loop—the result is the same.) Place the pretzel on the prepared sheet. Repeat with the remaining pretzels, working in sequence from the first ropes to the last and spacing them about 1 inch apart on the sheets. Let the pretzels stand, uncovered, in a warm place (90°F) just until they start to look puffy, about 10 minutes.

6. Fill an oil mister with olive oil and spray the pretzels lightly. Slip each sheet into a plastic bag and close tightly. Freeze overnight.

7. When ready to bake, preheat the oven to 450°F. Combine the water and baking soda in a large pot and bring to boil over high heat.

8. Remove the baking sheets from the freezer and slide off the parchment and pretzels. Lightly oil the sheets and sprinkle with semolina or cornmeal.

9. A few at a time, cook the frozen pretzels in the boiling water, 30 seconds per side. Using a wire-mesh skimmer, arrange the pretzels on the prepared baking sheets, about 1 inch apart. Lightly brush the pretzels with the egg glaze. Sprinkle with the salt, then the seeds, if desired.

10. Bake until the pretzels are puffed and browned, about 15 minutes. Transfer to a wire rack to cool. Serve warm or at room temperature.

Baker's Notes

WHEN ROLLING THE dough into ropes, the work surface must be clean of flour—any trace of flour on the board will reduce the traction and make the dough difficult to stretch. If necessary, mist the work surface with water to improve the grip of the dough on the board. One of the secrets to making pretzels is patience. Let the dough stand for 5- to 10-minute periods to relax the gluten before forming into ropes, and before forming the ropes into pretzels. Keep track of the ropes of dough, and start making pretzels with the first (and most relaxed) dough ropes.

Check to be sure that your baking sheets will fit into your freezer.

The pretzels must rise in a warm spot, about 90°F. If your kitchen isn't warm enough, turn the oven to its lowest setting for 5 minutes. Then turn it off and place the baking sheet with the pretzels inside the warm oven.

Spicy Cornmeal Crackers

MAKES TWO 16 × 12-INCH
SHEETS, ABOUT 12 SERVINGS

Fran Gage

Although grocery store shelves are chock-full of crackers of every description, there are many reasons to prepare the homemade version. They are fun to make, tasty, inexpensive, and versatile—serve them alone as a crunchy snack or pair them with a spread.

1 cup cold water
¼ cup extra virgin olive oil
2½ cups (12½ ounces) unbleached all-purpose flour
½ cup (2¾ ounces) yellow cornmeal
1½ teaspoons fine sea salt
½ teaspoon crushed red pepper flakes
2 teaspoons coarse sea salt or fleur de sel, for topping

1. In the bowl of a heavy-duty stand mixer fitted with the paddle attachment, combine the water and oil. In another bowl, mix the flour, cornmeal, fine salt, and red pepper flakes. With the machine on low speed, add the flour mixture all at once and mix thoroughly, but just until the dough comes together.

2. On a lightly floured surface, pat the dough into a thick rectangle, wrap in plastic wrap, and refrigerate for 30 minutes to 1 hour.

3. About 45 minutes before baking, place the rack in the center of the oven. Place a baking stone on the rack. Preheat the oven to 500°F.

4. Line two large baking sheets with parchment paper. Cut the dough into 2 equal pieces. Lightly flour the work surface. Working with one piece of dough at a time, roll out the dough into a very thin 16 × 12-inch rectangle. As you roll out the dough, it will resist and retract. When this happens, set the dough aside and let it rest while you roll the other piece of dough. Roll up one sheet of dough onto a rolling pin and unroll onto a baking sheet. Repeat with the other sheet of dough. Poke each sheet of dough thoroughly with a fork. Mist the dough with water and sprinkle with the coarse salt.

5. One sheet at a time, bake for 10 minutes, or until the dough is set. Flip the dough over and bake until browned, another 4 minutes. Transfer to a rack, still on the paper, to cool. Repeat with the other sheet of dough. Cool completely. Break the sheet of dough into irregularly shaped crackers. (Store in an airtight container for up to 3 days.)

Baker's Notes

DO NOT OVERMIX the dough, or the gluten will be activated and make the crackers tough. The dough must relax for at least 30 minutes, or the crackers will be difficult to roll out. If chilled for longer than 1 hour, the dough may crack; let the dough stand at room temperature for 10 minutes to lose its chill.

If you have two baking stones, you can bake two sheets of crackers at a time. Position the racks in the top and bottom thirds of the oven, place the stones on the racks, and preheat. Halfway through the baking time, switch the positions of the sheets to encourage even baking.

Focaccia di Recco

MAKES 1 ROUND FOCACCIA,
ABOUT 6 SERVINGS

Carol Field

This unleavened, double-crusted focaccia from Recco, a town just south of Genoa, bakes into a crunchy, thin casing that holds a filling of tangy cheese. In Italy it would often be made with Invernizzina, but that cheese isn't common in the States, and any soft, tangy Italian cheese will do. Eat this hot from the oven.

2 cups (10 ounces) unbleached all-purpose flour

1½ teaspoons fine sea salt, plus a little extra for the top

¾ cup water, or as needed

2½ to 3 tablespoons extra virgin olive oil, preferably Ligurian, plus a little extra for the top

¾ to 1 pound soft, tangy Italian cheese, such as Invernizzina, Stracchino, Crescenza, or Taleggio, rind trimmed

1. Combine the flour and salt in the bowl of a heavy-duty stand mixer fitted with the paddle blade. Mix the water and oil in a glass measuring cup. With the mixer on low speed, pour the water mixture into the flour in a slow, steady stream. Increase the speed to medium-low and mix until the dough comes together and cleans the sides of the bowl, 1 to 2 minutes. If the dough seems dry, add more water, 1 tablespoon at a time.

2. Turn the dough out onto a lightly floured work surface. Form it into 2 disks about 1 inch thick, one slightly larger than the other. Place the disks in a lightly oiled large bowl, turning to coat with the oil (the disks can touch each other). Cover the bowl with a damp tea towel and let stand at room temperature for 1 hour. The dough won't rise (it doesn't have any leavening), but the gluten will relax and make the dough easier to roll out.

3. Meanwhile, position a rack in the center of the oven and place a baking stone on the rack. Preheat the oven to 450°F, allowing at least 45 minutes. Lightly oil a 12-inch shallow pizza pan.

4. After the dough rests, it should be smooth, easily stretchable, and in no way sticky. Roll out the larger piece of dough on a lightly floured work surface into a 12-inch round about ¼ inch thick. Then stretch with your hands so that the dough is very thin. Place it on the pan, letting the excess hang over the sides. Break the cheese into walnut-sized pieces and scatter over the dough.

5. Roll out and stretch the smaller piece of dough into a 12-inch round. Lifting it as if you were shaking out a bedsheet, gently lay it over the cheese. Very gently press the dough around the cheese balls. Using a sharp knife, cut away the overhanging dough, leaving a small border all around. Crimp the edges of the dough together to seal tightly. Drizzle the top of the dough lightly with oil and sprinkle with a little sea salt.

6. Bake until both the top and bottom of the dough are golden, 15 to 20 minutes. Remove from oven and cool. Serve hot, while the cheese is still soft and a bit runny.

Custards and Other Egg-Based Desserts

The egg is often described as nature's most perfect food. Self-contained in its shell, incorporating both a fatty, rich yolk and a lean, austere white, it accomplishes many jobs in the kitchen. It can bind, aerate, glue, and glaze. With the addition of just a few ingredients, it can be turned into a smooth custard (baked until semifirm or cooked on the stove into a versatile sauce), an airy meringue, or light cream puffs, among other sweet treats.

But the egg can have a Jekyll-and-Hyde personality. It can be benign and helpful, or temperamental and troublesome. Exposed to excessive heat, the egg in your recipe can curdle and turn from dessert to disaster in no time.

Custard is the epitome of egg-based desserts. It's nothing more than a liaison between eggs, sugar, and cream or milk. It takes on many guises, from baked crème caramel and its cousin crème brûlée to the versatile stove-cooked dessert sauce, crème anglaise. A meringue is a foam of egg whites and sugar baked to hold its shape. Cheesecake is really a kind of custard—it would never hold together without eggs. And without eggs as the leavening, pâte à choux—cream puff dough—would not puff. We've written these recipes with lots of tips and tricks to be sure that you don't end up with egg on your face.

This committee was headed by David Lebovitz and Kathleen Stewart, and also consisted of Barbara Mooradian, Karen Smithson, and Mark Tachman. Thanks to Barbara Holzenrichter for valuable insight on caramelization.

Ingredients for Egg-Based Desserts

Eggs | All of the recipes in this chapter (and this book) were made with large eggs. If you use another size, you will change the amount of liquid in the recipe, which could be problematic.

Remove the eggs from the refrigerator 30 minutes to 1 hour before using when a recipe calls for room-temperature eggs. Or place the eggs in a bowl of warm tap water for 5 minutes before cracking. If warm liquids are whisked into cold eggs, the chances of curdling are greater.

Sugar | When making caramel, it is very important to use cane sugar, which is usually clearly labeled on the package. Some of our members who are cooking teachers report having trouble making caramel at schools in the Midwest, where beet sugar is often more common than cane sugar. It seems there are impurities in the beet sugar that make it resistant to smooth melting and caramelization.

Equipment for Egg-Based Desserts

Baking dishes | Custards can be prepared in 4-ounce ramekins or 6-ounce Pyrex custard cups. If you use classic crème brûlée dishes or pots de crème cups for their respective desserts, you will have to experiment with the cooking times. Two ceramic soufflé dishes, 1 and 2 quarts, will allow you to make soufflés of varying sizes, depending on the number of guests.

Wire strainer | Always strain a custard to remove any bits of egg white, which cook until firm more rapidly than yolks and will give the custard a gritty texture if not removed. A fine- or triple-mesh strainer does a good job.

The Ultimate Bread Pudding

3½ cups milk

1 cup sugar

3-inch piece of vanilla bean, split lengthwise

7 large eggs

5 large egg yolks

2½ cups heavy cream

6 cups day-old firm-textured bread, cut into 1-inch cubes

1. Position a rack in the center of the oven and preheat to 350°F. Butter a 13 × 9-inch baking dish.

2. Whisk the milk and sugar in a medium saucepan. Using the tip of a knife, scrape the seeds from the vanilla bean into the saucepan, then add the bean. Cook uncovered over low heat, stirring occasionally, until the mixture is hot but not boiling. Discard the vanilla bean, scraping any remaining seeds into the milk mixture.

3. Whisk the eggs and yolks in a large bowl. Gradually whisk in about 2 cups of the hot milk mixture, then pour this mixture into the saucepan. Strain the custard through a wire sieve back into the bowl. Whisk in the cream.

4. Spread the bread cubes in the prepared baking dish. Slowly pour the custard over the bread cubes, being sure to saturate all of the bread.

5. Bake until a small knife inserted in the center of the pudding comes out clean, about 1 hour. Serve warm or chilled.

MAKES 8 SERVINGS

Kathleen Stewart

A candidate for the comfort food hall of fame, bread pudding is certainly a great dessert, but it is also wonderful as a brunch main course, served with fruit salad on the side. This version comes from Downtown Bakery in Healdsburg, California. Kathleen Stewart, one of the bakery's owners, encourages you to use different breads to come up with your own variation.

Baker's Note

USE ANY FIRM-TEXTURED nonsavory bread for the pudding. Whole wheat cinnamon-raisin makes a dark and spicy pudding with the raisins that some bakers consider traditional in bread pudding. Use Italian panettone for a delicious fruit-filled variation, or try challah or brioche. Whatever you use, avoid soft supermarket bread (which makes a mushy pudding) and rustic, crusty loaves (the open crumb doesn't absorb the custard well, and the crust makes the pudding too firm).

*Custards
and Other
Egg-Based
Desserts*

Coffee Crème Brûlée

MAKES 6 SERVINGS

David Lebovitz

The name of the trendy dessert of the recent past, crème brûlée, *literally means "burned cream," but that's a misnomer if ever there was one. The cream is certainly not burned, but gently cooked into a custard—it is the caramelized sugar topping that gives the custard its name. Made with heavy cream and egg yolks, this is an unctuous, creamy custard that isn't firm enough to unmold. We bake our custards in ramekins, which are common equipment in the kitchens of most bakers. If you have classic crème brûlée dishes (which look like wide, deep saucers), see the variation at the end of the recipe.*

3 cups heavy cream
¼ cup sugar, plus 6 tablespoons for the topping
⅓ cup whole Italian- or French-roast coffee beans
    (do not use crushed or ground beans)
6 large egg yolks

1. In a medium saucepan, heat the cream, ¼ cup sugar, and the coffee beans over low heat, stirring occasionally, just until the cream is steaming and the sugar is dissolved. Cover and remove from the heat. Let stand for 1 hour to infuse the cream with the coffee. Reheat the mixture before adding to the egg yolks.

2. Position a rack in the center of the oven and preheat to 325°F.

3. Whisk the yolks in a medium bowl and gradually whisk in the hot cream mixture. Strain the custard through a fine-meshed sieve into a liquid measuring cup. Divide the custard among six 4-ounce ramekins. Arrange the ramekins in a large roasting pan. Place the pan in the oven and add enough hot water to come halfway up the sides of the ramekins.

4. Bake until the custards have barely set, about 1 hour. To check for doneness, shake a custard. It should look set around the edges, but the area in the center (about the size of a quarter) should jiggle slightly.

5. Remove the custards from the water and cool on a wire rack. Cover each custard with plastic wrap and refrigerate until chilled, at least 4 hours or overnight. (The custards can be prepared, covered, and refrigerated up to 3 days ahead.)

6. To serve, position the rack about 3 inches from the heat source and preheat the broiler. Sprinkle 1 tablespoon of the remaining sugar over the top of each custard. Arrange the ramekins in a jelly-roll pan. Broil until the sugar is melted and caramelized, about 2 minutes. Watch carefully so the sugar doesn't burn.

7. Serve immediately, or let stand at room temperature for up to 1 hour.

Classic Crème Brûlée: Many dessert bakers prefer crème brûlée dishes to ramekins because they allow for more of the caramelized topping. Because they're wider, you get more custard, too, and they'll bake in less time. Pour the custard into four 5-inch-diameter crème brûlée dishes. Bake in the water bath just until set, about 40 minutes.

Chocolate Pots de Crème: Melt 4 ounces finely chopped bittersweet chocolate over hot, not simmering, water until smooth. Add all of the warm egg custard at once and whisk until smooth. Strain and bake as directed above.

Baker's Notes

ALL OF THE Baker's Notes in the recipe for Cinnamon Crème Caramel (see page 306) apply to crème brûlée.

Instead of a broiler, a hand-held propane or butane torch can be used to caramelize the toppings. Sprinkle each custard with the sugar. Set the torch flame at medium and wave the tip of the flame over the sugar at close range until the sugar begins to melt. Rotate the ramekin with your other hand for even caramelization. Continue to melt the sugar with the blowtorch until it has darkened and caramelized.

Turbinado or Demerara sugar, pulverized in a blender or coffee grinder until the crystals look like granulated sugar, can be substituted for the regular sugar used to caramelize the tops.

Cinnamon Crème Caramel

MAKES 6 SERVINGS

David Lebovitz

The perfect crème caramel is firm enough to unmold without collapsing, yet silky-smooth on the tongue. Our tricks include a bit of heavy cream (which gives extra creaminess) and whole eggs (whites have a higher protein content than yolks, so this custard sets up better than yolk-only versions). Caramel is easy to overcook past the amber stage, and we like the trick of stopping the cooking with water. Cinnamon is a nontraditional flavoring, but it works beautifully with the deep flavor of the caramel. This gently spiced custard is easy to transform into any one of many variations.

The Baker's Dozen Cookbook

CUSTARD

2 cups milk
1 cup heavy cream
¾ cup sugar
Two 3-inch cinnamon sticks, slightly crushed
3 large eggs, at room temperature
3 large egg yolks, at room temperature

CARAMEL

½ cup water
¾ cup sugar
A few drops fresh lemon juice or a pinch
   of cream of tartar

1. To make the custard, heat the milk, cream, sugar, and cinnamon in a medium saucepan over low heat, stirring often, just until the cream is steaming and the sugar is dissolved. Remove from the heat and cover. Let stand for 1 hour so the cinnamon can release its flavor.

2. Meanwhile, to make the caramel, pour ¼ cup cold water into a medium saucepan, then evenly sprinkle in the sugar and add the lemon juice. Cover and bring to a boil over medium heat. Do not stir.

3. Uncover and increase the heat to medium-high. Cook until the caramel has colored to a deep red brown (about the color of an old penny) and a few wisps of smoke begin to appear. Being very careful to avoid splashes and steam (if you want, place a colander over the saucepan to act as a perforated lid), immediately pour the remaining ¼ cup water into the caramel. Whisk to dissolve any hardened caramel, being careful to avoid splatters.

4. Carefully divide the caramel among six 4- to 6-ounce ramekins. Immediately tilt and swirl the cups to line the insides with caramel. Place the cups in a deep roasting pan.

5. Position a rack in the center of the oven and preheat to 350°F.

6. Reheat the milk mixture until hot. Remove the cinnamon sticks. Gently whisk the eggs and yolks just until combined. Gradually whisk in the milk mixture. Strain into a 1-quart liquid measuring cup and divide among the ramekins.

7. Add enough hot water to the roasting pan to come halfway up the sides of the cups. Cover the pan tightly with aluminum foil.

8. Bake until the custards have barely set, 45 to 50 minutes. To check for doneness, remove the foil (watch out for steam) and shake a custard. It should look set around the edges, but the area in the center (about the size of a quarter) should jiggle slightly.

9. Remove the custards from the water and cool on a wire rack. Cover each custard with plastic wrap and refrigerate until chilled, at least 4 hours, or overnight. (The custards can be prepared, covered, and refrigerated up to 3 days ahead.)

10. To serve, run a knife around the inside of each cup to release the custard, pressing firmly as you go (don't cut into the custard, or you'll have little bits floating in the caramel). Center an upside-down dessert plate over the custard. Holding tightly, invert the cup and plate together. Give the plate a couple of shakes to dislodge the custard. Lift up the cup, tilting it slightly as you lift. If the custard doesn't unmold, slip your finger between the custard and the cup to break the air lock and try again. Serve chilled.

Baker's Notes

THE TEMPERATURE OF the milk/sugar mixture affects the custard's rate of cooking. It should be piping hot but not boiling, as boiled milk can develop a skin that would toughen the surface of the cooked custard.

Always strain a custard. The chalazae (tiny cords around the yolk) and whites cook to a semisolid firmness more quickly than the yolks and will need to be removed, or your custard will have little white lumps running through it.

Variations on a Custard Theme

It is a simple matter to vary the flavor of your custard. Usually all the baker has to do is infuse an ingredient in the milk and sugar mixture. Reheat the mixture until it is steaming hot before adding it to the eggs or yolks—a warm custard will set more quickly than a cold one. Here are some of our favorites.

Chocolate: Melt 4 ounces finely chopped bittersweet chocolate in a medium heat-proof bowl over hot, not simmering, water. Add all the warm custard at once and whisk until smooth.

Citrus: Working directly over the saucepan of the milk/sugar mixture, grate the zest of 3 oranges (about ⅓ cup) or 4 lemons (¼ cup) into the mixture. Heat, then infuse for 1 hour and strain.

Classic Vanilla: Split a vanilla bean lengthwise and scrape the tiny seeds from the bean into the milk/sugar mixture; add the bean to the saucepan, too. Heat, then infuse for at least 10 minutes and strain.

Coconut: Desiccated coconut (not sweetened flakes) is best for custard; don't bother to use fresh coconut. Toast ½ cup desiccated coconut in a preheated 325°F oven, stirring often, until lightly browned, about 5 minutes. Watch carefully, as it can burn easily. Add to the milk/sugar mixture. Heat, then infuse for 1 hour and strain.

Coffee: Add ¼ cup whole Italian- or French-roast coffee beans to the milk/sugar mixture. Do not use crushed or ground beans, or the custard may be bitter. Heat, then infuse for 1 hour and strain.

Ginger: Ginger contains an enzyme that keeps the custard from setting, so it must be blanched before using. Slice 6 to 8 quarter-sized rounds from a piece of fresh ginger (no need to peel it). Blanch in a small saucepan of boiling water over high heat for 2 minutes; drain. Add to the milk/sugar mixture. Heat, then infuse for 1 hour and strain.

Herb: Use ¼ cup packed herb leaves; mint or lemon verbena is a good choice. Crush the leaves gently before adding to the milk/sugar mixture. Heat, then infuse for 1 hour and strain.

Liquor: Add an additional large egg yolk to the custard. Add 3 tablespoons liquor (brandy, Cognac, golden rum, or bourbon) or liqueur (framboise, kirsch, or other eau-de-vie) to the finished custard. If added to the milk/sugar mixture, much of the liquor's flavor will escape in the steam.

Nut: Add 1 cup toasted almonds, walnuts, or hazelnuts to the milk/sugar mixture before heating. Heat, then infuse for 1 hour and strain.

Nutmeg: Add ⅛ teaspoon freshly grated nutmeg to the milk/sugar mixture before heating. No need to infuse.

Spiced: Add coarsely ground spices (use a mortar and pestle) to the milk/sugar mixture. Try about 1 tablespoon star anise, coriander seeds, or allspice, or 1 teaspoon cardamom seeds. Infuse for 1 hour, then reheat and strain.

Tea: Use ¼ cup tea leaves; aromatic teas such as Earl Grey, jasmine, fruit-flavored teas, or even green tea work well. Add them to the milk/sugar mixture, heat, then infuse for 30 minutes and strain.

Caramel Knowledge

Always add sugar to water in the saucepan, not the other way around. This moistens the sugar more efficiently and discourages crystallization.

• Crystallization of a syrup or caramel is the bane of the cook. A bit of lemon juice or cream of tartar, both acids, helps prevent the sugar crystals in the syrup from joining together into a gritty mass (caramel is simply a plain syrup that has been cooked until colored).

• Never stir a syrup while it is on its way to becoming a caramel. Stirring actually encourages crystallization. Sugar crystals can also attach themselves to foreign objects that are introduced into the syrup, such as a spoon. While you can stir the sugar mixture before it boils to help dissolve the sugar, we think it's much safer to avoid stirring altogether.

• If sugar crystals do form on the sides of the saucepan, they should be removed, or they could attract other crystals to join them. Cover the saucepan for the first minute of cooking, as the steam will often wash the crystals into the pan. Some cooks recommend pressing a wet pastry brush against the sides of the pan to wash the crystals into the syrup, but just be sure that you don't leave any bristles behind.

• Caramel can turn from the perfect color to burned in a flash, so watch carefully. Judge the caramel by its color but also by its aroma, which should smell rich with a hint of sharpness. You cannot use a candy thermometer when making caramel, as sugar crystals could form on the stem.

• Remember that caramel is very hot. If you are apprehensive, wear thick rubber gloves (the kind used for dishwashing) to protect yourself against splatter. But even the gloves can be awkward, causing their own problems, so common sense is your best protection.

• To clean a caramel-coated saucepan after cooking, fill halfway with water, cover, and bring to a boil over high heat. The water and steam will dissolve any hardened caramel.

• The darker the caramel, the deeper the flavor. Take the caramel to the farthest point that you dare before it burns. You may see a few wisps of smoke at this point. If there is a cloud of smoke and the caramel smells burned, it is.

Chocolate Budini

6 ounces bittersweet chocolate, finely chopped

12 tablespoons (1½ sticks) unsalted butter, cut into bits

¾ cup sugar

Pinch of fine sea salt

3 large eggs, separated, at room temperature

1 teaspoon vanilla extract

⅛ teaspoon cream of tartar

1 pint coffee or vanilla ice cream

Caramel Sauce (page 338)

½ cup whole blanched almonds, toasted (see page 16) and
    coarsely chopped

1. Position a rack in the lower third of the oven and preheat to 375°F.

2. Melt the chocolate and butter with 6 tablespoons sugar and the salt in a medium stainless steel bowl placed in a skillet of hot, not simmering, water, stirring frequently. Remove from the heat and cool slightly. Whisk in the egg yolks and vanilla.

3. In a greasefree medium bowl, using a hand-held electric mixer on high speed, beat the egg whites and cream of tartar until soft peaks form. Gradually beat in the remaining 6 tablespoons sugar and beat until the whites are stiff and glossy. Fold one-quarter of the beaten whites into the chocolate batter to lighten it. Scrape the chocolate batter into the bowl of whites and fold just until combined. Divide the batter evenly among six 12- to 16-ounce individual ceramic bowls. (The batter won't fill the bowls completely, allowing room for the ice cream, sauce, and almond toppings.) Place the bowls on a large baking sheet. (The budini can be prepared up to 2 days ahead to this point, loosely covered, and refrigerated.)

4. Bake until the budini are puffed with crusty, deeply cracked tops and a toothpick inserted in the centers comes out quite gooey, 20 to 25 minutes. (The budini can be completely baked up to a day ahead, cooled, covered, and refrigerated. To reheat, bake in a preheated 375°F oven until puffed, about 10 minutes.)

5. Serve within 10 minutes (the puddings will sink as they cool), topping each serving with a scoop of ice cream, a spoonful of caramel sauce, and some toasted almonds.

MAKES 6 SERVINGS

Jennifer Millar

Budino *is Italian for "pudding," although the similarity ends there for those of us raised on Jell-O Instant. Baker's Dozen member Jennifer Millar, pastry chef at Oakland's Restaurant Garibaldi, gave us the recipe for this oversized bowl of rich, warm chocolate, crusted on top and melting within, which we have adapted slightly for the home kitchen. The topping of coffee ice cream and toasted almonds makes it crunchy and creamy, hot and cold, all at once. And, this dessert adapts itself to a variety of situations: Bake the puddings immediately, make them up to 2 days ahead, or reheat the baked budini. You will need six 12- to 16-ounce individual porcelain bowls (such as café au lait cups or onion soup bowls) to make these.*

*Custards
and Other
Egg-Based
Desserts*

311

Riesling Sabayon

MAKES ABOUT 3¾ CUPS,
4 TO 6 SERVINGS

David Lebovitz

Sabayon (known as zabaglione in Italian) is a delicate marriage between egg yolks and wine, heated until light and foamy. It can be served on its own, layered with fresh berries and served with cookies, or used as a sauce for a cake or tart. Sabayon can be tricky, but once you master its secrets, you will have a dessert that can be quickly prepared from ingredients you probably have on hand. Serve it immediately, or it will deflate. To hold it longer, use the Creamy Sabayon variation.

7 large egg yolks, at room temperature
⅔ cup semi-dry white wine, such as Riesling or
**   Gewürztraminer**
⅓ cup sugar

1. Whisk the yolks, wine, and sugar in a 6-quart stainless steel or copper bowl. Place over a large saucepan of rapidly simmering water. The bowl should not touch the water.

2. Whisk constantly with a large, thin-wired balloon whisk, being sure to whip air into the mixture, until it is tripled in volume and light and fluffy in texture, about 5 minutes. (You can also use a hand-held electric mixer on medium-high speed.) The sabayon should form a thick ribbon that settles on top of the mass when the whisk is lifted. Serve immediately.

Creamy Sabayon: Place the sabayon in a large bowl of ice water. Let stand, stirring occasionally, until it cools to room temperature. Whip ½ cup heavy cream until very lightly whipped to soft peaks. Fold the whipped cream into the cooled sabayon. Cover tightly and refrigerate for up to 1 day.

Baker's Notes

ANY WHITE WINE (sweet or dry, still or sparkling) can be used, but semi-dry wines bring another sweet dimension to the sabayon. For a real treat, try a Moscato or late-harvest Riesling.

Don't let the sugar come into contact with the egg yolks until you are ready to whip the sabayon. The sugar crystals will "burn" the yolk and form small grains that will ruin your sabayon.

Sabayon rises to great heights thanks to the air that is beaten into it. Use a large wire balloon whisk, and be sure that you are whipping, not just stirring, the sabayon, reaching all areas of the bowl with a zigzag or figure-8 motion. Change arms if you get tired. Or simply use a hand-held mixer, which works beautifully.

Bittersweet Chocolate Soufflé

Softened unsalted butter and granulated sugar, for
    coating the soufflé dish
1 tablespoon unsalted butter
1 tablespoon all-purpose flour
¼ cup milk, heated
2 large eggs, separated, at room temperature
1 teaspoon vanilla extract
6 ounces bittersweet or semisweet chocolate,
    very finely chopped
1 large egg white, at room temperature
⅛ teaspoon cream of tartar
¼ cup granulated sugar
Confectioners' sugar, for dusting
Whipped Cream Topping (page 336), for serving

MAKES 4 SERVINGS

Alice Medrich

This rich, dark chocolate soufflé is easy to make and most impressive. You may even prepare it entirely ahead (except for baking), then pop it casually into a preheated oven 20 to 30 minutes before serving. Et voilà! But note that this is not a super high-riser; it will only puff an inch or so above the rim of the dish.

1. Position a rack in the lower third of the oven and preheat to 350°F. Butter the inside and rim of a 1-quart soufflé dish. Sprinkle about 3 tablespoons of sugar in the dish and tilt to coat the buttered areas. Tap out the excess sugar.

2. In a small saucepan, melt butter over low heat. Add the flour and let bubble, stirring constantly and without browning for 1½ minutes. Whisk in the milk. Cook, whisking constantly, until the sauce is thick and bubbling. Remove from heat. Let stand a few minutes to cool slightly, then whisk in the yolks and vanilla. Add the chocolate and whisk until smooth and melted.

3. In a greasefree medium bowl, using a hand-held electric mixer on high speed, beat the egg whites and cream of tartar until soft peaks form. Gradually beat in the sugar and beat until the eggs are stiff and glossy. Fold one-quarter of the beaten whites into the chocolate batter to lighten it. Scrape the chocolate batter into the bowl of whites and fold just until combined.

4. Transfer the batter to the soufflé dish. (The soufflé can be prepared up to 2 days ahead to this point, covered, and refrigerated.) Bake until the soufflé has risen with a cracked top, and a wooden skewer inserted in the center comes out with some thick, moist batter still clinging to it, 20 to 25 minutes (30 minutes if the soufflé was refrigerated).

5. Immediately sift confectioners' sugar over the top of the soufflé and serve with a large spoon, scraping against the sides of the dish so each guest gets a little crunchy sugar crust along with a gooey center portion. Top each serving with a dollop of whipped cream.

Raspberry Soufflé with Raspberry Sauce

MAKES 6 TO 8 SERVINGS

Kathleen Stewart

Anyone who can whip egg whites can make a soufflé. This one only has a few ingredients; pay attention to how the sugar is added to the different components. Raspberry puree is divided; one part is turned into the soufflé with egg yolks and whipped whites, and the other is sweetened to make a sauce for serving. Use other berries such as blueberries or blackberries. Just about any fruit puree can be turned into a soufflé. Soft fruits, such as berries and peaches, will only need to be pureed, but harder fruits, such as apples, should be cooked into a sauce before using.

Taste the raspberry purees (in the sauce and in the soufflé, just before adding the yolks) to judge their sweetness, and add a bit more sugar if needed. Balance their flavor with a few drops of lemon juice or raspberry liqueur.

The
Baker's
Dozen
Cookbook

6 cups fresh raspberries
1 cup sugar
4 large eggs, separated, at room temperature
4 large egg whites, at room temperature
⅛ teaspoon cream of tartar

1. Process the raspberries in a food processor fitted with the metal blade until pureed. Strain into a medium bowl. You should have 2 cups.

2. To make the sauce, combine 1 cup raspberry puree and 6 tablespoons sugar and cook over low heat, stirring often, until the sugar is completely dissolved, about 5 minutes. Set aside at room temperature.

3. Position a rack in the center of the oven and preheat to 400°F. Butter the inside of a 2-quart soufflé dish. Add 2 tablespoons of the remaining sugar to the dish and tilt to coat, tapping out the excess sugar.

4. In a large bowl, whisk the remaining 1 cup raspberry puree and 2 tablespoons of the remaining sugar. In a medium bowl, using a hand-held electric mixer at medium-high speed, beat the egg yolks with 2 tablespoons of the remaining sugar until the mixture is thick and pale yellow and falls back on itself in a thick ribbon when the beaters are lifted, about 3 minutes. Fold the egg yolk mixture into the puree.

5. Using clean beaters, whip the egg whites on low speed until foamy. Add the cream of tartar. Increase the speed to high and whip until soft peaks form. One tablespoon at a time, beat in the remaining ¼ cup sugar just until the peaks are shiny and firm but not stiff.

6. Stir about one-quarter of the whites into the egg yolk mixture to lighten the mixture, then fold in the remaining whites, being careful not to overmix (a few streaks are better than overmixing and deflating the mixture). Pour into the prepared dish.

7. Bake until the top is risen and golden brown, 25 to 28 minutes. Serve immediately, spooning some of the sauce over each portion.

Berry-Almond Vacherins

MERINGUES

⅓ cup plus 1 tablespoon sliced blanched almonds,
  toasted (see page 16)
1 cup sugar
½ cup egg whites (about 4 large), at room temperature
Pinch of cream of tartar

FILLING

3 cups assorted fresh berries, such as raspberries,
  golden raspberries, blackberries, currants,
  and strawberries
3 tablespoons framboise (raspberry eau-de-vie)
1 tablespoon fresh lemon juice
3 tablespoons sugar, or to taste
Mint sprigs, for garnish
Riesling Sabayon (page 312) or Whipped Cream Topping
  (page 336), optional

1. Position a rack in the center of the oven and preheat to 200°F. Line a large baking sheet with parchment paper.

2. To make the meringues, in a food processor fitted with the metal blade, process the almonds with ½ cup sugar until the nuts are ground to a powder.

3. In a greasefree large bowl, using a balloon whisk or hand-held electric mixer on low speed, beat the egg whites until foamy. Add the cream of tartar and continue beating (increase the mixer speed to high) until soft peaks form. One tablespoon at a time, beat in the remaining ½ cup sugar. Fold in the almond mixture with a large rubber spatula just until incorporated.

4. Using about ½ cup for each vacherin, drop mounds of the meringue onto the parchment paper, spacing them about 1 inch apart. Using a wet teaspoon, spread each mound into a 4-inch round and make an indentation in the center to form a shell.

5. Bake until the vacherins are crisp but barely beige, 2 to 2½ hours. Remove from the oven and cool completely on the pan. (The vacherins can be stored in an airtight container for up to 1 week.)

6. Meanwhile, make the filling. In a medium bowl, gently combine the berries, framboise, and lemon juice just until combined. Taste and add the

MAKES SIX 4-INCH VACHERINS

David Lebovitz

There is a round white French cheese called vacherin and when made without almonds, these meringue shells resemble small rounds of the cheese. You can fill the shells with any fruit salad that strikes your fancy (peaches and raspberries would be nice), but berries are especially tasty, as they play off the meringue's sweetness. This is the dessert to serve to guests who are low-fat fanatics; pass sabayon or whipped cream on the side to those who want to indulge. Note that the meringues aren't really baked, but dried in a very low oven. Before making vacherins, read "Egg Whites" on page 72.

sugar, if needed. Cover and refrigerate for at least 1 hour but no longer than 4 hours.

7. To serve, place a vacherin on each dessert plate. Use a slotted spoon to fill the vacherins with the berries, and garnish each with a mint sprig. Serve chilled, passing the sabayon on the side, if desired.

Baker's Notes

SUBSTITUTE TOASTED AND peeled hazelnuts for the almonds.

For the crispest shells, place them in a preheated 250°F oven and bake for 1 hour. Turn off the oven and let the vacherins stand in the oven for at least 12 hours, or overnight.

If the vacherins turn soggy from humidity during storage, bake them in a preheated 200°F oven until they recrisp, about 10 minutes. Cool completely.

Cream Puffs with Lemon Filling

CREAM PUFFS

1 cup water

6 tablespoons (¾ stick) unsalted butter,
    cut into small pieces

1 teaspoon sugar

¼ teaspoon salt

1 cup all-purpose flour

4 large eggs, at room temperature

1 large egg yolk beaten with 2 teaspoons milk,
    for the glaze

LEMON FILLING

1 cup heavy cream

1 cup Lemon Curd (page 340)

1 cup Caramel Sauce (page 338)

1. To make the puffs, position a rack in the center of the oven and preheat to 425°F. Line a large baking sheet with parchment paper or use an ungreased baking sheet.

2. In a medium saucepan, bring the water, butter, sugar, and salt to a boil over medium heat, stirring often to be sure the butter is completely melted by the time the water boils. Add the flour all at once, beating well, and continue stirring until the paste forms a mass that comes away from the sides of the pan, about 30 seconds.

3. Remove from the heat. Transfer to the bowl of a heavy-duty stand mixer fitted with the paddle blade, or to a medium bowl. Let stand for 3 minutes to cool the paste slightly. On low speed, one at a time, beat in the eggs (if not using a heavy-duty mixer, use a hand-held one), making sure each egg is incorporated before adding the next. The dough will be stiff and shiny.

4. Transfer the dough to a pastry bag fitted with a ½-inch-wide plain tube. Pipe the dough into 2-inch-diameter mounds about 1½ inches high about 2 inches apart on the prepared baking sheet. Lightly brush the tops of the mounds with the egg glaze, tamping down the pointed tips as you go. Be careful not to let the glaze drip down onto the parchment, or it will harden during baking and prevent the puffs from reaching their full expansion.

MAKES ABOUT 2 DOZEN PUFFS,
6 TO 8 SERVINGS

Kathleen Stewart
and David Lebovitz

Pâte à choux, like other French pastry doughs, can be turned into myriad desserts. But unlike other doughs, which are usually all about keeping the ingredients cold, it is a hot (chaud) dough. Through the years, chaud evolved into choux, which means cabbages, and it must be admitted that the little puffs do resemble them. Of all the choices for filling your puffs, this is a particularly elegant one, with tangy lemon curd lightened with whipped cream, and a caramel sauce to finish it off. For a very sophisticated, restaurant-style presentation, place ½ cup Caramel Sauce and ½ cup Mango Sauce (page 339) in plastic condiment squeeze bottles. Squirt abstract squiggles on each plate, and place the puffs on top.

5. Place the puffs in the oven and immediately lower the oven temperature to 375°F. Bake until the puffs are golden brown, 25 to 30 minutes. Remove the puffs from the oven and turn the oven off.

6. Using the tip of a small, sharp knife, pierce the side of each puff to release steam. Return the puffs to the oven for 5 minutes. Cool completely on the sheet before filling. (The puffs can be prepared up to 1 day ahead and stored in an airtight container at room temperature, or frozen for up to 3 months. To reheat and crisp the puffs, bake on a baking sheet in a preheated 350°F oven until heated through, about 5 minutes for room-temperature puffs and 10 minutes for frozen puffs. No need to thaw the frozen puffs before reheating.)

7. To make the filling, beat the cream in a chilled bowl until very stiff. Fold in the lemon curd. Transfer to a pastry bag fitted with a bismarck tip or a ½-inch-wide plain tip.

8. If you are using a bismarck tip, pierce the bottom of each puff and pipe in the filling. If using a plain tip, split each puff almost, but not fully, in half through its equator. Pipe the filling into the bottom of each puff, then replace the top. (The filled puffs can be prepared up to 2 hours ahead, loosely covered with plastic wrap, and refrigerated.)

9. To serve, spoon equal amounts of the sauce on 6 to 8 dessert plates. Arrange 3 or 4 puffs in the center of the sauce and serve immediately.

Baker's Notes

BECAUSE THE BUTTER must be completely melted by the time the water has evaporated, it is cut into small pieces and stirred often. If the water is allowed to boil, it will evaporate and throw off the formula, making the batter too dry. Dump in the flour all at once to avoid lumping.

Don't crack the eggs directly into the mixing bowl or you might end up with shell bits in your puffs. Crack them into a small bowl and check for shell fragments.

For uniformly shaped puffs, using a dark pencil or pen, draw three or four 1½-inch-wide strips onto the parchment paper, spacing them about 2 inches apart. Turn the paper over and place on the baking sheet. (You should be able to see the strips through the reverse side. If piped directly onto the pencil, the dough could pick up the markings.) Pipe the dough into mounds between the parallel lines.

A bismarck tip, available at bakery supply shops, is a pastry tip shaped like a long nozzle. It is perfect for squirting cream or jelly into puffs or doughnuts.

Our Favorite Cheesecake

CRUST

**1 cup graham cracker, gingersnap, or chocolate
    wafer crumbs**
1 tablespoon sugar
2 tablespoons unsalted butter, melted

FILLING

**2 pounds Philadelphia Brand cream cheese,
    at room temperature**
1¼ cups sugar
Grated zest of 1 lemon
¾ teaspoon vanilla extract
4 large eggs, at room temperature
2 tablespoons all-purpose flour
½ cup sour cream, at room temperature

1. Position a rack in the upper third of the oven and preheat to 375°F. Lightly butter a 9-inch springform pan.

2. To make the crust, stir the crumbs and sugar in a medium bowl, then stir in the melted butter until the crumbs are moistened. Pour into the pan and use the bottom of a wide glass to press evenly and firmly into the bottom of the pan.

3. Bake until the crust is beginning to brown at the edges, about 9 minutes. Transfer to a wire cooling rack and let stand while preparing the filling.

4. Increase the oven temperature to 500°F.

5. For the filling, in the bowl of a heavy-duty standing mixer fitted with the paddle attachment, beat the cream cheese and sugar on low speed just until the cheese is smooth and lump-free. Don't overbeat—too much air will make the top of the cheesecake crack. Beat in the lemon zest and vanilla. Beat in the eggs one at a time, scraping the bowl often to be sure the cheese is smooth. Mix in the flour, then the sour cream. Keep the machine on low and watch out for overbeating. Pour into the crust.

6. Bake for 11 minutes. Turn the oven down to 200°F and continue baking until the center of the cheesecake seems barely set when shaken, about 40 minutes. Do not overbake.

MAKES ONE 9½-INCH
CHEESECAKE, 12 TO 14 SERVINGS

David Lebovitz

As we discussed recipes for this book, cheesecake seemed to be in a class by itself. We also felt that cheesecake defies categorization, as it really isn't a cake. After consideration, we decided eggs play such an important role in a successful cheesecake that it belongs with the other egg-based desserts. If there is one thing we agreed on during our group cheesecake tasting, it is that we don't like fancy flavors, with the exception of Alice Medrich's Chocolate Mocha Cheesecake (see following recipe). A grating of lemon zest or a splash of vanilla is all a cheesecake wants or needs. Here is David Lebovitz's salute to the classic cheesecakes of New York City, incorporating the tips we learned from our tasting, including an unusual combination of oven temperatures.

*Custards
and Other
Egg-Based
Desserts*

7. Transfer the cake to a wire cooling rack. Cool completely, away from drafts, allowing at least 3 hours.

8. Cover with plastic wrap and refrigerate until completely chilled, at least 3 hours, or overnight. To serve, slice with a thin, sharp knife dipped into hot water.

Baker's Notes

PHILADELPHIA BRAND CREAM cheese gives the most traditional flavor and reliable results. It is so perfect for cheesecake that we hesitate to recommend alternatives. If you wish, you can use "natural" cream cheese without any gums or stabilizers; the flavor is superior, but the texture of the cheesecake will be drier, and creaminess is the goal here. Low-fat cream cheese or Neufchâtel cheese will also give drier results, and the baking time will be slightly reduced.

It is very important that the filling ingredients be at room temperature. Be sure to remove them from the refrigerator at least 1 hour before making the filling.

One more time: Be careful not to overbeat the filling.

A little flour makes a firmer cheesecake and absorbs excess liquid in the batter. Some recipes recommend cornstarch, but we prefer flour.

Here's the reasoning behind the two-tier baking temperature: The initial very high temperature gives the cheesecake its characteristic browned top, and the subsequent very low temperature keeps the eggs from overcooking, which can make for a tough, sodden filling. Some bakers insist on baking their cheesecakes in a steamy oven or in a water bath. We tried a variety of baking atmospheres and temperatures and concluded that our two-tier baking temperature, without any additional steam, was the easiest method with the best results.

Drafts can make a cheesecake cool too quickly, and the rapid contraction will cause cracking. Many of our bakers swear that the best place to let the cheesecake cool is in a turned-off oven with the oven door held ajar with a wooden spoon.

Always be sure to cool cheesecake completely before refrigerating. Chilling a warm cheesecake will trap condensation in the cake and make it soggy.

Chocolate Mocha Cheesecake

CRUST

**1½ cups chocolate wafer cookie or chocolate graham
cracker crumbs (about 16 single graham crackers)**
5 tablespoons unsalted butter, melted
¼ cup sugar
1½ teaspoons instant espresso powder

FILLING

⅓ cup plus 1 tablespoon boiling water
**6 ounces semisweet or bittersweet chocolate,
finely chopped**
1 ounce unsweetened chocolate, finely chopped
2 teaspoons instant espresso powder
1 pound cream cheese, at room temperature
¾ cup sugar
1 teaspoon vanilla extract
3 large eggs, at room temperature
2 cups sour cream, at room temperature

1. Position a rack in the lower third of the oven and preheat to 350°F. Lightly butter the inside of a 9-inch springform pan all the way to the top.

2. To make the crust, mix the cookie crumbs, melted butter, sugar, and espresso powder. Press firmly and evenly into the bottom and halfway up the sides of the pan. Bake until the crust looks set around the edges, about 10 minutes for wafer cookies or 15 minutes for graham crackers. Transfer to a wire cooling rack and cool completely. Keep the oven on.

3. To make the filling, place a 9 × 5-inch loaf pan on one side of the oven rack. Fill the pan halfway with hot water. Keep the pan in the oven throughout baking.

4. In a small bowl, pour the boiling water over the semisweet and unsweetened chocolates and the espresso powder. Let stand for a few minutes, then stir until the chocolate is smooth and melted; set aside.

5. In a large bowl, using a hand-held electric mixer on high speed, beat the cream cheese and sugar just until smooth. Scrape the bowl and beaters well. Add the vanilla, then the eggs, one at a time, making sure each egg is incorporated before adding another. Scrape the bowl and beaters well. Beat in the sour cream just until incorporated. Add the chocolate mixture and

MAKES ONE 9-INCH
CHEESECAKE, 10 TO 12
SERVINGS

Alice Medrich and Lily Gerson

A hefty dose of chocolate and a hint of espresso make this an especially satisfying example of the flavored-cheesecake school. The sugar is kept at a reasonable level so the tang of the cream cheese comes through, helping to balance the richness of the chocolate. If possible, make this a day or two before serving to allow the flavors to intensify.

*Custards
and Other
Egg-Based
Desserts*

beat on low speed just until blended. Pour into the cooled crust and smooth the top.

6. Place the cheesecake next to the loaf pan in the oven. Bake until the filling is puffed and set in a 1½-inch border around the sides but the center quivers when the pan is tapped, 35 to 40 minutes. The filling will look underdone, but it will firm upon chilling.

7. Transfer to a wire cooling rack. Slide a thin knife around the upper edge of the filling to release it from the sides of the pan. (There's no need to reach all the way down to the crust, as it only drags crumbs up into the filling.) Invert a very large pot over the pan, being sure it doesn't touch the cheesecake, and cool completely.

8. Cover the cheesecake with plastic wrap and refrigerate for at least 5 hours, preferably 24 to 48 hours. Run a hot, wet knife around the inside of the pan to release the entire cheesecake, and remove the side of the pan. Slice, dipping the knife into hot water between cuttings.

Baker's Notes

THIS RECIPE SHOWS how our members often disagree on technique but still achieve equally fine results. While some bakers think steam is unnecessary for their cheesecakes, Alice finds that steam in the oven prevents cracking.

Instead of cooling the cake in the turned-off oven, simulate it by placing a large pot over the cheesecake as it cools. This slows down the cooling process and helps prevent the sudden temperature changes that make the filling contract and crack into deep fissures.

The Finishing Touch:
Frostings, Glazes, and Sauces

When bakers choose to crown their cakes with smooth, creamy frostings and shiny glazes, or embellish them with spoonfuls of sauce, we are expressing our own personal artistry. While we love simple desserts that are served unadorned or only with a dusting of confectioners' sugar, an unfrosted birthday cake is unthinkable.

The frostings, glazes, icings, fillings, and sauces in this chapter can be used with your favorite cakes to make your own creations. There are other frostings in this book that we considered integral to the particular cake, but you may choose to use them in other applications. These include Golden Fluffy Frosting (page 89), Peanut Butter and White Chocolate Ganache (page 90), White Chocolate Cream (page 99), and Penuche Glaze (page 102).

The recipes in this chapter were created by Flo Braker, Nancy Kux, David Lebovitz, Evie Lieb, Alice Medrich, Lindsey Shere, and Kathleen Stewart.

Ingredients for Frostings, Glazes, and Sauces

OUR FROSTINGS AND GLAZES USE CLASSIC METHODS to create their smooth richness. We proudly present some scrumptious basic frostings, glazes, and sauces that are not just pretty faces that beautify baked goods—they taste great, too.

Butter | To ensure superb flavor and the creamiest consistency, always use pure unsalted Grade A butter for your frostings and glazes.

Chocolate | Be careful of using high-percentage chocolates in ganache recipes, as the fat-to-chocolate ratio will be skewed, and the ganache will separate. If a recipe can be prepared with a high-ratio chocolate, we will say so.

Eggs | The classic method for making buttercream incorporates a hot syrup into beaten egg yolks or whites. With today's concern for food-borne bacteria in raw eggs, we heat the yolks or whites in a hot water bath to 140°F, a temperature that kills the bacteria. Be mindful of cross-contamination, and wash your hands well with soap and hot water after separating eggs.

Sugar | For smooth-melting caramel that won't curdle or separate, use cane sugar, not beet sugar. The latter just doesn't melt smoothly. While beet sugar may not be so labeled on the package, cane sugar will be.

Heavy cream | We prefer the old-fashioned taste of pasteurized cream over cream that has been ultrapasteurized. You can find it at natural food stores, dairies, and many supermarkets.

Equipment for Frostings, Glazes, and Sauces

A HEAVY-DUTY STAND MIXER is almost essential for making buttercream. The whisk attachment works quickly to cool the hot yolks or whites. (This is important, because if the egg-sugar mixture is even slightly warm when the butter is added, the butter will melt and the buttercream will be too soft.) If you use a hand-held mixer, dip the bottom of the bowl in a larger bowl of ice water for a few seconds, then place the bowl of frosting on a wire cooling rack so air can circulate under the bowl to help speed the cooling.

A *metal icing spatula* is the ideal tool for spreading frostings and glazes on cakes. A *wire cooling rack* will hold a cake during the glazing process, lifting it above the glaze that drips off the cake. An *instant-read thermometer* is important to determine the temperatures of some ganache glazes and the egg-sugar mixtures for buttercream. A *food processor* or *blender* purees fruit into sauces. You'll need a *fine wire sieve* to strain the tiny seeds from berry sauces.

Techniques for Frostings, Glazes, and Sauces

INSTRUCTIONS ON FROSTING CAKES can be found on page 78.

Storing Frostings, Glazes, and Sauces

BUTTERCREAM FROSTINGS CAN BE MADE ahead and stored in the refrigerator or freezer, where they will harden.

To soften a chilled frosting to spreadable consistency, chop it into 1- to 2-inch chunks (if using frozen buttercream, first defrost it for a few hours in the refrigerator). Put the chunks of cold frosting in a metal mixing bowl, preferably the bowl of a heavy-duty stand mixer. Place the bowl in a larger bowl or pan of hot water and let stand until a third to half of the frosting is melted. Remove the bowl from the water and beat on low speed (with the paddle attachment, if using a standing mixer) to combine and restore the frosting to its original consistency. If the frosting is too firm or lumpy, return to the hot water to melt a bit more, then beat again. If the frosting is too soft, place the bowl in the refrigerator for about 15 minutes, then beat again.

Make-ahead tips for other frostings, glazes, and sauces are included with each recipe.

Classic Meringue Buttercream

MAKES ABOUT 3½ CUPS,
ENOUGH TO FROST A TWO- TO
THREE-LAYER 9-INCH CAKE

Nancy Kux

Made with egg whites, this buttercream has a luscious fluffy quality and a flavor that can be the springboard for many variations. We warm the whites briefly to reach the temperature that will kill harmful bacteria.

1 cup sugar
4 large egg whites, at room temperature
2 tablespoons water
1¾ cups (3½ sticks) unsalted butter, at room temperature (70°F)
1 teaspoon vanilla extract

1. Pour ½ inch of water into a skillet and bring it to a simmer over high heat. Reduce the heat to low and maintain a bare simmer.

2. In the bowl of a heavy-duty stand mixer, hand-whisk the sugar, egg whites, and water to combine. Place the bowl in the skillet and stir the mixture constantly with the whisk (don't bother to beat air into the mixture) until the sugar is completely dissolved and an instant-read thermometer reads 160°F.

3. Attach the bowl to the mixer and fit with the whisk attachment. Whip on medium-high speed until the meringue is cool, has tripled in volume, and forms stiff, shiny peaks, about 6 minutes.

4. Add the butter 1 tablespoon at a time, beating after each addition until it is absorbed into the meringue. Beat in the vanilla. (The buttercream can be used immediately or stored in an airtight container and refrigerated for up to 1 week. Or freeze the buttercream for up to 3 weeks. To defrost and use the frozen buttercream, see page 325.)

Orange Buttercream: Substitute 2 tablespoons freshly grated orange zest (from 2 large oranges) for the vanilla.

Lemon Buttercream: Substitute 2 tablespoons freshly grated lemon zest (from 4 medium lemons) for the vanilla.

Orange-Ginger Buttercream: Grate about 3 ounces fresh ginger on the large holes of a box grater. Place in cheesecloth or a clean kitchen towel and squeeze firmly over a bowl. (Or use bottled natural ginger juice from The Ginger People, available at many supermarkets, natural food stores, and at *www.gingerpeople.com.*) Add 2 tablespoons ginger juice to the Orange Buttercream along with the orange zest.

Baker's Notes

THE TEMPERATURE OF THE BUTTER is very important when making buttercream. The butter should be brought to cool room temperature, about 70°F. The easiest way to do this is to cut the butter sticks into 1-tablespoon slices and let them stand at room temperature for about 15 minutes. When you press the butter it will feel slightly firm, not squishy, and your finger will leave an impression. The butter will look dull, not oily or shiny.

If the buttercream separates, whip it on very high speed until it comes together. If this is not satisfactory, whip in a tablespoon of chilled butter on very high speed. This should emulsify the buttercream.

Chocolate Buttercream Frosting

MAKES ABOUT 3½ CUPS,
ENOUGH FOR A THREE-LAYER
8- TO 9-INCH CAKE

Alice Medrich

Here is the classic rich chocolate frosting, but with an extra step to ensure that the eggs are heated to a safe temperature. Depending on how the melted chocolate is added to the frosting, you can choose to make this frosting dark or light brown.

12 ounces semisweet or bittersweet chocolate,
   finely chopped
⅔ cup plus 6 tablespoons water
⅔ cup sugar
¼ teaspoon cream of tartar
3 large egg yolks
½ pound (2 sticks) unsalted butter, slightly softened,
   cut into 1-tablespoon pieces

1. In the top part of a double boiler over simmering water, melt the chocolate with 6 tablespoons water until smooth. Remove from the heat and let stand until tepid, stirring occasionally, while preparing the rest of the ingredients.

2. Place ⅓ cup water in a small (1-quart or less) saucepan, then add the sugar and cream of tartar. Stir just to moisten the sugar. Cover the pot and bring to a simmer over medium heat. Simmer, still covered, without stirring, until the sugar dissolves, about 2 minutes. Uncover and wash down the sides of the pan with a pastry brush dipped in water, just in case there are sugar crystals on the sides. Insert a candy thermometer in the syrup. Cook over high heat without stirring until the syrup reaches 238°F.

3. Meanwhile, bring about 1 inch of water to a simmer in a large skillet over high heat. Reduce the heat to low to maintain the simmer. Plug in a hand-held electric mixer near the stove.

4. Place the egg yolks in a medium stainless steel bowl. When the syrup is ready, start beating the yolks on high speed while pouring the syrup in a steady stream near, but not into, the beaters (this will reduce splashing). Remove the beaters from the mixer, rinse them in the simmering water to remove any raw egg, and reattach them to the mixer.

5. Place the bowl with the egg mixture in the simmering water. Using a heatproof silicone spatula, stir the egg mixture, being sure to scrape down any splatters from the inside of the bowl, until it reaches 160°F on an instant-read thermometer, 2 to 4 minutes. Remove the bowl from the skillet and beat with the mixer on high speed until the mixture is thick, pale yellow, and cooled to room temperature.

6. A tablespoon or two at a time, beat the butter into the egg mixture, being sure that each addition is almost incorporated before adding another, to make a smooth frosting.

7. For a dark chocolate buttercream, fold or stir the cooled chocolate into the frosting. For a lighter color, beat the cooled chocolate into the frosting. (The buttercream, covered airtight, can be refrigerated for up to 5 days or frozen for up to 3 months. To use chilled buttercream, see page 325.)

Baker's Notes

SEE THE BAKER'S Notes for Classic Meringue Buttercream (page 327) for tips on the temperature of the butter.

The chocolate buttercream uses egg yolks only. For a slightly lighter alternative (that also leaves the baker with 1 less egg white to discard or store), use 1 whole large egg and 1 egg white.

The chocolate is melted with water so it will harden into a softer state than it would without the water, keeping the buttercream smooth, creamy, and spreadable.

Creamy Chocolate Frosting

MAKES ABOUT 2½ CUPS,
ENOUGH FOR A 9-INCH TWO-
LAYER CAKE

Flo Braker
and Evie Lieb

*Here's an old-fashioned
frosting made in the American
style, with lots of
confectioners' sugar to give it
body. The result is a thick,
dark icing made for
slathering onto our Rich
Chocolate Cake (page 54).*

4 ounces unsweetened chocolate, coarsely chopped
3¾ cups (1 pound) confectioners' sugar
8 tablespoons (1 stick) unsalted butter, softened
⅛ teaspoon salt
½ cup whole milk
2 teaspoons vanilla extract

1. In a small bowl, melt the chocolate in a skillet of hot, not simmering, water, stirring occasionally until smooth. Remove from the heat and let stand until tepid.

2. In a food processor fitted with the metal blade, pulse the sugar, butter, and salt to combine. With the machine running, add the milk and vanilla and process until smooth. Add the cooled chocolate and process until well blended and creamy. Use immediately. (The frosting can be stored, covered airtight, in the refrigerator for up to 3 days, or frozen for up to 3 months. Bring the frosting to room temperature and beat vigorously before using.)

Alice's Light Ganache

2 cups heavy cream
6½ ounces semisweet or bittersweet chocolate,
 finely chopped

MAKES ABOUT 3 CUPS

1. At least 6 hours before frosting the cake, heat the cream in a large, heavy-bottomed saucepan over medium-high heat until it forms bubbles around the edges. Place the chocolate in a large bowl and pour the cream over it. Let stand until the chocolate is completely melted, about 15 minutes.

2. Stir with a rubber spatula, scraping the sides of the bowl often, until the mixture is smooth and evenly colored. Cool completely. Cover with plastic wrap and refrigerate until chilled and thick, at least 6 hours and up to 4 days before using.

3. Just before needed, using a hand-held electric mixer on medium speed, whip the thickened ganache until it is light in texture and spreadable. Use immediately, as the ganache will firm upon standing.

Alice Medrich

This simple but most luxurious of all fillings is essentially very rich chocolate whipped cream. Alice developed this wonderfully light ganache (the classic chocolate and cream mixture that bakers use for many chocolate applications, from fillings and glazes to truffles) as a filling for a layer cake that will be covered with a darker chocolate glaze. You must chill it for several hours in advance, then whip it just before using. Do not use bittersweet chocolate with more than 62 percent cocoa solids, or the ganache will be too dense to whip.

Baker's Note

THE FLAVOR INTENSIFIES upon standing, so if you have the time, make the ganache the day before using.

Chocolate Glaze

MAKES 1½ CUPS

Alice Medrich

This glaze is actually a rich ganache. This is a good glaze for chilled or room-temperature cakes.

Baker's Note

Some bakers heat the cream for the ganache just until warm, but the storage life of the glaze is increased if the cream comes to a full boil.

¾ cup heavy cream
8 ounces semisweet or bittersweet chocolate, finely
   chopped

1. In a small saucepan, heat the cream over medium-high heat until it comes to a boil—watch carefully to avoid boiling over. Place the chocolate in a medium bowl and pour the cream over it.

2. Let stand for a few minutes to soften the chocolate, then stir gently until completely smooth and melted. Do not whisk or beat the ganache, or you will make bubbles that will show up in the glazed cake. Cool until the ganache is thick and spreadable, about 30 minutes, depending on the kitchen temperature.

3. If desired, place the cake on a cardboard cake round before glazing. Using a metal icing spatula, spread less than one-fourth of the glaze in a very thin layer over the top and sides of the cake, smoothing rough surfaces and filling in any cracks. Be careful not to get any crumbs into the bowl of glaze. This is called a "crumb coat," and it serves to give the cake a smooth, even undercoat for the final glaze. Clean and dry the spatula.

4. Rewarm the cooled glaze by placing it in a skillet of barely simmering water for a few seconds, stirring gently until the glaze is smooth and the consistency of thick heavy cream (an instant-read thermometer will read 85° to 90°F). Do not overheat, or it will melt the crumb coat. If necessary, cool to the proper temperature. Strain the glaze to remove any crumbs, if necessary.

5. Center the crumb-coated cake on a decorating turntable or round platter. Pour all of the glaze onto the center of the cake. Working quickly, use just two or three strokes to spread the glaze over the cake so it runs over the sides, rotating the turntable as you spread. Use the spatula to scoop up any dripped glaze and touch it to any bare spots on the sides of the cake (you can cover small spots by dipping your finger into the glaze and applying it). Jiggle or gently rap the turntable to settle the glaze. Do not respread the glaze once it has started to set, or the glaze will have marks and dull streaks.

6. Using a wide spatula, transfer the cake to a wire cooling rack. Let stand at room temperature (or refrigerate, depending on the cake recipe), until the glaze sets, about 15 minutes.

Chocolate Butter Glaze

8 ounces semisweet or bittersweet chocolate, finely
  chopped
8 tablespoons (1 stick) unsalted butter, cut into bits
1 teaspoon light corn syrup

1. Combine the chocolate, butter, and corn syrup in a heatproof medium bowl. Place in a skillet of barely simmering water and stir often until almost completely melted.

2. Remove the bowl from the water and stir occasionally, until completely smooth. Do not whisk or beat the glaze. Then let stand at room temperature without stirring until cooled, thick, and spreadable, about 30 minutes, depending on the kitchen temperature.

3. If desired, place the cake on a cardboard cake round before glazing. Using a metal icing spatula, spread less than one-fourth of the glaze in a very thin layer over the top and sides of the cake, being sure to smooth rough surfaces and filling in any cracks. Be careful not to get any crumbs into the bowl of glaze. This is called a "crumb coat" and it serves to give the cake a smooth, even undercoat for the final glaze. Clean and dry the spatula.

4. Rewarm the cooled glaze by placing it in a skillet of barely simmering water for a few seconds, stirring gently until the glaze is perfectly smooth and the consistency of heavy cream (an instant-read thermometer will read 90°). Do not overheat the glaze, or it will not dry with a shiny finish. If necessary, cool to the proper temperature. Strain the glaze to remove any crumbs, if necessary.

5. Center the crumb-coated cake on a decorating turntable or round platter. Pour all of the glaze onto the center of the cake. Working quickly, use just two or three strokes to spread the glaze over the cake so it runs over the sides, rotating the turntable or platter as you spread. Use the spatula to scoop up any dripped glaze and touch it to any bare spots on the sides of the cake (you can cover small spots by dipping your finger into the glaze and applying it). Jiggle or gently rap the turntable to settle the glaze. Do not respread the glaze once it has started to set, or the glaze will have marks and dull streaks.

6. Using a wide spatula, transfer the cake to a wire cooling rack. Let stand at room temperature until the glaze sets, about 15 minutes.

MAKES 1½ CUPS, ENOUGH FOR
A 9-INCH CAKE

Alice Medrich

Choose this glaze for a cake that does not require refrigeration. Unlike cream-based ganache, this dark, glossy glaze can be prepared with high-percentage chocolate, without adjusting the recipe, making it the choice of those who like a bittersweet edge to their icing. The cake must be at room temperature before glazing. This glaze must be used at 90°F for it to retain its shiny finish. Store and serve the cake at room temperature.

Pastry Cream

MAKES ABOUT 1¼ CUPS

Lindsey Shere

Pastry cream, basically a custard sauce that has been thickened, can be used as a base for a fruit tart under berries, or as a filling for cream puffs. Vanilla is the classic flavoring, but there are other options, such as chocolate or liqueur.

1 cup milk

1 large egg plus 1 large egg yolk, or
   3 large egg yolks

½ cup sugar

¼ cup all-purpose flour

1 teaspoon vanilla extract

1. In a nonreactive medium pan, heat the milk over medium heat until bubbles form around the edges.

2. In a medium bowl, using a hand-held mixer on high speed or a whisk, beat the egg, yolk, and sugar until thick and pale yellow. Beat in the flour. On low speed, gradually beat in about half of the hot milk. Pour the mixture into the saucepan.

3. Cook over medium heat, stirring constantly, until the pastry cream comes to a full boil, taking care that it doesn't scorch.

4. Rub the pastry cream through a wire sieve into a medium bowl. Stir in the vanilla. Press plastic wrap directly on the surface of the pastry cream and poke a few holes in the plastic so the steam can escape. Refrigerate until chilled, at least 2 hours. (The pastry cream can be prepared, covered, and refrigerated for up to 1 week.)

Chocolate Pastry Cream: Stir 2 ounces bittersweet chocolate, finely chopped and melted, into the hot pastry cream.

Brandied Pastry Cream: Stir 1 tablespoon brandy, Cognac, or dark rum into the hot pastry cream. If you wish, use a fruit-based liqueur or eau-de-vie, such as Grand Marnier, kirsch, or framboise.

Baker's Notes

FOR A SUCCESSFUL PASTRY cream that holds its shape when cut, be sure to use flour or cornstarch, not arrowroot or other root-based starches such as tapioca flour. Root starches will not set enough to cut.

The pastry cream must come to a full boil—the flour will insulate the eggs and keep them from curdling. If it doesn't come to a boil, the enzymes in the yolks will react with the starch gels and break down the pastry cream as it stands, making it soupy.

There are a number of options for the milk in the pastry cream. Milk and half-and-half give the richest flavor, but low-fat milk makes a firm cream. This texture may be desirable in a tart under very juicy fruit. However, pastry cream made with low-fat milk burns more quickly, so special care must be taken.

If the pastry cream seems very stiff after chilling, it can be whisked to break some of the milk-engorged starch molecules, which will thin the cream. On the other hand, if your cream is the perfect thickness but it looks a bit lumpy, resist the temptation to whisk it, or it will thin out too much. Don't worry—pastry cream smooths out when it is spread in the shell. For a lighter version, whip ¼ cup heavy cream with 1 teaspoon sugar until stiff peaks form, then fold into the pastry cream.

Whipped Cream Topping

MAKES ABOUT 2½ CUPS

Alice Medrich

So many desserts need a little something extra to put them over the top, and that usually means a dollop of whipped cream. There are a few secrets to making whipped cream that is worthy of your best baked goods, detailed in the Baker's Notes. But whatever you do, don't leave out the sugar and vanilla, or you'll end up with a flat-tasting mound of cream that is well on its way to being butter.

1 cup heavy cream
1 tablespoon sugar
1 teaspoon vanilla extract

In a chilled medium bowl, using a hand-held electric mixer on medium speed or a whisk, beat the cream, sugar, and vanilla just until stiff peaks begin to form. Cover and refrigerate. (The whipped cream can be prepared ahead, covered, and refrigerated for up to 1 day.)

Baker's Notes

BE SURE the cream and bowl are well chilled—cold helps stabilize the cream and give it more body. If you have the time, freeze the cream in the bowl (with the beaters or whisk, if you remember) for a few minutes before whipping.

For the best flavor, use pasteurized (not ultrapasteurized) heavy cream, available at natural food markets and dairy stores.

Add the granulated sugar at the beginning of whipping, so it has time to dissolve. If you wish, substitute confectioners' sugar. If you taste the whipped cream and think it needs more sweetening, use confectioners' or superfine sugar so it dissolves readily.

Toasted Almond Crème Anglaise

2 cups milk
½ cup coarsely chopped toasted almonds
6 tablespoons sugar
Pinch of salt
½ vanilla bean, split
6 large egg yolks

MAKES ABOUT 2½ CUPS

David Lebovitz

Almond enhances many desserts and makes something special out of the familiar vanilla custard sauce. For the classic version, delete the almonds and skip the infusion.

1. Mix the milk, almonds, sugar, and salt in a heavy medium saucepan. Using the tip of a knife, scrape the seeds from the vanilla bean into the mixture. Heat over low heat until the milk is warm but not simmering. Remove from the heat, cover, and let stand for 1 hour, until the milk is flavored with the almonds.

2. Strain the milk mixture through a wire sieve and discard the almonds. Return the milk to the saucepan and reheat.

3. Whisk the yolks in a medium bowl and gradually whisk in the hot milk. Pour into the saucepan.

4. Cook over medium-low heat, stirring constantly with a wooden spatula and being sure to scrape the bottom and sides of the pan, until the custard is thick enough to cling heavily to the spatula and your finger drawn through the custard cuts a swath, about 3 minutes. (An instant-read thermometer inserted in the custard will read 185°F.)

5. Strain through the sieve into a medium bowl placed in a larger bowl of ice water. Let stand, stirring often with a clean spatula, until chilled. (The sauce can be made ahead, covered, and refrigerated for up to 3 days.)

Baker's Note

FOR OTHER flavor ideas, see "Variations on a Custard Theme," page 308.

Caramel Sauce

MAKES 1¾ CUPS

David Lebovitz

Caramel sauce is a versatile complement to many desserts. Playing with layers of richness, it can set off a dark chocolate cake, or it can make something special out of a selection of ripe seasonal fruits.

½ cup cold water

1 cup sugar

¼ teaspoon fresh lemon juice

½ cup heavy cream, at room temperature

¼ cup boiling water

4 tablespoons (½ stick) unsalted butter, at room temperature

1 tablespoon corn syrup

1. Pour the cold water into a heavy-bottomed medium saucepan. Add the sugar and lemon juice and stir just enough to dampen the sugar. Cover and bring to a boil over medium heat, swirling the pan by the handle to help dissolve the sugar. Occasionally press a wet pastry brush against any sugar crystals that form on the inside of the pan to wash them back into the syrup.

2. Uncover and increase the heat to medium-high. Cook until the caramel has colored to a deep red brown (about the color of an old penny). Being very careful to avoid splashes and steam (if you want, place a colander over the saucepan to act as a perforated lid), immediately pour the boiling water into the caramel. If the caramel hardens, whisk over low heat to dissolve.

3. Remove from the heat and whisk in the cream. The mixture will bubble up, so be careful. Return to low heat and whisk until the hardened caramel dissolves. Add the butter and corn syrup and whisk until the sauce comes to a boil. Strain to remove any undissolved sugar crystals. Whisk again before serving. Serve warm, at room temperature, or chilled.

Baker's Notes

READ "CARAMEL KNOWLEDGE" on page 310.

A tall saucepan is best for making caramel sauce, as the addition of cream always makes the caramel bubble up dramatically. The tall sides prevent boiling over.

A Rainbow of Fruit Sauces

Many soft fruits can be pureed to make fast, colorful, and tasty sauces for dressing up your desserts. Small amounts of lemon juice and liquor are used to enhance the fruit flavor. When making these sauces, taste them carefully for sweetness, and add more sugar or lemon juice until you get the right equilibrium. These additions are meant not as flavorings but as enhancements.

Of course, you can experiment with other fruits. Blackberries, boysenberries, and raspberries can be made into sauces following the strawberry sauce formula. (Blueberry skins don't puree smoothly, so don't use them for an uncooked sauce.) Nectarines and white peaches are a fine substitute for regular peaches, but they are sweeter, so use less sugar.

Strawberry Sauce: In a food processor, puree 1 pint strawberries (rinsed, hulled, and sliced), 2 tablespoons sugar, ¼ teaspoon kirsch, and a few drops of fresh lemon juice. Do not overprocess the berries, or you will crush the seeds and add an unpleasant flavor to the sauce. Strain, but leave some of the seeds in the sauce for texture. Cover and refrigerate for up to 2 days. Makes about 2 cups.

Raspberry Sauce: In a food processor, puree two 6-ounce containers of raspberries, 2 tablespoons sugar, 1 teaspoon framboise or Chambord, and ½ teaspoon fresh lemon juice. Strain through a fine wire sieve to remove the seeds. Cover and refrigerate for up to 2 days. Makes about 1 cup.

Peach Sauce: In a food processor, puree 1 pound ripe peaches (peeled, pitted, and sliced), 3 tablespoons sugar, 2 teaspoons fresh lemon juice, and ¼ teaspoon kirsch until very smooth. Cover tightly and refrigerate until serving. Serve within 12 hours, or the peaches may oxidize and turn brown. Makes about 1 cup.

Cooked Peach Sauce: This sauce is a good choice for making ahead, as the cooking keeps the peaches from turning brown. In a medium nonreactive saucepan, cook 1 pound ripe peaches (peeled, pitted, and sliced) with ½ cup water over medium heat until the peaches are very tender, about 5 minutes. Transfer to a food processor and puree with 3 tablespoon sugar, ¼ teaspoon kirsch, and a few drops of lemon juice. Cool, cover, and refrigerate for up to 2 days. Makes about 1½ cups.

Mango Sauce: In a food processor, puree 1 large mango (peeled, with the flesh cut from the pit and coarsely chopped), 2 tablespoons sugar, 2 teaspoons fresh lime juice, and 2 teaspoons dark rum until very smooth. Cover and refrigerate for up to 2 days. Makes about 1¼ cups.

David Lebowitz

Lemon Curd

MAKES ABOUT 1½ CUPS

Kathleen Stewart

Luscious is the word for this lemon curd, which can be used by itself as a spread for biscuits and toast or as a cake filling, or folded into whipped cream to make a filling for cream puffs or a cake frosting. This recipe, from Healdsburg's Downtown Bakery in the Sonoma, California, wine country, has the added advantage of being cooked directly over a low flame, which saves time compared with the traditional double-boiler method.

2 large eggs, at room temperature

3 large egg yolks, at room temperature

¾ cup lemon juice (about 4 lemons)

Grated zest of 4 lemons

6 tablespoons (¾ stick) unsalted butter, chilled,
    cut into ½-inch cubes

¼ cup sugar

2 tablespoons water

1. Combine all the ingredients in a heavy-bottomed medium saucepan. Using a heat-resistant silicone or wooden spatula, stir constantly over medium-low heat, being careful not to let the mixture come to a boil, until it is thick enough to coat the spatula (if you run a finger through the curd on the spatula, it will cut a swath) and an instant-read thermometer inserted in the mixture reads 185°F, about 7 minutes. Do not overcook; the curd will thicken as it cools. Immediately strain the curd through a wire sieve into a bowl.

2. Press a sheet of plastic wrap directly on the surface of the curd. With the tip of a sharp knife, poke a few holes in the plastic to allow steam to escape. Cool to room temperature. Transfer to an airtight container and refrigerate. (The curd can be stored, covered and refrigerated, for up to 5 days.)

Baker's Notes

THE KEY TO a smooth lemon curd is to avoid overcooking. If the mixture comes to a boil, it will curdle. The butter must be completely melted by the time the mixture reaches 185°F, so adjust the heat.

Don't be concerned about straining out the lemon zest. The oils in the zest will have transferred their flavor to the curd during cooking. And the little bits of zest would spoil the curd's silky smoothness.

Whipped Cream Frosting

2 cups heavy cream, preferably not ultrapasteurized
2 tablespoons sugar
1 teaspoon vanilla extract

1. In a chilled large bowl, using a hand-held electric mixer at medium speed or a whisk, whip the cream, sugar, and vanilla just until the cream holds its shape. Transfer half of the softly whipped cream to a chilled medium bowl, cover with plastic wrap, and refrigerate.

2. Beat the remaining cream just until it forms stiff peaks—overwhipping will give the cream a grainy texture. Using a metal icing spatula, apply a crumb coat to the cake (see page 78). Refrigerate until the cream firms, about 15 minutes.

3. Carefully whip the remaining cream just until it forms soft peaks; do not overbeat. Frost the coated cake with this cream—note that the more you work the cream with the spatula, the stiffer and denser it will become, making it difficult to spread, so handle it lightly.

MAKES 3½ CUPS

Flo Braker

Homemade angel food or chiffon cake with whipped cream frosting is one of life's simple pleasures. In order to give the cake a smooth crumb coat, then a fluffy outer layer, the cream is prepared differently from the standard method.

Baker's Note

FOR PIPED WHIPPED cream decorations, the cream should be piped just past the soft peak stage, but not stiff. A large (½-inch) open star tip will make a design with the most detail. Use a plain round tip for creating designs with softly whipped cream.

Sources

The Baker's Catalogue
P.O. Box 876
Norwich, VT 05055-0876
(800) 827-6836

One-stop shopping for bread baking supplies, but a good selection for the cake and pastry baker, too. Look here for malt powder, loaf pans, popover pans, baker's peels, baking stones, bench knives, semolina, durum, flours, electric scales, baker's lame, ginger juice, crystallized ginger, Grade B maple syrup, sanding sugar, pearl sugar, and more.

Bridge Kitchenware
214 East 52nd Street
New York, NY 10022
(212) 688-4220
www.bridgekitchenware.com

The place for high-quality baking pans (or any kitchen utensil, for that matter), and a reliable source for professional-grade parchment paper.

The Broadway Panhandler
477 Broome Street
New York, NY 10013
(212) 966-3434

A wide selection of pans and utensils for the baker.

La Cuisine
323 Cameron Street
Alexandria, VA 22314
(800) 521-1176

Quality hardware for the cook, with some edibles (such as sanding sugars and extracts), too.

New York Cake and Baking Supply
56 West 22nd Street
New York, NY 10010
(212) 675-2253
(800) 942-2539

Another three-star baking supply source, with everything from a wide selection of chocolates to countless pans, molds, and utensils.

Penzeys, Ltd.
P.O. Box 933
Muskego, WI 53150
(414) 679-7207
www.penzeys.com

Fine spices for baking, plus vanilla beans and extracts.

Royal Pacific Foods (The Ginger People)
2700 Garden Road, Suite G
Monterey, CA 93940
(831) 645-1090
(800) 551-5284
www.gingerpeople.com

All things ginger, including crystallized ginger and ginger juice.

Surfas
8825 National Boulevard
Culver City, CA 90232
(310) 559-4770
Fax (310) 559-4983
e-mail: surfas@pacbell.net

If Michelin gave stars to kitchenware shops, this one would deserve three stars to designate "worth a journey." In business since 1937, their motto is "A Chef's Paradise," and they are right. They have an incredible array of baking equipment, as well as fresh, frozen, and bottled ingredients, including such hard-to-find items as pistachio extract.

Sur La Table
Catalog Division
1765 Sixth Avenue South
Seattle, WA 98134-1608
(800) 243-0852
www.surlatable.com

This kitchenware chain is all over the country, and many of our bakers teach at the cooking schools in the stores. Look at their website for locations and dates. Their "Tools for the Cook" catalog is especially useful for hard-to-find baking utensils.

Sweet Celebrations
P.O. Box 39426
Edina, MN 55436-0426
(800) 328-6722
www.sweetc.com

Formerly known as Maid of Scandinavia, You'll find an amazing array of cake and pastry making supplies here—offset metal icing spatulas, pastry bags and tips, cardboard cake rounds, and more.

Williams-Sonoma
P.O. Box 7456
San Francisco, CA 94120
(800) 541-2233

In spite of growing competition, Williams-Sonoma remains one of the best choices for well-made baking tools. Their famous catalog is packed with beautiful things for the kitchen.

Index

Alice's light ganache, 331
  in chocolate raspberry
    cake, 94–95
almond(s):
  -anise biscotti, classic,
    205
  -berry vacherins, 315–16
  in caramel ice cream roll,
    103–5
  in chocolate budini, 311
  and chocolate sandwich
    cookies, 202–3
  and dried cherry cake, 88
  in French noisette shells,
    220–21
  in plum-frangipane tart,
    168–69
  in Queen of Sheba torte,
    108–9
  toasted, crème anglaise,
    337
angel food cake:
  five-spice, *see* five-spice
    angel food cake
  Flo's, 70–71
  testing and tasting of,
    72–74
anise-almond biscotti,
  classic, 205

Anjou pears, in pear crisp,
  184
Anna's Daughter's Rye
  Bread, 23
apple(s):
  baked, with walnut-orange
    stuffing, 194
  brown Betty, 186
  cinnamon, pie, 148
  mincemeat pie, 146–47
  muffins, 229
  -raisin pandowdy, 188
Apple Farm, The, 21
apple-polenta tart:
  double-crusted, 172–73
  quince and, 173
applesauce:
  -carrot layer cake,
    56–57
  -carrot layer cake with
    golden fluffy frosting,
    89
  gingerbread, 241
appliances, small electric,
  26–27
apricot streusel bars,
  214–15
artichoke and potato
  turnovers, 153

baguettes, French, 276–78
baked apples with walnut-
  orange stuffing, 194
baking pans, 28–31
banana:
  bread, Kona Inn, 240
  cream pie, 134
bars:
  apricot streusel, 214–15
  buttermilk, 246–47
  date streusel, 215
  maple, 243–44
  prune streusel, 215
basic tart dough (pâte
  brisée), 159
Beaumes-de-Venise and
  honey, pears baked
  in, 195
berry(ies):
  -almond vacherins,
    315–16
  cobbler, mixed, 185
  -lemon meringue tart, 171
  in summer pudding,
    192–93
  tart, summer, 176
  see also specific berries
best chocolate chip cookies,
  211

Betty, 183
    apple brown, 186
biscotti:
    chocolate-hazelnut, 205
    classic almond-anise, 205
    pine nut–orange, 205
    pistachio-golden raisin,
        204–5
biscuits:
    buttermilk, 231–32
    testing and tasting, 233
bittersweet chocolate:
    in Alice's light ganache,
        331
    in almond and chocolate
        sandwich cookies,
        202–3
    in caramel ice cream roll,
        103–5
    in chocolate budini, 311
    in chocolate buttercream
        frosting, 328–29
    in chocolate butter glaze,
        333
    in chocolate glaze, 332
    in chocolate-hazelnut
        biscotti, 205
    in chocolate-hazelnut
        meringue cookies,
        210
    in chocolate mocha
        cheesecake, 321–22
    in chocolate noisette
        sandwiches, 221
    in chocolate pastry cream,
        335
    in chocolate pots de
        crème, 305
    in chocolate tartlets,
        174–75
    in gateau victoire, 106–7
    in molten chocolate cakes,
        110–11
    in peanut butter and fudge
        pie, 135
    pudding pie, 136–37
    in Queen of Sheba torte,
        108–9
    soufflé, 313
    in triple chocolate cake,
        83
blackberries:
    in berry-almond
        vacherins, 315–16

in deep-dish summer pie,
    150
in mixed berry cobbler,
    185
in summer berry tart, 176
in summer pudding,
    192–93
blood orange chiffon pie with
    chocolate crumb
    crust, 144–45
blueberry(ies):
    in deep-dish summer pie,
        150
    grunt, 187
    in mixed berry cobbler,
        185
    muffins, 228–29
    in raspberry-lemon tart,
        170–71
Bosc pears, in warm pear
    tart, 164–65
bourbon pecan pie, 128
bowls, 32
boysenberries:
    in summer berry tart, 176
    in summer pudding,
        192–93
Braker, Flo, 52–62, 65–71,
    83–93, 96–105, 330,
    341
brandy:
    in brandied pastry cream,
        335
    in Queen of Sheba torte,
        108–9
    in warm pear tart, 164–65
bran-raisin muffins, 230
bread dough:
    dividing and shaping of,
        260–61
    kneading of, 258–59
    making of, 256–57
    risings of, 259–60,
        261–62
    temperatures of, 258
bread pudding, the ultimate,
    303
breads, 251–97
    baking of, 262–63
    buttery dinner rolls,
        292–93
    classic rye, 283–85
    dinner rolls of multigrain
        bread dough, 274

dinner rolls of white
    sandwich dough,
    264–65
double fig focaccia,
    294–95
durum, 270–72
French baguettes,
    276–78
hamburger buns, 265
ingredients for, 252–56
Italian whole wheat,
    270–72
morning buns, 290–91
multigrain, 273–75
orange-rum sweet,
    288–89
pita, 286–87
quick, see quick breads
round rye loaves, 284–85
soft pretzels, 296–97
sourdough, 279–82
storing of, 263
white sandwich, 264–66
brioche:
    molds, individual, 268
    raisin, 267–69
brownies, double chocolate,
    209
brown sugar thins, 206–7
budini, chocolate, 311
buns:
    hamburger, 265
    morning, 290–91
bushberries, in deep-dish
    summer pie, 150
butter cakes:
    mixing of, 48–49
    our favorite, 52–53
buttercream:
    classic meringue,
        326–27
    frosting, chocolate,
        328–29
    lemon, 327
    orange, 327
    orange-ginger, see orange-
        ginger buttercream
buttermilk:
    bars, 246–47
    biscuits, 231–32
    currant scones, 234–35
    spice doughnuts, 245–46
butter pie dough, 123
buttery dinner rolls, 292–93

cakes:
    baking of, 50–51
    basics of, 44–74
    butter, *see* butter cakes
    carrot-applesauce layer,
        see carrot-applesauce
        layer cake
    classic genoise, 60–61
    cooling of, 51
    decorating of, 77–82
    equipment for, 46–47
    five-spice angel food, *see*
        five-spice angel food
        cake
    Flo's angel food, 70–71
    frosting of, 78–79
    ingredients for, 44–46
    layer, *see* layer cake
    Meyer lemon chiffon,
        68–69
    our favorite butter, 52–53
    our favorite chocolate
        genoise, *see* our
        favorite chocolate
        genoise
    peanut butter layer, 58–59
    rich chocolate, 54–55
    sponge, *see* espresso
        sponge cake; sponge
        cakes
    storing of, 51
    techniques for, 47–51
    trimming and splitting of,
        77–78
cakes for family and friends,
        75–111
    caramel ice cream roll,
        103–5
    chocolate raspberry,
        94–95
    coconut cupcakes with
        nougatine sticks,
        96–98
    dried cherry and almond,
        88
    equipment for, 76
    gateau victoire, 106–7
    heavenly hazelnut, with
        chocolate rum glaze,
        86–87
    molten chocolate, 110–11
    orange-ginger gateau, 91
    peanut butter and
        strawberry jam, 90

pistachio roulade with
        white chocolate
        cream, 99–101
    Queen of Sheba torte,
        108–9
    sour cream pound, 84–85
    storing of, 82
    techniques for, 76–77
    triple chocolate, 83
caramel:
    cinnamon crème, 306–7
    crunch topping, for
        espresso sponge
        cake, 92–93
    ice cream roll, 103–5
    knowledge, 310
caramel sauce, 338
    for cream puffs with
        lemon filling, 317–18
    pineapple, warm
        pineapple in puff
        pastry with, 189–91
Carroll, John Phillip,
        228–40, 242–47,
        249–50
carrot-applesauce layer
        cake, 56–57
    with golden fluffy frosting,
        89
Chambord, in chocolate
        raspberry cake,
        94–95
cheese and tomato galette,
        178–79
cheesecake:
    chocolate mocha,
        321–22
    our favorite, 319–20
cherry, dried, and almond
        cake, 88
chess pie, cranberry, 133
chiffon cake, Meyer lemon,
        68–69
chiffon pies:
    blood orange, with
        chocolate crumb
        crust, 144–45
    lemon or lime, 145
chocolate, 3–7
    almond and, sandwich
        cookies, 202–3
    bittersweet, *see* bittersweet
        chocolate
    budini, 311

buttercream frosting,
        328–29
    buying and storing of, 8
    -cinnamon sauce for
        caramel ice cream
        roll, 103–5
    in creamy mocha pie,
        138–39
    crumb crust, 127
    custard, 308
    double, brownies, 209
    frosting, creamy, 330
    genoise, our favorite, *see*
        our favorite chocolate
        genoise
    -hazelnut biscotti, 205
    -hazelnut meringue
        cookies, 210
    melting of, 7–8
    mocha cheesecake,
        321–22
    noisette sandwiches, 221
    noisette shells, 221
    pastry cream, 335
    pots de crème, 305
    raspberry cake, 94–95
    rum glaze, for heavenly
        hazelnut cake,
        86–87
    semisweet, *see* semisweet
        chocolate
    tartlets, 174–75
    types of, 4–7
    wafers, in chocolate
        crumb crust, 127
    white, *see* white chocolate
chocolate butter glaze, 333
    for Queen of Sheba torte,
        108–9
chocolate cakes:
    genoise, our favorite,
        63–64
    molten, 110–11
    raspberry cake, 94–95
    rich, 54–55
    triple, 83
chocolate chip cookies, best,
        211
chocolate crumb crust, 127
    blood orange chiffon pie
        with, 144–45
chocolate glaze, 332
    for chocolate raspberry
        cake, 94–95

cinnamon:
  apple pie, 148
  -chocolate sauce for
    caramel ice cream
    roll, 103–5
  crème caramel, 306–7
  -sugar doughnuts, 247
citrus custard, 308
cobbler, 183
  mixed berry, 185
cocoa:
  in molten chocolate cakes,
    110–11
  in our favorite chocolate
    genoise, 63–64
  types of, 4–7
coconut:
  cupcakes with nougatine
    sticks, 96–98
  -pecan macaroons, 208
coconut custard, 308
  pie, toasted, 129
coconut milk, in coconut
    cupcakes with
    nougatine sticks,
    96–98
coffee:
  in chocolate mocha
    cheesecake,
    321–22
  in creamy mocha pie,
    138–39
  crème brûlée, 304–5
  custard, 308
  in gateau victoire, 106–7
Cognac:
  in brandied pastry cream,
    335
  in chocolate tartlets,
    174–75
  in Queen of Sheba torte,
    108–9
Comice pears, in pear crisp,
    184
Cookenboo, Julia, 106–7,
    202–7, 210, 212–13,
    218–19, 222
cookies, 196–222
  almond and chocolate
    sandwich, 202–3
  apricot streusel bars,
    214–15
  best chocolate chip, 211
  brown sugar thins, 206–7

chocolate-hazelnut
    biscotti, 205
chocolate-hazelnut
    meringue, 210
chocolate noisette
    sandwiches, 221
chocolate noisette shells,
    221
classic almond-anise
    biscotti, 205
classic Scottish
    shortbread, 222
coconut-pecan macaroons,
    208
crispy oatmeal wafers,
    212
date streusel bars, 215
diamonds, 213
double chocolate
    brownies, 209
equipment for, 198–99
French noisette shells,
    220–21
fresh ginger-spice,
    216–17
ingredients for, 197
lemon-poppy seed
    shortbread, 222
lemon stars, 218–19
making of, 199–200
pine nut–orange biscotti,
    205
pistachio-golden raisin
    biscotti, 204–5
prune streusel bars, 215
storage of, 201
cookware, 31–32
corn bread, melt-in-your-
    mouth, 238–39
cornmeal:
  crackers, spicy, 298–99
  in double-crusted apple-
    polenta tart, 172–73
Cowgirl Creamery, 22–23
crackers, spicy cornmeal,
    298–99
cranberry(ies):
  chess pie, 133
  dried, in apple mincemeat
    pie, 146–47
cream:
  pastry, see pastry cream
  whipped, see whipped
    cream

white chocolate, pistachio
    roulade with, 99–101
cream cheese:
  in chocolate mocha
    cheesecake, 321–22
  in our favorite
    cheesecake, 319–20
  pie dough, 125
cream pie, banana, 134
cream puffs with lemon
    filling, 317–18
creamy:
  chocolate frosting, 330
  mocha pie, 138–39
  sabayon, 312
crème anglaise, toasted
    almond, 337
crème brûlée:
  classic, 305
  coffee, 304–5
crème caramel, cinnamon,
    306–7
Crescenza, in focaccia di
    Recco, 300
crisp, 183
  pear, 184
crispy oatmeal wafers, 212
crumb crust, 127
  chocolate, see chocolate
    crumb crust
  vanilla, 127
Cunningham, Marion, 1–2,
    124
cupcakes, coconut, with
    nougatine sticks,
    96–98
currant(s):
  in apple-raisin pandowdy,
    188
  in berry-almond
    vacherins, 315–16
  buttermilk, scones, 234–35
  dried, in apple mincemeat
    pie, 146–47
  red, in summer pudding,
    192–93
  red, jelly, in summer berry
    tart, 176
custard:
  cinnamon crème caramel,
    306–7
  toasted coconut, pie, 129
  variations on, 308–9
  see also crème brûlée

date(s):
pumpkin bread with
walnuts and, 242
streusel bars, 215
decorating, cake, 77–82
deep-dish summer pie, 150
diamonds, 213
dinner rolls:
buttery, 292–93
multigrain bread dough
for, 274
white sandwich bread
dough for, 264–65
double chocolate brownies,
209
double-crusted apple-
polenta tart, 172–73
double crust pie dough:
butter, 123
cream cheese, 125
lard, 126
shortening, 124
double fig focaccia, 294–95
dough, *see specific kinds of
dough*
doughnuts:
buttermilk spice, 245–46
cinnamon-sugar, 247
dos and don'ts, 248
dried cherry and almond
cake, 88
durum bread, 270–72

egg-based desserts, 301–22
berry-almond vacherins,
315–16
bittersweet chocolate
soufflé, 313
chocolate budini, 311
chocolate mocha
cheesecake, 321–22
chocolate pots de crème,
305
cinnamon crème caramel,
306–7
classic crème brûlée,
305
coffee crème brûlée,
304–5
cream puffs with lemon
filling, 317–18
creamy sabayon, 312

ingredients and
equipment for, 302
our favorite cheesecake,
319–20
raspberry soufflé with
raspberry sauce, 314
Riesling sabayon, 312
the ultimate bread
pudding, 303
see also custard
eggs, 8–10
Empire apples, in apple-
raisin pandowdy, 188
equipment:
for cakes, 46–47
for cakes for family and
friends, 76
for cookies, 198–99
for egg-based desserts,
303
for frostings, glazes, and
sauces, 324
for fruit desserts, 181–82
for measuring, 32–35
miscellaneous small,
36–40
for pies, 116–18
for quick breads, 224–25
for tarts, 155
espresso sponge cake, 65–66
with caramel crunch
topping, 92–93

fall squash pie, 130–31
fats, 10–11
for pie dough, 113–14
feta, spinach, and ricotta pie,
152
Field, Carol, 172–73,
270–72, 288–89,
300
fig focaccia, double, 294–95
five-spice angel food cake,
70–71
with penuche glaze, 102
flatbreads:
focaccia di Recco, 300
spicy cornmeal crackers,
298–99
Flatt, Letty, 125
Fleischmann's Yeast, 23
Flo's angel food cake, 70–71

flour, 11–14
foam-based cakes:
blood orange chiffon pie
with chocolate crumb
crust, 144–45
mixing of, 49–50
see also angel food cake;
sponge cakes
focaccia:
di Recco, 300
double fig, 294–95
framboise (raspberry eau-de-
vie):
in berry-almond
vacherins, 315–16
in brandied pastry cream,
335
frangipane-plum tart,
168–69
French baguettes, 276–78
French noisette shells,
220–21
fresh ginger–spice cookies,
216–17
frosting(s):
of cake, 78–79
chocolate buttercream,
328–29
creamy chocolate, 330
equipment for, 324
golden fluffy, for carrot-
applesauce layer
cake, 89
ingredients for, 323–24
storing of, 325
whipped cream, 341
see also glazes; sauces
fruit:
Queen of Sheba torte with,
109
sauces, 339
see also specific fruits
fruit desserts, 180–95
apple brown Betty, 186
apple-raisin pandowdy,
188
baked apples with walnut-
orange stuffing, 194
blueberry grunt, 187
defined, 183
equipment for, 181–82
ingredients for, 181
mixed berry cobbler, 185
pear crisp, 184

fruit desserts (*continued*)
pears baked in Beaumes-
de-Venise and honey,
195
storing of, 182
summer pudding,
192–93
techniques for, 182
warm pineapple in puff
pastry with pineapple
caramel sauce,
189–91
fudge and peanut butter, pie,
135

Gage, Fran, 267–68,
286–87, 290–91,
294–95, 298–99
galettes:
simple nectarine, 166–67
tomato and cheese,
178–79
ganache:
Alice's light, *see* Alice's
light ganache
peanut butter and white
chocolate, for peanut
butter and strawberry
jam cake, 90
gateau victoire, 106–7
genoise:
chocolate, our favorite, *see*
our favorite chocolate
genoise
classic, 60–61
lemon, 61
orange, *see* orange genoise
testing and tasting flour
for, 62
see also sponge cakes
Gerson, Lily, 63–64,
168–69, 321–22
Gewürztraminer, in Riesling
sabayon, 312
ginger:
custard, 309
-orange buttercream, *see*
orange-ginger
buttercream
-orange gateau, 91
-spice cookies, fresh,
216–17

ginger, crystallized:
in applesauce
gingerbread, 241
in orange-ginger gateau,
91
gingerbread, applesauce,
21
glazes:
chocolate, *see* chocolate
glaze
chocolate butter, *see*
chocolate butter
glaze
chocolate rum, for
heavenly hazelnut
cake, 86–87
equipment for, 324
ingredients for, 323–24
penuche, for five-spice
angel food cake,
102
storing of, 325
see also frosting(s);
sauces
Golden Delicious apples, in
apple brown Betty,
186
golden fluffy frosting for
carrot-applesauce
layer cake, 89
golden raisins:
in apple mincemeat pie,
146–47
in carrot-applesauce layer
cake, 56–57
-pistachio biscotti,
204–5
graham cracker crumbs, in
crumb crust, 127
Grand Marnier:
in brandied pastry cream,
335
in orange-ginger gateau,
91
Granny Smith apples, in
apple brown Betty,
186
Greenleaf Produce, 21
grunt, 183
blueberry, 187
Gruyère cheese, in tomato
and cheese galette,
178–79
Guittard Chocolate, 22

hamburger buns, 265
hazelnut:
cake, heavenly, with
chocolate rum glaze,
86–87
-chocolate biscotti, 205
-chocolate meringue
cookies, 210
heavenly hazelnut cake with
chocolate rum glaze,
86–87
herb custard, 309
high-altitude baking, 41–43
honey, pears baked in
Beaumes-de-Venise
and, 195
huckleberries, in deep-dish
summer pie, 150
Huppin-Fleck, Rochelle,
144–45

ice cream roll, caramel,
103–5
ingredients:
for cakes, 44–46
for cookies, 197
for egg-based desserts,
302
for frostings, glazes, and
sauces, 323–24
for fruit desserts, 181
glossary of, 3–20
for pies, 113
for quick breads, 223–24
for tarts, 154–55
for yeast bread, 252–56
Invernizzina, in focaccia di
Recco, 300
Italian whole wheat bread
(pane integrale),
270–72

jam, raspberry, in summer
berry tart, 176
jam, strawberry:
and peanut butter cake,
90
in summer berry tart, 176
jelly, red currant, in summer
berry tart, 176

Jewett, Tami, 211
Just Desserts, 24

Key lime pie, 132
kirsch:
    in brandied pastry cream,
        335
    in chocolate tartlets,
        174–75
    in dried cherry and
        almond cake, 88
    in summer pudding,
        192–93
    in warm pear tart,
        164–65
    in warm pineapple in puff
        pastry with pineapple
        caramel sauce,
        189–91
Kona Inn banana bread,
    240
Kux, Nancy, 91, 326–27

lard pie dough, old-fashioned,
    126
layer cakes:
    carrot-applesauce, 56–57
    carrot-applesauce, with
        golden fluffy frosting,
        89
    peanut butter, 58–59
    sponge, 66
leavenings, 14–15
Lebovitz, David, 304–7, 312,
    315–20, 337–39
lemon:
    -berry meringue tart, 171
    buttercream, 327
    chiffon pie, 145
    filling, cream puffs with,
        317–18
    genoise, 61
    meringue pie, 140–41
    Meyer, chiffon cake,
        68–69
    -poppy seed shortbread,
        222
    -raspberry tart, 170–71
    sponge cake, 66
    stars, 218–19

lemon curd, 340
    for cream puffs with
        lemon filling, 317–18
Lieb, Evie, 54–55, 330
lime chiffon pie, 145
liqueur:
    orange, in orange-ginger
        gateau, 91
    raspberry, in chocolate
        raspberry cake,
        94–95
liquor custard, 309
Lloyd, Baird, 264–65

macaroons, coconut-pecan,
    208
madeleine molds, 221
mango sauce, 339
maple bars, 243–44
measuring:
    equipment for, 32–35
    techniques for, 34–35
Medrich, Alice, 62, 83,
        94–95, 108–11, 313,
        321–22, 328–29,
        331–33, 336
melt-in-your-mouth corn
        bread, 238–39
meringue:
    buttercream, classic,
        326–27
    chocolate-hazelnut,
        cookies, 210
    pie, lemon, 140–41
    tart, lemon-berry, 171
    testing and tasting of,
        142–43
Meyer lemon chiffon cake,
    68–69
Millar, Jennifer, 311
mincemeat apple pie,
    146–47
mixed berry cobbler, 185
mixers, 26–27
mocha:
    chocolate, cheesecake,
        321–22
    pie, creamy, 138–39
molten chocolate cakes,
    110–11
Mooradian, Barbara, 216–17
morning buns, 290–91

Morocco, Robert, 208–9,
    220–21
muffins:
    apple or pear, 229
    blueberry, 228–29
    raisin-bran, 230
Mulroony, Stephanie A. E.,
    142–43
multigrain bread, 273–75
Murray, Patti, 214–15
mushroom and potato tart,
    177

nectarine galette, simple,
    166–67
noisette shells:
    chocolate, 221
    French, 221–22
nougatine sticks, coconut
        cupcakes with,
        96–98
nut(s), 16
    in best chocolate chip
        cookies, 211
    custard, 309
    see also specific nuts
nutmeg custard, 309

oatmeal wafers, crispy, 212
old-fashioned lard pie
        dough, 126
orange:
    blood, chiffon pie with
        chocolate crumb
        crust, 144–45
    buttercream, 327
    -ginger gateau, 91
    -pine nut biscotti, 205
    -rum sweet bread (crescia
        cingolana), 288–89
    sponge cake, 66
    -walnut stuffing, baked
        apples with, 194
orange genoise, 61
    for orange-ginger gateau,
        91
orange-ginger buttercream,
    327
    for orange-ginger gateau,
        91

orange liqueur, in orange-
ginger gateau, 91
our favorite:
butter cake, 52–53
cheesecake, 319–20
our favorite chocolate
genoise, 63–64
in chocolate raspberry
cake, 94–95
ovens, 25–26

pandowdy, 183
apple-raisin, 188
pans, baking, 28–31
using of, 81–82
parchment cones, 81–82
Parmesan cheese, in tomato
and cheese galette,
178–79
pastry bags, 80–81
pastry cream, 334–35
brandied, 335
chocolate, 335
peach sauce, 339
cooked, 339
peach vanilla pie, 149
peanut butter:
and fudge pie, 135
layer cake, 58–59
and strawberry jam cake,
90
and white chocolate
ganache, 90
pear(s):
baked in Beaumes-de-
Venise and honey,
195
crisp, 184
muffins, 229
tart, warm, 164–65
pearl sugar:
in diamonds, 213
in double fig focaccia,
294–95
pecan(s):
bourbon, pie, 128
-coconut macaroons, 208
in crispy oatmeal wafers,
212
penuche glaze, for five-spice
angel food cake, 102
Pettigrew Farms, 21–22

pie dough:
butter, 123
cream cheese, 125
double crust, see double
crust pie dough
fats for, 113–14
flour for, 114
mixing of, 118–19
old-fashioned lard, 126
rolling out of, 119–20
savory, 123
shortening, 124
pie fillings, thickeners for,
114–15
pies:
ingredients for, 113
serving and storage of,
122
shaping and baking of,
120–22
pies, savory:
artichoke and potato
turnovers, 153
spinach, feta, and ricotta,
152
pies, sweet:
apple mincemeat, 146–47
banana cream, 134
bittersweet chocolate
pudding, 136–37
bourbon, pecan, 128
chiffon, 144–45
cinnamon apple, 148
cranberry chess, 133
creamy mocha, 138–39
deep-dish summer, 150
equipment for, 116–18
fall squash, 130–31
Key lime, 132
lemon meringue, 140–41
peanut butter and fudge,
135
pineapple, warm, in puff
pastry with caramel
sauce, 189–91
raspberry-rhubarb, 151
sweet potato, 131
toasted coconut custard,
129
vanilla peach, 149
pine nut–orange biscotti,
205
Pippin apples, in apple
brown Betty, 186

pistachio:
-golden raisin biscotti,
204–5
roulade with white
chocolate cream,
99–101
pita bread, 286–87
plum-frangipane tart,
168–69
polenta tart:
double-crusted apple-,
172–73
quince and apple-, 173
Ponsford, Craig, 276–78
popovers, 236–37
poppy seed–lemon
shortbread, 222
potato:
and artichoke turnovers,
153
and mushroom tart, 177
pots de crème, chocolate,
305
pound cake, sour cream,
84–85
pretzels, soft, 296–97
prune streusel bars, 215
pudding:
bread, the ultimate, 303
chocolate budini, 311
pie, bittersweet chocolate,
136–37
summer, 192–93
puff pastry:
quick, 163
warm pineapple in, with
pineapple caramel
sauce, 189–91
pumpkin bread with dates
and walnuts, 242

Queen of Sheba torte,
108–9
with fruit, 109
quick breads, 223–50
applesauce gingerbread,
241
equipment for, 224–25
ingredients for, 223–24
Kona Inn banana, 240
melt-in-your-mouth corn,
238–39

pumpkin, with dates and
walnuts, 242
rum raisin zucchini,
249–50
storing of, 227
techniques for, 225–26
see also biscuits;
doughnuts; muffins;
popovers
quick puff pastry, 163
quince and apple-polenta
tart, 173

raisin:
-apple pandowdy, 188
-bran muffins, 230
brioche, 267–68
golden, *see* golden raisins
rum, zucchini bread,
249–50
raspberry(ies):
in berry-almond
vacherins, 315–16
chocolate cake, 94–95
in deep-dish summer pie,
150
-lemon tart, 170–71
in mixed berry cobbler, 185
-rhubarb pie, 151
soufflé, with raspberry
sauce, 314
in summer berry tart, 176
in summer pudding,
192–93
raspberry liqueur, in
chocolate raspberry
cake, 94–95
raspberry sauce, 339
raspberry soufflé with, 314
for summer pudding,
192–93
Reinhart, Peter, 273–74,
279–85, 292–93,
296–97
rhubarb-raspberry pie, 151
rich chocolate cake, 54–55
ricotta, spinach, and feta pie,
152
Riesling:
in baked apples with
walnut-orange
stuffing, 194

sabayon, *see* sabayon,
Riesling
rolls, dinner, *see* dinner rolls
roulade:
caramel ice cream roll,
103
pistachio, with white
chocolate cream,
99–101
round rye loaves, 284–85
rum:
chocolate, glaze for
heavenly hazelnut
cake, 86–87
-orange sweet bread
(crescia cingolana),
288–89
raisin zucchini bread,
249–50
rum, dark:
in apple mincemeat pie,
146–47
in brandied pastry cream,
335
in warm pear tart,
164–65
rye:
bread, classic, 283–85
loaves, round, 284–85
pastry dough, 159

sabayon, Riesling, 312
in berry-almond
vacherins, 315
creamy, 312
salt, 16–17
sandwich cookies:
almond and chocolate,
202–3
chocolate noisette, 221
Santa Rosa plums, in plum-
frangipane tart,
168–69
sauces:
caramel, *see* caramel
sauce
chocolate-cinnamon, for
caramel ice cream
roll, 103–5
equipment for, 324
fruit, 339
ingredients for, 323–24

pineapple caramel, for
warm pineapple in
puff pastry, 189–91
raspberry, *see* raspberry
sauce
storing of, 325
see also frosting(s); glazes
savory pie dough, 123
scones, buttermilk currant,
234–35
semisweet chocolate:
in Alice's light ganache,
331
in almond and chocolate
sandwich cookies,
202–3
in bittersweet chocolate
soufflé, 313
in chocolate buttercream
frosting, 328–29
in chocolate butter glaze,
333
in chocolate glaze, 332
in chocolate mocha
cheesecake, 321–22
in chocolate noisette
shells, 221
in double chocolate
brownies, 209
in gateau victoire, 106–7
in molten chocolate cakes,
110–11
in peanut butter and fudge
pie, 135
in Queen of Sheba torte,
108–9
in triple chocolate cake,
83
serving of pies, 122
Shere, Lindsey, 159–79,
189–95, 334–35
shortbread:
classic Scottish, 222
lemon-poppy seed, 222
shortening pie dough, 124
short pastry dough (pâte
sablée), 160
simple nectarine galette,
166–67
soft pretzels, 296–97
soufflé:
bittersweet chocolate, 313
raspberry, with raspberry
sauce, 314

sources for ingredients and
equipment, 343–45
sour cream pound cake,
84–85
sourdough bread, 279–82
spice(d):
buttermilk doughnuts,
245–46
custard, 309
-fresh ginger cookies,
216–17
spicy cornmeal crackers,
298–99
spinach, feta, and ricotta pie,
152–53
sponge, 275
sponge cakes:
classic, 65–66
espresso, *see* espresso
sponge cake
layer, 66
lemon, 66
orange, 66
see also genoise
squash pie, fall, 130–31
stars, lemon, 218–19
Stewart, Kathleen, 140–41,
303, 314, 317–18,
340
storing:
of cakes, 51, 82
of cookies, 201
of frostings, glazes, and
sauces, 325
of fruit desserts, 182
of pies, 122
of quick breads, 227
of tarts, 158
of yeast breads, 263
stracchino, in focaccia di
Recco, 300
strawberry(ies):
in berry-almond
vacherins, 315–16
in mixed berry cobbler,
185
sauce, 339
in summer berry tart, 176
strawberry jam:
and peanut butter cake,
90
in summer berry tart, 176
sugar:
-cinnamon doughnuts, 247

pearl, *see* pearl sugar
types of, 17–18
summer berry tart, 176
summer pudding, 192–93
sweet potato pie, 131
sweet tart pastry (pâte
sucrée), 161

Taleggio, in focaccia di
Recco, 300
tart doughs, 159–63
basic, 159
mixing of, 156
quick puff pastry, 163
rolling out of, 156–57
rye pastry, 159
short pastry, 160
sweet tart pastry, 161
tartlet, 162
tartlets:
chocolate, 174–75
dough, 162
tarts, 154–79
baking of, 157
chocolate tartlets,
174–75
double-crusted apple-
polenta, 172–73
equipment for, 155
ingredients for, 154–55
lemon-berry meringue,
171
plum-frangipane, 168–69
potato and mushroom, 177
quince and apple-polenta,
173
raspberry-lemon, 170–71
simple nectarine galette,
166–67
storing of, 158
summer berry, 176
tomato and cheese galette,
178–79
warm pear, 164–65
tea custard, 309
techniques:
for bread dough, 256–63
for cakes, 47–51
for cakes for family and
friends, 76–77
for cookies, 199–200
for fruit desserts, 182

for pies, 118–22
for quick breads,
225–27
thermometers, 35–36
thins, brown sugar, 206–7
toasted:
almond crème anglaise,
337
coconut custard pie, 129
tomato and cheese galette,
178–79
tools, 25–40
topping:
caramel crunch, for
espresso sponge
cake, 92–93
whipped cream, *see*
whipped cream
topping
torte, Queen of Sheba,
108–9
triple chocolate cake, 83
turnovers, artichoke and
potato, 153

ultimate bread pudding, the,
303

vacherins, berry-almond,
315–16
vanilla, 19–20
crumb crust, 127
custard, classic, 308
peach pie, 149
vanilla wafers, in vanilla
crumb crust, 127

wafers:
crispy oatmeal, 212
vanilla, in vanilla crumb
crust, 127
walnut(s):
in carrot-applesauce layer
cake, 56–57
in crispy oatmeal wafers,
212
in double chocolate
brownies, 209

in Kona Inn banana
bread, 240
-orange stuffing, baked
apples with, 194
pumpkin bread with dates
and, 242
warm pear tart, 164–65
warm pineapple in puff
pastry with pineapple
caramel sauce,
189–91
Weil, Carolyn B., 123,
126–41, 146–53,
184–88, 241
whipped cream:
in berry-almond
vacherins, 315–16
frosting, 341
whipped cream topping,
336
for Key lime pie, 132

white chocolate:
cream, pistachio roulade
with, 99–101
and peanut butter ganache
for peanut butter and
strawberry jam cake,
90
white sandwich bread,
264–66
testing and tasting of,
266
whole wheat bread, Italian
(pane integrale),
270–72
wine, semi-dry white in
Riesling sabayon,
312
wine, sweet:
in baked apples with
walnut-orange
stuffing, 194

in pears baked in
Beaumes-de-Venise
and honey, 195
Winesap apples in apple-
raisin pandowdy,
188
Winter Nelis pears, in
warm pear tart,
164–65
winter squash puree, in
fall squash pie,
130–31

yeast, 15

zucchini bread, rum raisin,
249–50